Hands-On Infrastructure Monitoring with Prometheus

Implement and scale queries, dashboards, and alerting across machines and containers

Joel Bastos
Pedro Araújo

Packt>

BIRMINGHAM - MUMBAI

Hands-On Infrastructure Monitoring with Prometheus

Copyright © 2019 Packt Publishing

All rights reserved. No part of this book may be reproduced, stored in a retrieval system, or transmitted in any form or by any means, without the prior written permission of the publisher, except in the case of brief quotations embedded in critical articles or reviews.

Every effort has been made in the preparation of this book to ensure the accuracy of the information presented. However, the information contained in this book is sold without warranty, either express or implied. Neither the authors, nor Packt Publishing or its dealers and distributors, will be held liable for any damages caused or alleged to have been caused directly or indirectly by this book.

Packt Publishing has endeavored to provide trademark information about all of the companies and products mentioned in this book by the appropriate use of capitals. However, Packt Publishing cannot guarantee the accuracy of this information.

Commissioning Editor: Pavan Ramchandani
Acquisition Editor: Rohit Rajkumar
Content Development Editor: Nithin George Varghese
Technical Editor: Rutuja Patade
Copy Editor: Safis Editing
Project Coordinator: Jagdish Prabhu
Proofreader: Safis Editing
Indexer: Pratik Shirodkar
Graphics: Jayalaxmi Raja
Production Coordinator: Jisha Chirayil

First published: May 2019

Production reference: 2221119

Published by Packt Publishing Ltd.
Livery Place
35 Livery Street
Birmingham
B3 2PB, UK.

ISBN 978-1-78961-234-9

www.packtpub.com

Packt.com

Subscribe to our online digital library for full access to over 7,000 books and videos, as well as industry leading tools to help you plan your personal development and advance your career. For more information, please visit our website.

Why subscribe?

- Spend less time learning and more time coding with practical eBooks and Videos from over 4,000 industry professionals

- Improve your learning with Skill Plans built especially for you

- Get a free eBook or video every month

- Fully searchable for easy access to vital information

- Copy and paste, print, and bookmark content

Did you know that Packt offers eBook versions of every book published, with PDF and ePub files available? You can upgrade to the eBook version at www.packt.com and as a print book customer, you are entitled to a discount on the eBook copy. Get in touch with us at customercare@packtpub.com for more details.

At www.packt.com, you can also read a collection of free technical articles, sign up for a range of free newsletters, and receive exclusive discounts and offers on Packt books and eBooks.

Contributors

About the authors

Joel Bastos is an open source supporter and contributor, with a background in infrastructure security and automation. He is always striving for the standardization of processes, code maintainability, and code reusability. He has defined, led, and implemented critical, highly available, and fault-tolerant enterprise and web-scale infrastructures in several organizations, with Prometheus as the cornerstone. He has worked at two unicorn companies in Portugal and at one of the largest transaction-oriented gaming companies in the world. Previously, he has supported several governmental entities with projects such as the Public Key Infrastructure for the Portuguese citizen card. You can find him on Twitter with the handle `@kintoandar`.

> I would like to thank the Prometheus maintainers and community, without whom you wouldn't be reading this book, and specifically Brian Brazil for taking the time to help this project become a reality.
>
> On a more personal note, I would like to thank my soulmate, Ana Sofia, for giving meaning to my life and keeping me sane (ish), and my family and friends for all the unconditional support.

Pedro Araújo is a site reliability and automation engineer and has defined and implemented several standards for monitoring at scale. His contributions have been fundamental in connecting development teams to infrastructure. He is highly knowledgeable about infrastructure, but his passion is in the automation and management of large-scale, highly-transactional systems. Pedro has contributed to several open source projects, such as Riemann, OpenTSDB, Sensu, Prometheus, and Thanos. You can find him on Twitter with the handle `@phcrva`.

> My thanks to Brian Brazil for his insightful observations and valuable feedback, to the creators and maintainers of Prometheus for their truly amazing work, and to everyone at Packt for making this book come true.
>
> Lastly, I would like to thank my wife Inês and my children Gui and Mia for their patience, love, and support, as well as my family and friends for their encouragement.

About the reviewer

Brian Brazil is a Prometheus developer and the founder of Robust Perception. He works across the Prometheus ecosystem, and is involved in areas such as best practices, exporters, PromQL semantics, and client libraries. He is the main writer of the Reliable Insights blog, which regularly covers Prometheus topics, and is the author of the book *Prometheus: Up and Running*.

Packt is searching for authors like you

If you're interested in becoming an author for Packt, please visit authors.packtpub.com and apply today. We have worked with thousands of developers and tech professionals, just like you, to help them share their insight with the global tech community. You can make a general application, apply for a specific hot topic that we are recruiting an author for, or submit your own idea.

Table of Contents

Preface   1

Section 1: Introduction

Chapter 1: Monitoring Fundamentals   9
  Definition of monitoring   9
    The value of monitoring   10
    Organizational contexts   10
    Monitoring components   12
  Whitebox versus blackbox monitoring   12
  Understanding metrics collection   14
    An overview of the two collection approaches   14
    Push versus pull   15
    What to measure   16
      Google's four golden signals   16
      Brendan Gregg's USE method   16
      Tom Wilkie's RED method   16
  Summary   17
  Questions   17
  Further reading   18

Chapter 2: An Overview of the Prometheus Ecosystem   19
  Metrics collection with Prometheus   19
    High-level overview of the Prometheus architecture   20
  Exposing internal state with exporters   22
    Exporter fundamentals   23
  Alert routing and management with Alertmanager   24
    Alerting routes   25
  Visualizing your data   25
  Summary   27
  Questions   28
  Further reading   28

Chapter 3: Setting Up a Test Environment   29
  Code organization   29
  Machine requirements   31
    Hardware requirements   32
    Recommended software   33
      VirtualBox   33
      Vagrant   34
      Minikube   34

kubectl	34
Spinning up a new environment	34
Automated deployment walkthrough	35
Prometheus	36
Grafana	36
Alertmanager	38
Cleanup	38
Advanced deployment walkthrough	39
Prometheus	39
Grafana	41
Alertmanager	43
Node Exporter	44
Validating your test environment	45
Summary	46
Questions	46
Further reading	46

Section 2: Getting Started with Prometheus

Chapter 4: Prometheus Metrics Fundamentals	49
Understanding the Prometheus data model	49
Time series data	50
Time series databases	50
Prometheus local storage	51
Data flow	51
Memory	51
Write ahead log	51
Disk	52
Layout	52
Prometheus data model	53
Notation	53
Metric names	53
Metric labels	54
Samples	54
Cardinality	54
A tour of the four core metric types	55
Counter	55
Gauge	57
Histogram	60
Summaries	61
Longitudinal and cross-sectional aggregations	63
Cross-sectional aggregation	64
Longitudinal aggregation	64
Summary	65
Questions	66
Further reading	66
Chapter 5: Running a Prometheus Server	67

[ii]

Deep dive into the Prometheus configuration	67
Prometheus startup configuration	68
The config section	68
The storage section	68
The web section	69
The query section	70
Prometheus configuration file walkthrough	71
Global configuration	72
Scrape configuration	74
Managing Prometheus in a standalone server	77
Server deploy	77
Configuration inspection	78
Cleanup	81
Managing Prometheus in Kubernetes	81
Static configuration	81
Kubernetes environment	82
Prometheus server deployment	83
Adding targets to Prometheus	86
Dynamic configuration – the Prometheus Operator	89
Kubernetes environment	90
Prometheus Operator deployment	90
Prometheus server deployment	92
Adding targets to Prometheus	94
Summary	98
Questions	98
Further reading	99
Chapter 6: Exporters and Integrations	101
Test environments for this chapter	101
Static infrastructure test environment	102
Kubernetes test environment	104
Operating system exporter	106
The Node Exporter	106
Configuration	107
Deployment	108
Container exporter	109
cAdvisor	110
Configuration	111
Deployment	111
kube-state-metrics	115
Configuration	116
Deployment	117
From logs to metrics	121
mtail	121
Configuration	122
Deployment	123
Grok exporter	125

Table of Contents

Configuration	125
Deployment	127
Blackbox monitoring	**129**
Blackbox exporter	129
Configuration	131
Deployment	133
Pushing metrics	**136**
Pushgateway	136
Configuration	137
Deployment	137
More exporters	**141**
JMX exporter	142
HAProxy exporter	143
Summary	**144**
Questions	**144**
Further reading	**145**
Chapter 7: Prometheus Query Language - PromQL	**147**
The test environment for this chapter	**147**
Getting to know the basics of PromQL	**150**
Selectors	150
Label matchers	150
Instant vectors	155
Range vectors	156
The offset modifier	158
Subqueries	159
Operators	160
Binary operators	160
Arithmetic	160
Comparison	161
Vector matching	162
One-to-one	162
Many-to-one and one-to-many	163
Logical operators	163
Aggregation operators	165
Binary operator precedence	167
Functions	167
absent()	168
label_join() and label_replace()	169
predict_linear()	170
rate() and irate()	170
histogram_quantile()	173
sort() and sort_desc()	174
vector()	174
Aggregation operations over time	174
Time functions	175
Info and enum	176
Common patterns and pitfalls	**177**

[iv]

Patterns	178
Service-level indicators	178
Percentiles	179
The health of scrape jobs	180
Pitfalls	180
Choosing the right functions for the data type	180
Sum-of-rates versus rate-of-sums	181
Having enough data to work with	182
Unexpected results when using increase	183
Not using enough matchers to select a time series	183
Losing statistical significance	183
Knowing what to expect when constructing complex queries	184
The query of death	184
Moving on to more complex queries	**185**
In which node is Node Exporter running?	185
Scenario rationale	185
PromQL approach	185
Comparing CPU usage across different versions	186
Scenario rationale	187
PromQL approach	187
Summary	**189**
Questions	**189**
Further reading	**189**
Chapter 8: Troubleshooting and Validation	**191**
The test environment for this chapter	**191**
Deployment	191
Cleanup	192
Exploring promtool	**192**
Checks	193
check config	193
check rules	193
check metrics	194
Queries	194
query instant	195
query range	195
query series	195
query labels	196
Debug	196
debug pprof	197
debug metrics	199
debug all	199
Tests	200
Logs and endpoint validation	**200**
Endpoints	200
Logs	201
Analyzing the time series database	**202**
Using the tsdb tool	203

Summary	205
Questions	206
Further reading	206

Section 3: Dashboards and Alerts

Chapter 9: Defining Alerting and Recording Rules — 209
Creating the test environment — 209
- Deployment — 210
- Cleanup — 211
Understanding how rule evaluation works — 211
- Using recording rules — 211
- Naming convention for recording rules — 215
Setting up alerting in Prometheus — 217
- What is an alerting rule? — 217
- Configuring alerting rules — 218
  - Prometheus server configuration file — 218
  - Rule file configuration — 219
- Labels and annotations — 223
- Delays on alerting — 225
Testing your rules — 226
- Recording rules tests — 226
- Alerting rules tests — 230
Summary — 232
Questions — 232
Further reading — 233

Chapter 10: Discovering and Creating Grafana Dashboards — 235
Test environment for this chapter — 236
- Deployment — 236
- Cleanup — 237
How to use Grafana with Prometheus — 238
- Login screen — 239
- Data source — 240
- Explore — 242
- Dashboards — 244
- Grafana running on Kubernetes — 245
Building your own dashboards — 249
- Dashboard fundamentals — 249
  - Panels — 250
  - Variables — 251
  - Time picker — 252
- Creating a basic dashboard — 253
- Exporting dashboards — 260
Discovering ready-made dashboards — 260
- Grafana dashboards gallery — 261

Publishing your dashboards	263
Default Prometheus visualizations	264
Out-of-the-box console templates	265
Console template basics	266
Summary	269
Questions	269
Further reading	269
Chapter 11: Understanding and Extending Alertmanager	271
Setting up the test environment	272
Deployment	272
Cleanup	273
Alertmanager fundamentals	274
The notification pipeline	274
Dispatching alert groups to the notification pipeline	275
Inhibition	276
Silencing	276
Routing	278
Alertmanager clustering	279
Alertmanager configuration	281
Prometheus configuration	281
Configuration file overview	282
global	283
route	283
inhibit_rules	285
receiver	288
templates	288
The amtool command-line tool	289
alert	289
silence	290
check-config	292
config	292
Kubernetes Prometheus Operator and Alertmanager	294
Common Alertmanager notification integrations	297
Email	298
Chat	299
Pager	300
Webhook	300
null	301
Customizing your alert notifications	302
Default message format	302
Creating a new template	304
Who watches the Watchmen?	308
Meta-monitoring and cross-monitoring	308
Dead man's switch alerts	310
Summary	312

Table of Contents

Questions — 312
Further reading — 313

Section 4: Scalability, Resilience, and Maintainability

Chapter 12: Choosing the Right Service Discovery — 317
Test environment for this chapter — 317
Deployment — 319
Cleanup — 320
Running through the service discovery options — 320
Cloud providers — 321
Container orchestrators — 323
Service discovery systems — 326
DNS-based service discovery — 327
File-based service discovery — 329
Using a built-in service discovery — 331
Using Consul service discovery — 331
Using Kubernetes service discovery — 338
Building a custom service discovery — 342
Custom service discovery fundamentals — 343
Recommended approach — 344
The service discovery adapter — 344
Custom service discovery example — 345
Using the custom service discovery — 347
Summary — 350
Questions — 350
Further reading — 351

Chapter 13: Scaling and Federating Prometheus — 353
Test environment for this chapter — 353
Deployment — 354
Cleanup — 355
Scaling with the help of sharding — 356
Logical grouping of jobs — 356
The single job scale problem — 358
What to consider when sharding — 360
Alternatives to sharding — 360
Having a global view using federation — 362
Federation configuration — 362
Federation patterns — 365
Hierarchical — 366
Cross-service — 367
Using Thanos to mitigate Prometheus shortcomings at scale — 368
Thanos' global view components — 369
Sidecar — 371
Query — 372

Summary	374
Questions	374
Further reading	374

Chapter 14: Integrating Long-Term Storage with Prometheus — 375
- Test environment for this chapter — 375
  - Deployment — 376
  - Cleanup — 377
- Remote write and remote read — 378
  - Remote write — 378
  - Remote read — 379
- Options for metrics storage — 381
  - Local storage — 381
  - Remote storage integrations — 384
- Thanos remote storage and ecosystem — 385
  - Thanos ecosystem — 385
  - Thanos components — 387
    - Test environment specifics — 388
    - Thanos query — 389
    - Thanos sidecar — 390
    - Thanos store gateway — 392
    - Thanos compact — 392
    - Thanos bucket — 394
    - Thanos receive — 395
    - Thanos rule — 398
- Summary — 398
- Questions — 399
- Further reading — 399

Assessments — 401

Other Books You May Enjoy — 413

Index — 417

Preface

Introduction to the book and the technology

This book about Prometheus, the second project to graduate within the **Cloud Native Computing Foundation** (**CNCF**), will help you to crystallize the core fundamentals of monitoring and the approaches available to ensure the required infrastructure visibility. It relies on practical examples, using test environments and diagrams, to communicate knowledge in an easy-to-digest manner.

The content was designed to ensure that all the important Prometheus stack concepts are tackled. Our main goal during the writing process was to aim the book at our past selves and ensure that they would have everything they needed to know about this technology in this book.

From running one Prometheus server, to what scaling options are available, from creating and testing alerting rules, to templating slack notifications; and from useful dashboards, to automating target discovery; many other topics will be explained to ensure a full knowledge base on infrastructure monitoring using Prometheus as its cornerstone.

Who this book is for

If you're a software developer, cloud specialist, site reliability engineer, DevOps enthusiast, or a system administrator looking to set up a reliable monitoring and alerting system to sustain infrastructure security and performance, this book is for you. Basic networking and infrastructure monitoring knowledge will help you understand the concepts covered in this book.

What this book covers

Chapter 1, *Monitoring Fundamentals*, lays the foundations of several key concepts that are used throughout the book. This chapter also explores the approach Prometheus takes to metric collection and why some controversial decisions are vital for the design and architecture of its stack.

Preface

Chapter 2, *An Overview of the Prometheus Ecosystem*, introduces a high-level overview of the entire Prometheus ecosystem, which components perform which jobs, and how everything interoperates logically.

Chapter 3, *Setting Up a Test Environment*, presents the fundamentals of how to use the test environments provided throughout the book, and how to tinker with them to validate different configurations.

Chapter 4, *Prometheus Metrics Fundamentals*, explores metrics, the core resource of Prometheus. Understanding them correctly is essential to fully utilize, manage, or even extend the Prometheus stack.

Chapter 5, *Running a Prometheus Server*, focuses on the Prometheus server, providing common patterns of usage and full setup process scenarios for virtual machines and containers.

Chapter 6, *Exporters and Integrations*, introduces some of the most useful exporters available, as well as providing examples on how to use them.

Chapter 7, *Prometheus Query Language – PromQL*, dives into the powerful and flexible Prometheus query language to leverage its multi-dimensional data model, which allows ad hoc aggregation and the combination of time series.

Chapter 8, *Troubleshooting and Validation*, provides useful guidelines on how to quickly detect and fix problems. It also presents useful endpoints that expose critical information and explores `promtool`, the Prometheus command-line interface and validation tool.

Chapter 9, *Defining Alerting and Recording Rules*, covers the usage and testing of recording and alerting rules, providing examples along the way.

Chapter 10, *Discovering and Creating Grafana Dashboards*, delves into the visualization components of the Prometheus stack, covering not only the built-in console functionality but also exploring Grafana and how to build, share, and reuse dashboards.

Chapter 11, *Understanding and Extending Alertmanager*, introduces the alerting component of the stack, showing how to integrate it with several different alerting providers, and how to correctly set up clustering to enable high-availability with the deduplication of alerts.

Chapter 12, *Choosing the Right Service Discovery*, explores multiple service discovery integrations, as well as providing you with the requirements and knowledge to build your own integration if required.

Chapter 13, *Scaling and Federating Prometheus*, tackles the scaling of a Prometheus stack and introduces concepts such as sharding and global views, while providing context and explaining them.

Chapter 14, *Integrating Long-Term Storage with Prometheus*, covers the concepts of the Prometheus read and write endpoints. Then, it deep-dives into considerations for external and long-term metric storage. Finally, it introduces an end-to-end example using Thanos.

To get the most out of this book

Basic knowledge of monitoring, networking, and containers is useful but is not mandatory.

All the test environments were validated using macOS and Linux, while enforcing specific software versions for added compatibility, so those are the best candidates to guarantee you won't run into issues. Chapter 3, *Setting Up a Test Environment*, provides all the technical information on this subject.

Decent internet connectivity is required to download the software dependencies, as is a modern browser to ensure access to all the web interfaces presented in the book.

Download the example code files

You can download the example code files for this book from your account at www.packt.com. If you purchased this book elsewhere, you can visit www.packtpub.com/support and register to have the files emailed directly to you.

You can download the code files by following these steps:

1. Log in or register at www.packt.com.
2. Select the **Support** tab.
3. Click on **Code Downloads**.
4. Enter the name of the book in the **Search** box and follow the onscreen instructions.

Once the file is downloaded, please make sure that you unzip or extract the folder using the latest version of:

- WinRAR/7-Zip for Windows
- Zipeg/iZip/UnRarX for Mac
- 7-Zip/PeaZip for Linux

The code bundle for the book is also hosted on GitHub at https://github.com/PacktPublishing/Hands-On-Infrastructure-Monitoring-with-Prometheus. In case there's an update to the code, it will be updated on the existing GitHub repository.

We also have other code bundles from our rich catalog of books and videos available at https://github.com/PacktPublishing/. Check them out!

Download the color images

We also provide a PDF file that has color images of the screenshots/diagrams used in this book. You can download it here: https://www.packtpub.com/sites/default/files/downloads/9781789612349_ColorImages.pdf.

Conventions used

There are a number of text conventions used throughout this book.

`CodeInText`: Indicates code words in text, database table names, folder names, filenames, file extensions, pathnames, dummy URLs, user input, and Twitter handles. Here is an example: "Now, you can run `vagrant status`."

A block of code is set as follows:

```
annotations:
    description: "Node exporter {{ .Labels.instance }} is down."
    link: "https://example.com"
```

When we wish to draw your attention to a particular part of a code block, the relevant lines or items are set in bold:

```
annotations:
    description: "Node exporter {{ .Labels.instance }} is down."
    link: "https://example.com"
```

Any command-line input or output is written as follows:

```
vagrant up
```

Bold: Indicates a new term, an important word, or words that you see onscreen. For example, words in menus or dialog boxes appear in the text like this. Here is an example: "You can find this page by going into **Status** | **Rules** on the top bar."

Warnings or important notes appear like this.

Tips and tricks appear like this.

Get in touch

Feedback from our readers is always welcome.

General feedback: If you have questions about any aspect of this book, mention the book title in the subject of your message and email us at `customercare@packtpub.com`.

Errata: Although we have taken every care to ensure the accuracy of our content, mistakes do happen. If you have found a mistake in this book, we would be grateful if you would report this to us. Please visit `www.packtpub.com/submit/errata`, selecting your book, clicking on the Errata Submission Form link, and entering the details.

Piracy: If you come across any illegal copies of our works in any form on the Internet, we would be grateful if you would provide us with the location address or website name. Please contact us at `copyright@packt.com` with a link to the material.

If you are interested in becoming an author: If there is a topic that you have expertise in and you are interested in either writing or contributing to a book, please visit `authors.packtpub.com`.

Reviews

Please leave a review. Once you have read and used this book, why not leave a review on the site that you purchased it from? Potential readers can then see and use your unbiased opinion to make purchase decisions, we at Packt can understand what you think about our products, and our authors can see your feedback on their book. Thank you!

For more information about Packt, please visit `packt.com`.

Section 1: Introduction

On completion of this section, the reader will have the basic knowledge they need to proceed with a deep dive into the Prometheus stack.

The following chapters are included in this section:

- `Chapter 1`, *Monitoring Fundamentals*
- `Chapter 2`, *An Overview of the Prometheus Ecosystem*
- `Chapter 3`, *Setting Up a Test Environment*

Monitoring Fundamentals

This chapter lays the foundation for several key concepts that will be used throughout this book. Starting with the definition of monitoring, we will explore various views and factors that emphasize why systematic analysis assumes different levels of importance and makes an impact on organizations. You will learn about the advantages and disadvantages of different monitoring mechanics, taking a closer look at the Prometheus approach regarding collecting metrics. Finally, we will discuss some of the controversial decisions that were vital for the design and architecture of the Prometheus stack and why you should take them into account when designing your own monitoring system.

We will be covering the following topics in this chapter:

- Defining of monitoring
- Whitebox versus blackbox monitoring
- Understanding metrics collection

Definition of monitoring

A consensual definition of monitoring is hard to come by because it quickly shifts between industry- or even job-specific contexts. The diversity of viewpoints, the components comprising the monitoring system, and even how the data is collected or used are all factors that contribute to the struggle of reaching a clear definition.

Without a common ground, it is difficult to sustain a discussion and, usually, expectations are mismatched. Therefore, in the following topics, we will outline a baseline, orientated to obtain a definition of monitoring that will guide us throughout this book.

The value of monitoring

With the growing complexity of infrastructures, exponentially driven by the adoption of microservices-oriented architectures, it has become critical to attain a global view of all the different components of an infrastructure. It is unthinkable to manually validate the health of each instance, caching service, database, or load balancer. There are way too many moving pieces to count—let alone keep a close eye on.

Nowadays, it is expected that monitoring will keep track of data from those components. However, data might come in several forms, allowing it to be used for different purposes.

Alerting is one of the standard uses of monitoring data, but the application of such data can go far beyond it. You may require historical information to assist you in capacity planning or incident investigations, or you may need a higher resolution to drill down into a problem and even higher freshness to decrease the mean time to recovery during an outage.

You can look at monitoring as a source of information for maintaining healthy systems, production- and business-wise.

Organizational contexts

Looking into an organizational context, roles such as system administrators, quality assurance engineers, **Site Reliability Engineers** (**SREs**), or product owners have different expectations from monitoring. Understanding the requirements of what each role surfaces makes it easier to comprehend why context is so useful when discussing monitoring. Let's expand the following statements while providing some examples:

- System administrators are interested in high-resolution, low-latency, and high-diversity data. For a system administrator, the main objective of monitoring is to obtain visibility across the infrastructure and manage data from CPU usage to **Hypertext Transfer Protocol** (**HTTP**) request rate so that problems are quickly discovered and the root causes are identified as soon as possible. In this approach, exposing monitoring data in high resolution is critical to be able to drill down into the affected system. If a problem is occurring, you don't have the privilege to wait several hours for your next data point, and so data has to be provided in near real time or, in other words, with low latency. Lastly, since there is no easy way to identify or predict which systems are prone to be affected, we need to collect as much data as possible from all systems; namely, a high diversity of data.

- Quality assurance engineers are interested in high-resolution, high-latency, and high-diversity data. Besides being important for quality assurance engineers to have high resolution monitoring data collected, which enables a deeper drill down into effects, the latency is not as critical as it is for system administrators. In this case, historical data is much more critical for comparing software releases than the freshness of the data. Since we can't wholly predict the ramifications of a new release, the available data needs to be spread across as much of the infrastructure as possible, touching every system the software release might use and invoke it or generally interact with it (directly or indirectly), so that we have as much data as possible.
- SREs focused on capacity planning are interested in low-resolution, high-latency, and high-diversity data. In this scenario, historical data carries much more importance for SREs than the resolution that this data is presented in. For example, to predict the increase in infrastructure, it is not critical for a SRE to know that some months ago at 4 A.M., one of the nodes had a spike of CPU usage reaching 100% in 10 seconds, but is useful to understand the trend of the load across the fleet of nodes to infer the number of nodes required to handle new scale requirements. As such, it is also important for SREs to have a broad visualization of all the different parts of the infrastructure that are affected by those requirements to predict, for example, the amount of storage for logs, network bandwidth increase, and so on, making the high diversity of monitoring data mandatory.
- Product owners are interested in low-resolution, high-latency, and low-diversity data. Where product owners are concerned, monitoring data usually steps away from infrastructure to the realm of business. Product owners strive to understand the trends of specific software products, where historical data is fundamental and resolution is not so critical. Keeping in mind the objective of evaluating the impact of software releases on the customers, latency is not as essential for them as it is for system administrators. The product owner manages a specific set of products, so a low diversity of monitoring data is expected, comprised mostly of business metrics.

The following table sums up the previous examples in a much more condensed form:

	Data resolution	Data latency	Data diversity
Infrastructure alerting	High	Low	High
Software release view	High	High	High
Capacity planning	Low	High	High
Product/business view	Low	High	Low

Monitoring components

The same way the monitoring definition changes across contexts, its components follow the same predicament. Depending on how broad you want to be, we can find some or all of these components in the following topics:

- **Metrics**: This exposes a certain system resource, application action, or business characteristic as a specific point in time value. This information is obtained in an aggregated form; for example, you can find out how many requests per second were served but not the exact time for a specific request, and without context, you won't know the ID of the requests.
- **Logging**: Containing much more data than a metric, this manifests itself as an event from a system or application, containing all the information that's produced by such an event. This information is not aggregated and has the full context.
- **Tracing**: This is a special case of logging where a request is given a unique identifier so that it can be tracked during its entire life cycle across every system. Due to the increase of the dataset with the number of requests, it is a good idea to use samples instead of tracking all requests.
- **Alerting**: This is the continuous threshold validation of metrics or logs, and fires an action or notification in the case of a transgression of the said threshold.
- **Visualization**: This is a graphical representation of metrics, logs, or traces.

Recently, the term monitoring has been overtaken by a superset called **observability**, which is regarded as the evolution of monitoring, or a different wrapping to spring a hype and revive the concept (the same way it happened with DevOps). From where it stands, observability does indeed include all the components we described here.

Throughout this book, our monitoring definition incorporates metrics, alerting, and visualization.

> Monitoring is metrics with associated alerting and visualization.

Whitebox versus blackbox monitoring

There are many ways we could go about monitoring, but they largely fall into two main categories, that is, blackbox and whitebox monitoring.

In blackbox monitoring, the application or host is observed from the outside and, consequently, this approach can be fairly limited. Checks are made to assess whether the system under observation responds to probes in a known way:

- Does the host respond to **Internet Control Message Protocol (ICMP)** echo requests (more commonly known as ping)?
- Is a given TCP port open?
- Does the application respond with the correct data and status code when it receives a specific HTTP request?
- Is the process for a specific application running in its host?

On the other hand, in whitebox monitoring, the system under observation surfaces data about its internal state and the performance of critical sections. This type of introspection can be very powerful as it exposes the operating telemetry, and consequently the health, of the different internal components, which otherwise would be difficult or even impossible to ascertain. This telemetry data is usually handled in the following ways:

- **Exported through logging**: This is by far the most common case and how applications exposed their inner workings before instrumentation libraries were widespread. For instance, an HTTP server's access log can be processed to monitor request rates, latencies, and error percentages.
- **Emitted as structured events**: This approach is similar to logging but instead of being written to disk, the data is sent directly to processing systems for analysis and aggregation.
- **Maintained in memory as aggregates**: Data in this format can be hosted in an endpoint or read directly from command-line tools. Examples of this approach are `/metrics` with Prometheus metrics, HAProxy's stats page, or the varnishstats command-line tool.

Not all software is instrumented and ready to have its internal state exposed for metrics collection. For example, it can be a third-party, closed-source application that has no means of surfacing its inner workings. In these cases, external probing can be a viable option to gather the data that's deemed essential for a proper service state validation.

Regardless, not only third-party applications benefit from blackbox monitoring. It can be useful to validate your applications from their clients' standpoint by going through, for example, load balancers and firewalls. Probing can be your last line of defense—if all else fails, you can rely on blackbox monitoring to assess availability.

Understanding metrics collection

The process by which metrics are by monitoring systems can generally be divided into two approaches—push and pull. As we'll see in the following topics, both approaches are valid and have their pros and cons, which we will thoroughly discuss. Nonetheless, it is essential to have a solid grasp on how they differ to understand and fully utilize Prometheus. After understanding how collecting metrics works, we will delve into what should be collected. There are several proven methods to achieve this, and we will give an overview of each one.

An overview of the two collection approaches

In push-based monitoring systems, emitted metrics or events are sent either directly from the producing application or from a local agent to the collecting service, like so:

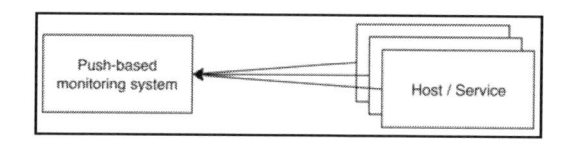

Figure 1.1: Push-based monitoring system

Systems that handle raw event data generally prefer push since the frequency of event generation is very high—in the order of hundreds, thousands, or even tens of thousands per second, per instance—which would make polling data impractical and complex. Some sort of buffering mechanism would be needed to keep events generated between polls, and event freshness would still be a problem compared with just pushing data. Some examples that use this approach include Riemann, StatsD, and the **Elasticsearch**, **Logstash**, and the **Kibana** (**ELK**) stack.

That is not to say that only these types of systems use push. Some monitoring systems such as Graphite, OpenTSDB, and the **Telegraf**, **InfluxDB**, **Chronograph**, and **Kapacitor** (**TICK**) stack have been designed using this approach. Even good old Nagios supports push through the **Nagios Service Check Acceptor** (**NSCA**), commonly known as passive checks:

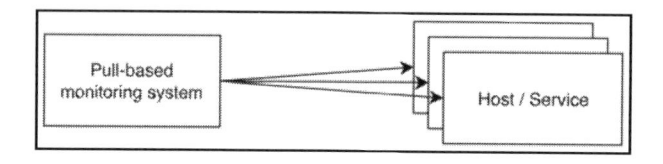

Figure 1.2: Pull-based monitoring system

In contrast, pull-based monitoring systems collect metrics directly from applications or from proxy processes that make those metrics available to the system. Some notable monitoring software that uses pull are Nagios and Nagios-style systems (Icinga, Zabbix, Zenoss, and Sensu, to name a few). Prometheus is also one of those that embraces the pull approach and is very opinionated about this.

Push versus pull

There is much debate in the monitoring community around the merits of each of these design decisions. The main point of contention is usually about target discovery, which we will discuss in the following paragraphs.

In push-based systems, the monitored hosts and services make themselves known by reporting to the monitoring system. The advantage here is that no prior knowledge of new systems is required for them to be picked up. However, this means that the monitoring service's location needs to be propagated to all targets, usually with some form of configuration management. Staleness is a big drawback of this approach: if a system hasn't reported in for some time, does that mean it's having problems or was it purposely decommissioned?

Furthermore, when you manage a distributed fleet of hosts and services that push data to a central point, the risk of a thundering herd (overload due to many incoming connections at the same time) or a misconfiguration causing an unforeseen flood of data becomes much more complex and time-consuming to mitigate.

In pull-based monitoring, the system needs a definitive list of hosts and services to monitor so that their metrics are ingested. Having a central source of truth provides some level of assurance that everything is where it's supposed to be, with the drawback of having to maintain said source of truth and keeping it updated with any changes. With the rapid rate of change in today's infrastructures, some form of automated discovery is needed to keep up with the full picture. Having a centralized point of configuration enables a much faster response in the case of issues or misconfigurations.

In the end, most of the drawbacks from each approach can be reduced or effectively solved by clever design and automation. There are other more important factors when choosing a monitoring tool, such as flexibility, ease of automation, maintainability, or broad support for the technologies being used.

Even though Prometheus is a pull-based monitoring system, it also provides a way of ingesting pushed metrics by using a gateway that converts from push to pull. This is useful for monitoring a very narrow class of processes, which we will see later in this book.

What to measure

When planning metrics collection, there is a question that's bound to come up, which is defining what metrics to observe. To answer this question, we should turn to the current best practices and methodologies. In the following topics, we will look at an overview of the most influential and best-regarded methods for reducing noise and improving visibility on performance and general reliability concerns.

Google's four golden signals

Google's rationale regarding monitoring is quite simple. It states, pretty straightforwardly, that the four most important metrics to keep track of are the following:

- **Latency**: The time required to serve a request
- **Traffic**: The number of requests being made
- **Errors**: The rate of failing requests
- **Saturation**: The amount of work not being processed, which is usually queued

Brendan Gregg's USE method

Brendan's method is more machine-focused and it states that for each resource (CPU, disk, network interface, and so on), the following metrics should be monitored:

- **Utilization**: Measured as the percentage of the resource that was busy
- **Saturation**: The amount of work the resource was not able to process, which is usually queued
- **Errors**: Amount of errors that occurred

Tom Wilkie's RED method

The RED method is more focused on a service-level approach and not so much on the underlying system itself. Obviously, being useful to monitor services, this strategy is also valuable to predict the experience of external clients. If a service's error rate increases, it is reasonable to assume those errors will impact, directly or indirectly, on the customer's experience. These are the metrics to be aware of:

- **Rate**: Translated as requests per second
- **Errors**: The amount of failing requests per second
- **Duration**: The time taken by those requests

Summary

In this chapter, we had the chance to understand the true value of monitoring and how to approach the term in a specific context, including the context that's used in this book. This will help you avoid any misunderstandings and ensure a clear perception of where the book stands on this topic. We also went through different aspects of monitoring, such as metrics, logging, tracing, alerting, and visualizations, while presenting observability and the benefits it brings. Whitebox and blackbox monitoring were addressed, which provide the basis to comprehend the benefits of using metrics. Armed with this knowledge about metrics, we went through the mechanics of push and pull and all the arguments regarding each one, before ending with what the metrics to track on the systems you manage are.

In the next chapter, we will look at an overview of the Prometheus ecosystem, and talk about several of its components.

Questions

1. Why is monitoring definition so hard to clearly define?
2. Does a high latency of metrics impact the work of a system administrator who's focused on fixing a live incident?
3. What are the monitoring requirements to properly do capacity planning?
4. Is logging considered monitoring?
5. Regarding the available strategies for metrics collection, what are the downsides of using the push-based approach?
6. If you had to choose three basic metrics from a generic web service to focus on, which would they be?
7. When a check verifies whether a given process is running on a host by way of listing the running processes in said host, is that whitebox or blackbox monitoring?

Further reading

- **The Prometheus blog**: https://prometheus.io/blog/2016/07/23/pull-does-not-scale-or-does-it
- **Site Reliability Book**: https://landing.google.com/sre/sre-book/chapters/monitoring-distributed-systems
- **The USE Method**: http://www.brendangregg.com/usemethod.html
- **The RED Method**: https://www.weave.works/blog/the-red-method-key-metrics-for-microservices-architecture

2
An Overview of the Prometheus Ecosystem

With such a vast collection of components available for use, it can be daunting to choose the ones that are required to solve a given monitoring gap. In this chapter, we will go over the Prometheus ecosystem, which components perform what job, and understand how everything works together logically.

Striving for simplicity and having a clear understanding of all the moving parts of a Prometheus stack is invaluable to keep things manageable and reliable.

In brief, the following topics will be covered in this chapter:

- Metrics collection with Prometheus
- Exposing internal state with exporters
- Alert routing and management with Alertmanager
- Visualizing your data

Metrics collection with Prometheus

Prometheus is a time series-based, open source monitoring system. It collects data by sending HTTP requests to hosts and services on metrics endpoints, which it then makes available for analysis and alerting using a powerful query language.

Even though Prometheus has graduated with the **Cloud Native Computing Foundation** (**CNCF**) by demonstrating stability, maturity, and solid governance, it is still evolving at a very rapid pace. At the time of writing, the current stable version of Prometheus is 2.9.2, and every component or feature that is going to be discussed will be based on this version. While there should be no major architectural changes within version 2, care should be taken when applying specific configuration that's been learned from this book to earlier or even later versions.

High-level overview of the Prometheus architecture

The Prometheus ecosystem is composed of several components, each with its own responsibility and clearly defined scope. Prometheus itself is essential as it sits squarely in the middle of most interactions, but many components are in fact optional, depending on your monitoring needs.

As we can see in the following diagram, the main components in the Prometheus ecosystem are as follows:

- The Prometheus server collects time series data, stores it, makes it available for querying, and sends alerts based on it.
- The Alertmanager receives alert triggers from Prometheus and handles routing and dispatching of alerts.
- The Pushgateway handles the exposition of metrics that have been pushed from short-lived jobs such as cron or batch jobs.
- Applications that support the Prometheus exposition format make internal state available through an HTTP endpoint.
- Community-driven exporters expose metrics from applications that do not support Prometheus natively.
- First-party and third-party dashboarding solutions provide a visualization of collected data.

Each one will be explored in depth later in this book:

Figure 2.1: High-level overview of the main components in the Prometheus ecosystem

> The Prometheus server has its own internal processes, such as recording rules and service discovery, which are thoroughly explained in `Chapter 9`, *Defining Alerting and Recording Rules*, and `Chapter 12`, *Choosing the Right Service Discovery*, respectively.

Prometheus was originally created by Matt T. Proud and Julius Volz while working at SoundCloud. It was inspired by Google's Borgmon, which influenced a lot of its earlier design: scraping plain text from metrics endpoints; exporters as proxies for metrics collection; time series as multi-dimensional vectors, which can then be transformed and filtered; and the use of ruleset evaluations for recording and alerting, among other features.

> You might be tempted to try and make Prometheus fit into a push-based metrics collection model, but this is ill-advised. Prometheus' core design is around pull, so naturally, many assumptions break down when converting from push to pull. This will be further explained when we approach the Pushgateway.

A singular attribute of Prometheus is that it unabashedly does not try to do any type of clustering. By not relying on the network for coordination and storage (although remote write is possible, as we'll see by the end of this book), it makes a great argument for reliability and ease of use. It's trivial to just pick up the appropriate binary distribution of Prometheus and run it locally on your computer, and yet the same binary might be able to handle thousands of scrape targets and the ingestion of millions of samples per second on server hardware.

Exposing internal state with exporters

Not all applications are built with Prometheus-compatible instrumentation. Sometimes, no metrics are exposed at all. In these cases, we can rely on exporters. The following diagram shows how they work:

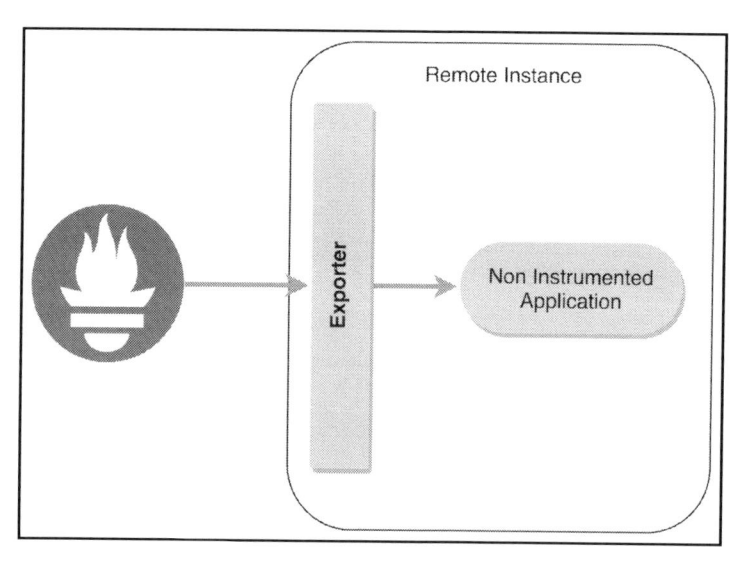

Figure 2.2: A high-level overview of an exporter

An exporter is nothing more than a piece of software that collects data from a service or application and exposes it via HTTP in the Prometheus format. Each exporter usually targets a specific service or application and as such, their deployment reflects this one-to-one synergy.

Nowadays, you can find exporters for pretty much any service you need, and if a particular third-party service doesn't have an exporter available, it's quite simple to build your own.

Exporter fundamentals

When the exporter starts, it binds to a configured port and exposes the internal state of whatever is being collected in an HTTP endpoint of your choosing (the default being `/metrics`). The instrumentation data is collected when an HTTP GET request is made to the configured endpoint. For example, node exporter, one of the most commonly used exporters, relies on a number of kernel statistics to present data such as disk I/O, CPU, memory, network, filesystem usage, and much, much more. Every single time that endpoint is scraped, the information is quickly gathered and exposed in a synchronous operation.

> The HTTP GET request that's made by the Prometheus server to the observed system for metric collection is called a **scrape**.

If you are the one writing the service, the best option is to instrument the code directly using a Prometheus client library. There are official client libraries available for the following programming languages:

- Go
- Java/JVM
- Python
- Ruby

There are community-driven client libraries for the following programming languages:

- Bash
- C++
- Common Lisp
- Elixir
- Erlang
- Haskell
- Lua for NGINX
- Lua for Tarantool
- .NET

- C#
- Node.js
- Perl
- PHP
- Rust

Due to an ever-growing community around Prometheus, this list is constantly expanding.

Usually, exporters are very light and the performance footprint is mostly negligible but, as always, there are exceptions for this rule, on which we will go into considerable detail later in this book.

Alert routing and management with Alertmanager

Alertmanager is the component from the Prometheus ecosystem that's responsible for the notifications that are triggered by the alerts that are generated from the Prometheus server. As such, its availability is of the essence and the design choices reflect this need. It's the only component that's truly conceived to work in a highly available cluster setup, and uses gossip as the communication protocol:

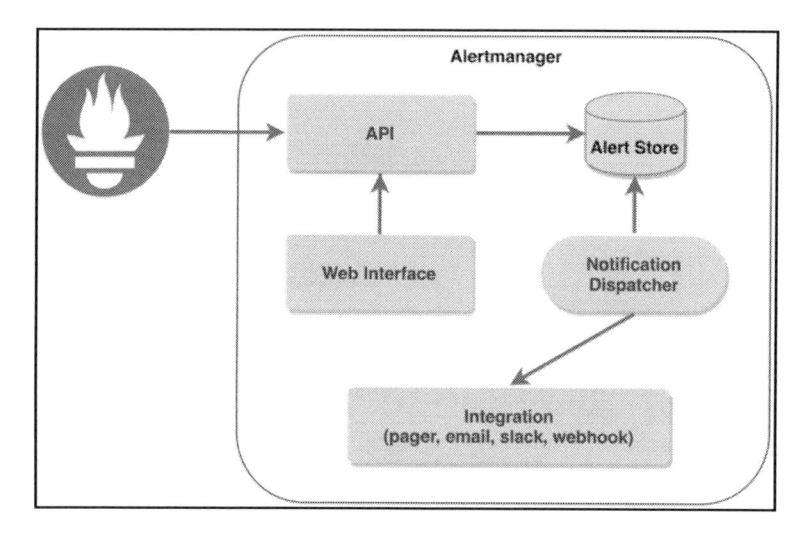

Figure 2.3: A high-level overview of Alertmanager

At a very high level, Alertmanager is a service that receives HTTP POST requests from Prometheus servers via its API, which it then deduplicates and acts on by following a predefined set of routes.

Alertmanager also exposes a web interface to allow, for instance, the visualization and silencing of firing alerts or applying inhibition rules for them.

One of the core design choices is to value delivery over deduplication. This means that if a network partition occurs between a cluster of Alertmanager instances, notifications will be sent from both sides of the partition.

Alerting routes

A route, in its essence, can be seen as a tree-like structure. If an incoming alert has a specific payload that triggers a particular route (branch), a pre-defined integration will be invoked.

There are multiple out-of-the-box integrations available for the most common use cases, such as the following:

- Email
- Hipchat
- PagerDuty
- Slack
- Opsgenie
- VictorOps
- WeChat

There's also the webhook integration that issues an HTTP POST request with the JSON payload of the firing alert to an endpoint of your choosing, opening a world of possibilities for custom integrations.

Visualizing your data

Data visualization is one of the simplest ways to produce or consume information. Prometheus exposes a well-defined API, where PromQL queries can produce raw data for visualizations.

An Overview of the Prometheus Ecosystem

Currently, the best external software for visualization is Grafana, which we will explain thoroughly in `Chapter 10`, *Discovering and Creating Grafana Dashboards*. The Grafana team has made its integration with Prometheus seamless, and the result is a delightful user experience.

The Prometheus server also ships with two internal visualizations components:

- **Expression browser**: Here, you can run PromQL directly to quickly query data and visualize it instantly:

Figure 2.4: The Prometheus expression browser interface

[26]

- **Consoles**: These are web pages that are built using the Golang templating language and are served by the Prometheus server itself. This approach allows you to have pre-defined data visualization interfaces without you having to constantly type PromQL:

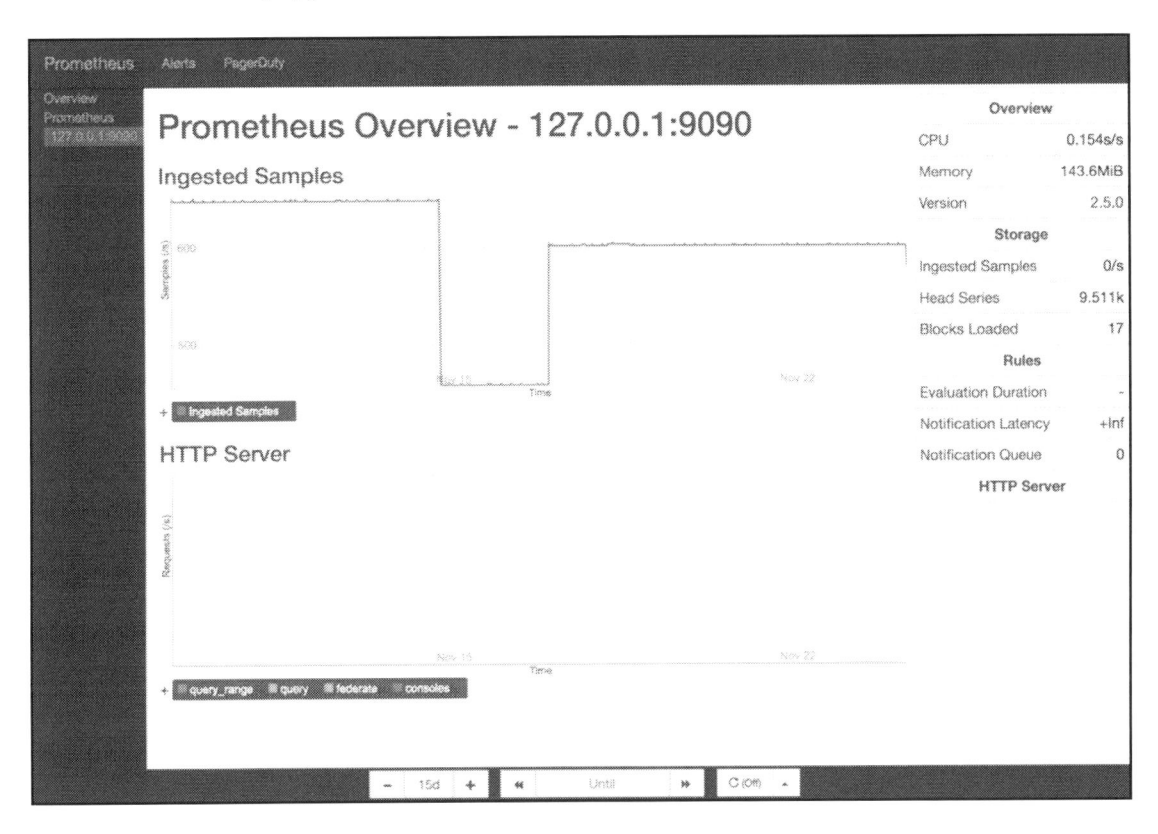

Figure 2.5: The Prometheus console interface

Summary

To better understand the Prometheus philosophy, it is essential to have an insight – even if it's at a high level—into the main components of the Prometheus ecosystem, from data collection via exporters to reliable alerting using Alertmanager, as well as the available visualization options. This is what we covered in this chapter.

In the next chapter, we'll start building a test environment, so that all the concepts we've discussed so far can start to materialize.

Questions

1. What are the main components of the Prometheus ecosystem?
2. Which components are essential and which are optional for a Prometheus deployment?
3. Why are out-of-process exporters needed?
4. When an HTTP GET request hits the metrics endpoint of an exporter, what ensues?
5. What happens to a triggering alert in an Alertmanager cluster if a network partition occurs?
6. You realize you need to integrate Alertmanager with a custom-made API. What would be your quickest option?
7. What visualizations options are included in a standard Prometheus server installation?

Further reading

- **Prometheus overview**: https://prometheus.io/docs/introduction/overview/

3
Setting Up a Test Environment

The best way to learn is by doing. This chapter will help you quickly spin up an environment for testing so that you can safely experiment without worrying too much. It will provide several configuration examples and tips on how to get things running. This type of environment will also be used throughout this book in several different scenarios.

In brief, the following topics will be covered in this chapter:

- Code organization
- Machine requirements
- Spinning up a new environment

Code organization

While the examples and code listings in this book can be used directly without any supporting material, a companion Git repository is also provided to help you with the setup process and the automation of test environments so that you can follow along easily.

In this section, we're going to explore how that repository is organized, explain some choices that are made in terms of the automation of the test environments, and give some pointers on how to customize them:

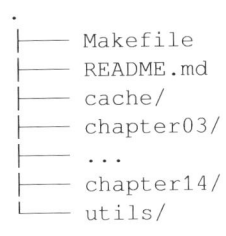

```
.
├── Makefile
├── README.md
├── cache/
├── chapter03/
├── ...
├── chapter14/
└── utils/
```

Setting Up a Test Environment

The root structure of the repository shown here should be fairly easy to understand:

- One directory per chapter that needs its own test environment (aptly named `chapter`, followed by the chapter number)
- A `cache` directory, which will hold downloaded packages so that rebuilding test environments becomes as fast as possible
- A `utils` directory, where default versions and parameters of the test environments can be found (and changed if wanted), along with some helper functions

Next, we are going to drill down and have a closer look at each of these, like so:

```
.
├── ...
└── utils/
    ├── defaults.sh
    ├── helpers.sh
    └── vagrant_defaults.rb
```

In the `utils` directory, the following files can be found:

- `defaults.sh`: Here, the versions of each component in the Prometheus stack (such as Prometheus itself, along with exporters and Alertmanager, among others) that will be used in the test environments can be found.
- `vagrant_defaults.rb`: This file controls a couple of tunable parameters for the virtual machines that are used to run the test environments, like the amount of RAM each virtual machine will have, which base image to use, and what the environment's internal network will look like.
- `helpers.sh`: This is a shell library that's used by the provisioning scripts with some helper functions to manage the downloading and caching of archives:

```
.
├── ...
├── chapter03/
│   ├── Vagrantfile
│   ├── configs/
│   └── provision/
└── ...
```

While each test environment will differ in some ways between chapters, the basic structure will remain the same:

- A `Vagrantfile` to describe how many virtual machines are needed for the test environment, along with how to configure and provision them
- A `configs` directory to house configuration files that will be used in the provision step
- A `provision` directory with scripts to download, install, and configure each of the Prometheus components that are required for the current test environment

We can see an example of this by looking at the tree structure for this chapter:

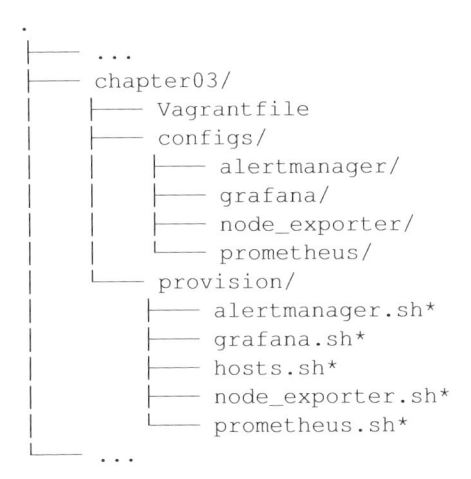

```
.
├── ...
├── chapter03/
│   ├── Vagrantfile
│   ├── configs/
│   │   ├── alertmanager/
│   │   ├── grafana/
│   │   ├── node_exporter/
│   │   └── prometheus/
│   └── provision/
│       ├── alertmanager.sh*
│       ├── grafana.sh*
│       ├── hosts.sh*
│       ├── node_exporter.sh*
│       └── prometheus.sh*
└── ...
```

The `configs` directory has sub-directories for each of the components that's used in this chapter. The `provision` directory follows the same model, with an added `hosts.sh` shell script to automate the management of `/etc/hosts` file on the guests.

By now, the question of *Why not just use configuration management?* might have risen in the minds of some. All the provisioning automation was done in a shell for a couple of reasons:

- This was a conscious effort to expose every detail, not abstract them away.
- Shell scripting is the lowest common denominator of automation in Unix-like systems.
- The purpose of this book is to focus on the inner workings of Prometheus, not the specific implementation of a given configuration management tool.

Machine requirements

The machine requirements for this setup can comfortably run on a modern laptop, as long it has CPU virtualization extensions enabled and its operating system is compatible with the software requirements. All the software requirements that are covered here were thought-out. We will be using free and open source software, so no extra cost should be necessary when you try out the test environments.

Hardware requirements

The minimal requirements for the host deploying the provided examples are as follows:

- At least 2 CPU cores
- At least 4 GB of memory
- At least 20 GB of free disk space

With these specifications, you should be able to spin up the test environment without encountering any issues.

Regarding connectivity, the host machine should have internet access and the ability to resolve external DNS records. The provision scripts will have to download dependencies during their execution, though most of the dependencies will be cached locally to avoid being downloaded in every deployment.

The default network for the example environment is `192.168.42.0/24`, and the following diagram illustrates the configuration you would get when running this chapter's example:

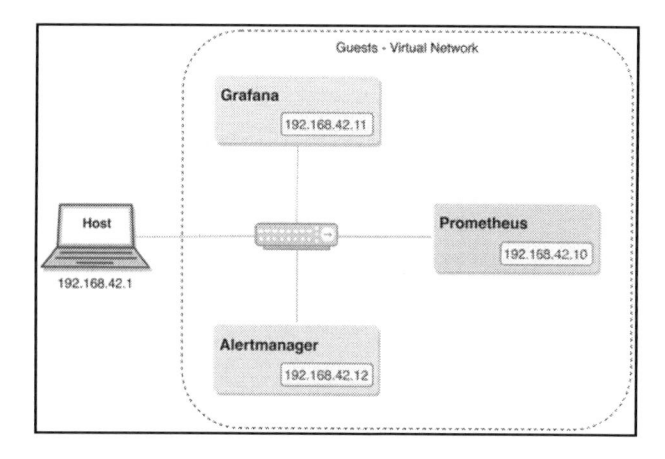

Figure 3.1: Virtual network configuration

> **TIP**
>
> When launching a test environment, the subnet `192.168.42.0/24` will be used. Each environment belongs to a specific chapter, and should be destroyed before switching to a new one. If you encounter a conflict with your local address space, you can change the test environment subnet by editing the NETWORK option in the provided `./utils/vagrant_defaults.rb` file.

Recommended software

The environment was tested using the following software, and so the standard disclaimer applies: although other versions within their respective major releases might work without additional changes, care should be taken when using versions that are different from the ones we've recommended:

Software	Version
VirtualBox	6.0.4
Vagrant	2.2.4
Minikube	1.0.1
kubectl	1.14.1

Regarding supported operating systems, all the tests were conducted using the following versions of Linux and macOS:

- Ubuntu 18.04 LTS (Bionic Beaver)
- macOS 10.14.3 (Mojave)

Other operating systems/distributions might be able to run the test environments, although it's not ensured.

VirtualBox

Oracle VirtualBox is a free and open source hypervisor, which runs on all major operating systems (macOS, Linux, and Windows). It allows you to not only launch virtual machine images, but also create virtual networks and mount host filesystem paths into the guests, among other features. This software requires hardware virtualization to be enabled.

> You can find all the installation files for VirtualBox at `https://www.virtualbox.org/wiki/Downloads`

Vagrant

HashiCorp Vagrant allows for the creation of portable environments. In the context of this book, it will become the interface with VirtualBox, allowing for the launch and configuration of virtual machines. In our examples, we chose to use Chef Bento as the virtual machine image, as recommended by HashiCorp.

> You can find all the installation files for Vagrant at https://www.vagrantup.com/downloads.html

Minikube

Minikube is the easiest way to test Kubernetes locally. We will be using Minikube in conjunction with VirtualBox to guarantee that the examples in this book behave the same way across operating systems.

> You can find all the installation information for Minikube at https://kubernetes.io/docs/tasks/tools/install-minikube/#install-minikube.

kubectl

The client tool for interacting with the Kubernetes API is called **kubectl**, and is fundamental for some of the examples in this book.

> You can find all the installation information for kubectl at https://kubernetes.io/docs/tasks/tools/install-minikube/#install-kubectl.

Spinning up a new environment

After you have ensured that all the required software is available on your host, you may proceed with one or both of the following walkthroughs.

Automated deployment walkthrough

This method will abstract all the deployment and configuration details, allowing you to have a fully running test environment with only a couple of commands. You'll still be able to connect to each of the guest instances and change configurations.

The steps to spin up the environment are as follows:

1. Clone this book's repository:

   ```
   git clone
   https://github.com/PacktPublishing/Hands-On-Infrastructure-Monitori
   ng-with-Prometheus.git
   ```

2. Step into the newly created directory and chapter number:

   ```
   cd Hands-On-Infrastructure-Monitoring-with-Prometheus/chapter03
   ```

3. Spin up this chapter's test environment:

   ```
   vagrant up
   ```

   The first run will take a few minutes because the Vagrant image and some of the software dependencies will have to be downloaded. After this setup process, subsequent runs will be much faster since all those assets will be kept in the cache.

4. Now, you can run `vagrant status`. You will be presented with the following output:

   ```
   Current machine states:

   prometheus running (virtualbox)
   grafana running (virtualbox)
   alertmanager running (virtualbox)

   This environment represents multiple VMs. The VMs are all listed
   above with their current state. For more information about a
   specific
   VM, run `vagrant status NAME`.
   ```

Prometheus

You can find the Prometheus HTTP endpoint at `http://192.168.42.10:9090/targets`:

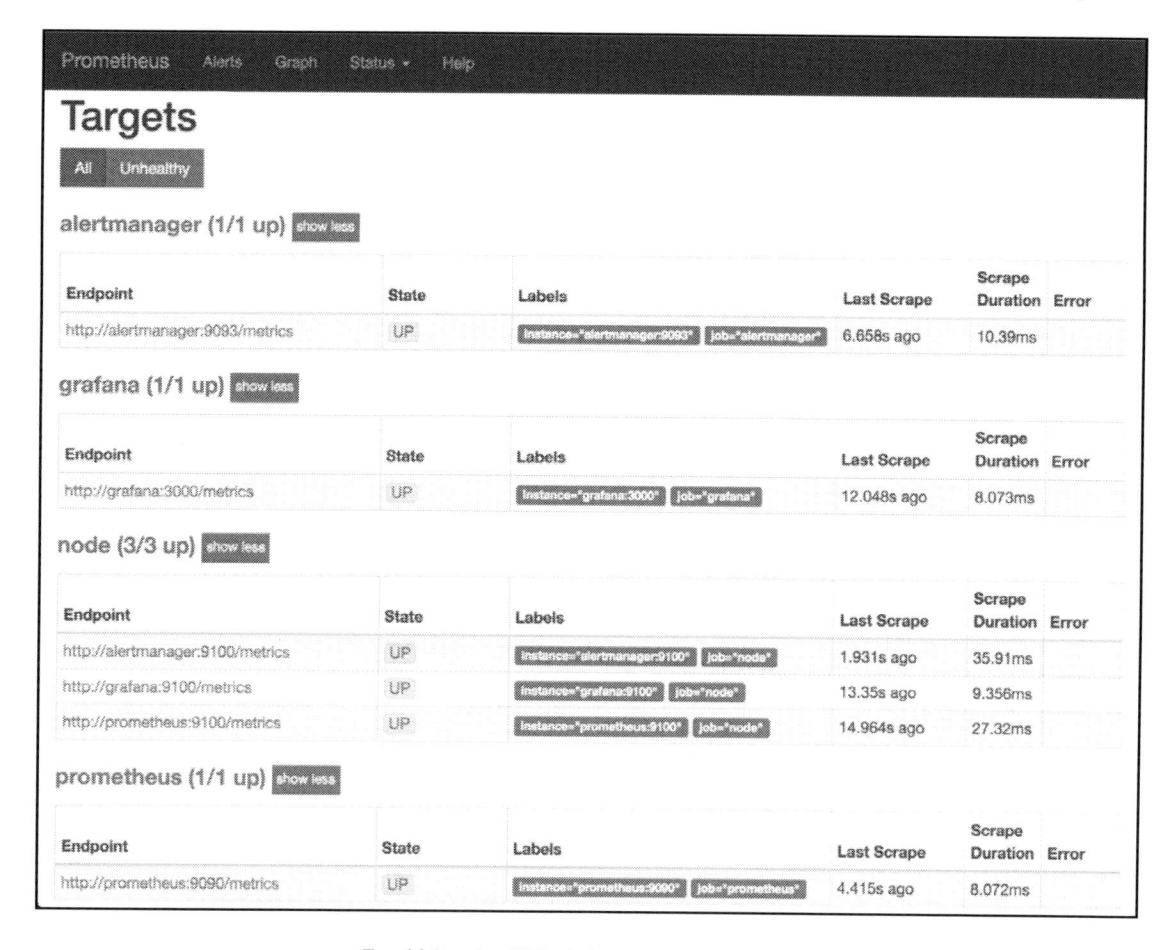

Figure 3.2: Prometheus HTTP endpoint – showing all configured targets

Grafana

You can find the Grafana HTTP endpoint at `http://192.168.42.11:3000`.

Grafana's default credentials are as follows:

Username	Password
`admin`	`admin`

You'll be greeted by two automatically provisioned dashboards. We'll have an entire chapter dedicated to Grafana and dashboards later in this book, in `Chapter 10`, *Discovering and Creating Grafana Dashboards*:

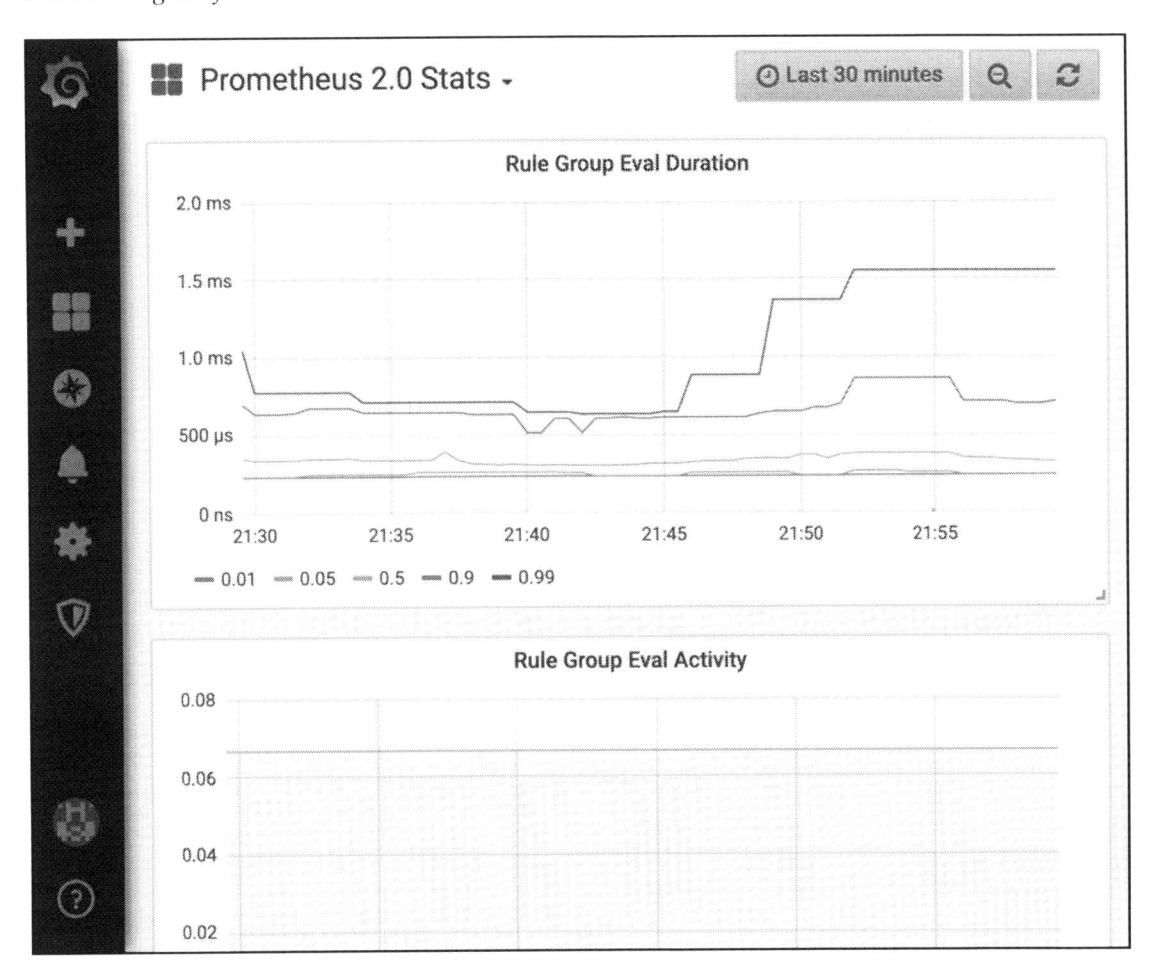

Figure 3.3: An automatically provisioned Grafana dashboard

Alertmanager

You can find the Alertmanager HTTP endpoint at `http://192.168.42.12:9093`.

We also configured an always-firing alert on Prometheus and a custom Alertmanager integration via webhook so that you can start to get a feel for how both are related. We'll go into much more detail on Alertmanager in a different chapter, but for now, you may look at the logs that the example alert generates in the code repository root at `./cache/alerting.log`:

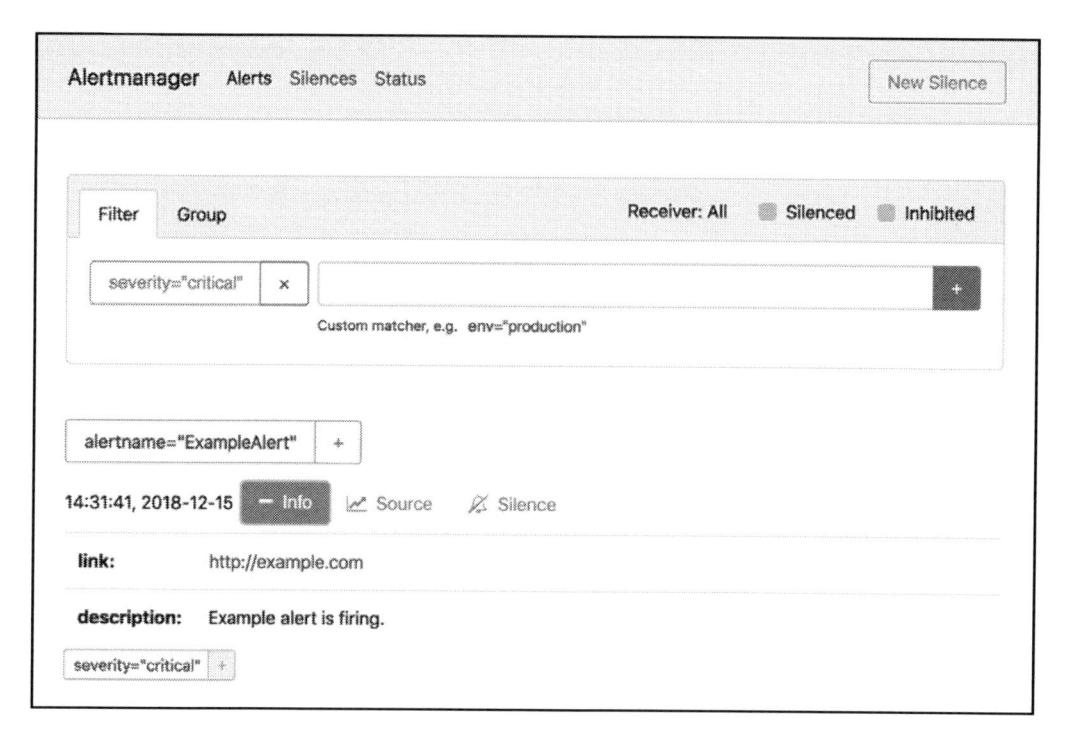

Figure 3.4: Alertmanager – firing an example alert

Cleanup

When you've finish testing, just make sure that's you're inside `chapter03` and execute the following:

```
vagrant destroy -f
```

Don't worry too much – you can easily spin up the environment again if you so desire.

Advanced deployment walkthrough

Using this method, the guest virtual machines will be spun up but no provision will take place, so you'll need to set up the environment yourself with a hands-on approach. We won't go into detailed explanations of the available configuration files and command-line arguments – those will be thoroughly explored in the following chapters. So, as a high-level overview, for each software component, we are going to do the following:

- Set up basic networking between the virtual machines in the environment
- Create an individual system user
- Download and install the software
- Create support files and directories
- Start the daemon

To start, clone this book's repository:

```
git clone
https://github.com/PacktPublishing/Hands-On-Infrastructure-Monitoring-with-
Prometheus.git
```

Step into the newly created directory and chapter number and run Vagrant without provisioning the guest instances. This will leave you with just off-the-shelf virtual machines:

```
cd Hands-On-Infrastructure-Monitoring-with-Prometheus/chapter03
vagrant up --no-provision
```

After all the guests have started, we will continue by configuring our instances one by one.

Prometheus

Perform the following steps:

1. Log in to the Prometheus guest instance:

    ```
    vagrant ssh prometheus
    ```

Setting Up a Test Environment

2. Inside the guest instance, drop to the root:

   ```
   sudo -i
   ```

3. Add all the guests' addresses to the instance host's file:

   ```
   cat <<EOF >/etc/hosts
   127.0.0.1        localhost
   192.168.42.10    prometheus.prom.inet    prometheus
   192.168.42.11    grafana.prom.inet       grafana
   192.168.42.12    alertmanager.prom.inet  alertmanager


   # The following lines are desirable for IPv6 capable hosts
   ::1       localhost ip6-localhost ip6-loopback
   ff02::1 ip6-allnodes
   ff02::2 ip6-allrouters
   EOF
   ```

4. Create a new system user:

   ```
   useradd --system prometheus
   ```

5. Go into /tmp and download the Prometheus archive:

   ```
   cd /tmp
   curl -sLO
   "https://github.com/prometheus/prometheus/releases/download/v2.9.2/
   prometheus-2.9.2.linux-amd64.tar.gz"
   ```

6. Uncompress the archive:

   ```
   tar zxvf prometheus-2.9.2.linux-amd64.tar.gz
   ```

7. Place every file in its correct location:

   ```
   install -m 0644 -D -t /usr/share/prometheus/consoles
   prometheus-2.9.2.linux-amd64/consoles/*

   install -m 0644 -D -t /usr/share/prometheus/console_libraries
   prometheus-2.9.2.linux-amd64/console_libraries/*

   install -m 0755 prometheus-2.9.2.linux-amd64/prometheus
   prometheus-2.9.2.linux-amd64/promtool /usr/bin/

   install -d -o prometheus -g prometheus /var/lib/prometheus

   install -m 0644 -D
   ```

```
/vagrant/chapter03/configs/prometheus/prometheus.yml
/etc/prometheus/prometheus.yml

install -m 0644 -D
/vagrant/chapter03/configs/prometheus/first_rules.yml
/etc/prometheus/first_rules.yml
```

8. Add a `systemd` unit file for the Prometheus service:

   ```
   install -m 0644
   /vagrant/chapter03/configs/prometheus/prometheus.service
   /etc/systemd/system/

   systemctl daemon-reload
   ```

9. Enable and start the Prometheus service:

   ```
   systemctl enable prometheus
   systemctl start prometheus
   ```

   You should now have the Prometheus HTTP endpoint available on your host.

10. Exit the root account and then the Vagrant user account:

    ```
    exit
    ```

    ```
    exit
    ```

Grafana

Perform the following steps:

1. Log in to the Grafana guest instance:

   ```
   vagrant ssh grafana
   ```

2. Inside the guest instance, drop to the root:

   ```
   sudo -i
   ```

Setting Up a Test Environment

3. Add all the guests' addresses to the instance host's file:

   ```
   cat <<EOF >/etc/hosts
   127.0.0.1          localhost
   192.168.42.10      prometheus.prom.inet     prometheus
   192.168.42.11      grafana.prom.inet        grafana
   192.168.42.12      alertmanager.prom.inet   alertmanager


   # The following lines are desirable for IPv6 capable hosts
   ::1       localhost ip6-localhost ip6-loopback
   ff02::1 ip6-allnodes
   ff02::2 ip6-allrouters
   EOF
   ```

4. Go into /tmp and download the Grafana package:

   ```
   cd /tmp
   curl -sLO
   "https://dl.grafana.com/oss/release/grafana_6.1.6_amd64.deb"
   ```

5. Install the package and all dependencies:

   ```
   DEBIAN_FRONTEND=noninteractive apt-get install -y libfontconfig

   dpkg -i "grafana_6.1.6_amd64.deb"
   ```

6. Place all the provided configurations on their correct location:

   ```
   rsync -ru
   /vagrant/chapter03/configs/grafana/{dashboards,provisioning}
   /etc/grafana/
   ```

7. Enable and start the Grafana service:

   ```
   systemctl daemon-reload
   systemctl enable grafana-server
   systemctl start grafana-server
   ```

   You should now have the Grafana HTTP endpoint available on your host.

8. Exit the root account and then the Vagrant user account:

   ```
   exit

   exit
   ```

Alertmanager

Perform the following steps:

1. Log in to the Alertmanager guest instance:

   ```
   vagrant ssh alertmanager
   ```

2. Inside the guest instance, drop to the root:

   ```
   sudo -i
   ```

3. Add all the guests' addresses to the instance host's file:

   ```
   cat <<EOF >/etc/hosts
   127.0.0.1         localhost
   192.168.42.10     prometheus.prom.inet      prometheus
   192.168.42.11     grafana.prom.inet         grafana
   192.168.42.12     alertmanager.prom.inet    alertmanager


   # The following lines are desirable for IPv6 capable hosts
   ::1     localhost ip6-localhost ip6-loopback
   ff02::1 ip6-allnodes
   ff02::2 ip6-allrouters
   EOF
   ```

4. Create a new system user:

   ```
   useradd --system alertmanager
   ```

5. Go into /tmp and download the Alertmanager archive:

   ```
   cd /tmp
   curl -sLO
   "https://github.com/prometheus/alertmanager/releases/download/v0.17
   .0/alertmanager-0.17.0.linux-amd64.tar.gz"
   ```

6. Uncompress the archive:

   ```
   tar zxvf alertmanager-0.17.0.linux-amd64.tar.gz
   ```

7. Place every file in its correct location:

   ```
   install -m 0755 alertmanager-0.17.0.linux-amd64/{alertmanager,amtool}
   /vagrant/chapter03/configs/alertmanager/alertdump /usr/bin/

   install -d -o alertmanager -g alertmanager /var/lib/alertmanager

   install -m 0644 -D
   /vagrant/chapter03/configs/alertmanager/alertmanager.yml
   /etc/alertmanager/alertmanager.yml
   ```

8. Add a `systemd` unit file for the Alertmanager service:

   ```
   install -m 0644
   /vagrant/chapter03/configs/alertmanager/alertmanager.service
   /etc/systemd/system/

   systemctl daemon-reload
   ```

9. Enable and start the Alertmanager service:

   ```
   systemctl enable alertmanager
   systemctl start alertmanager
   ```

   You should now have the Alertmanager HTTP endpoint available on your host.

10. Exit the root account and then the Vagrant user account:

    ```
    exit

    exit
    ```

Node Exporter

To ensure that system-level metrics will be collected, Node Exporter must be installed in all three virtual machines. To log in to each virtual machine, use the commands that we explored in the previous sections:

1. Inside the guest instance, drop to the root:

   ```
   sudo -i
   ```

2. Create a new system user:

   ```
   useradd --system node_exporter
   ```

[44]

3. Go into `/tmp` and download the Node Exporter archive:

   ```
   cd /tmp
   curl -sLO "https://github.com/prometheus/node_exporter/releases/download/v0.17.0/node_exporter-0.17.0.linux-amd64.tar.gz"
   ```

4. Place every file in its correct location:

   ```
   tar zxvf "node_exporter-0.17.0.linux-amd64.tar.gz" -C /usr/bin --strip-components=1 --wildcards */node_exporter
   ```

5. Add a `systemd` unit file for the Node Exporter service:

   ```
   install -m 0644 /vagrant/chapter03/configs/node_exporter/node-exporter.service /etc/systemd/system/
   ```

   ```
   systemctl daemon-reload
   ```

6. Enable and start the Node Exporter service:

   ```
   systemctl enable node-exporter
   systemctl start node-exporter
   ```

7. Exit the root account and then the Vagrant user account:

   ```
   exit
   ```

   ```
   exit
   ```

Validating your test environment

After running through these steps, you'll be able to validate your environment by using the following endpoints on your host machine:

Service	Endpoint
Prometheus	`http://192.168.42.10:9090`
Grafana	`http://192.168.42.11:3000`
Alertmanager	`http://192.168.42.12:9093`

Summary

With a test environment at your disposal, you can now inspect, change, and validate configurations without worrying about breaking things. Throughout this book, this approach to testing will be used extensively, because nothing beats experimenting when learning new skills.

In the next chapter, we'll go over the fundamentals of Prometheus metrics. The test environment we just built will be helpful to demonstrate them.

Questions

1. What are the recommended tools to set up a reproducible test environment?
2. Where can you change the default versions of the Prometheus components for the test environment?
3. What is the default subnet that's used on all examples?
4. At a high level, what are the steps to get a Prometheus instance up and running?
5. Node Exporter is installed on every guest instance. How can you quickly validate if all of them are exposing metrics correctly?
6. In our test environment, where can you find the alert log?
7. How can you create a clean test environment from scratch?

Further reading

- **Bash manual**: https://www.gnu.org/software/bash/manual/html_node/index.html
- **Recommended Vagrant boxes**: https://www.vagrantup.com/docs/boxes.html

Section 2: Getting Started with Prometheus

With the testing environment up and running, it is time to dive into the Prometheus stack. This section will look at metrics, configurations, and best practices.

The following chapters are included in this section:

- `Chapter 4`, *Prometheus Metrics Fundamentals*
- `Chapter 5`, *Running a Prometheus Server*
- `Chapter 6`, *Exporters and Integrations*
- `Chapter 7`, *Prometheus Query Language – PromQL*
- `Chapter 8`, *Troubleshooting and Validation*

4
Prometheus Metrics Fundamentals

Metrics are the core resources that the Prometheus stack ingests to provide you with useful information. Understanding them correctly is essential to fully utilize, manage, or even extend the realm of possibilities this stack has to offer. From data to information, and finally to knowledge, metrics are here to help you.

In brief, the following topics will be covered in this chapter:

- Understanding the Prometheus data model
- A tour of the four core metric types
- Longitudinal and cross-sectional aggregations

Understanding the Prometheus data model

To understand the Prometheus data model, we need to go through what makes a time series and the storage of such data. These concepts will be invaluable throughout this book.

Time series data

Time series data can usually be defined as a sequence of numerical data points that are indexed chronologically from the same source. In the scope of Prometheus, these data points are collected at a fixed time interval. As such, this kind of data, when represented in graphical form, will most commonly plot the evolution of the data through time, with the x axis being time and the y axis being the data value.

Time series databases

It all starts with the need to collect, store, and query measurements over time. When dealing with massive amounts of data from collectors and sensors (such as those that make up the Internet of Things), querying the resulting datasets is extremely slow if the database isn't designed with that use case in mind. Nothing prevents you from using standard relational or NoSQL databases to store time series data, but the performance penalty and scalability concerns should make you ponder on that decision. Prometheus chose to implement a time series database that was tailored to its unique problem space.

Besides the write-heavy aspect of these types of databases, which in turn implies the storage of a massive volume of measurements, it is also important to understand that a simple query can span over several hours, days, or even months, returning a tremendous amount of data points, but is still expected to return data reasonably fast.

As such, modern time series databases store the following components:

- A timestamp
- A value
- Some context about the value, encoded in a metric name or in associated key/value pairs

An abstract example of data that fits this time series database specification is as follows:

```
timestamp=1544978108, company=ACME, location=headquarters, beverage=coffee, value=40172
```

As you can see, this kind of data can be easily stored into a single table in a database:

timestamp	company	location	beverage	value
1544978108	ACME	headquarters	coffee	40172

In this simple example, we can check the cups of coffee being served by a vending machine located at the headquarters of the ACME company. This example has all the required components of a time series if it's continually measured through time.

> This example does not map directly to the Prometheus data model, as it also requires a metric name, but illustrates the logic we're aiming to address.

Prometheus local storage

Local storage is the standard approach for storing data in Prometheus and, as such, we must understand its basics. At a very high level, Prometheus storage design is a combination of an index implementation using posting lists for all currently stored labels with their values, and its own time series data format.

Data flow

The way Prometheus stores collected data locally can be seen as a three-part process. The following topics depict the stages that data goes through until it's successfully persisted.

Memory

The freshest batch of data is kept in memory for up to two hours. This includes one or more chunks of data that are gathered during the two-hour time window. This approach dramatically reduces disk I/O two fold; the most recent data is available in memory, making it blazingly fast to query; and the chunks of data are created in memory, avoiding constant disk writes.

Write ahead log

While in memory, data is not persisted and could be lost if the process terminates abnormally. To prevent this scenario, a **write-ahead log** (**WAL**) in disk keeps the state of the in-memory data so that it can be replayed if Prometheus, for any reason, crashes or restarts.

Disk

After the two-hour time window, the chunks get written to disk. These chunks are immutable and, even though data can be deleted, it's not an atomic operation. Instead, tombstone files are created with the information of the data that's no longer required.

Layout

The way data gets stored in Prometheus, as we can see in the following example, is organized into a series of directories (blocks) containing the data chunks, the LevelDB index for that data, a `meta.json` file with human-readable information about the block, and tombstones for data that's no longer required. Each one of these blocks represents a database.

At the top level, you can also see the WAL for the data that's not been flushed into its own chunk yet:

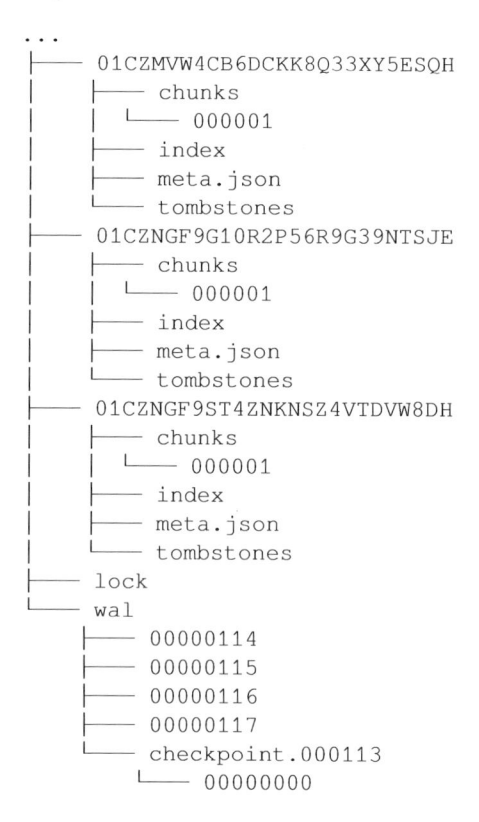

```
...
├── 01CZMVW4CB6DCKK8Q33XY5ESQH
│   ├── chunks
│   │   └── 000001
│   ├── index
│   ├── meta.json
│   └── tombstones
├── 01CZNGF9G10R2P56R9G39NTSJE
│   ├── chunks
│   │   └── 000001
│   ├── index
│   ├── meta.json
│   └── tombstones
├── 01CZNGF9ST4ZNKNSZ4VTDVW8DH
│   ├── chunks
│   │   └── 000001
│   ├── index
│   ├── meta.json
│   └── tombstones
├── lock
└── wal
    ├── 00000114
    ├── 00000115
    ├── 00000116
    ├── 00000117
    └── checkpoint.000113
        └── 00000000
```

Prometheus data model

As we have seen so far, Prometheus stores data as time series, which includes key/value pairs known as labels, a timestamp, and finally a value. The following topics will expand on these components and provide the basics for each one, which we will be utilizing in depth in `Chapter 7`, *Prometheus Query Language - PromQL*, dedicated to PromQL.

Notation

A time series in Prometheus is represented as follows:

```
<metric_name>[{<label_1="value_1">,<label_N="value_N">}]
<datapoint_numerical_value>
```

As you can see, it's represented as a metric name, optionally followed by one or more set of label names/values inside curly brackets, and then the value of the metric. Additionally, a sample will also have a timestamp with millisecond precision.

Metric names

Even though this is an implementation detail, a metric name is nothing more than the value of a special label called "__name__". So, if you have a metric named `"beverages_total"`, internally, it's represented as "__name__=beverages_total". Keep in mind that labels surrounded by "__" are internal to Prometheus, and any label prefixed with "__" is only available in some phases of the metrics collection cycle.

The combination of labels (key/values) and the metric name defines the identity of a time series.

Every metric name in Prometheus must match the following regular expression:

```
"[a-zA-Z_:][a-zA-Z0-9_:]*"
```

This, in layman's terms, means that metric names only allow lowercase and uppercase letters of the English alphabet (`a-z`), underscores (`_`), colons (`:`), and Arabic numerals (`0-9`), except on the first character, where numbers are not allowed.

> Colons are reserved for a special kind of metric-designated recording rule. We will expand on this subject in another chapter.

Metric labels

Labels, or the key/value pairs associated with a certain metric, add dimensionality to the metrics. This is an essential part of what makes Prometheus so good at slicing and dicing time series, as we'll see in `Chapter 7`, *Prometheus Query Language – PromQL*.

While label values can be full UTF-8, label names have to match a regular expression to be considered valid; for example, `"[a-zA-Z0-9_]*"`.

Their main difference in regard to metric names is that label names don't allow the colon (:).

Samples

Samples are the collected data points, and they represent the numerical value of time series data. The components that are required to define a sample are a float64 value, and a timestamp with millisecond precision. Something to keep in mind is that samples collected out of order will be discarded by Prometheus. The same happens to samples with the same metric identity and different sample values.

Cardinality

Depending on the computing resources being assigned to a Prometheus instance (that is, CPU, memory, disk space, and IOPS), it will gracefully handle a number of time series. This number can be thought of as the primary indicator of capacity for that instance, and it will inform your scraping decisions: will you have thousands of targets with relatively few metrics, fewer targets with a thousand metrics each, or something in between? In the end, Prometheus will only be able to handle that amount of time series without performance degradation.

It is in this context that the concept of cardinality appears. This term is often used to mean the number of unique time series that are produced by a combination of metric names and their associated label names/values. As an example, a single metric with no additional dimensions (such as labels) from an application that has one hundred instances will naturally mean that Prometheus will store 100 time series, one for each instance (the instance, here, is a dimension that's added outside of the application); another metric from that application that had a label with ten possible values will translate into 1,000 time series (10 time series per instance, times 100 instances). This shows that cardinality is multiplicative—each additional dimension will increase the number of produced time series by repeating the existing dimensions for each value of the new one. Having multiple dimensions with a large number of possible values in a metric will cause what is called a cardinality explosion in Prometheus, which is the creation of a very large number of time series.

When you have label values that don't have a clear limit, which can increase indefinitely or above hundreds of possible values, you will also have a cardinality problem. These metrics might be better suited to be handled in logs-based systems.

The following are some examples of data with high or unbound cardinality that should not be used as label values (or in metric names, for that matter):

- Email addresses
- Usernames
- Request/process/order/transaction ID

A tour of the four core metric types

Prometheus metrics are divided into four main types: counters, gauges, histograms, and summaries. It is essential to understand them in depth, as most functions provided by Prometheus only work correctly with a given data type. So, to that end, here is an overview of each.

Counter

This is a strictly cumulative metric whose value can only increase. The only exception for this rule is when the metric is reset, which brings it back to zero.

Prometheus Metrics Fundamentals

This is one of the most useful metric types because even if a scrape fails, you won't lose the cumulative increase in the data, which will be available on the next scrape. To be clear, in the case of a failed scrape, granularity would be lost as fewer points will be saved.

To help visualize this type of metric, here are some examples of counters and their graphical representation based on the test environment we created in the previous chapter:

- The total number of packets received by the Prometheus instance:

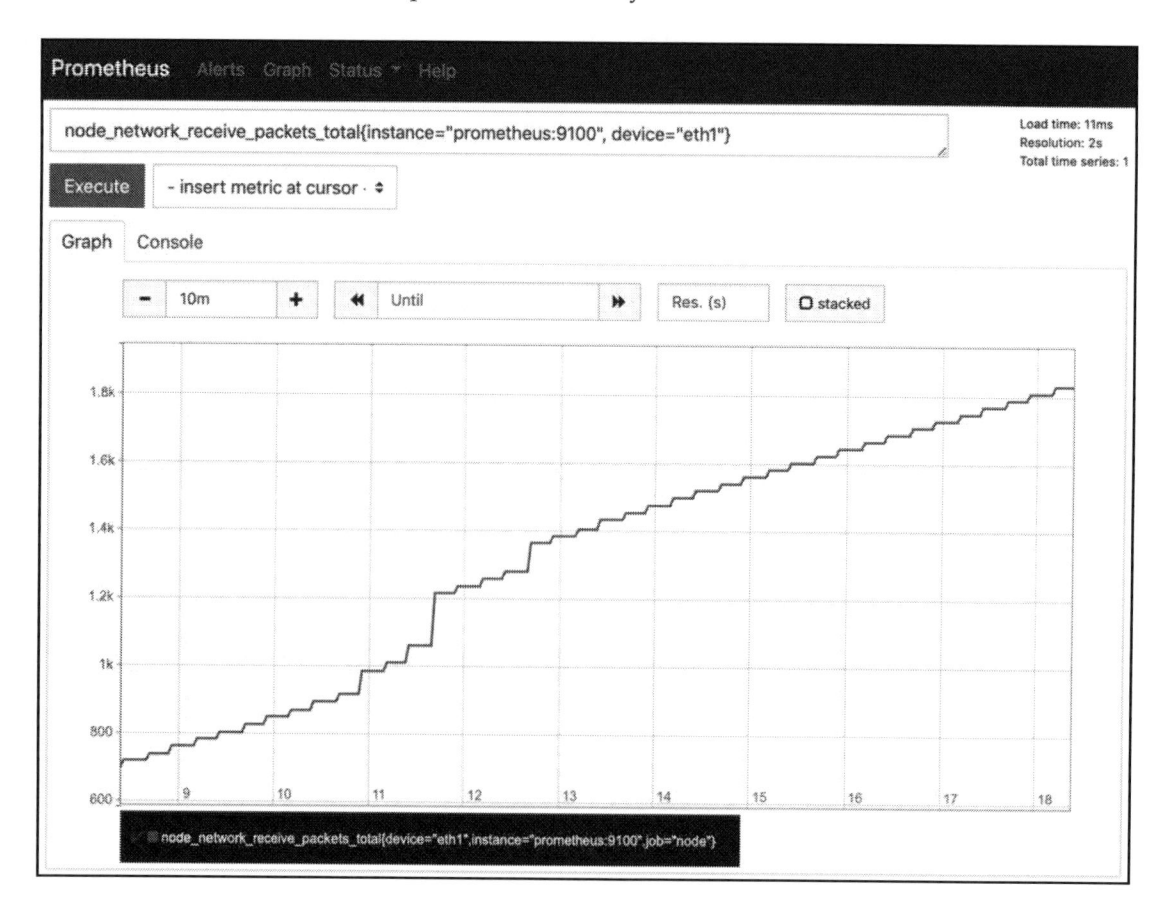

- The total number of bytes written to disk by the Grafana instance – notice the middle gap caused by an instance restart, forcing the counter to reset:

Gauge

A gauge is a metric that snapshots a given measurement at the time of collection, which can increase or decrease (such as temperature, disk space, and memory usage).

If a scrape fails, you will lose that sample, as the next scrape might encounter the metric on a different value (higher/lower).

Prometheus Metrics Fundamentals

To help visualize this type of metric, here are some examples of gauges and their graphical representation based on the test environment we created in the previous chapter:

- The number of established TCP connections on the Alertmanager instance:

- The amount of free memory on the Grafana instance – notice the middle gap caused by an instance restart, preventing any assumption about the possible value during that period:

Histogram

Recording numerical data that's inherent to each event in a system can be expensive, so some sort of pre-aggregation is usually needed to conserve at least partial information about what happened. However, by pre-calculating aggregations on each instance (such as average since process start, rolling window, exponentially weighted, and so on), a lot of granularity is lost and some calculations can be computationally costly. Adding to this, a lot of pre-aggregations can't generally be re-aggregated without losing meaning—the average of a thousand pre-calculated 95th percentiles has no statistical meaning. Similarly, having the 99th percentile of request latency collected from each instance of a given cluster (for example) gives you no indication of the overall cluster's 99th percentile and no way to accurately calculate it.

Histograms allow you to retain some granularity by counting events into buckets that are configurable on the client side, and also by providing a sum of all observed values. Prometheus histograms produce one time series per configured bucket, plus an additional two that track the sum and the count of observed events. Furthermore, histograms in Prometheus are cumulative, which means each bucket will have the value of the previous bucket, plus the number of its own events. This is done so that some buckets can be dropped for performance or storage reasons without losing the overall ability to use the histogram.

The downside of using histograms is that the selected buckets need to fit the range and distribution of values that are expected to be collected. The error margin for quantile calculation will be directly related with this fit: too few or poorly selected buckets will increase the error margins for quantile calculations.

This type of metric is especially useful to track bucketed latencies and sizes (for example, request durations or response sizes) as it can be freely aggregated across different dimensions. Another great use is to generate heatmaps (the evolution of histograms over time).

To help visualize this type of metric, here is an example of a histogram and its graphical representation based on the test environment we created in the previous chapter:

- A Prometheus HTTP request duration in seconds, divided into buckets. This is shown in a Grafana heatmap to better illustrate the concept of buckets:

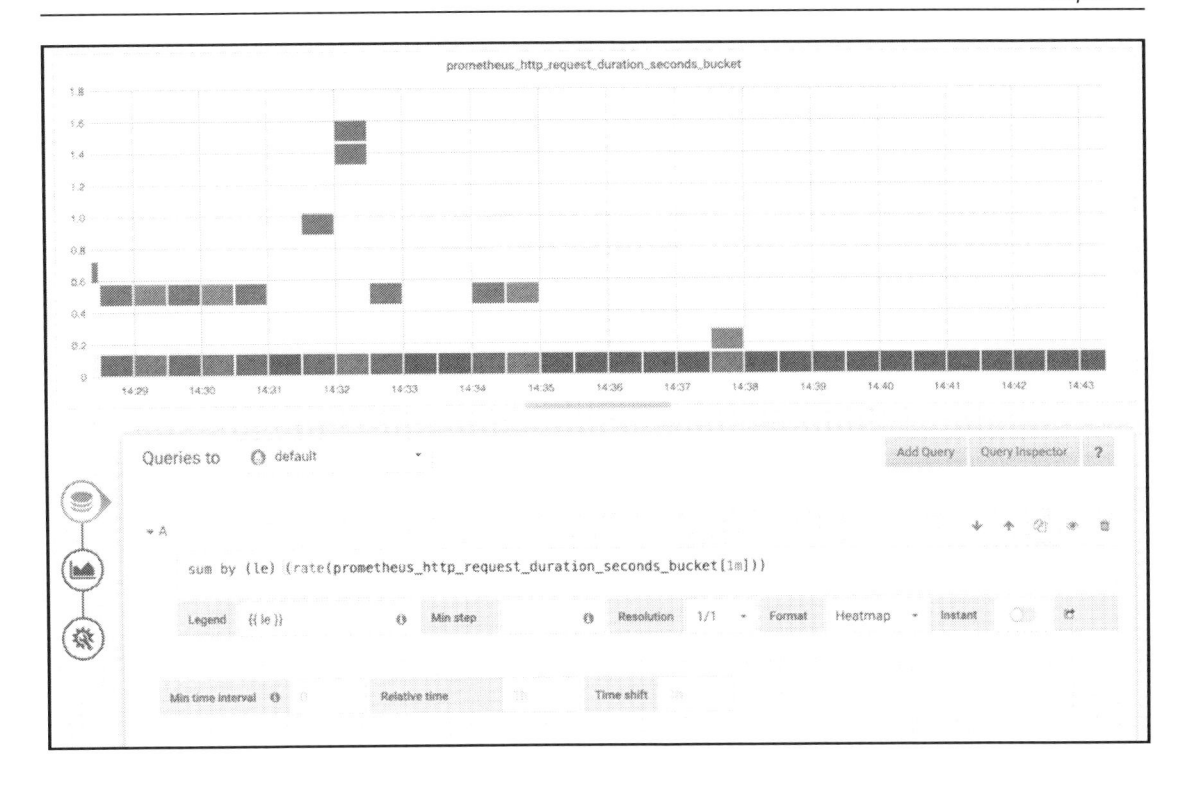

Summaries

Summaries are similar to histograms in some ways, but present different trade-offs and are generally less useful. They are also used to track sizes and latencies, and also provide both a sum and a count of observed events. Additionally (and if the client library used supports it), summaries can also provide pre-calculated quantiles over a predetermined sliding time window. The main reason to use summary quantiles is when accurate quantile estimation is needed, irrespective of the distribution and range of the observed events.

> Quantiles in Prometheus are referred to as φ-quantiles, where $0 \leq \varphi \leq 1$.

Both quantiles and sliding window size are defined in the instrumentation code, so it's not possible to calculate other quantiles or window sizes on an ad hoc basis. Doing these calculations on the client side also means that the instrumentation and computational cost is a lot higher. The last downside to mention is that the resulting quantiles are not aggregable and thus of limited usefulness.

One benefit that summaries have is that, without quantiles, they are quite cheap to generate, collect, and store.

To help visualize this type of metric, here is an example of a summary and its graphical representation, based on the test environment we created in the previous chapter:

- The maximum duration of the Prometheus rule group in seconds by quantile:

Longitudinal and cross-sectional aggregations

The last concept to grasp when thinking about time series is how aggregations work on an abstract level. One of Prometheus' core strengths is that it makes the manipulation of time series data easy, and this slicing and dicing of data usually boils down to two kinds of aggregations, which are often used together: longitudinal and cross-sectional aggregations.

In the context of time series, an aggregation is a process that reduces or summarizes the raw data, which is to say that it receives a set of data points as input and produces a smaller set (often a single element) as output. Some of the most common aggregation functions in time series databases are minimum, maximum, average, count, and sum.

To better understand how these aggregations work, let's look at some data using the example time series we presented earlier in this chapter. To be clear, the next few sections will explain how these aggregations work on an abstract level and will hint at what their Prometheus counterparts are, but are not supposed to be a one-to-one match with PromQL (which we will explore thoroughly in `Chapter 7`, *Prometheus Query Language – PromQL*).

Let's pretend we've selected `{company=ACME, beverage=coffee}` and we're now looking at the raw counters over time per location. The data would look something like this:

Location/Time	t=0	t=1	t=2	t=3	t=4	t=5	t=6
Factory	1,045	1	2	3	4	5	6
Warehouse	223	223	223	223	224	224	224
Headquarters	40,160	40,162	40,164	40,166	40,168	40,170	40,172

> Actual data wouldn't look exactly like this, as each time series is collected at slightly different times. The data points would have their own timestamps associated, which means they would be out of alignment. This, in turn, impacts on the results of aggregations, as some method of interpolation would be applied to align data points.

For argument's sake, let's say that the samples were collected every minute. The metric type is probably a counter, as it's monotonically increasing, with the exception of the counter that's reset at `t=1` for `location=factory`.

Cross-sectional aggregation

Cross-sectional aggregations are the easiest to understand. As we can see in the following data representation, we take a column of data and apply an aggregation function to it:

Location/Time	t=0	t=1	t=2	t=3	t=4	t=5	t=6
Factory	1,045	1	2	3	4	5	6
Warehouse	223	223	223	223	224	224	224
Headquarters	40160	40,162	40,164	40,166	40,168	40,170	40,172

If we apply the `max()` aggregation, we can find out which location reported more coffees were dispensed—in this case, the result would be 40,172. Applying `count()` would give us the number of offices reporting data for the dimensions that were selected (`{company=ACME, beverage=coffee}`): 3.

> **TIP**
> It's not generally sane to apply `max()` to a counter, as we'll see in Chapter 7, *Prometheus Query Language – PromQL*. This is a simple and abstract example to help you understand the basics of time series.

This type of aggregation usually applies to the last data points in the requested set. The most common case where this is not true is when graphing the aggregation over time, as it needs to be calculated for each point in the graph.

You will notice that the selected data resembles a traditional column vector from linear algebra. As we'll see in Chapter 7, *Prometheus Query Language – PromQL*, dedicated to PromQL, these will be referred to as instant vectors.

Longitudinal aggregation

Longitudinal aggregations are trickier to use because you need to select a time window over which to apply the aggregation. This means they work over rows, as we can see in the following representation:

Location/Time	t=0	t=1	t=2	t=3	t=4	t=5	t=6
Factory	1,045	1	2	3	4	5	6
Warehouse	223	223	223	223	224	224	224
Headquarters	40,160	40,162	40,164	40,166	40,168	40,170	40,172

Since the current selectors we're using return three rows of data, this means we'll have three results when applying longitudinal aggregations. In this example, we've selected the last three minutes of data for aggregation (as we mentioned previously, we're considering a 1-minute sample interval). If we apply the `max()` aggregation over time, since these are counters and there wasn't a reset in the selected window, we will get the latest values in the selected set: 6 for `location=factory`, **224** for `location=warehouse`, and **40,172** for `location=headquarters`. `count()` will return the number of points that were selected in the specified time range—in this case, since the collection occurs every minute and we requested it for three minutes, it will return **3** for each location.

A more interesting aggregation of this kind that wasn't mentioned before is `rate()`. It is a particularly useful aggregation to use with counters, as you can calculate the rate of change per unit of time—we will explore this in detail later in this book. In this example, `rate()` would return 1, 0, and 2 for each location, respectively.

Once again, we would like to point out the resemblance of the selected data to a traditional matrix from mathematics. These type of selections will be referred to as range vectors in PromQL.

Summary

In this chapter, we came to understand what time series data is, and looked at an overview of how a modern time series database such as Prometheus works, not only logically, but physically as well. We went through the Prometheus metrics notation and how metric names and labels relate to each other, and also covered what defines a sample. Prometheus metrics have four types, and we had the chance to go through every one of them and provide some useful examples. Finally, we dived into how longitudinal and cross-sectional aggregations work, which is essential to fully take advantage of Prometheus' query language.

In the next chapter, we'll return to a more hands-on approach and go into Prometheus server configuration, and how to manage it on both virtual machines and Kubernetes.

Questions

1. What is the mandatory requirement of any graphical time series representation?
2. What are the components for a data point to be considered as time series data?
3. When a Prometheus server crashes, what prevents it from losing data?
4. What is the Prometheus in-memory database time window for storing data?
5. What are the components of a Prometheus sample?
6. What are the common use cases for both histograms and summaries?
7. What is the difference between a cross-sectional and a longitudinal aggregation?

Further reading

- **Prometheus storage layout**: https://prometheus.io/docs/prometheus/latest/storage/
- **Prometheus storage format**: https://github.com/prometheus/tsdb/blob/master/docs/format/README.md
- **Fabian Reinartz – Writing a Time Series Database from Scratch**: https://fabxc.org/tsdb/
- **Prometheus data model**: https://prometheus.io/docs/concepts/data_model/
- **Histograms and Summaries**: https://prometheus.io/docs/practices/histograms/

5
Running a Prometheus Server

It's time to get our hands on some Prometheus configurations. This chapter will explore the core component of the stack, you will be introduced to common patterns of usage and full setup process scenarios under virtual machines and containers. This will allow you to truly validate the knowledge you've gathered so far and provide you with real examples to test your knowledge.

In brief, the following topics will be covered in this chapter:

- Deep dive into the Prometheus configuration
- Managing Prometheus in a standalone server
- Managing Prometheus in Kubernetes

Deep dive into the Prometheus configuration

One of the key features of Prometheus is, owing to incredibly sane default configurations, that it can scale from a quick test running on a local computer to a production-grade instance, handling millions of samples per second without having to touch almost any of its many knobs and dials. Having said that, it is very useful to know what configuration options are available to be able to get the most value out of Prometheus.

There are two main types of configuration on a Prometheus server—command-line flags and operating logic that provided through configuration files. Command-line flags control the parameters that cannot be changed at runtime, such as the storage path or which TCP port to bind to, and need a full server restart to apply any change done at this level. The configuration files control runtime configuration, such as scrape job definitions, rules files locations, or remote storage setup. In the following sections, we're going to explore both of these types of configurations in depth.

Prometheus startup configuration

While running a Prometheus server with no startup configuration can be good enough for local instances, it is advisable to configure a couple of basic command-line flags for any serious deployment.

At the time of writing, Prometheus has almost 30 command-line flags for tweaking several aspects of its operational configuration, grouped by the following namespaces: `config`, `web`, `storage`, `rules`, `alertmanager`, `query`, and `log`. The `--help` flag does a good job of describing most options, but it can be a bit terse in a few places, so we're going to highlight the ones that are either important for any deployment or whose function is not readily apparent.

The config section

The first thing that is usually important to set is the Prometheus configuration file path, through the `--config.file` flag. By default, Prometheus will look for a file named `prometheus.yml` in the current working directory. While this is great for local tests, production deployments usually place server binaries and configuration files in their own paths, and so this flag is commonly needed. As a side note, this and a storage directory are the only hard requirements for starting a Prometheus server; without a configuration file, Prometheus refuses to start.

The storage section

Following the same logic from the previous section, the `--storage.tsdb.path` flag should be set to configure the base path to the data storage location. This defaults to `data/` on the current working directory, and so it is advisable to point this to a more appropriate path—possibly to a different drive/volume, where data can be safely persisted and I/O contention can be mitigated. To note that NFS (AWS EFS included) is not supported, as it doesn't support the POSIX locking primitives needed for safe database files management. Placing the Prometheus data storage directory in a network share is also ill-advised as transient network failures would impact the monitoring system's ability to keep functioning - just when you'd need it the most.

The Prometheus local storage can only be written to by a single Prometheus instance at a time. To make sure this is the case, it uses a lock file in the data directory. On startup, it tries to lock this file using OS-specific system calls, and will refuse to start if the file is already locked by another process.

There can be an edge case to this behavior; when using persistent volumes to store the data directory, there is a chance that, when relaunching Prometheus as another container instance using the same volume, the previous instance might not have unlocked the database. This problem would make a setup of this kind susceptible to race conditions. Luckily, there is the `--storage.tsdb.no-lockfile` flag, which can be used in exactly this type of situation. Be warned though that, in general (and namely, in most Prometheus deployments), it is a bad idea to disable the lock file, as doing so makes unintended data corruption easier.

The web section

The next step is to configure what address users are going to utilize to get to the Prometheus server. The `--web.external-url` flag sets this base URL so that weblinks generated both in the web user interface and in outgoing alerts link back to the Prometheus server or servers correctly. This might be the DNS name for a load balancer/reverse proxy, a Kubernetes service, or, in the simplest deployments, the publicly accessible, fully qualified domain name of the host running the server. For completeness, and as stated in the official documentation, a URL path can also be supplied here when Prometheus is behind some layer seven reverse proxy with content switching (also referred to as location-based switching or URL prefix routing).

The Prometheus server behaves as a conventional `*nix` daemon by reloading its configuration file (along with rules files) when it receives a `SIGHUP`. However, there are situations where sending this signal isn't convenient (for example, when running in a container orchestration system such as Kubernetes or using custom-built automation) or even impossible (when running Prometheus on Windows). In these situations, the `--web.enable-lifecycle` flag can be used to enable the `/-/reload` and `/-/quit` HTTP endpoints, which can be used to control, reload, and shut down, respectively. To prevent accidental triggering of these endpoints, and because a `GET` wouldn't be semantically correct, a `POST` request is needed. This flag is turned off by default as unfettered access to these endpoints pose a security concern.

Similarly, the `--web.enable-admin-api` flag is also turned off by default for the same reason. This flag enables HTTP endpoints that provide some advanced administration actions, such as creating snapshots of data, deleting time series, and cleaning tombstones.

As you may have noticed in Chapter 3, *Setting Up a Test Environment*, the official Prometheus tarballs also bring two additional directories, `consoles` and `console_libraries`. These are needed to enable the native dashboarding capabilities of Prometheus, which are often overlooked. These directories contain some preconfigured dashboards (referred to as consoles) and support template libraries, written in the Go templating language. Prometheus can be configured to load these by using the `--web.console.templates` and `--web.console.libraries` flags. After that, those dashboards will be available at the `/consoles` endpoint (a link will be available in the main web UI if an index.html file exists).

The query section

This section is all about tuning the inner workings of the query engine. Some are fairly straightforward to understand, such as how long a given query can run before being aborted (`--query.timeout`), or how many queries can run simultaneously (`--query.max-concurrency`).

However, two of them set limits that can have non-obvious consequences. The first is `--query.max-samples`, which was introduced in Prometheus 2.5.0, that sets the maximum number of samples that can be loaded onto memory. This was done as a way of capping the maximum memory the query subsystem can use (by using it together with `--query.max-concurrency`) to try and prevent the dreaded *query-of-death*—a query that loaded so much data to memory that it made Prometheus hit a memory limit and then killing the process. The behavior post 2.5.0 is that if any query hits the limit set by this flag (which defaults to 50,000,000 samples), the query simply fails.

The second one is `--query.lookback-delta`. Without going into too much detail regarding how PromQL works internally, this flag sets the limit of how far back Prometheus will look for time series data points before considering them stale. This implicitly means that if you collect data at a greater interval than what's set here (the default being five minutes), you will get inconsistent results in alerts and graphs, and as such, two minutes is the maximum sane value to allow for failures.

Prometheus configuration file walkthrough

The configuration file we mentioned in the previous section declares the runtime configuration for the Prometheus instance. As we will see, everything related to scrape jobs, rule evaluation, and remote read/write configuration is all defined here. As we mentioned previously, these configurations can be reloaded without shutting down the Prometheus server by either sending a `SIGHUP` to the process, or by sending an HTTP POST request to the `/-/reload` endpoint (when `--web.enable-lifecycle` is used at startup).

At a high level, we can split the configuration file into the following sections:

- `global`
- `scrape_configs`
- `alerting`
- `rule_files`
- `remote_read`
- `remote_write`

Once again, the official Prometheus documentation includes the schema for this file, which is written in YAML format. In this chapter, we will introduce an example configuration for us to analyze, but only go into detail on the `global` and `scrape_configs` sections. The alerting and `rule_files` are covered in Chapter 9, *Defining Alerting and Recording Rules*, while `remote_read` and `remote_write` are explained in Chapter 14, *Integrating Long-Term Storage with Prometheus*.

> **TIP**: A configuration file with the most comprehensive list of options available can be found in the Prometheus project GitHub repository, located in the following address: https://github.com/prometheus/prometheus/blob/v2.9.2/config/testdata/conf.good.yml.

Our example configuration looks as follows:

```
global:
  scrape_interval: 1m
...
scrape_configs:
  - job_name: 'prometheus'
    scrape_interval: 15s
    scrape_timeout: 5s
    sample_limit: 1000
    static_configs:
      - targets: ['localhost:9090']
```

```
    metric_relabel_configs:
      - source_labels: [ __name__ ]
        regex: expensive_metric_.+
        action: drop
```

At first glance, it may seem a bit dense, but for clarity's sake, we're making some configurations whose defaults values don't usually need to be touched explicit.

Let's examine each section in detail.

Global configuration

The `global` configuration defines the default parameters for every other configuration section, as well as outlining what labels should be added to metrics going to external systems, as shown in the following code block:

```
global:
  scrape_interval: 1m
  scrape_timeout: 10s
  evaluation_interval: 1m
  external_labels:
    dc: dc1
    prom: prom1
```

> Duration can only be integer values and can only have one unit. This means that trying to use 0.5 minutes instead of 30 seconds or one minute 30 seconds instead of 90 seconds will be considered a configuration error.

`scrape_interval` sets the default frequency targets that should be scraped. This is usually between 10 seconds and one minute, and the default `1m` is a good conservative value to start. Longer intervals are not advisable as the lost granularity (especially in gauges) starts to impact the ability to properly alert on issues and makes querying finicky as you need to be aware that some shorter intervals might not return data. Additionally, considering the default loopback delta of five minutes (mentioned in the command-line flags), any `scrape_interval` longer than 150 seconds (2 minutes 30 seconds) will mean every time series for a given target will be considered stale if a single scrape fails.

`scrape_timeout` defines how long Prometheus should wait by default for a response from a target before closing the connection and marking the scrape as failed (10 seconds if not declared). Bear in mind that even though it is expected that targets respond to scrapes fairly quickly, the guidelines for metrics exposition mandate that collection should happen at scrape time and not cached, which means there can be some exporters that take a bit longer to respond.

Similar to `scrape_interval`, `evaluation_interval` sets the default frequency recording and alerting rules are evaluated. For sanity, both should have the same. This is going to be discussed in more detail in Chapter 9, *Defining Alerting and Recording Rules*:

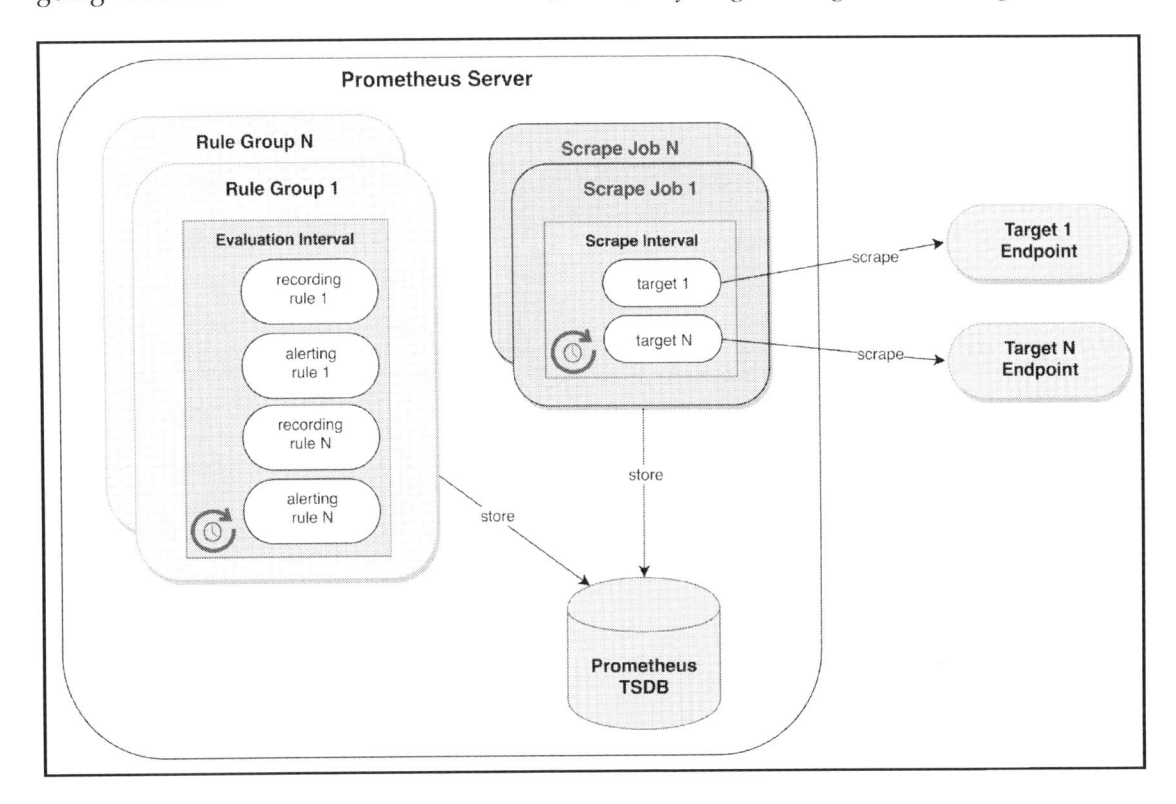

Figure 5.1: Representation of scrape intervals and evaluation intervals inside Prometheus

Lastly, `external_labels` allows you to set label name/value pairs that are added to time series or alerts going to external systems, such as Alertmanager, remote read and write infrastructure, or even other Prometheis through federation. This functionality is usually employed to uniquely identify the source of a given alert or time series; therefore, it is common to identify the region, datacenter, shard, or even the instance identifier of a Prometheus server.

> As per the official documentation, the plural form of *Prometheus* is *Prometheis*: https://prometheus.io/docs/introduction/faq/#what-is-the-plural-of-prometheus.

Scrape configuration

Even though Prometheus accepts an empty file as a valid configuration file, the absolute minimum useful configuration needs a `scrape_configs` section. This is where we define the targets for metrics collection, and if some post-scrape processing is needed before actual ingestion.

In the configuration example we introduced previously, we defined two scrape jobs: `prometheus` and `blackbox`. In Prometheus terms, a scrape is the action of collecting metrics through an HTTP request from a targeted instance, parsing the response, and ingesting the collected samples to storage. The default HTTP endpoint used in the Prometheus ecosystem for metrics collection is aptly named `/metrics`.

A collection of such instances is called a **job**. The instances in a job are usually all running copies of the same service, and so there is usually a job definition for each kind of monitored software, though this can be a bit different when using service discovery, as we'll see in `Chapter 12`, *Choosing the Right Service Discovery*. The combination of instance and job identify the source of the collected samples, and so these are automatically added as labels to the ingested data, as shown in the following code block:

```
scrape_configs:
  - job_name: 'prometheus'
    static_configs:
      - targets: ['localhost:9090']
...

  - job_name: 'blackbox'
    static_configs:
      - targets:
        - http://example.com
        - https://example.com:443
...
```

A scrape job definition needs at least a `job_name` and a set of targets. In this example, `static_configs` was used to declare the list of targets for both scrape jobs. While Prometheus supports a lot of ways to dynamically define this list, `static_configs` is the simplest and most straightforward method:

```
scrape_configs:
  - job_name: 'prometheus'
    scrape_interval: 15s
    scrape_timeout: 5s
    sample_limit: 1000
    static_configs:
      - targets: ['localhost:9090']
```

```
metric_relabel_configs:
  - source_labels: [ __name__ ]
    regex: expensive_metric_.+
    action: drop
```

Analyzing the `prometheus` scrape job in detail, we can see that both `scrape_interval` and `scrape_timeout` can be redeclared at the job level, thus overriding the global values. As stated before, having varying intervals is discouraged, so only use this when absolutely necessary.

By setting `sample_limit`, Prometheus will ensure that whatever value was set, it will be collected per scrape by not ingesting those samples when their number goes over the limit and marking the scrape as failed. This is a great safety net for preventing a cardinality explosion from a target outside of your control impacting the monitoring system.

The last relevant configuration here is `metric_relabel_configs`. This is a powerful rewrite engine that allows a collected metrics' identity to be transformed, or even dropped, before being saved to storage. The most common use cases for this feature is to blacklist a set of misbehaving metrics, dropping labels without compromising a metric's identity, or changing labels to better match Prometheus semantics. Ideally, `metric_relabel_configs` should be used as a stopgap while the problems aren't fixed at the source and so using it often can be a red flag. The preceding example is using `metric_relabel_configs` to drop every metric that starts with `expensive_metric_`:

```
- job_name: 'blackbox'
  metrics_path: /probe
  scheme: http
  params:
    module: [http_2xx]
  static_configs:
    - targets:
      - http://example.com
  relabel_configs:
    - source_labels: [__address__]
      target_label: __param_target
    - source_labels: [__param_target]
      target_label: instance
    - target_label: __address__
      replacement: 127.0.0.1:9115
```

While we are going to explore blackbox exporter in depth in the next chapter, its configuration is used here to help explain the following important configurations:

- `metrics_path` is used to change which endpoint Prometheus should scrape
- `scheme` defines whether HTTP or HTTPS is going to be used when connecting to targets
- `params` allows you to define a set of optional HTTP parameters

However, the most important and most useful configuration is `relabel_configs`. It provides the same powerful semantics as `metric_relabel_configs`, but it has a very different function; `relabel_configs` is used to manipulate the scrape job's list of targets. The relabel actions are performed in sequence, and so it is possible to create or modify labels and then use those in the next action. By default, a target will have a couple of labels that have been generated automatically and that will be available for relabeling: the `job` label will be set to the `job_name` configuration, `__address__` label will be created with the target's host and port, `__scheme__` and `__metrics_path__` labels will be set to their respective configurations (`scheme` and `metrics_path`), and a `__param_<name>` label will be created for each of the parameters defined in the `params` configuration. Additionally, `__meta_` labels will be available when using a service discovery mechanism, as we'll see in Chapter 12, *Choosing the Right Service Discovery*. If the `instance` label is not set by the end of the relabeling phase, `__address__` will be used to set it. Labels that start with two underscores (`__`) will be removed when the relabeling phase ends. As a final note, if you need temporary labels during the relabeling process, always use the `__tmp` prefix, as it is guaranteed to not overlap with Prometheus internal labels.

In the case of the blackbox exporter, this functionality is very useful as we need to send the probe requests to the exporter, which will then use the `target` GET parameter to perform its job. So, going through the example, for each target specified in `static_configs`, this configuration does the following:

- Copies the target's address into a `__param_target` label, which will be used to set the `target` GET parameter in the scrape
- Copies the content of this newly created label into the `instance` label so that it is explicitly set, bypassing the automatic generation based on the `__address__`
- Replaces the `__address__` label with the address of the blackbox exporter so that scrapes are done to the exporter and not directly to the target we specified in `static_configs`

> **TIP:** While `relabel_configs` is used to rewrite the target list (it runs before the scrape is performed), `metric_relabel_configs` is used to rewrite labels or drop samples (it runs after the scrape is performed).

> The example configuration used in this section is for demonstration purposes only. For example, there should be no need to set `sample_limit` on Prometheus itself, or to drop metrics without a concrete reason.

A very useful metric that must be introduced is the up metric. This metric exposes the status of a scrape job. It includes, at least, a label with the correspondent job name and another with the targeted instance. In its sample, we can have the value 1 for a successful scrape or 0 for a failed one.

Next, we're going to start managing Prometheus in different deployment environments.

Managing Prometheus in a standalone server

As we previously went through several configuration definitions, we're now ready to put them to practice by managing a standalone instance of Prometheus. In these examples, we'll be exposing several configurations while providing an environment to validate them.

Server deploy

To create a new instance of Prometheus, move into the correct repository path, as shown here:

```
cd chapter05/
```

Ensure that no other test environments are running and spin up this chapter's environment, like so:

```
vagrant global-status
vagrant up
```

After a few moments, the new instance will be available for inspection, and the Prometheus web interface will be accessible at `http://192.168.42.10:9090`.

Configuration inspection

With the newly created instance running, it's time to log in using the following command:

```
vagrant ssh prometheus
```

We can validate the startup configuration in use by looking into its `systemd` unit file by using the following command:

```
cat /etc/systemd/system/prometheus.service
```

The following excerpt shows the flags that are currently in place:

```
ExecStart=/usr/bin/prometheus \
    --config.file=/etc/prometheus/prometheus.yml \
    --storage.tsdb.path=/var/lib/prometheus/data \
    --web.console.templates=/usr/share/prometheus/consoles \
    --web.console.libraries=/usr/share/prometheus/console_libraries
```

The configuration file for Prometheus itself, as defined by the `--config.file` flag, can be reviewed as follows:

```
cat /etc/prometheus/prometheus.yml
```

As we can see, the configuration in use is similar to the one that was presented previously, in the Prometheus configuration file walkthrough. We can now validate a couple of concepts we mentioned previously.

- Due to `metric_relabel_configs` in the `prometheus` job, we can use two of Prometheus' per-scrape metrics to determine the number of samples being dropped by our configuration as follows:
    - `scrape_samples_scraped`: This metric provides the total of samples collected
    - `scrape_samples_post_metric_relabeling`: This metric provides the total of samples available after the metric relabeling takes place

If we subtract these two metrics, we obtain the number of dropped samples (in our example, this is all of the metric names starting with `go_`):

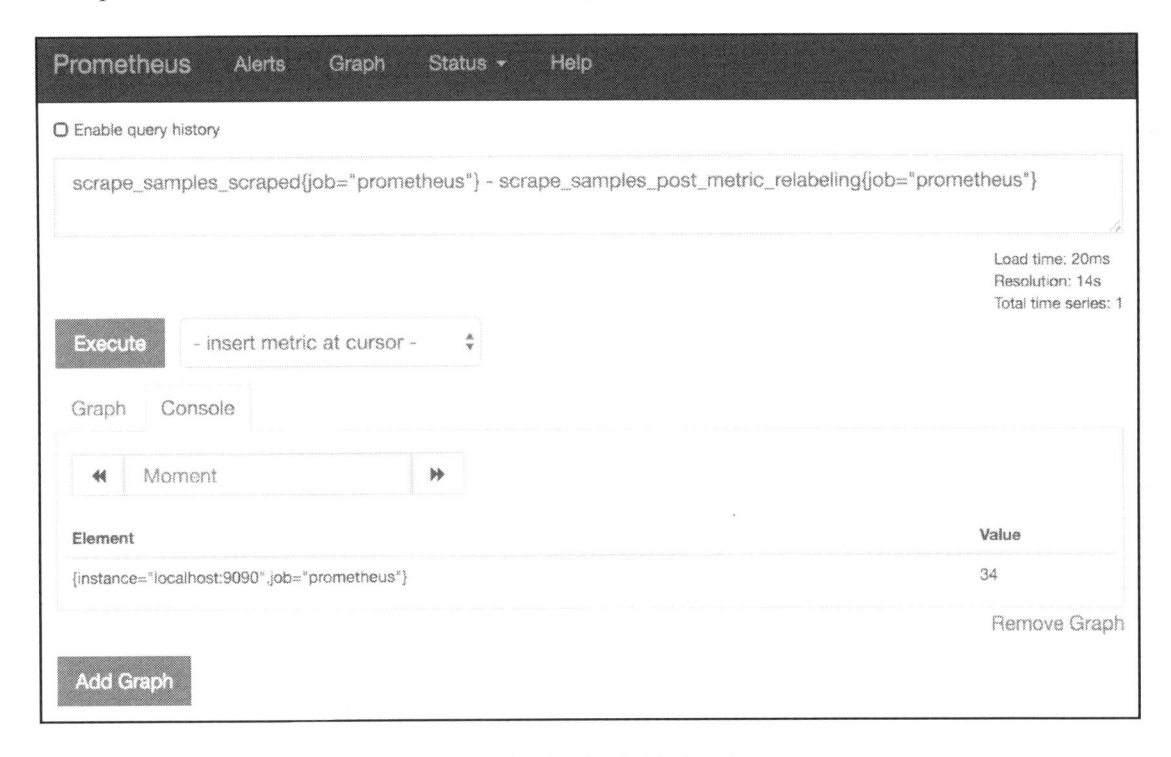

Figure 5.2: Number of metrics being dropped

Running a Prometheus Server

We can confirm the outcome of the configuration relabeling, which in our example, generates the instance labels under the `blackbox` job:

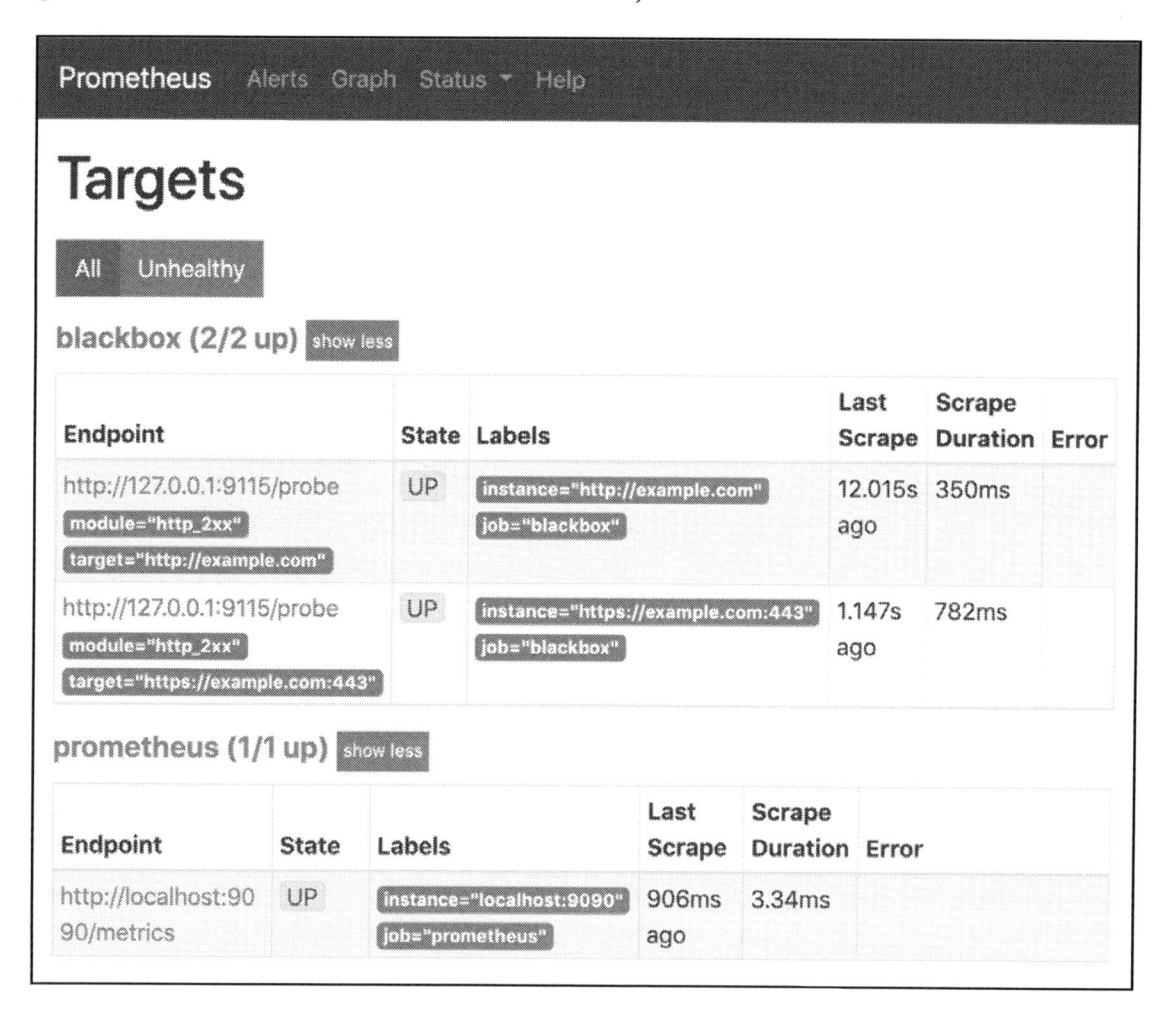

Figure 5.3: Instance labels generated by *relabel_configs*

You can validate the Prometheus configuration by using a provided utility called `promtool`, which will be thoroughly dissected on `Chapter 8`, *Troubleshooting and Validation*. When reloading Prometheus with a new configuration, you also have the option to look at the `prometheus_config_last_reload_successful` metric to assess whether the configuration was successfully parsed and applied.

Cleanup

When you've finish testing, just make sure you're inside the `chapter05/` path and execute the following:

```
vagrant destroy -f
```

Don't worry too much – you can easily spin up the environment again if you so require.

Managing Prometheus in Kubernetes

Kubernetes is the first project to graduate from the CNCF and is currently the de facto standard for container orchestration. Early on, Heapster was widely used as a monitoring solution that came out-of-the-box with Kubernetes. It started out as a tool to send monitoring data to external systems but then grew to become a monitoring system itself. However, it didn't take long for Prometheus to become the de facto standard monitoring system for Kubernetes clusters. Nowadays, most of the components that make up a Kubernetes cluster have native Prometheus instrumentation.

In the following sections, we'll go into how to integrate Prometheus in a Kubernetes environment by employing examples based on the Kubernetes project and the Prometheus Operator project.

> You can find the complete source code of the Kubernetes project and the Prometheus Operator at the following addresses, respectively: `https://github.com/kubernetes/kubernetes` and `https://github.com/coreos/prometheus-operator`.

Ensure that you have all the software requirements that were defined in Chapter 3, *Setting Up a Test Environment*, available in their specific versions, particularly the following:

- Minikube
- kubectl

Static configuration

Although this approach is quite far from being advised, it provides the foundations to better understand and troubleshoot a Prometheus server running in Kubernetes. In this example, we'll create a Prometheus deployment using a ConfigMap to define the server configuration.

Running a Prometheus Server

Kubernetes environment

Ensure that there's no instance of `minikube` running the following commands:

```
minikube status
minikube delete
```

> `minikube delete` is a destructive instruction, so be sure you save your work before proceeding.

Start a new `minikube` instance with the following specifications:

```
minikube start \
  --cpus=2 \
  --memory=2048 \
  --kubernetes-version="v1.14.0" \
  --vm-driver=virtualbox
```

When the previous command finishes, a new Kubernetes environment should be ready to be used. You may access its dashboard by using the following command, which will open the Kubernetes dashboard address in your default browser:

```
minikube dashboard
```

To proceed with our example, ensure that you move into the correct repository path, like so:

```
cd chapter05/provision/kubernetes/static
```

For the sake of organization, we'll be creating a new namespace called `monitoring` using the following manifest with the help of `kubectl`:

```
apiVersion: v1
kind: Namespace
metadata:
  name: monitoring
```

Apply the previous manifest using the following command:

```
kubectl apply -f monitoring-namespace.yaml
```

We can validate the successful namespace creation on the Kubernetes dashboard:

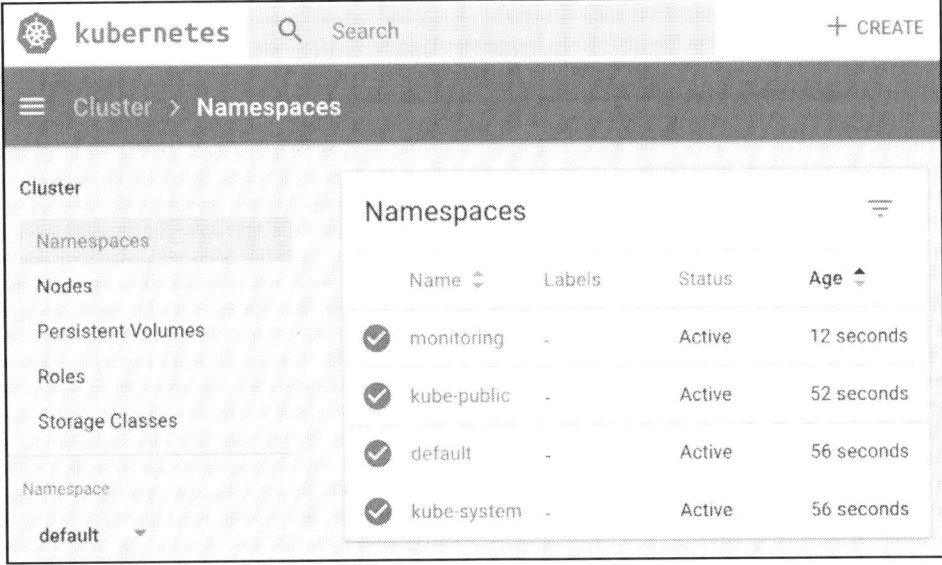

Figure 5.4: Kubernetes dashboard - monitoring namespace

Prometheus server deployment

With our new namespace available, it's time to create a very simple Prometheus configuration and save it on a ConfigMap using the following manifest:

```
apiVersion: v1
kind: ConfigMap
metadata:
  name: prometheus-config
  namespace: monitoring
data:
  prometheus.yml: |
    scrape_configs:
    - job_name: prometheus
      static_configs:
      - targets:
        - localhost:9090
```

Apply the previous manifest using the following command:

```
kubectl apply -f prometheus-configmap.yaml
```

Running a Prometheus Server

Now, it's time to start a new deployment of Prometheus, making sure we mount the previously configured ConfigMap into the pod we are deploying. The Deployment object is configured with the following metadata:

```yaml
apiVersion: apps/v1
kind: Deployment
metadata:
  name: prometheus-deployment
  namespace: monitoring
  labels:
    app: prometheus
```

The Prometheus container will be started with its configuration file and data directory coming from volume mounts, shown as follows:

```yaml
args:
  - --config.file=/etc/config/prometheus.yml
  - --storage.tsdb.path=/data
volumeMounts:
  - name: config-volume
    mountPath: /etc/config/prometheus.yml
    subPath: prometheus.yml
  - name: prometheus-data
    mountPath: /data
    subPath: ""
```

The `config-volume` volume is created from a ConfigMap, while the `prometheus-data` volume is created with an empty directory. This can be seen in the following snippet:

```yaml
volumes:
  - name: config-volume
    configMap:
      name: prometheus-config
  - name: prometheus-data
    emptyDir: {}
```

Apply the previous manifest using the following command:

`kubectl apply -f prometheus-deployment.yaml`

We can follow the deployment status using this snippet:

`kubectl rollout status deployment/prometheus-deployment -n monitoring`

We should look at the logs of our Prometheus instance using the following command:

`kubectl logs --tail=20 -n monitoring -l app=prometheus`

After a successful deployment, we're ready to assign a new service to our instance, choosing `NodePort` so we can access it without requiring port-forwarding, like so:

```yaml
kind: Service
apiVersion: v1
metadata:
  name: prometheus-service
  namespace: monitoring
spec:
  selector:
    app: prometheus
  type: NodePort
  ports:
  - name: prometheus-port
    protocol: TCP
    port: 9090
    targetPort: 9090
```

Apply the previous manifest using the following:

```
kubectl apply -f prometheus-service.yaml
```

And you're ready to check your new Prometheus service using the following code snippet:

```
minikube service prometheus-service -n monitoring
```

This will open your browser on the Prometheus service endpoint. You can now check the running configuration and targets using the Prometheus web interface:

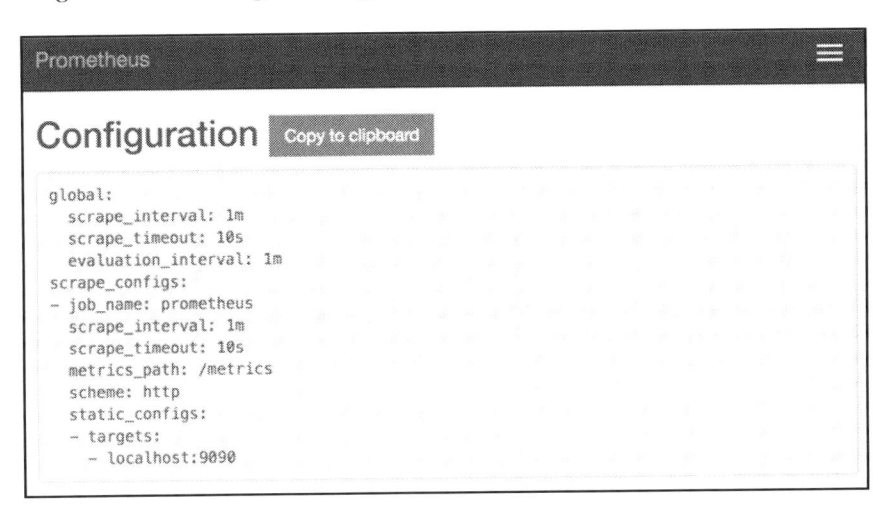

Figure 5.5: Prometheus initial configuration

Adding targets to Prometheus

For the sake of this example, we'll deploy yet another service and add it to our Prometheus server, going step by step on how to do it. We'll use a small *Hello World* type of application called *Hey* for our setup.

> The code for the *Hey* application can be inspected at https://github.com/kintoandar/hey.

These steps are quite similar to the deployment of the Prometheus server. Start by creating a new deployment for *Hey* using the following manifest:

```yaml
apiVersion: apps/v1
kind: Deployment
metadata:
  name: hey-deployment
  namespace: monitoring
  labels:
    app: hey
...
    - name: hey
      image: kintoandar/hey:v1.0.1
...
    - name: http
      containerPort: 8000
...
```

Apply the previous manifest using the following command:

```
kubectl apply -f hey-deployment.yaml
```

We can follow the deployment status using this code snippet:

```
kubectl rollout status deployment/hey-deployment -n monitoring
```

We can validate the logs of our *Hey* instance using the following command:

```
kubectl logs --tail=20 -n monitoring -l app=hey
```

After a successful deployment, we're ready to assign a new service to our instance choosing `NodePort` so that we can access it without requiring port-forwarding, like so:

```yaml
kind: Service
apiVersion: v1
metadata:
  name: hey-service
  namespace: monitoring
spec:
  selector:
    app: hey
  type: NodePort
  ports:
  - name: hey-port
    protocol: TCP
    port: 8000
    targetPort: 8000
```

Apply the previous manifest using the following command:

```
kubectl apply -f hey-service.yaml
```

Now, you're ready to check your new *Hey* service like so:

```
minikube service hey-service -n monitoring
```

Since Prometheus is statically managed in our example, we need to add the new *Hey* target for metric collection. This means that we need to change the Prometheus ConfigMap to reflect the newly added service, like so:

```yaml
kind: ConfigMap
metadata:
  name: prometheus-config
  namespace: monitoring
data:
  prometheus.yml: |
    scrape_configs:
    - job_name: prometheus
      static_configs:
      - targets:
        - localhost:9090
    - job_name: hey
      static_configs:
      - targets:
        - hey-service.monitoring.svc:8000
```

Running a Prometheus Server

Apply the previous manifest using the following command:

```
kubectl create -f prometheus-configmap-update.yaml -o yaml --dry-run |
kubectl apply -f -
```

If you check the running Prometheus configuration, nothing has changed; this is because a new deployment wasn't triggered. For that to happen, something needs to change on the deployment definition, so we just change the version annotation and apply the new manifest like so:

```
kubectl apply -f prometheus-deployment-update.yaml
```

We can follow the deployment status using the following command:

```
kubectl rollout status deployment/prometheus-deployment -n monitoring
```

After a moment, a new deployment will take place, changing the Prometheus configuration and a new target will present itself, which you can validate in the Prometheus web user interface:

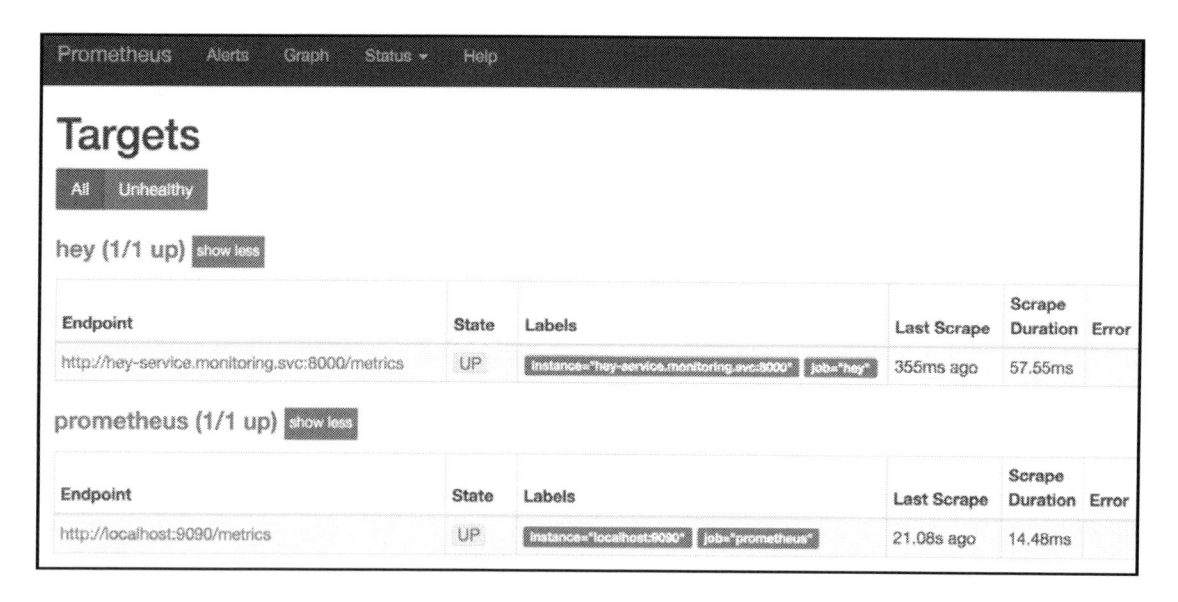

Figure 5.6: Prometheus targeting the Hey application

> **TIP**
> You may have noticed that no **role-based access control (RBAC)** configuration was required in this example. This is because all pods run in the same namespace and Prometheus didn't require access to the Kubernetes API yet. We strongly believe RBAC is fundamental in a secure Kubernetes setup.

[88]

Dynamic configuration – the Prometheus Operator

CoreOS was the pioneer in building a pattern called Operator, which abstracts the complexity of packaging, deployment, and the management of Kubernetes applications. The Operator synthesizes the knowledge required for the operation of an application (such as configuration and deploy logic) into Kubernetes custom resources and custom controllers.

> A custom resource is an object that extends the Kubernetes API, allowing custom API definitions. Custom controller strives to achieve the user's required state for a resource, continuously working on maintaining such a state.

The combination of both a Kubernetes custom resource and custom controller into a pattern is what brings the Operator definition to life.

When implementing this type of pattern, instead of defining for example, the persistent storage for an application, as well as the specific configuration for their environment, the user would rather just request an instance of that application, and the Operator would abstract all the required dependencies and provide the final result automatically.

In our case, besides managing the deployment, including the number of pods and persistent volumes of the Prometheus server, the Prometheus Operator will also update the configuration dynamically using the concept of ServiceMonitor, which targets services with matching rules against the labels of running containers:

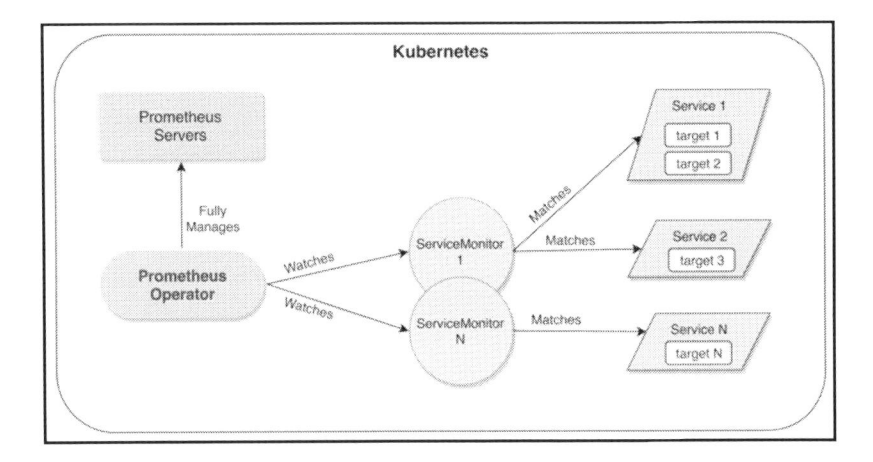

Figure 5.7: Prometheus Operator logic diagram

Running a Prometheus Server

Empowered with this knowledge, we'll provide an example on how to deploy and configure Prometheus using the Prometheus Operator, including collecting metrics from an application, this time running on a different namespace.

Kubernetes environment

Ensure that there's no instance of `minikube` running, like so:

```
minikube status
minikube delete
```

Start a new `minikube` instance with the following specifications:

```
minikube start \
   --cpus=2 \
   --memory=2048 \
   --kubernetes-version="v1.14.0" \
   --vm-driver=virtualbox
```

When the previous command finishes, a new Kubernetes environment should be ready to be used. You may access its dashboard by using the following command, which will open the Kubernetes dashboard address in your default browser:

```
minikube dashboard
```

To proceed with the deployment of our example, ensure that you move into the correct repository path, as shown here:

```
cd chapter05/provision/kubernetes/operator
```

Like the previous example, we'll be creating a new namespace called `monitoring` with the help of `kubectl`, like so:

```
kubectl apply -f monitoring-namespace.yaml
```

Prometheus Operator deployment

With the new namespace available, it's time to ensure that all access permissions are in place for the Prometheus Operator, as shown in the next few configuration snippets. The first one defines the `ClusterRole`:

```
apiVersion: rbac.authorization.k8s.io/v1
kind: ClusterRole
metadata:
  name: prometheus-operator
```

```
  rules:
  - apiGroups: [apiextensions.k8s.io]
    verbs: ['*']
    resources: [customresourcedefinitions]
  - apiGroups: [monitoring.coreos.com]
    verbs: ['*']
    resources:
      - alertmanagers
      - prometheuses
      - servicemonitors
  ...
```

Then, we apply the ClusterRole to a ClusterRoleBinding:

```
apiVersion: rbac.authorization.k8s.io/v1
kind: ClusterRoleBinding
metadata:
  name: prometheus-operator
roleRef:
  apiGroup: rbac.authorization.k8s.io
  kind: ClusterRole
  name: prometheus-operator
subjects:
- kind: ServiceAccount
  name: prometheus-operator
  namespace: monitoring
```

Finally, we create a ServiceAccount for the ClusterRoleBinding:

```
apiVersion: v1
kind: ServiceAccount
metadata:
  name: prometheus-operator
  namespace: monitoring
```

Apply the manifest containing the previous snippets using the following command:

```
kubectl apply -f prometheus-operator-rbac.yaml
```

Having the new service account configured, we're ready to deploy the Operator itself, like so:

```
apiVersion: apps/v1beta2
kind: Deployment
metadata:
  labels:
    k8s-app: prometheus-operator
  name: prometheus-operator
```

Running a Prometheus Server

```
    namespace: monitoring
spec:
  replicas: 1
  selector:
    matchLabels:
      k8s-app: prometheus-operator
...
      serviceAccountName: prometheus-operator
```

Apply the previous manifest using the following command:

```
kubectl apply -f prometheus-operator-deployment.yaml
```

We can follow the deployment status using the following code snippet:

```
kubectl rollout status deployment/prometheus-operator -n monitoring
```

With the Operator deployed, we can now use it to deploy and manage Prometheus instances.

Prometheus server deployment

Before proceeding with the setup of Prometheus, we'll need to grant its instances with the right access control permissions. The following snippets from the Prometheus RBAC manifest do just that. First we need to create a `ClusterRole` that allows Prometheus access to /metrics through GET requests:

```
apiVersion: rbac.authorization.k8s.io/v1
kind: ClusterRole
metadata:
  name: prometheus-k8s
rules:
...
- nonResourceURLs:
  - /metrics
  verbs:
  - get
```

Next, we create a `ClusterRoleBinding` to grant the permissions from the aforementioned `ClusterRole` to a user, which in our case will be a `ServiceAccount`:

```
apiVersion: rbac.authorization.k8s.io/v1
kind: ClusterRoleBinding
metadata:
  name: prometheus-k8s
roleRef:
```

```
    apiGroup: rbac.authorization.k8s.io
    kind: ClusterRole
    name: prometheus-k8s
subjects:
- kind: ServiceAccount
  name: prometheus-k8s
  namespace: monitoring
```

Finally, we create a `ServiceAccount` for Prometheus:

```
apiVersion: v1
kind: ServiceAccount
metadata:
  name: prometheus-k8s
  namespace: monitoring
```

Apply the manifest containing the previous snippets using the following command:

```
kubectl apply -f prometheus-rbac.yaml
```

Having the service account ready, we can now use the Prometheus Operator to deploy our Prometheus servers using the following manifest:

```
apiVersion: monitoring.coreos.com/v1
kind: Prometheus
metadata:
  labels:
    prometheus: k8s
  name: k8s
  namespace: monitoring
spec:
  baseImage: quay.io/prometheus/prometheus
  version: v2.9.2
  replicas: 2
  ...
  serviceAccountName: prometheus-k8s
  serviceMonitorNamespaceSelector: {}
  serviceMonitorSelector: {}
```

Apply the previous manifest using the following command:

```
kubectl apply -f prometheus-server.yaml
```

We can follow the deployment progress using the following command:

```
kubectl rollout status statefulset/prometheus-k8s -n monitoring
```

Running a Prometheus Server

When the deployment is finished, we'll be ready to create a new service for our Prometheus servers and launch the web interface to validate the current settings, like so:

```
kubectl apply -f prometheus-service.yaml

minikube service prometheus-service -n monitoring
```

Following is the Prometheus default configuration created by the Prometheus Operator:

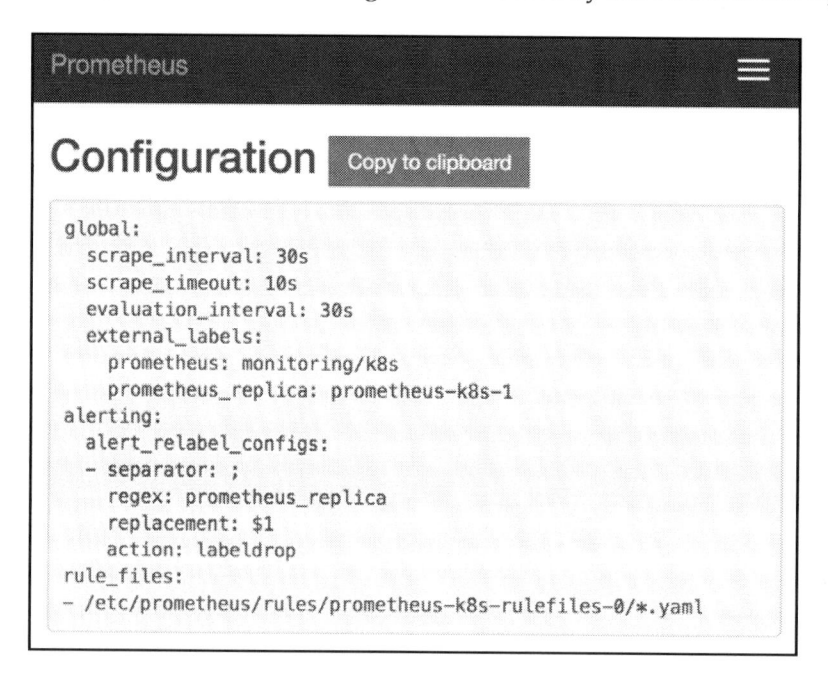

```
Prometheus

Configuration  [Copy to clipboard]

global:
  scrape_interval: 30s
  scrape_timeout: 10s
  evaluation_interval: 30s
  external_labels:
    prometheus: monitoring/k8s
    prometheus_replica: prometheus-k8s-1
alerting:
  alert_relabel_configs:
  - separator: ;
    regex: prometheus_replica
    replacement: $1
    action: labeldrop
rule_files:
- /etc/prometheus/rules/prometheus-k8s-rulefiles-0/*.yaml
```

Figure 5.8: Prometheus default configuration created by the Prometheus Operator

Adding targets to Prometheus

So far, we've deployed the Operator and used it to deploy Prometheus itself. Now, we're ready to add targets and go over the logic of how to generate them.

Before proceeding, we'll also deploy an application to increase the number of available targets. For this, we'll be using the *Hey* application once again, this time using the default namespace:

```
apiVersion: apps/v1
kind: Deployment
metadata:
```

```
  name: hey-deployment
  namespace: default
spec:
  replicas: 3
  selector:
    matchLabels:
      app: hey
```

Pay close attention to the labels and the port name, as shown in the following code block; they'll be used by the service monitor:

```
template:
  metadata:
    labels:
      app: hey
  spec:
    containers:
    - name: hey
      image: kintoandar/hey:v1.0.1
      ports:
      - name: hey-port
        containerPort: 8000
...
```

Apply the manifest containing the previous snippets using the following command:

```
kubectl apply -f hey-deployment.yaml
```

We can follow the status of the deployment using the following command:

```
kubectl rollout status deployment/hey-deployment -n default
```

After the deployment finishes, we'll create a new service, as shown in the following code block. Pay close attention to the labels that will be used by the service monitor to target this service:

```
kind: Service
metadata:
  labels:
    squad: frontend
  name: hey-service
  namespace: default
spec:
  selector:
    app: hey
  type: NodePort
  ports:
  - name: hey-port
```

Running a Prometheus Server

```
    protocol: TCP
    port: 8000
    targetPort: hey-port
```

Apply the previous manifest using the following command:

```
kubectl apply -f hey-service.yaml
```

```
minikube service hey-service -n default
```

Finally, we are going to create service monitors for both the Prometheus instances and the *Hey* application, which will instruct the Operator to configure Prometheus, adding the required targets. Pay close attention to the selector configuration – it will be used to match the services we created previously.

The following is the service monitor for Prometheus:

```
apiVersion: monitoring.coreos.com/v1
kind: ServiceMonitor
metadata:
  labels:
    k8s-app: prometheus
  name: prometheus
  namespace: monitoring
spec:
  endpoints:
  - interval: 30s
    port: web
  selector:
    matchLabels:
      prometheus: k8s
```

The service monitor for the *Hey* application is as follows:

```
apiVersion: monitoring.coreos.com/v1
kind: ServiceMonitor
metadata:
  labels:
    app: hey
  name: hey-metrics
  namespace: default
spec:
  endpoints:
  - interval: 30s
    port: hey-port
  selector:
    matchLabels:
      squad: frontend
```

Apply the previous manifests using the following command:

```
kubectl apply -f prometheus-servicemonitor.yaml
```

```
kubectl apply -f hey-servicemonitor.yaml
```

You can validate the successful deployment of the service monitors using the following command:

```
kubectl get servicemonitors --all-namespaces
```

After the Operator reconfigures Prometheus, which might take a few seconds, the added targets should be available on your Prometheus web interface:

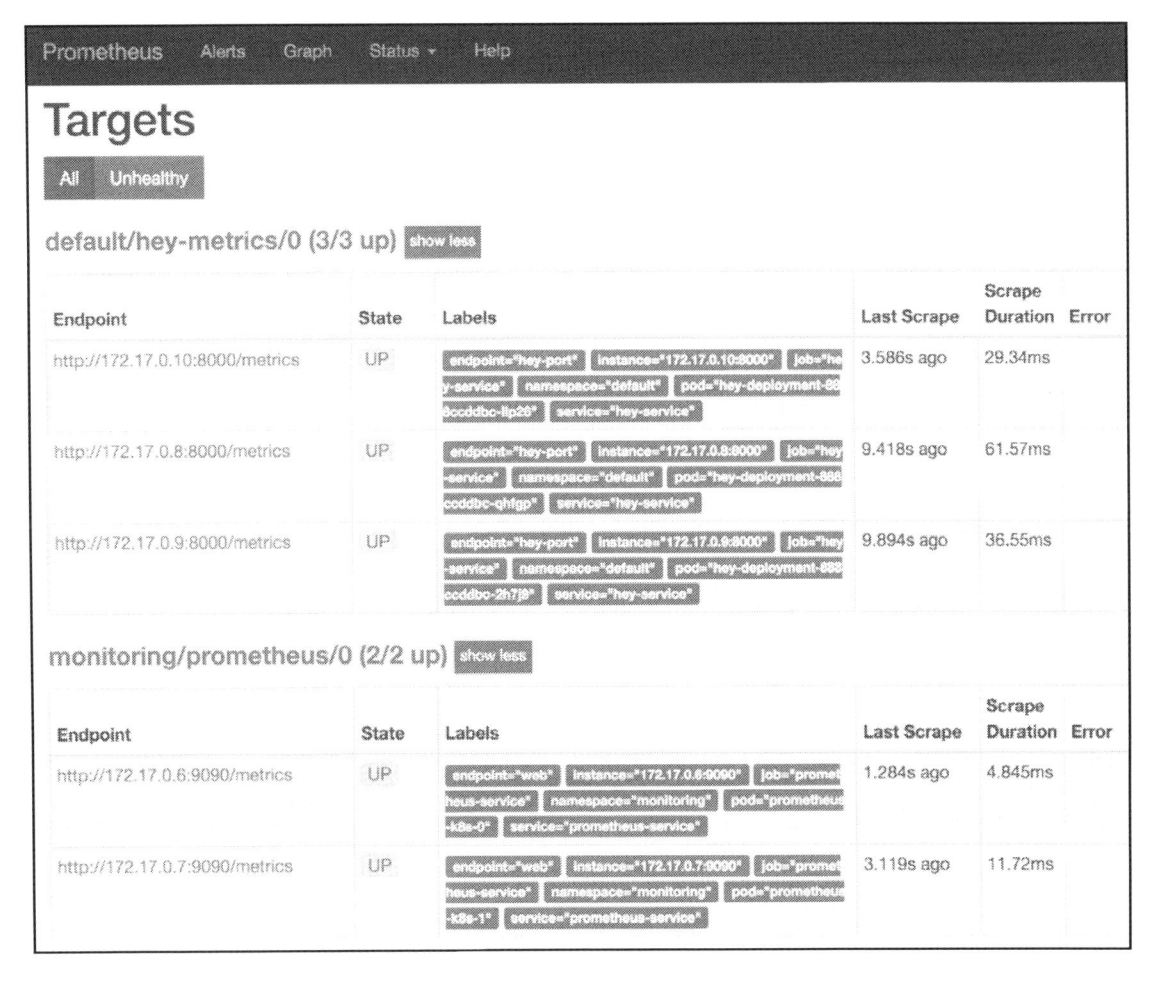

Figure 5.9: Prometheus targets after the service monitors' configuration

ServiceMonitors are the main building block when using the Prometheus Operator. You can configure anything that goes into a scrape job, such as scrape and timeout intervals, metrics endpoint to scrape, HTTP query parameters, and so on. You can find the documentation for these configurations at https://github.com/coreos/prometheus-operator/blob/master/Documentation/api.md#endpoint.

Summary

In this chapter, we were introduced to some of the most important configuration concepts for setting up a Prometheus server. This knowledge is fundamental for tailoring Prometheus for your specific scenario. From startup flags to the configuration file, we also spun up an instance to experiment and validate the knowledge we obtained.

As more and more workloads are transitioning to containers, and specifically to Kubernetes, we dived into how to set up and manage Prometheus on such an environment. We began experimenting with static configurations as a stepping stone to understand a more robust approach, the Prometheus Operator.

In the next chapter, we'll go into the most common exporters and build upon what we've learned so that we can successfully collect data from various different sources on Prometheus.

Questions

1. What happens if `scrape_timeout` is not declared explicitly?
2. How can Prometheus be made to reload its configuration file?
3. How far back does Prometheus look for data before considering a time series stale?
4. What is the difference between `relabel_configs` and `metric_relabel_configs`?
5. On the static deployment example, we added a Kubernetes service for the Hey application as a target in Prometheus. What problems will arise if we increase the number of *Hey* pods?
6. Does static Prometheus static configuration make sense on a Kubernetes environment? Why?
7. In which Kubernetes facilities does the Prometheus Operator rely upon to achieve its goals?

Further reading

- **Prometheus configuration**: https://prometheus.io/docs/prometheus/latest/configuration/configuration/
- **Prometheus TSDB APIs**: https://prometheus.io/docs/prometheus/latest/querying/api/#tsdb-admin-apis
- **Prometheus security**: https://prometheus.io/docs/operating/security/
- **Kubernetes custom controllers**: https://kubernetes.io/docs/concepts/extend-kubernetes/api-extension/custom-resources/#custom-controllers
- **Kubernetes custom resources**: https://kubernetes.io/docs/concepts/extend-kubernetes/api-extension/custom-resources/#customresourcedefinitions
- **Prometheus Operator**: https://github.com/coreos/prometheus-operator/blob/master/Documentation/design.md

6
Exporters and Integrations

Even though first-party exporters cover the basics pretty well, the Prometheus ecosystem provides a wide variety of third-party exporters that cover everything else. In this chapter, we will be introduced to some of the most useful exporters available—from **operating system** (**OS**) metrics and **Internet Control Message Protocol** (**ICMP**) probing to generating metrics from logs, or how to collect information from short-lived processes, such as batch jobs.

In brief, the following topics will be covered in this chapter:

- Test environments for this chapter
- Operating system exporter
- Container exporter
- From logs to metrics
- Blackbox monitoring
- Pushing metrics
- More exporters

Test environments for this chapter

In this chapter, we'll be using two test environments: one based on **virtual machines** (**VMs**) that mimic traditional static infrastructure and one based on Kubernetes for modern workflows. The following topics will guide you through the automated setup procedure for both of them, but will gloss over the details from each exporter—these will be explained in depth in their own sections.

Static infrastructure test environment

This method will abstract all the deployment and configuration details, allowing you to have a fully provisioned test environment with a couple of commands. You'll still be able to connect to each of the guest instances and tinker with the example configurations.

To launch a new test environment, move into this chapter path, relative to the repository root:

```
cd ./chapter06/
```

Ensure no other test environments are running and spin up this chapter's environment:

```
vagrant global-status
vagrant up
```

You can validate the successful deploy of the test environment using:

```
vagrant status
```

Which will output the following:

```
Current machine states:

prometheus                running (virtualbox)
target01                  running (virtualbox)

This environment represents multiple VMs. The VMs are all listed
above with their current state. For more information about a specific
VM, run `vagrant status NAME`.
```

The end result will be an environment like the one depicted in the following diagram:

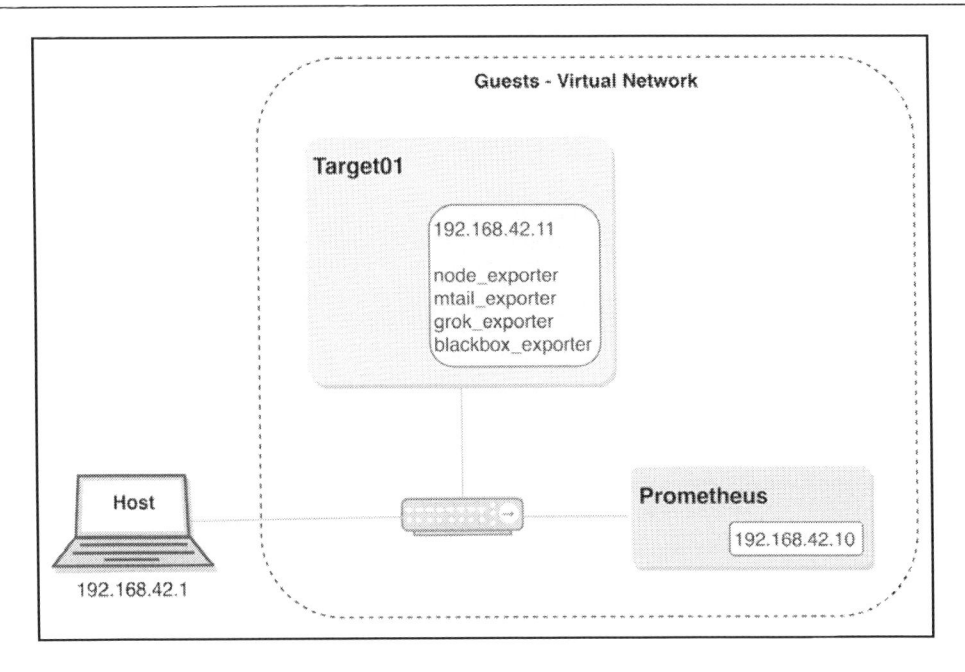

Figure 6.1: Diagram of the static infrastructure test environment

To connect to the `target01` instance, just run the following:

```
vagrant ssh target01
```

To connect to the Prometheus instance, use the following code snippet:

```
vagrant ssh prometheus
```

When you're finished with this environment, move into this chapter path, relative to the repository root as follows:

```
cd ./chapter06/
```

And execute the following instruction:

```
vagrant destroy -f
```

Kubernetes test environment

To start the Kubernetes test environment, we first must ensure there's no instance of `minikube` running as follows:

```
minikube status
minikube delete
```

Start a new `minikube` instance with the following specifications:

```
minikube start \
  --cpus=2 \
  --memory=3072 \
  --kubernetes-version="v1.14.0" \
  --vm-driver=virtualbox
```

When the previous command finishes, a new Kubernetes environment should be ready to be used.

For our Kubernetes test environment, we'll be building upon the lessons learned in Chapter 5, *Running a Prometheus Server*, and using Prometheus Operator in our workflow. Since we already covered the Prometheus Operator setup, we'll deploy all the required components without going over each one of them.

Step into the following chapter number:

```
cd ./chapter06/
```

Deploy the Prometheus Operator and validate the successful deploy as follows:

```
kubectl apply -f ./provision/kubernetes/operator/bootstrap/
```

```
kubectl rollout status deployment/prometheus-operator -n monitoring
```

Use the Prometheus Operator to deploy Prometheus and ensure the deploy was successful like so:

```
kubectl apply -f ./provision/kubernetes/operator/deploy/
```

```
kubectl rollout status statefulset/prometheus-k8s -n monitoring
```

Add ServiceMonitors as shown in the following code, which will configure Prometheus jobs:

```
kubectl apply -f ./provision/kubernetes/operator/monitor/
```

```
kubectl get servicemonitors --all-namespaces
```

After a moment, you should have Prometheus available and ready; the following instruction will provide its web interface:

```
minikube service prometheus-service -n monitoring
```

You can validate the Kubernetes StatefulSet for Prometheus using the following instruction, which will open the Kubernetes dashboard:

```
minikube dashboard
```

> **TIP**: More information regarding the Kubernetes objects, including the StatefulSet controller, is available at https://kubernetes.io/docs/concepts/.

The following screenshot illustrates the correct deployment of the Prometheus StatefulSet:

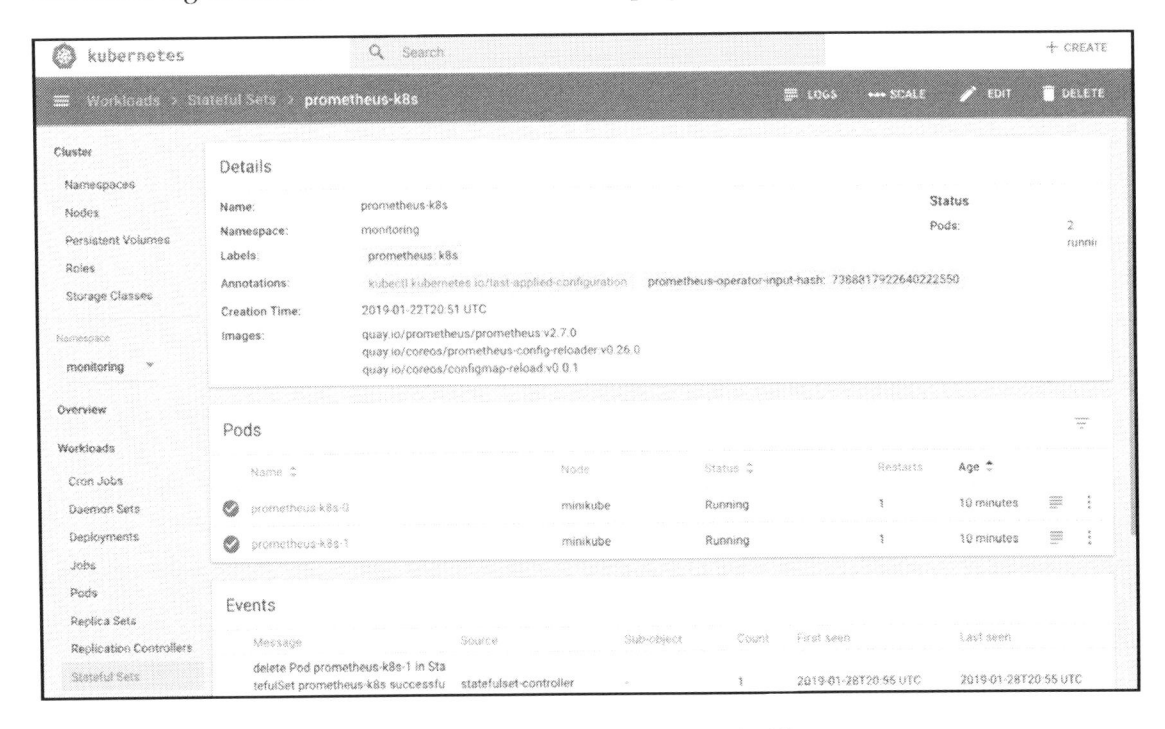

Figure 6.2 - Kubernetes dashboard depicting Prometheus StatefulSet

Operating system exporter

When monitoring infrastructure, the most common place to start looking is at the OS level. Metrics for resources such as CPU, memory, and storage devices, as well as kernel operating counters and statistics provide valuable insight to assess a system's performance characteristics. For a Prometheus server to collect these types of metrics, an OS-level exporter is needed on the target hosts to expose them in an HTTP endpoint. The Prometheus project provides such an exporter that supports Unix-like systems called the Node Exporter, and the community also maintains an equivalent exporter for Microsoft Windows systems called the WMI exporter.

The Node Exporter

The Node Exporter is the most well-known Prometheus exporter, for good reason. It provides over 40 collectors for different areas of the OS, as well as a way of exposing local metrics for cron jobs and static information about the host. Like the rest of the Prometheus ecosystem, the Node Exporter comes with a sane default configuration and some smarts to identify what can be collected, so it's perfectly reasonable to run it without much tweaking.

> In this context, *node* refers to a computer node or host and is not related to Node.js in any way.

Although this exporter was designed to be run as a non-privileged user, it does need to access kernel and process statistics, which aren't normally available when running inside a container. This is not to say that it doesn't work in containers—every Prometheus component can be run in containers—but that additional configuration is required for it to work. It is, therefore, recommended that the Node Exporter be run as a system daemon directly on the host whenever possible.

Node Exporter collectors might gather different metrics depending on the system being run, as OS kernels vary in the way they expose internal state and what details they make available. As an example, metrics exposed by `node_exporter` on macOS will be substantially different from the ones on Linux. This means that, even though the Node Exporter supports Linux, Darwin (macOS), FreeBSD, OpenBSD, NetBSD, DragonFly BSD, and Solaris, each collector within the Node Exporter will have their own compatibility matrix, with Linux being the kernel with the most support.

> **TIP**
> Metric names exposed by the Node Exporter changed in version 0.16.0 due to a standardization effort across the Prometheus project. This was a breaking change, which means that dashboards and tutorials made for earlier versions of this exporter won't work out of the box. An upgrade guide (https://github.com/prometheus/node_exporter/blob/v0.17.0/docs/V0_16_UPGRADE_GUIDE.md) can be found in the Node Exporter's repository.

> The source code and installation files for the Node Exporter are available at https://github.com/prometheus/node_exporter.

By design, this exporter only produces aggregated metrics about processes (such as how many are running, and so on) and not individual metrics per process. In the Prometheus model, each process of relevance needs to expose its own metrics, or have a companion exporter to do that job for it. This is one of the reasons why it is ill-advised in most cases to run a generic process exporter without an explicit whitelist.

Configuration

Exporters in the Prometheus ecosystem usually collect a specific set of metrics from a given process. The Node Exporter differs from most other exporters as machine-level metrics span a wide range of subsystems, and so it is architected to provide individual collectors, which can be turned on and off, depending on the instrumentation needs. Enabling collectors that are turned off by default can be done with the `--collector.<name>` set of flags; enabled collectors can be disabled by using the `--no-collector.<name>` flag variant.

Exporters and Integrations

From all the collectors enabled by default, one needs to be singled out due to its usefulness as well as its need of configuration to properly work. The `textfile` collector enables the exposition of custom metrics by watching a directory for files with the `.prom` extension that contain metrics in the Prometheus exposition format. The `--collector.textfile.directory` flag is empty by default and so needs to be set to a directory path for the collector to do its job. It is expected that only instance-specific metrics be exported through this method, for example:

- Local cron jobs can report their exit status through a metric (finish timestamp is not useful to record, as the metrics file modification timestamp is already exported as a metric)
- Informational metrics (that only exist for the labels they provide), such as VM flavor, size, or assigned role
- How many package upgrades are pending, if a restart is required
- Anything else not covered by the built-in collectors

Deployment

The test environment for static infrastructure for this chapter should already have `node_exporter` up and running through the automatic provisioning. Nevertheless, we can inspect it by connecting, for example, to the `target01` VM as follows:

```
cd ./chapter06/
vagrant ssh target01
```

Then check the configuration of the provided `systemd` unit file like so:

```
vagrant@target01:~$ systemctl cat node-exporter
```

In this snippet, we can see the `textfile` collector directory being set so that custom metrics can be exported:

```
...
ExecStart=/usr/bin/node_exporter --collector.textfile.directory=/var/lib/node_exporter
...
```

Let's try creating a custom metric. To do that, we only need to write the metric to a file inside the `textfile` collector directory with a `.prom` extension as follows:

```
vagrant@target01:~$ echo test_metric 1 | sudo tee /var/lib/node_exporter/test.prom
```

> **TIP**
>
> In a real-world scenario, you would need to make sure the file was written atomically so that `node_exporter` wouldn't see a half-written (thus corrupted) file. You could either write it out to a temporary file and then `mv` it into place (taking care to not cross mount point boundaries), or use the `sponge` utility, which is usually found in the `moreutils` package.

We can then request the `/metrics` endpoint and search for our test metric like so:

```
vagrant@target01:~$ curl -qs 0:9100/metrics | grep test_metric
```

The output should be something like the following:

```
# HELP test_metric Metric read from /var/lib/node_exporter/test.prom
# TYPE test_metric untyped
test_metric 1
```

This exporter produces a large number of metrics, depending on which collectors are enabled. Some of the more interesting metrics available from `node_exporter` are the following:

- `node_cpu_seconds_total`, which provides the number of seconds cumulatively used per core for all the available CPU modes, is very useful for understanding the CPU utilization
- `node_memory_MemTotal_bytes` and `node_memory_MemAvailable_bytes`, which allow calculating the ratio of memory available
- `node_filesystem_size_bytes` and `node_filesystem_avail_bytes`, which enable the calculation of filesystem utilization
- `node_textfile_scrape_error`, which tells you if the textfile collector couldn't parse any of the metrics files in the textfile directory (when this collector is enabled)

Container exporter

In the constant pursuit for workload isolation and resource optimization, we witnessed the move from physical to virtualized machines using hypervisors. Using virtualization implies a certain degree of resource usage inefficiency, as the storage, CPU, and memory need to be allocated to each running VM whether it uses them or not. A lot of work has been done in this area to mitigate such inefficiencies but, in the end, fully taking advantage of system resources is still a difficult problem.

Exporters and Integrations

With the rise of operating-system-level virtualization on Linux (that is, the use of containers), the mindset changed. We no longer want a full copy of an OS for each workload, but instead, only properly isolated processes to do the desired work. To achieve this, and focusing specifically on Linux containers, a set of kernel features responsible for isolating hardware resources (named cgroups or control groups) and kernel resources (named namespaces) were made available. Resources managed by cgroups are as follows:

- CPU
- Memory
- Disk I/O
- Network

These kernel features allow the user to have fine control over what resources a given workload has available, thus optimizing resource usage. Cgroups metrics are invaluable to any modern monitoring system.

cAdvisor

Container Advisor (cAdvisor) is a project developed by Google that collects, aggregates, analyzes, and exposes data from running containers. The data available covers pretty much anything you might require, from memory limits to GPU metrics, all available and segregated by container and/or host.

cAdvisor isn't tied to Docker containers but it's usually deployed as one. Data is collected from the container daemon and Linux cgroups, making the discovery of containers transparent and completely automatic. It also exposes process limits and throttling events whenever these limits are reached, which is important information to keep an eye on to maximize infrastructure resource usage without negatively impacting workloads.

Besides exposing metrics in the Prometheus format, cAdvisor also ships with a useful web interface, allowing the instant visualization of the status of hosts and their containers.

> The source code and installation files for cAdvisor are available at https://github.com/google/cadvisor.

Configuration

When launching cAdvisor as a container, some host paths are required to be available in read-only mode. This will allow, for example, the collection of kernels, processes, and container data.

There are quite a few runtime flags, so we'll feature some of the most relevant for our test case in the following table:

Flag	Description
`--docker`	Docker endpoint, defaults to `unix:///var/run/docker.sock`
`--docker_only`	Only report containers in addition to root stats
`--listen_ip`	IP to bind on, default to `0.0.0.0`
`--port`	Port to listen on, defaults to `8080`
`--storage_duration`	How long to store data, defaults to `2m0s`

> **TIP**: You can inspect the available runtime configurations using the following address: https://github.com/google/cadvisor/blob/release-v0.33/docs/runtime_options.md.

Deployment

Although historically the cAdvisor code was embedded in the Kubelet binary, it is currently scheduled to be deprecated there. Therefore, we'll be launching cAdvisor as a DaemonSet to future proof this example and to expose its configurations, while also enabling its web interface, as a Kubernetes service, to be explored.

Ensure you move into the correct repository path as shown here:

```
cd ./chapter06/provision/kubernetes/
```

Next, we must create a DaemonSet, because we want cAdvisor running in every single node:

```
apiVersion: apps/v1
kind: DaemonSet
metadata:
  name: cadvisor
  namespace: monitoring
...
```

Exporters and Integrations

Notice all the volume mounts allowing the collection of data from the Docker daemon and various Linux resources as shown here:

```
...
    spec:
     containers:
      - name: cadvisor
        volumeMounts:
         - {name: rootfs, mountPath: /rootfs, readOnly: true}
         - {name: var-run, mountPath: /var/run, readOnly: true}
         - {name: sys, mountPath: /sys, readOnly: true}
         - {name: docker, mountPath: /var/lib/docker, readOnly: true}
         - {name: disk, mountPath: /dev/disk, readOnly: true}
...
```

Apply the previous manifest using the following instruction:

```
kubectl apply -f ./cadvisor/cadvisor-daemonset.yaml
```

We can follow the deployment status using the following:

```
kubectl rollout status daemonset/cadvisor -n monitoring
```

When the deployment finishes, it's time to add a new service. Notice the port name that will be used in the ServiceMonitor. Here's the manifest we'll be using:

```
apiVersion: v1
kind: Service
metadata:
  labels:
    p8s-app: cadvisor
  name: cadvisor-service
  namespace: monitoring
spec:
  selector:
    p8s-app: cadvisor
  type: NodePort
  ports:
   - {name: http, protocol: TCP, port: 8080, targetPort: http}
```

The manifest can be applied using the following:

```
kubectl apply -f ./cadvisor/cadvisor-service.yaml
```

We can now connect to the cAdvisor web interface using the following instruction:

```
minikube service cadvisor-service -n monitoring
```

This will open a browser window with an interface similar to the following figure:

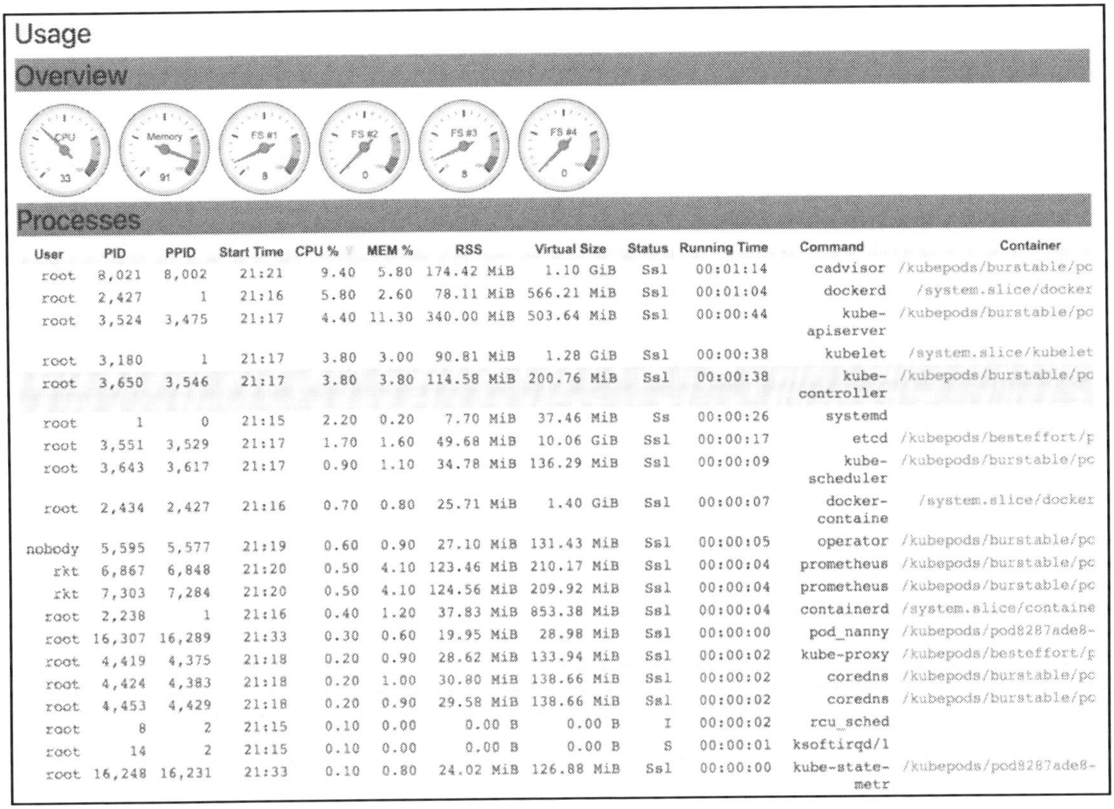

Figure 6.3: cAdvisor web interface

It's time to add cAdvisor exporters as new targets for Prometheus. For that, we'll be using the next `ServiceMonitor` manifest as shown here:

```
apiVersion: monitoring.coreos.com/v1
kind: ServiceMonitor
metadata:
  labels:
    p8s-app: cadvisor
  name: cadvisor-metrics
  namespace: monitoring
spec:
  endpoints:
  - interval: 30s
    port: http
    selector:
```

Exporters and Integrations

```
        matchLabels:
            p8s-app: cadvisor
```

The previous manifest can be applied using:

```
kubectl apply -f ./cadvisor/cadvisor-servicemonitor.yaml
```

After a few moments, you can inspect the newly added targets in the Prometheus web interface, using the following instruction to open its web interface:

```
minikube service prometheus-service -n monitoring
```

The following figure illustrates the Prometheus `/targets` endpoint showing cAdvisor target:

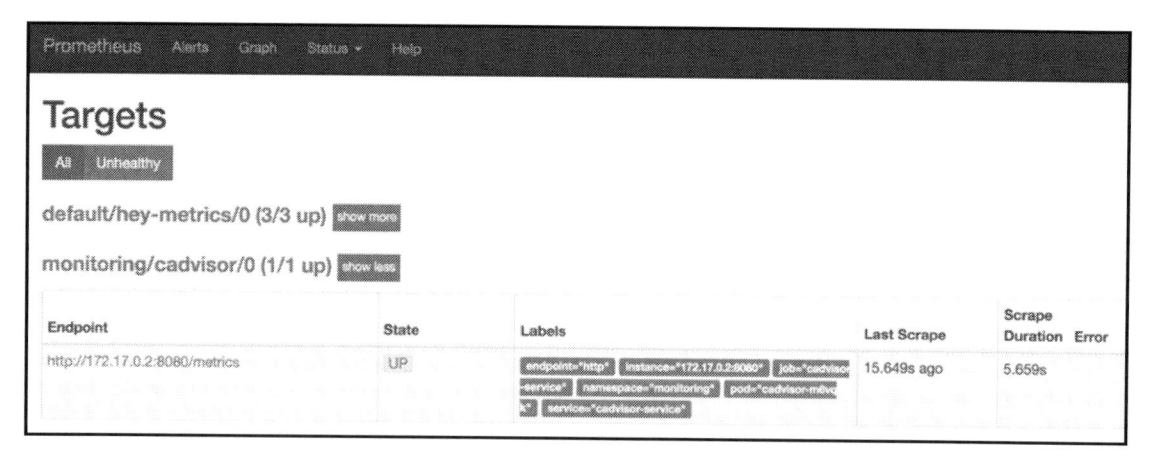

Figure 6.4: Prometheus /targets endpoint showing cAdvisor target

With this, we now have container-level metrics. Do note that cAdvisor exports a large amount of samples per container, which can easily balloon exported metrics to multiple thousands of samples per scrape, possibly causing cardinality-related issues on the scraping Prometheus.

> You can find every metric exposed by cAdvisor at their Prometheus documentation: https://github.com/google/cadvisor/blob/release-v0.33/docs/storage/prometheus.md.

From the thousands of metrics exported by cAdvisor, these are generally useful for keeping an eye out for problems:

- `container_last_seen`, which keeps track of the timestamp the container was last seen as running
- `container_cpu_usage_seconds_total`, which gives you a counter of the number of CPU seconds per core each container has used
- `container_memory_usage_bytes` and `container_memory_working_set_bytes`, which keep track of container memory usage (including cache and buffers) and just container active memory, respectively
- `container_network_receive_bytes_total` and `container_network_transmit_bytes_total`, which let you know how much traffic in the container receiving and transmitting, respectively

When running on Kubernetes, cAdvisor doesn't provide you with insight into how the cluster is running—application-level metrics from Kubernetes itself. For this, we need another exporter: kube-state-metrics.

kube-state-metrics

kube-state-metrics does not export container-level data, as that's not its function. It operates at a higher level, exposing the Kubernetes state, providing metrics regarding the API internal objects such as pods, services, or deployments. The object metric groups currently available when using this exporter are the following:

- CronJob metrics
- DaemonSet metrics
- Deployment metrics
- Job metrics
- LimitRange metrics
- Node metrics
- PersistentVolume metrics
- PersistentVolumeClaim metrics
- Pod metrics
- Pod Disruption Budget metrics
- ReplicaSet metrics

- ReplicationController metrics
- Resource quota metrics
- Service metrics
- StatefulSet metrics
- Namespace metrics
- Horizontal Pod Autoscaler metrics
- Endpoint metrics
- Secret metrics
- ConfigMap metrics

There are two endpoints exposed by kube-state-metrics: one provides the API objects metrics and the other presents the internal metrics from the exporter itself.

> The source code and installation files for kube-state-metrics are available at https://github.com/kubernetes/kube-state-metrics.

Configuration

When configuring kube-state-metrics, other than all the required RBAC permissions, there are also several runtime flags to be aware of. We will provide an overview of the more relevant ones for our test case in the following table:

Flag	Description
`--host`	IP to bind and expose Kubernetes metrics on, defaults to `0.0.0.0`
`--port`	Port to expose Kubernetes metrics, defaults to `80`
`--telemetry-host`	IP to expose internal metrics, defaults to `0.0.0.0`
`--telemetry-port`	Port to expose internal metrics, defaults to `80`
`--collectors`	Comma-separated list of metrics groups to enable, defaults to ConfigMap, CronJobs, DaemonSets, Deployments, endpoints, horizontalpodautoscalers, Jobs, LimitRanges, namespaces, Nodes, PersistentVolumeClaims, PersistentVolumes, PodDisruptionBudgets, pods, ReplicaSets, ReplicationControllers, resource quotas, Secrets, services, StatefulSets

`--metric-blacklist`	Comma-separated list of metrics to disable, mutually exclusive with the whitelist
`--metric-whitelist`	Comma-separated list of metrics to enable, mutually exclusive with the blacklist

> Due to the unpredictable amount of objects required to be exported, which are directly proportional to the size of the cluster, a common pattern when deploying kube-state-metrics is to use a special container called **addon-resizer**, which can vertically resize the exporter pod dynamically. Information regarding *addon-resizer* can be found at https://github.com/kubernetes/autoscaler/tree/addon-resizer-release-1.8.

Deployment

We'll be building upon the Kubernetes test environment started previously. To begin the deployment, ensure you move into the correct repository path, relative to the repository root as follows:

```
cd ./chapter06/provision/kubernetes/
```

As access to the Kubernetes API is required, the **role-based access control** (**RBAC**) configuration for this deploy is quite extensive, which includes a Role, a RoleBinding, a ClusterRole, a ClusterRoleBinding, and a ServiceAccount. This manifest is available at `./kube-state-metrics/kube-state-metrics-rbac.yaml`.

It should be applied using the following command:

```
kubectl apply -f ./kube-state-metrics/kube-state-metrics-rbac.yaml
```

We'll be creating a deployment for kube-state-metrics with just one instance, as, in this case, no clustering or special deployment requirements are necessary:

```
apiVersion: apps/v1
kind: Deployment
metadata:
  name: kube-state-metrics
  namespace: monitoring
spec:
  selector:
    matchLabels:
      k8s-app: kube-state-metrics
  replicas: 1
...
```

Exporters and Integrations

This deployment will run an instance of the `kube-state-metrics` exporter, along with `addon-resizer` to scale the exporter dynamically:

```
...
  template:
    spec:
      serviceAccountName: kube-state-metrics
      containers:
      - name: kube-state-metrics
...
      - name: addon-resizer
...
```

This can be applied using the following instruction:

```
kubectl apply -f ./kube-state-metrics/kube-state-metrics-deployment.yaml
```

We can follow the deployment status using the following:

```
kubectl rollout status deployment/kube-state-metrics -n monitoring
```

After a successful deployment, we'll be creating a service for this exporter, this time with two ports: one for the Kubernetes API object metrics and another for the exporter's internal metrics themselves:

```
apiVersion: v1
kind: Service
metadata:
  name: kube-state-metrics
  namespace: monitoring
  labels:
    k8s-app: kube-state-metrics
  annotations:
    prometheus.io/scrape: 'true'
spec:
  type: NodePort
  ports:
  - {name: http-metrics, port: 8080, targetPort: http-metrics, protocol: TCP}
  - {name: telemetry, port: 8081, targetPort: telemetry, protocol: TCP}
  selector:
    k8s-app: kube-state-metrics
```

The previous manifest can be applied as follows:

```
kubectl apply -f ./kube-state-metrics/kube-state-metrics-service.yaml
```

With the service in place, we are able to validate both metrics endpoints using the following command:

```
minikube service kube-state-metrics -n monitoring
```

This will open two different browser tabs, one for each metrics endpoint:

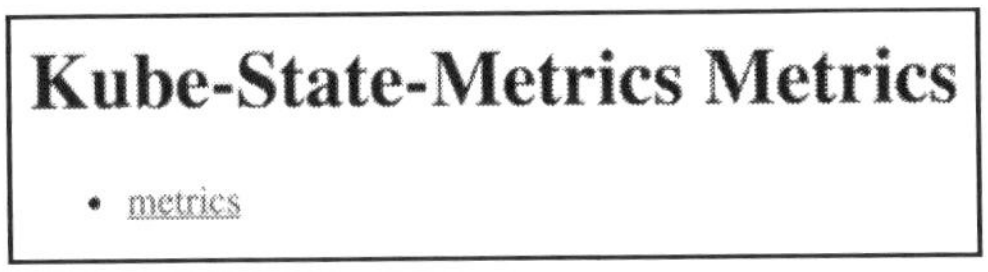

Kube-State-Metrics Metrics

- metrics

Figure 6.5: The kube-state-metrics web interface

Finally, it is time to configure Prometheus to scrape both endpoints using the `ServiceMonitor` manifest as shown here:

```yaml
apiVersion: monitoring.coreos.com/v1
kind: ServiceMonitor
metadata:
  labels:
    k8s-app: kube-state-metrics
  name: kube-state-metrics
  namespace: monitoring
spec:
  endpoints:
  - interval: 30s
    port: http-metrics
  - interval: 30s
    port: telemetry
  selector:
    matchLabels:
      k8s-app: kube-state-metrics
```

And it can now be applied using the following command:

```
kubectl apply -f ./kube-state-metrics/kube-state-metrics-servicemonitor.yaml
```

Exporters and Integrations

We can now validate the correct configuration of scrape targets in Prometheus, using the following instruction to open its web interface:

```
minikube service prometheus-service -n monitoring
```

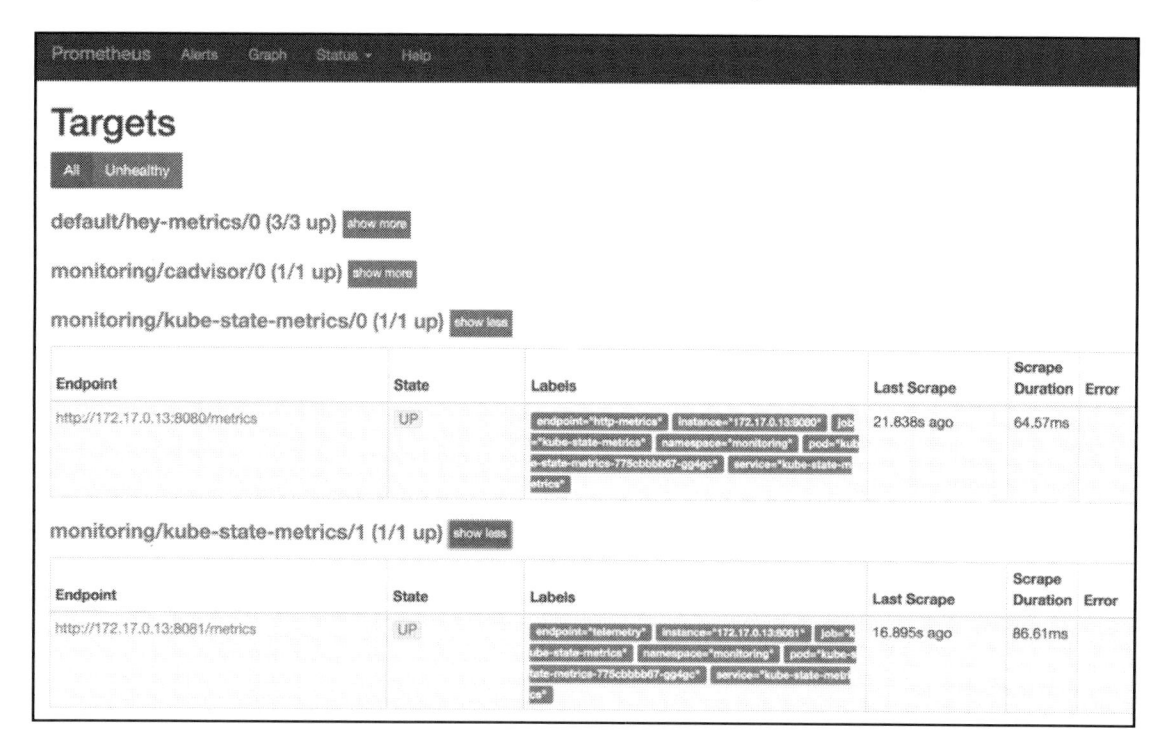

Figure 6.6: Prometheus /targets endpoint showing kube-state-metrics targets for metrics and telemetry

Some interesting metrics from kube-state-metrics that can be used to keep an eye on your Kubernetes clusters are:

- `kube_pod_container_status_restarts_total`, which can tell you if a given pod is restarting on a loop;
- `kube_pod_status_phase`, which can be used to alert on pods that are in a non-ready state for a long time;
- Comparing `kube_<object>_status_observed_generation` with `kube_<object>_metadata_generation` can give you a sense when a given object has failed but hasn't been rolled back

From logs to metrics

In a perfect world, all applications and services would have been properly instrumented and we would only be required to collect metrics to gain visibility. External exporters are a stop-gap approach that simplifies our work, but not every service exposes its internal state through a neat API. Older daemon software, such as Postfix or ntpd, makes use of logging to relay their inner workings. For these cases, we're left with two options: either instrument the service ourselves (which isn't possible for closed source software) or rely on logs to gather the metrics we require. The next topics go over the available options for extracting metrics from logs.

mtail

Developed by Google, mtail is a very light log processor that is capable of running programs with pattern matching logic, allowing the extraction of metrics from said logs. It supports multiple export formats, such as Prometheus, StatsD, Graphite, and more.

Besides the `/metrics` endpoint, the `/` endpoint for the mtail service exposes valuable debug information. This endpoint is available in the static infrastructure test environment at `http://192.168.42.11:9197`:

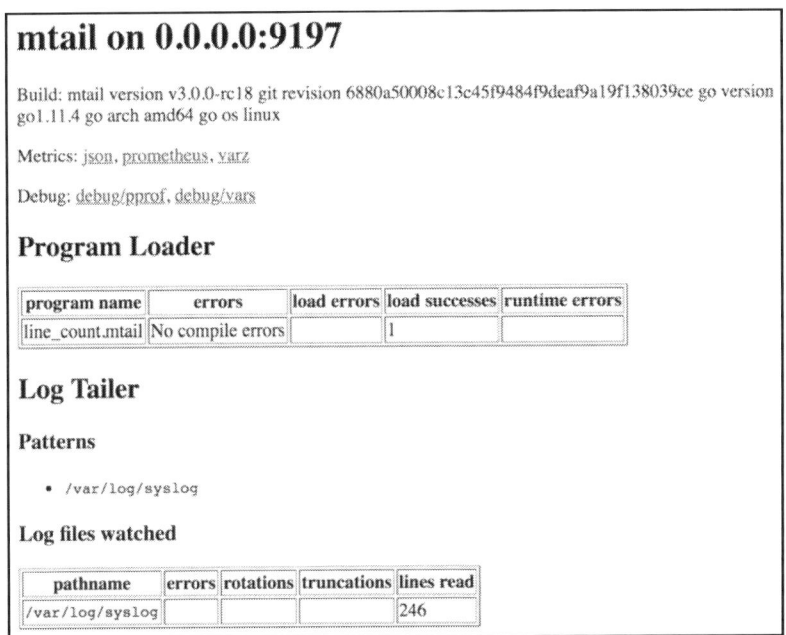

Figure 6.7: mtail web interface

> The source code and installation files for mtail are available at `https://github.com/google/mtail`.

Configuration

To configure mtail, we require a program with the pattern matching logic. Let's look at a very straightforward example available in the official repository:

```
# simple line counter
counter line_count
/$/ {
  line_count++
}
```

This program defines the `line_count` metric of the `counter` type, an RE2-compatible expression `/$/` matching the end of a line, and finally, an action between `{ }`, which, in this case, increments the `line_count` counter.

To run this program, we are only required to start mtail with command line flags to point it to our program and to the log we want to monitor. Here are some of the most useful flags for our test case:

-address	Host or IP to bind
-port	Listener port, defaults to `3903`
-progs	Path to the programs
-logs	Comma-separated list of files to monitor (this flag can be set multiple times)

> You can find the mtail programming guide at `https://github.com/google/mtail/blob/master/docs/Programming-Guide.md` and the RE2 syntax at `https://github.com/google/re2/wiki/Syntax`.

Deployment

In our static infrastructure test environment, we can validate the configuration of mtail by connecting to the `target01` instance as shown here:

```
cd ./chapter06/

vagrant ssh target01
```

Then checking the configuration of the provided `systemd` unit file as shown in the following command:

```
vagrant@target01:~$ systemctl cat mtail-exporter
```

As in this example, `mtail` is counting the lines of the `syslog` file so it needs to have proper permissions to access system logs, and thus, we run the `mtail` daemon with `Group=adm` to make this work. We can see all the required arguments for the `mtail` service in the following snippet from the unit file, including the path to the line count program:

```
...
Group=adm
ExecStart=/usr/bin/mtail -address 0.0.0.0 -port 9197 -progs /etc/mtail_exporter/line_count.mtail -logs /var/log/syslog
...
```

On the Prometheus instance, we added the following job:

```
- job_name: 'mtail'
  scrape_interval: 15s
  scrape_timeout: 5s
  static_configs:
    - targets: ['target01:9197']
```

> In a real-world scenario, you would name the scrape job as the daemon whose logs mtail is monitoring, such as ntpd or Postfix.

Exporters and Integrations

Using the Prometheus expression browser, available at `http://192.168.42.10:9090`, we can validate, not only that the scrapes are being successful through the `up` metric, but also that our metric is available:

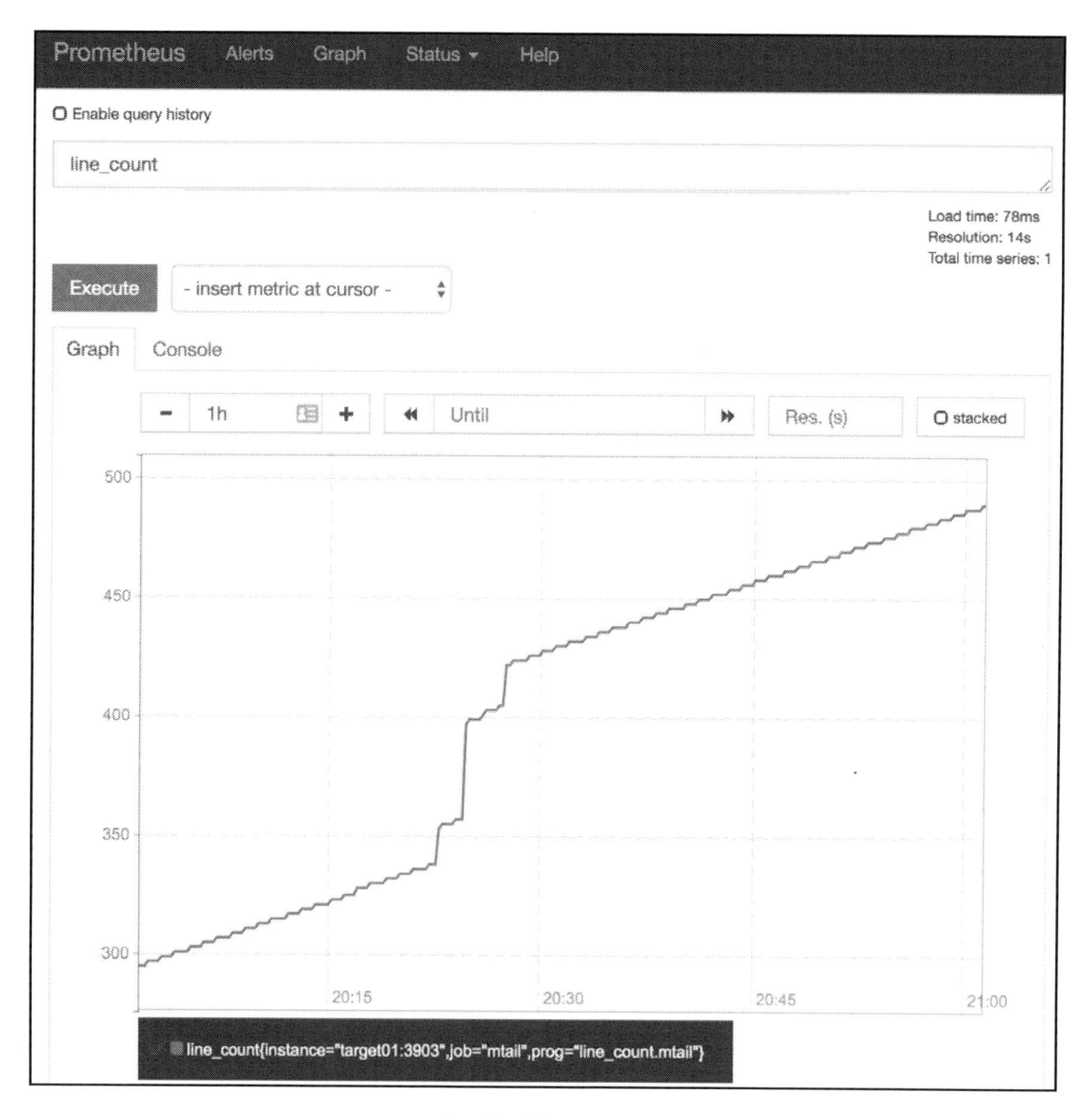

Figure 6.8: mtail line_count metric

Some interesting metrics from mtail that can be used to keep an eye on this exporter are:

- `mtail_log_watcher_error_count`, which counts the number of errors received from `fsnotify` (kernel-based notification system for filesystem events)
- `mtail_vm_line_processing_duration_milliseconds_bucket`, a histogram which provides the line processing duration distribution in milliseconds per mtail program

Grok exporter

Similarly to `mtail`, `grok_exporter` parses unstructured log data and generates metrics from it. However, as the name suggests, the main difference is the domain-specific language for this exporter being modeled after the Logstash pattern language (Grok), which enables the reuse of patterns you might already have built.

> The source code and installation files for `grok_exporter` are available at https://github.com/fstab/grok_exporter.

Configuration

This exporter requires a configuration file for its setup. There are five main sections in the configuration, which we can dissect in the following snippets from the exporter's configuration file deployed in our static infrastructure test environment. The `global` section sets the configuration format version. Version 2 is currently the standard configuration version, and so we set it here:

```
global:
    config_version: 2
```

The input section defines the location of the logs to be parsed. If `readall` is set to `true`, the file will be completely parsed before waiting for new lines; as we can see, we're not doing that in our example:

```
input:
    type: file
    path: /var/log/syslog
    readall: false
```

The `grok` section loads the patterns to use for parsing. These are configured in a separate location, as can be seen here:

```
grok:
    patterns_dir: /etc/grok_exporter/patterns
```

The `metrics` section is where the magic happens. It defines what metrics to extract from the parsed logs. Every Prometheus metric type is natively supported in this exporter. The configuration for each `type` can be slightly different, so you should check its documentation. However, we're going to provide an overview of the configuration that is common among them:

- The `match` configuration defines the regular expression for data extraction; in our example, LOGLEVEL is a predefined pattern to match log levels.
- The `labels` configuration is able to use Go's templating syntax to output whatever was extracted from the match definition; in this case, we used `level` as our variable in the match pattern and so it is available as `.level` in the template:

```
metrics:
    - type: counter
      name: grok_loglevel_example_total
      help: Total log level events triggered.
      match: '.*\(echo %{LOGLEVEL:level}\)$'
      labels:
          level: '{{.level}}'
```

> **TIP**
> The full configuration documentation is available at https://github.com/fstab/grok_exporter/blob/v0.2.7/CONFIG.md

Finally, the `server` section is where the bind address and port for the exporter are defined:

```
server:
    host: 0.0.0.0
    port: 9144
```

Now that we have a better understanding of what goes into the configuration file, it is time for us to try this exporter out in our test environment.

Deployment

In our static infrastructure test environment, we can validate the configuration of `grok_exporter` by connecting to the `target01` instance as shown here:

```
cd ./chapter06/
```

```
vagrant ssh target01
```

Outputting the configuration of the provided `systemd` unit file is shown in the following code snippet:

```
vagrant@target01:~$ systemctl cat grok-exporter
```

Just as with the `mtail` exporter, we need to run `grok_exporter` with `Group=adm` so that it has access to `syslog` without requiring being run as a privileged user. We can see all the required arguments for the `grok_exporter` service in the following snippet from the unit file, including the path to the configuration file mentioned before:

```
...
Group=adm
ExecStart=/usr/bin/grok_exporter -config /etc/grok_exporter/config.yml
...
```

On the Prometheus instance, we added the following job:

```
  - job_name: 'grok'
    scrape_interval: 15s
    scrape_timeout: 5s
    static_configs:
      - targets: ['target01:9144']
```

Exporters and Integrations

Using the Prometheus expression browser, available at `http://192.168.42.10:9090`, we can validate not only whether the scrapes are successful but also that our metric is available:

Figure 6.9: *grok_exporter* example metric

Some interesting metrics from `grok_exporter` that can be used to keep an eye on this exporter are:

- `grok_exporter_line_buffer_peak_load`, a summary which provides the number of lines that are read from the log file and waiting to be processed
- `grok_exporter_line_processing_errors_total`, which exposes the total number of processing errors for each defined metric

Blackbox monitoring

Introspection is invaluable to gather data about a system, but sometimes we're required to measure from the point of view of a user of that system. In such cases, probing is a good option to simulate user interaction. As probing is made from the outside and without knowledge regarding the inner workings of the system, this is classified as blackbox monitoring, as discussed in `Chapter 1`, *Monitoring Fundamentals*.

Blackbox exporter

`blackbox_exporter` is one of the most peculiar of all the currently available exporters in the Prometheus ecosystem. Its usage pattern is ingenious and usually, newcomers are puzzled by it. We'll be going to dive into this exporter with the hope of making its use as straightforward as possible.

The `blackbox_exporter` service exposes two main endpoints:

- `/metrics`: Where its own metrics are exposed
- `/probe`: It is the query endpoint that enables blackbox probes, returning their results in Prometheus exposition format

Besides the two previous endpoints, the `/` of the service also provides valuable information, including logs for the probes performed. This endpoint is available in the static infrastructure test environment at `http://192.168.42.11:9115`.

The blackbox exporter supports probing endpoints through a wide variety of protocols natively, such as TCP, ICMP, DNS, HTTP (versions 1 and 2), as well as TLS on most probes. Additionally, it also supports scripting text-based protocols such as IRC, IMAP, or SMTP by connecting through TCP and configuring what messages should be sent and what responses are expected; even plain HTTP would be possible to script but, as HTTP probing is such a common use case, it's already built in.

Exporters and Integrations

Having said that, this exporter doesn't cover all the blackbox-style monitoring needs. For those cases, writing your own exporter might be needed. As an example, you can't use `blackbox_exporter` to test a Kafka topic end to end, so you might need to look for an exporter able to produce a message to Kafka and then consume it back:

Figure 6.10: blackbox_exporter web interface

The `/probe` endpoint, when hit with an HTTP GET request with the parameters module and target, it executes the specified `prober` module against the defined target, and the result is then exposed as Prometheus metrics:

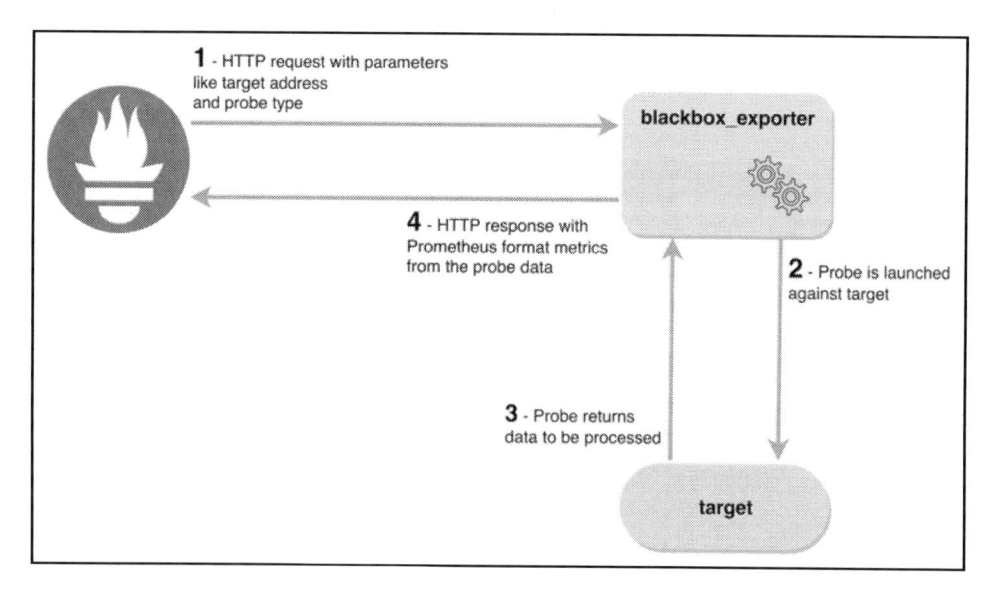

Figure 6.11: blackbox_exporter high-level workflow

For example, a request such as `http://192.168.42.11:9115/probe?module=http_2xx&target=example.com` will return something like the following snippet (a couple of metrics were discarded for briefness):

```
# HELP probe_duration_seconds Returns how long the probe took to complete in seconds
# TYPE probe_duration_seconds gauge
probe_duration_seconds 0.454460181
# HELP probe_http_ssl Indicates if SSL was used for the final redirect
# TYPE probe_http_ssl gauge
probe_http_ssl 0
# HELP probe_http_status_code Response HTTP status code
# TYPE probe_http_status_code gauge
probe_http_status_code 200
# HELP probe_ip_protocol Specifies whether probe ip protocol is IP4 or IP6
# TYPE probe_ip_protocol gauge
probe_ip_protocol 4
# HELP probe_success Displays whether or not the probe was a success
# TYPE probe_success gauge
probe_success 1
```

> **TIP**
> When debugging probes, you can append `&debug=true` to the HTTP GET URL to enable debug information.

> The source code and installation files for `blackbox_exporter` are available at `https://github.com/prometheus/blackbox_exporter`.

A quirk to be aware of when using `blackbox_exporter` is that the `up` metric does not reflect the status of the probe, but merely that Prometheus can reach the exporter. As can be seen in the previous metrics output, there is a `probe_success` metric that represents the status of the probe itself. This means that it is common for the `up` metric to appear healthy, but the probe might be failing, which is a common source for confusion.

Configuration

The scrape job configuration for blackbox probes is unusual, in the sense that both the `prober` module and the list of targets, whether static or discovered, need to be relayed to the exporter as HTTP GET parameters to the `/probe` endpoint. To make this work, a bit of `relabel_configs` magic is required, as seen in Chapter 5, *Running a Prometheus Server*.

Using the following Prometheus configuration snippet as an example, we're setting up an ICMP probe against the Prometheus instance, while `blackbox_exporter` is running on `target01`:

```
- job_name: 'blackbox-icmp'
  metrics_path: /probe
  params:
    module: [icmp]
  static_configs:
    - targets:
      - prometheus.prom.inet
  relabel_configs:
    - source_labels: [__address__]
      target_label: __param_target
    - source_labels: [__param_target]
      target_label: instance
    - target_label: __address__
      replacement: target01:9115
```

> Due to the nature of the ICMP probe, it requires elevated privileges to be run. In our environment, we're setting the capability to use raw sockets (`setcap cap_net_raw+ep /usr/bin/blackbox_exporter`) to guarantee such privileges.

The goal is to replace the address of the target with the address of `blackbox_exporter`, ensuring the internal `__param_target` keeps the address of the target. Focusing on how the `relabel_configs` is processed, the following happens:

- The `__address__` value (which contains the address of the target) is stored into `__param_target`.
- `__param_target` value is then stored into the instance label.
- The `blackbox_exporter` host is then applied to `__address__`.

This enables to Prometheus to query `blackbox_exporter` (using `__address__`), keep the instance label with the target definition, and pass the parameters module and target (using the internal `__param_target`) to the `/probe` endpoint, which returns the metrics data.

Deployment

In our static infrastructure test environment, we can validate the configuration of `blackbox_exporter` by connecting to the `target01` instance as shown here:

```
cd ./chapter06/

vagrant ssh target01
```

Then checking the configuration of the provided `systemd` unit file as shown in the following command:

```
vagrant@target01:~$ systemctl cat blackbox-exporter
```

> **TIP**: The configuration can be reloaded in runtime by sending an HTTP POST to the `/-/reload` endpoint or a `SIGHUP` to the `blackbox_exporter` process. If there are configuration errors, it will not be applied.

We can see all the required arguments for the `blackbox_exporter` service in the following snippet from the unit file, including the path to the configuration file:

```
...
ExecStart=/usr/bin/blackbox_exporter --
config.file=/etc/blackbox_exporter/blackbox.yml
...
```

The configuration we tailored for our example can be found in the following snippet:

```
modules:
  http_2xx:
    prober: http
    http:
      preferred_ip_protocol: ip4

  icmp:
    prober: icmp
    icmp:
      preferred_ip_protocol: ip4
```

> Notice `preferred_ip_protocol: ip4` is used, as `blackbox_exporter` prefers `ipv6`, but we're forcing `ipv4` in our probes.

Exporters and Integrations

On the Prometheus instance, we added the following jobs:

```
- job_name: 'blackbox-http'
  metrics_path: /probe
  params:
    module: [http_2xx]
  static_configs:
    - targets: [ 'http://example.com', 'https://example.com:443' ]
...
- job_name: 'blackbox-icmp'
  metrics_path: /probe
  params:
    module: [icmp]
  static_configs:
    - targets:
      - prometheus
...
```

Using the Prometheus web interface, available at `http://192.168.42.10:9090/targets`, we can validate whether the scrapes are successful (independently of the return status of the probes):

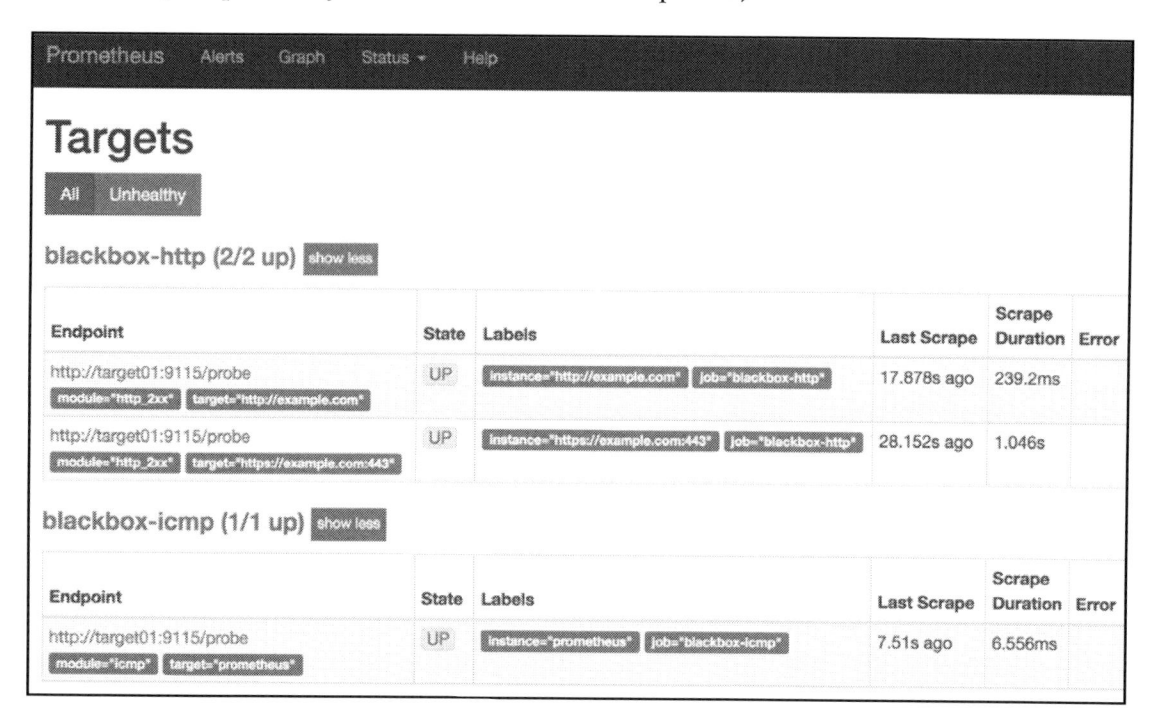

Figure 6.12: Prometheus /targets endpoint showing the blackbox_exporter targets

[134]

As mentioned before, the `/targets` page doesn't tell you whether a probe was successful or not. This needs to be validated in the expression browser by querying the `probe_success` metric:

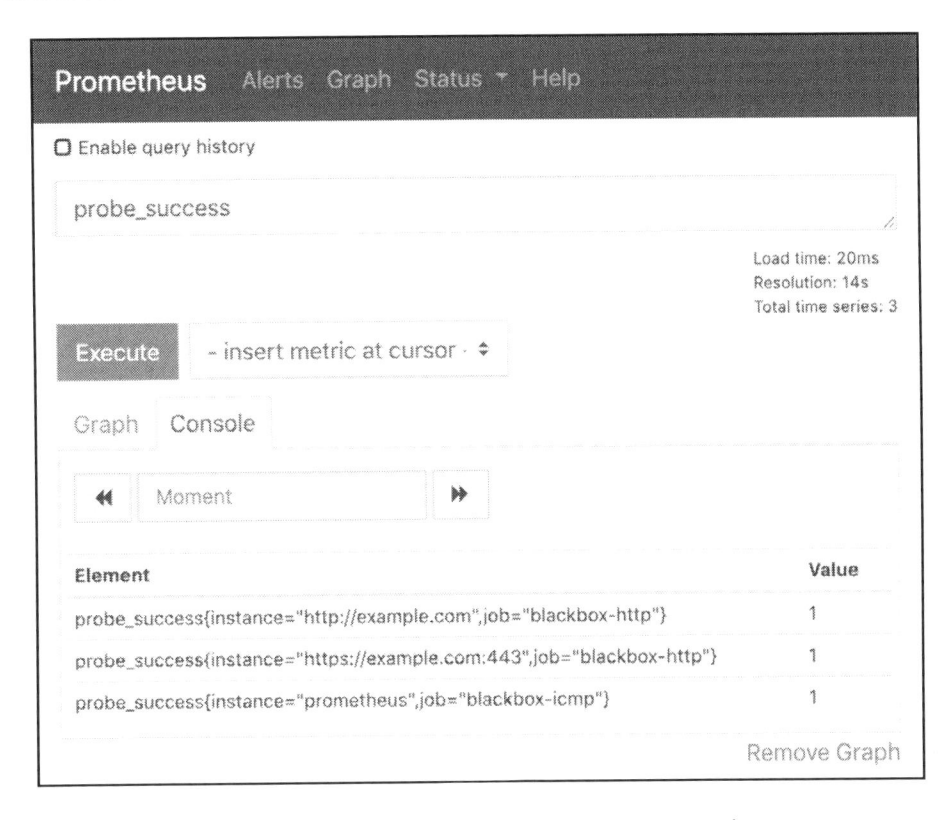

Figure 6.13: Prometheus expression browser showing the probe_success query results

Some interesting metrics that can be collected from `blackbox_exporter` (both about the exporter itself and from probes) are:

- `blackbox_exporter_config_last_reload_successful`, which exposes if the exporter's configuration file was reloaded successfully after a `SIGHUP`
- `probe_http_status_code`, which allows you to understand what HTTP status code is being returned when using the HTTP `prober` module
- `probe_ssl_earliest_cert_expiry`, which returns the timestamp for when the certificate chain from a SSL probe becomes invalid due to one of the certificates in the chain expiring

Exporters and Integrations

Pushing metrics

Despite the intense debate regarding push versus pull and the deliberate decision of using pull in the Prometheus server design, there are some legitimate situations where push is more appropriate.

One of those situations is batch jobs, though, for this statement to truly make sense, we need to clearly define what is considered a batch job. In this scope, a service-level batch job is a processing workload not tied to a particular instance, executed infrequently or on a schedule, and as such is not always running. This kind of job makes it very hard to generate successful scrapes if instrumented, which, as discussed previously in `Chapter 5`, *Running a Prometheus Server*, results in metric staleness, even if running for long enough to be scraped occasionally.

There are alternatives to relying on pushing metrics; for example, by using the textfile collector from `node_exporter` as described previously. Nevertheless, this option does not come without downsides. If the workload is not specific to a particular instance, you'll end up with multiple time series plus the cleanup logic of the textfile collector files, unless the lifetime of the metric matches the lifetime of the instance, which can then work out well in practice.

As a last resort, you have Pushgateway, which we'll be covering next.

Pushgateway

This exporter should only be employed in very specific use cases, as stated previously, and we should be aware of some common pitfalls. One possible problem is the lack of high availability, making it a single point of failure. This also impacts scalability as the only way to accommodate more metrics/clients is to either scale the instance vertically (adding more resources) or sharding (having different Pushgateway instances for different logical groups). By using Pushgateway, Prometheus does not scrape an application instance directly, which prevents having the `up` metric as a proxy for health monitoring. Additionally, and similarly to the textfile collector from `node_exporter`, metrics need to be manually deleted from Pushgateway via its API, or they will forever be exposed to Prometheus.

To push a metric, you need to send an HTTP POST request to the Pushgateway endpoint, using the following URL path definition. This will be demonstrated in the following deployment section:

```
http://<pushgateway_address>:<push_port>/metrics/job/<job_name>/[<label_name1>/<label_value1>]/[<label_nameN>/<label_valueN>]
```

Here, `<job_name>` will become the value of the label job for the metrics pushed and the `<label_name>/<label_value>` pairs will become additional label/value pairs. Keep in mind that metrics will be available until manually deleted, or in the case of a restart, when persistence is not configured.

> The source code and installation files for Pushgateway are available at `https://github.com/prometheus/pushgateway`.

Configuration

As Pushgateway is a centralized point where instances push their metrics, when a scrape is performed by Prometheus, the label instance will be automatically set to the Pushgateway server address/port for every single metric it exposes, and the label job to whatever name was set in the Prometheus scrape job definition. On label collision, Prometheus renames the original labels to `exported_instance` and `exported_job`, respectively. To avoid this behavior, `honor_labels: true` should be used in the scrape job definition to guarantee the labels that prevail are the ones coming from Pushgateway.

The noteworthy runtime configuration for our test case is as follows:

Flag	Description
`--web.listen-address`	Bind address, defaults to `0.0.0.0:9091`
`--persistence.file`	Persistence file location, if empty metrics are only kept in memory
`--persistence.interval`	Interval to write to the persistence file, defaults to 5m

Deployment

We'll be building upon the Kubernetes test environment started previously. In this particular scenario, we'll deploy an instance of Pushgateway and we'll be adding it as a target in Prometheus. To validate the correctness of our setup, we'll create a Kubernetes CronJob to emulate a batch job style of workload, and push its metrics to the Pushgateway service to ensure Prometheus collects our data.

Exporters and Integrations

To begin the deployment, ensure you move into the correct repository path, relative to the code repository root:

```
cd ./chapter06/provision/kubernetes/
```

To deploy an instance of Pushgateway, you can use the following manifest. Keep in mind that this service does not support high availability or clustering:

```yaml
apiVersion: apps/v1
kind: Deployment
metadata: {name: pushgateway, namespace: monitoring}
spec:
  selector:
    matchLabels: {p8s-app: pushgateway}
  replicas: 1
  template:
    metadata:
      labels: {p8s-app: pushgateway}
    spec:
      containers:
      - name: pushgateway
...
```

Apply the manifest by executing the following command:

```
kubectl apply -f ./pushgateway/pushgateway-deployment.yaml
```

And follow the deployment using the following:

```
kubectl rollout status deployment/pushgateway -n monitoring
```

After a successful deployment, it's time to provide a `Service` to our new instance, using the following manifest:

```yaml
apiVersion: v1
kind: Service
metadata:
  name: pushgateway-service
  namespace: monitoring
  labels:
    p8s-app: pushgateway
spec:
  type: NodePort
  ports:
  - {name: push-port, port: 9091, targetPort: push-port, protocol: TCP}
  selector:
    p8s-app: pushgateway
```

The following instruction applies to the previous manifest:

```
kubectl apply -f ./pushgateway/pushgateway-service.yaml
```

You may now validate the web interface for Pushgateway using the following command:

```
minikube service pushgateway-service -n monitoring
```

This will open a new browser tab pointing to the newly created Pushgateway instance web interface, which should look like the following figure:

Figure 6.14: Pushgateway web interface without any metric being pushed

Now, we need to instruct Prometheus to scrape Pushgateway. This can be accomplished via a new `ServiceMonitor` manifest as follows:

```
apiVersion: monitoring.coreos.com/v1
kind: ServiceMonitor
metadata:
  labels:
    p8s-app: pushgateway
  name: pushgateway
  namespace: monitoring
spec:
  endpoints:
  - interval: 30s
    port: push-port
    honorLabels: true
  selector:
    matchLabels:
      p8s-app: pushgateway
```

To apply this ServiceMonitor, we just type the following command:

```
kubectl apply -f ./pushgateway/pushgateway-servicemonitor.yaml
```

Now that we have our monitoring infrastructure in place, we need to simulate a batch job to validate our setup.

Exporters and Integrations

We can rely on the following manifest, which pushes a dummy `batchjob_example` metric with several labels to the Pushgateway service endpoint using a handcrafted `curl` payload:

```
apiVersion: batch/v1beta1
kind: CronJob
metadata:
  name: batchjob
spec:
  schedule: "*/1 * * * *"
  jobTemplate:
    spec:
      template:
        spec:
          containers:
          - name: batchjob
            image: kintoandar/curl:7.61.1
            args:
            - -c
            - 'echo "batchjob_example $(date +%s)" | curl -s --data-binary @- http://pushgateway-service.monitoring.svc.cluster.local:9091/metrics/job/batchjob/app/example/squad/yellow'
          restartPolicy: OnFailure
```

To apply the previous manifest, use the following command:

`kubectl apply -f ./pushgateway/batchjob-cronjob.yaml`

After a minute, the web interface for Pushgateway will look similar to this screenshot:

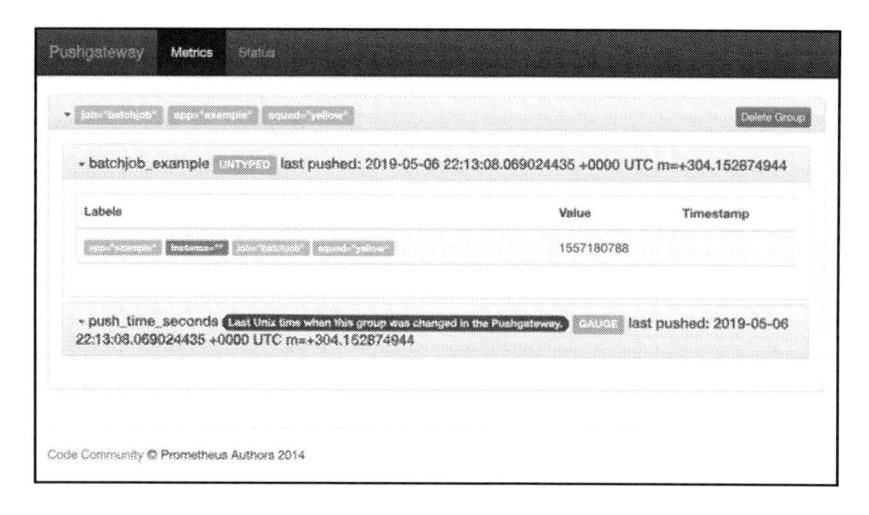

Figure 6.15: Pushgateway web interface presenting the batchjob_example metric

We can now use the Prometheus expression browser to validate the metric is being scraped from Pushgateway:

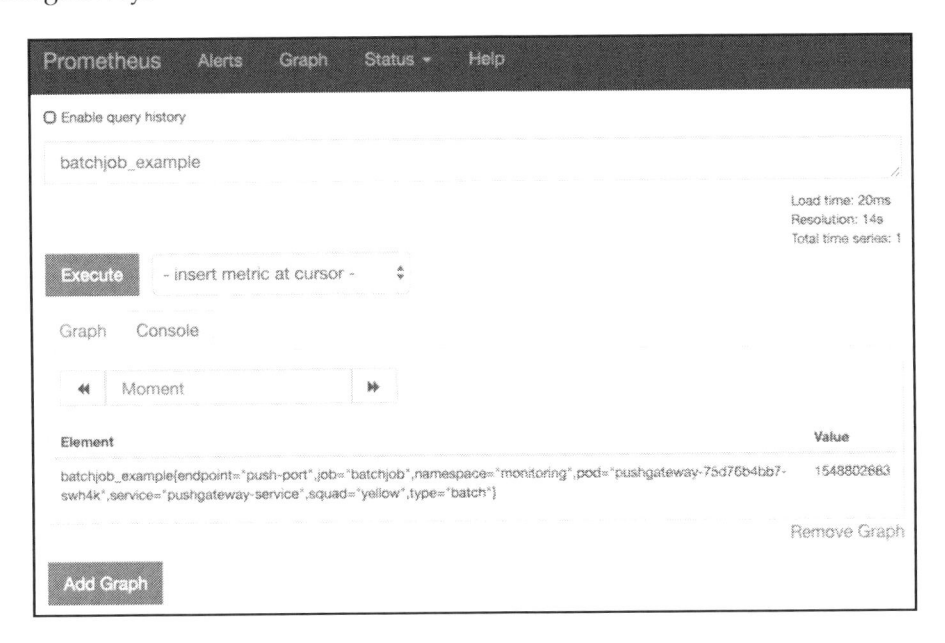

Figure 6.16: Prometheus expression browser showing the batchjob_example metric

As Pushgateway's job is to proxy metrics from other sources, it provides very little metrics of its own - just the standard Go runtime metrics, process metrics, HTTP handler metrics and build info. However, there is one application metric to note, which is `push_time_seconds`. This will tell you the last time a specific group (combination of labels used in the HTTP API when pushing) was seen. This can be used to detect missing or delayed jobs.

More exporters

The Prometheus community has produced a great number of exporters for just about anything you might need. However, making an intentional choice to deploy a new piece of software in your infrastructure has an indirect price to pay upfront. That price translates into the deployment automation code to be written, the packaging, the metrics to be collected and alerting to be created, the logging configuration, the security concerns, the upgrades, and other things we sometimes take for granted. When choosing an open source exporter, or any other open source project for that matter, there are a few indicators to keep in mind.

We should validate the community behind the project, the general health of contributions, if issues are being addressed, pull requests are being timely managed, and whether the maintainers are open to discuss and interact with the community. Technically, we should also check whether the official Prometheus client libraries are being used by the particular project. With that said, we'll be covering a few noteworthy exporters.

JMX exporter

The **Java Virtual Machine** (**JVM**) is a popular choice for core infrastructure services, such as Kafka, ZooKeeper, and Cassandra, among others. These services, like many others, do not natively offer metrics in the Prometheus exposition format and instrumenting such applications is far from being a trivial task. In these scenarios, we can rely on the **Java Management Extensions** (**JMX**) to expose the application's internal state through the **Managed Beans** (**MBeans**). The JMX exporter extracts numeric data from the exposed MBeans and converts it into Prometheus metrics, exposing them on an HTTP endpoint for ingestion.

The exporter is available in the following two forms:

- **Java agent**: In this mode, the exporter is loaded inside the local JVM where the target application is running and exposes a new HTTP endpoint.
- **Standalone HTTP server**: In this mode, a separate JVM instance is used to run the exporter that connects via JMX to the target JVM and exposes collected metrics on its own HTTP server.

The documentation strongly advises deploying the exporter using the Java agent, for good reason; the agent produces richer sets of metrics as compared with the standalone exporter, as it has access to the full JVM being instrumented. However, both have trade-offs that are important to be aware of so that the right tool for the job is chosen.

Although the standalone server does not have access to the JVM specific metrics, such as garbage collector statistics or process memory/CPU usage, it's easier to deploy and manage on static infrastructure when Java applications already have JMX enabled and are long-running processes that might not be convenient to touch. Adding to that, the exporter upgrade cycle becomes decoupled with the application life cycle, even though new releases are infrequent.

On the other hand, the Java agent provides the full range of available metrics in the JVM, but needs to be loaded into the target application at startup. This might be simpler to do on regularly deployed applications or when those applications run in containers.

Another benefit of running the agent is that the target JVM is also responsible to serve its own metrics, so the `up` metric from the scrape job can represent the process status without ambiguity.

Both options require a configuration file that can whitelist, blacklist, and/or relabel metrics from MBeans into the Prometheus format. An important performance consideration is the use of whitelists whenever possible. Some applications expose a very large amount of MBeans (such as Kafka or Cassandra) and frequent scrapes do have a significant performance impact.

> **TIP:** You can find useful examples of configuration files for the most used applications at `https://github.com/prometheus/jmx_exporter/tree/master/example_configs`.

> The source code for `jmx_exporter` is available at `https://github.com/prometheus/jmx_exporter`.

HAProxy exporter

HAProxy, a well-known load balancing solution, at the time of writing does not expose Prometheus metrics natively. Fortunately, it has an exporter, made by the Prometheus maintainers, to ensure its metrics can be collected, which is the `haproxy_exporter`. HAProxy natively exposes its metrics in **comma-separated value** (**CSV**) format via a configurable HTTP endpoint by using the `stats enable` configuration. The `haproxy_exporter`, which runs as a separate daemon, is able to connect to the HAProxy stats endpoint, consume the CSV, and convert its contents to the Prometheus metric format, exposing it in a synchronous manner when triggered by a scrape.

Instrumenting the load-balancer layer can be quite useful when the applications in the backend pools aren't properly instrumented and thus don't expose access metrics. For example, dashboards and alerts can be created for HTTP error rates or backend availability without any development effort from the application side. This is not meant to be a long-term solution, but can help in transitioning from legacy monitoring systems to Prometheus.

> You can find the source code and installation files for the `haproxy_exporter` at `https://github.com/prometheus/haproxy_exporter`

[143]

Summary

In this chapter, we had the opportunity to discover some of the most used Prometheus exporters available. Using test environments, we were able to interact with operating-system-level exporters running on VMs and container-specific exporters running on Kubernetes. We found that sometimes we need to rely on logs to obtain metrics and went through the current best options to achieve this. Then, we explored blackbox probing with the help of `blackbox_exporter` and validated its unique workflow. We also experimented with pushing metrics instead of using the standard pull approach from Prometheus, while making clear why sometimes this method does indeed make sense.

All these exporters enable you to gain visibility without having to natively instrument code, which sometimes is much more costly than relying on community-driven exporters.

With so many sources of metrics, now is the time to understand how to extract useful information from their data. In the next chapter, we'll go over PromQL and how best to leverage it.

Questions

1. How would you collect custom metrics with the Node Exporter?
2. What resources does cAdvisor consult to generate metrics?
3. kube-state-metrics expose numerous API objects. Is there a way to restrict that number?
4. How could you debug a `blackbox_exporter` probe?
5. If an application does not expose metrics, in Prometheus format or otherwise, what could an option to monitor it be?
6. What are the downsides of using Pushgateway?
7. If a particular batch job is host specific, is there any alternative to the use of Pushgateway?

Further reading

- **Prometheus exporters**: `https://prometheus.io/docs/instrumenting/exporters/`
- **Prometheus port allocations**: `https://github.com/prometheus/prometheus/wiki/Default-port-allocations`
- **Manpages cgroups**: `http://man7.org/linux/man-pages/man7/cgroups.7.html`
- **Manpages namespaces**: `http://man7.org/linux/man-pages/man7/namespaces.7.html`
- **Kubernetes resource usage monitoring**: `https://kubernetes.io/docs/tasks/debug-application-cluster/resource-usage-monitoring/`

Prometheus Query Language - PromQL

Prometheus offers a powerful and flexible query language in order to leverage its multi-dimensional data model that allows ad hoc aggregation and a combination of time series data. In this chapter, we'll introduce PromQL, its syntax, and semantics. Armed with the knowledge and features of this language, we'll be able to unlock the true potential of Prometheus.

In brief, the following topics will be covered in this chapter:

- The test environment for this chapter
- Getting to know the basics of PromQL
- Common patterns and pitfalls
- Moving on to more complex queries

The test environment for this chapter

In this chapter, we will be using a Kubernetes-based environment to generate all the metrics we need to test the PromQL examples that are covered in this chapter. Using the Prometheus Operator, the setup of this environment is quite simple; go through the following steps to get yourself up and running:

1. To start the Kubernetes test environment, we first must ensure there's no instance of `minikube` running:

   ```
   minikube status
   minikube delete
   ```

2. Start a new `minikube` instance with the following specifications:

   ```
   minikube start \
     --cpus=2 \
     --memory=3072 \
     --kubernetes-version="v1.14.0" \
     --vm-driver=virtualbox
   ```

   When the previous command finishes, a new Kubernetes environment should be ready to be used.

   For our Kubernetes test environment, we'll be building upon the lessons we learned about in Chapter 5, *Running a Prometheus Server*, and will employ the Prometheus Operator in our workflow. Since we've already covered the Prometheus Operator setup, we'll deploy all the required components without dwelling on each one of them.

3. Step into this chapter number, relative to the code repository root path:

   ```
   cd ./chapter07/
   ```

4. Deploy the Prometheus Operator and validate the successful deploy:

   ```
   kubectl apply -f ./provision/kubernetes/bootstrap/
   kubectl rollout status deployment/prometheus-operator -n monitoring
   ```

5. Wait a few seconds for the Prometheus Operator to be able to execute requests and deploy the Prometheus server:

   ```
   kubectl apply -f ./provision/kubernetes/prometheus/
   kubectl rollout status statefulset/prometheus-k8s -n monitoring
   ```

So that we have a few metric providers, we'll be deploying some of the exporters we covered in Chapter 6, *Exporters and Integrations*, specifically the following:

- Node Exporter
- cAdvisor
- kube-state-metrics

We'll also be deploying a type of *Hello World* application, *Hey*, that we introduced in Chapter 5, *Running a Prometheus Server*, so that Prometheus gathers web application metrics as well.

To ease the effort required to deploy all of the components and configurations, the following command abstracts all the steps needed, which we also went through in previous chapters:

```
kubectl apply -f ./provision/kubernetes/services/
kubectl get servicemonitors --all-namespaces
```

After a moment, you should have Prometheus and all the services ready and available. The following instruction should open the Prometheus web interface in your default web browser:

```
minikube service prometheus-service -n monitoring
```

If you browse the /targets endpoint, you'll be presented with something similar to the following:

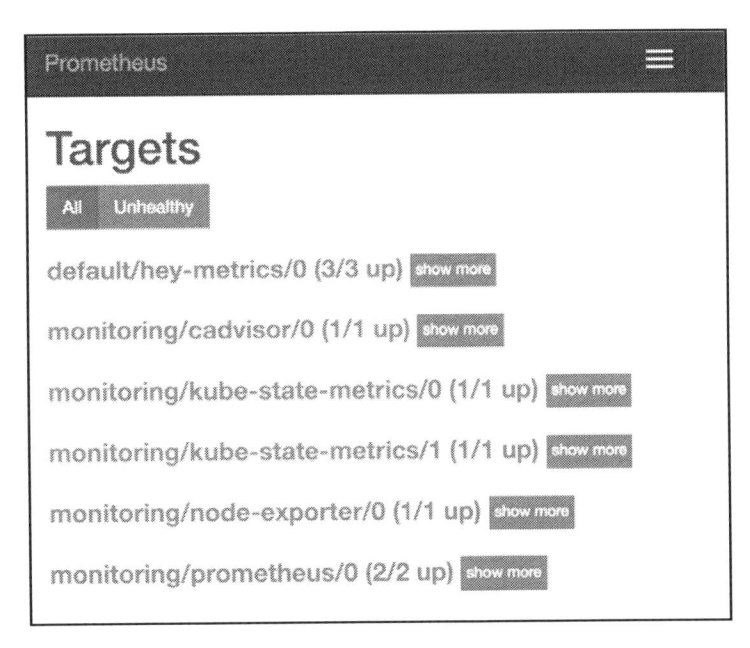

Figure 7.1: Prometheus /targets endpoint showing all the configured targets

You can now follow along with the examples in this chapter using this newly created test environment.

Getting to know the basics of PromQL

Understanding the Prometheus Query Language is essential to be able to perform insightful dashboarding, capacity planning, and alerting. But for that, we need to begin by learning the basics. The following topics will cover the components that available to construct queries and look into how they behave together.

Selectors

Prometheus is designed to handle hundreds of thousands of time series. Each metric name can have several different time series, depending on the combination of labels; querying the right data can look difficult, or even downright perplexing, when similarly-named metrics from different jobs are mixed together. In Prometheus, a selector refers to a set of label matchers. The metric name is also included in this definition as, technically, its internal representation is also a label, albeit a special one: __name__. Each label name/value pair in a selector is called a label matcher, and multiple matchers can be used to further filter down the time series matched by the selector. Label matchers are enclosed in curly brackets. If no matcher is needed, the curly brackets can be omitted. Selectors can return instant or range vectors. Here's an example selector:

```
prometheus_build_info{version="2.9.2"}
```

This selector is equivalent to the following:

```
{__name__="prometheus_build_info", version="2.9.2"}
```

Let's now see how to label matchers work.

Label matchers

Matchers are employed to restrict a query search to a specific set of label values. We'll be using the node_cpu_seconds_total metric to exemplify the four available label matcher operators: =, !=, =~, and !~. Without any matching specification, this metric alone returns an instant vector with all the available time series containing the metric name, as well as all combinations of the CPU core numbers (cpu="0", cpu="1") and CPU modes (mode="idle", mode="iowait", mode="irq", mode="nice", mode="softirq", mode="steal", mode="user", mode="system"), which makes a grand total of 16 time series, as shown in the following screenshot:

Chapter 7

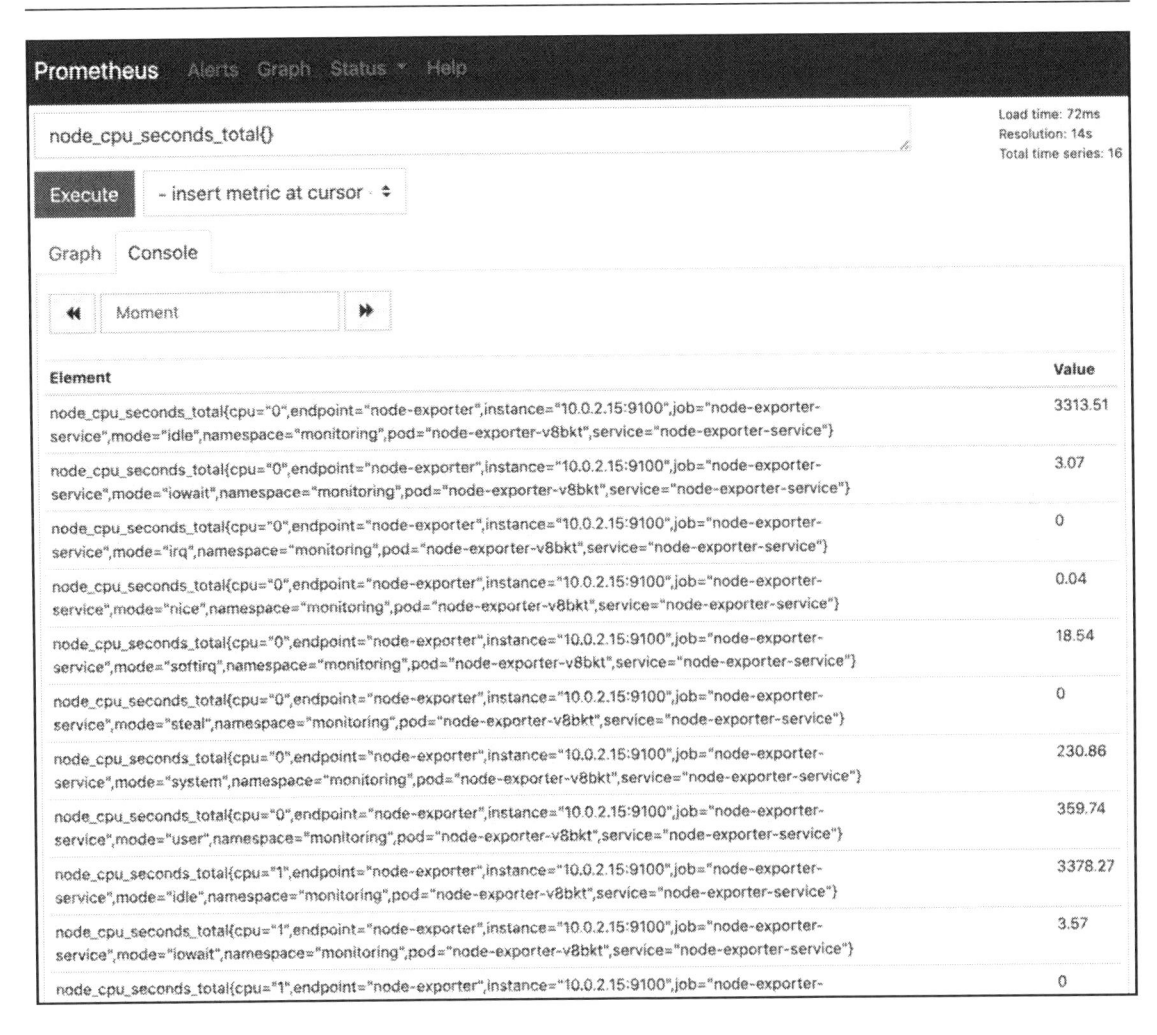

Figure 7.2: node_cpu_seconds_total query resulting in 16 time series being returned

Now, let's use each of the four available label matchers (=, !=, =~, and !~) to restrict the query differently and analyze the produced results.

Prometheus Query Language - PromQL

Using =, we can perform an exact match on the label value. For instance, if we only match CPU core 0, it will return an instant vector with half of the time series from the previous query:

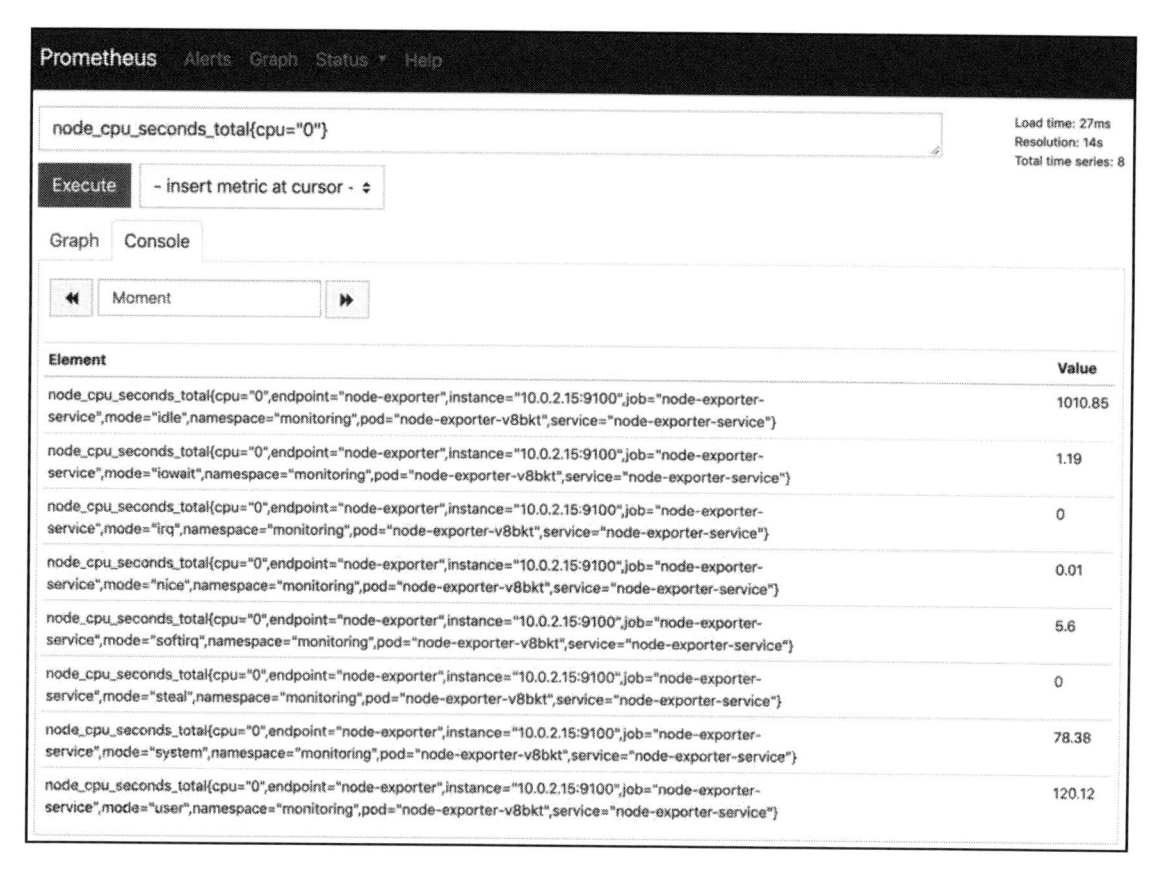

Figure 7.3: Query node_cpu_seconds_total only on CPU core 0

We can also negate a match to obtain all the remaining time series using the != matcher. Once applied to our example, it will return the remaining eight time series only, as follows:

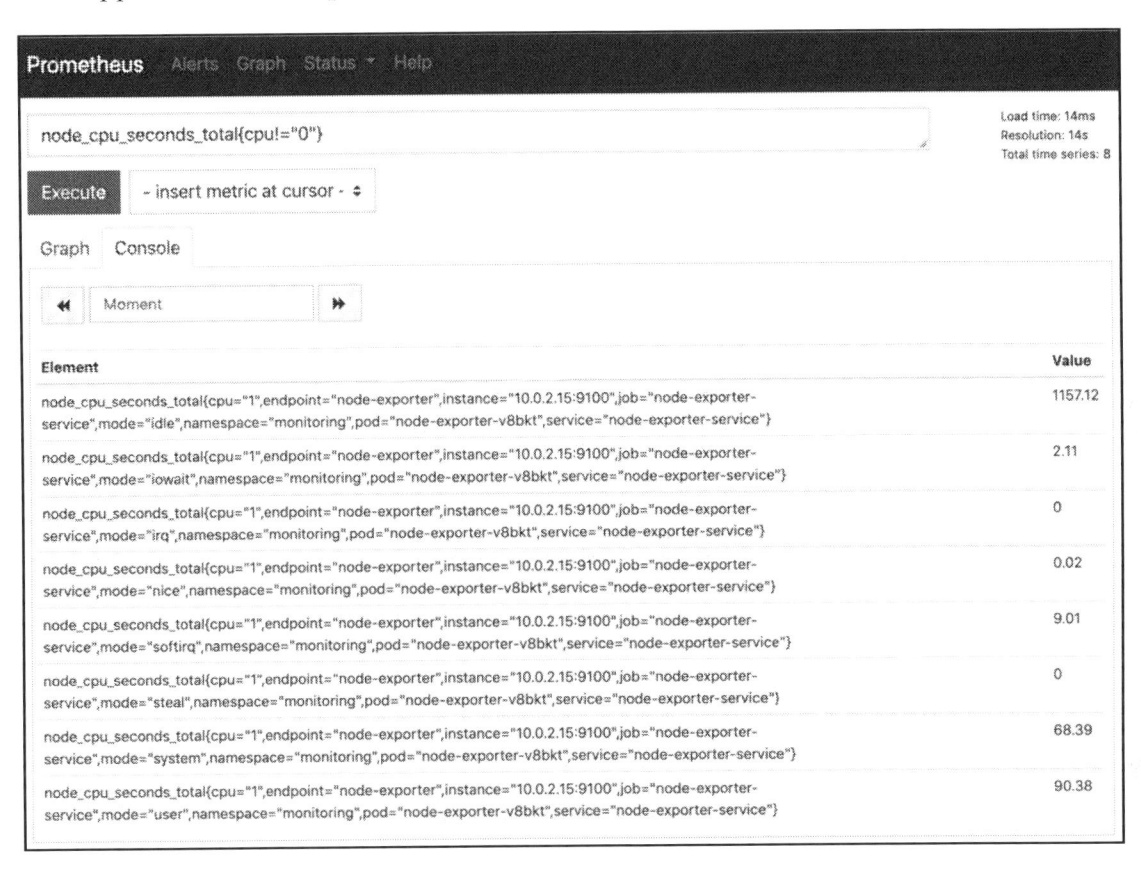

Figure 7.4: Query node_cpu_seconds_total for all time series except core 0

When selecting time series, instead of relying solely on exact matches, it is also important to be able to apply regular expressions. Hence, =~ and !~ are PromQL matchers for this operation and they both accept RE2 type regex syntax. Keep in mind that the regular expressions are anchored when using these matchers. This means they need to match the full label value. You can unanchor an expression by adding .* at the beginning and end of the regex.

Prometheus Query Language - PromQL

> **TIP**
> The regular expression syntax that's accepted by RE2 can be found at: `https://github.com/google/re2/wiki/Syntax`.

Looking at our example, if we were only interested in two CPU modes, `mode="user"` and `mode="system"`, we could easily perform a query like the following, effectively selecting only the modes we require:

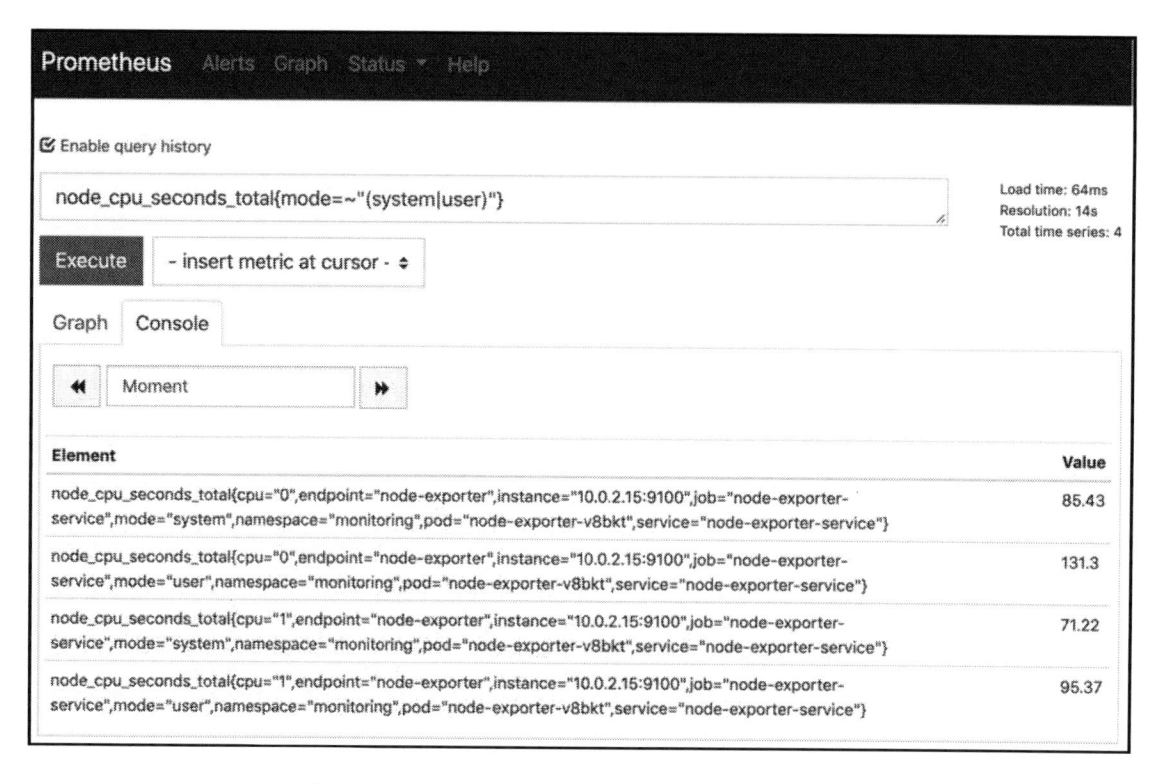

Figure 7.5: Query node_cpu_seconds_total only for mode="user" and mode="system"

Considering that RE2 does not support negative lookahead, and similar to the negate matcher, Prometheus provides a way to negate the regex matcher, by using `!~`. This matcher excludes results that match the expression and allows all the remaining time series. Here's an example:

[154]

Chapter 7

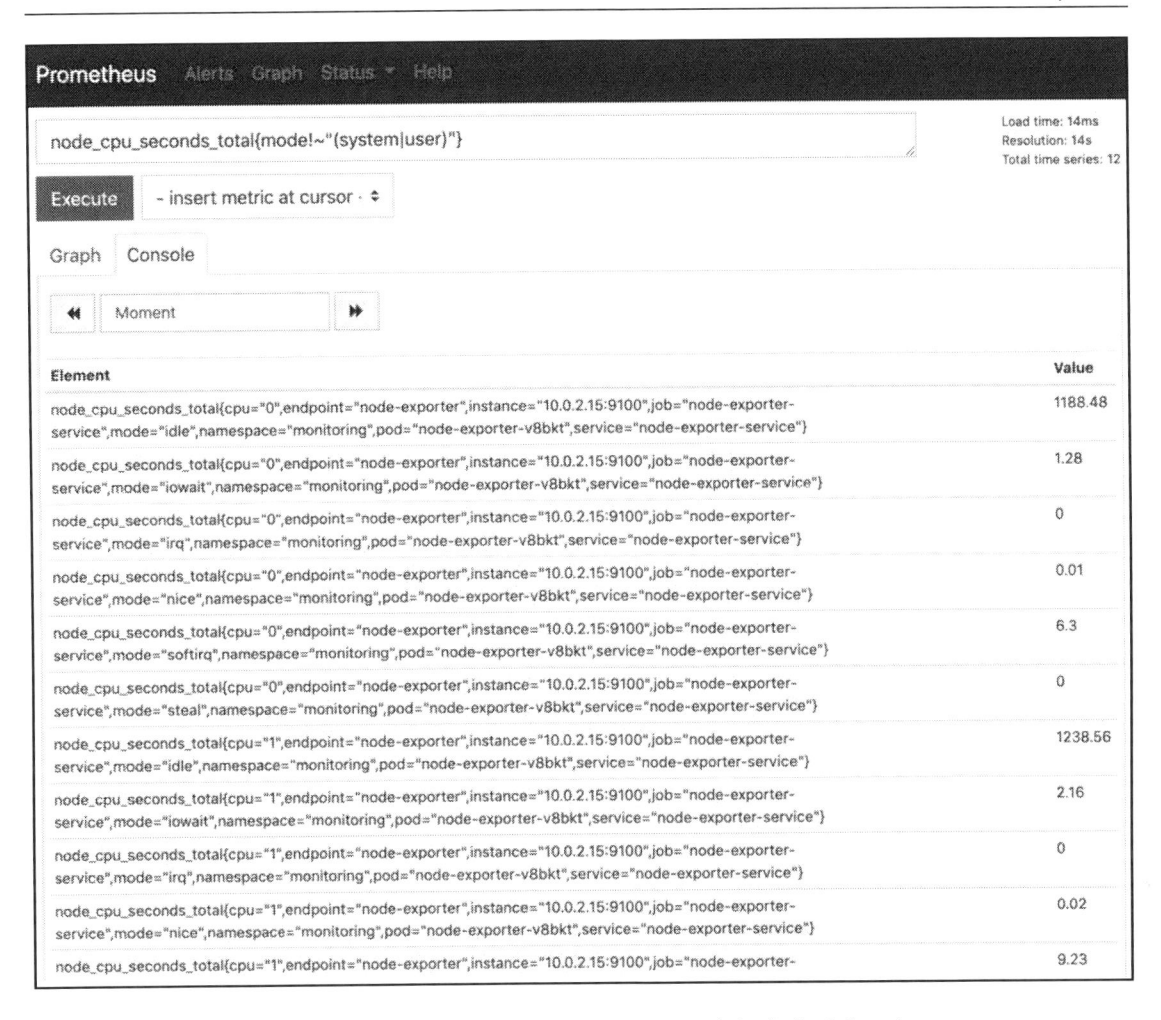

Figure 7.6: Query node_cpu_seconds_total for all time series except mode="user" and mode="system"

Now that we have a good understanding on how label matchers work, let's have a look at instant vectors.

Instant vectors

Instant vector selectors are named as such because they return a list of samples, relative to the query evaluation time, for the time series that match them. This list is called an **instant vector**, as it's a result at a given instant.

A sample is a data point of a time series, composed of a value and a timestamp. This timestamp, in most cases, reflects the time when the scrape occurred and that value was ingested, with the exception of metrics pushed to the Pushgateway, which, due to their nature, will never have timestamps. However, if functions are applied or operations are performed on the time series, the timestamp for the instant vector samples will reflect the query time and not the ingested time.

The way instant vectors operate – by only returning the most recent samples relative to query time that match the selector - means that Prometheus will not return time series that are considered stale (as we mentioned in `Chapter 5`, *Running a Prometheus Server*). A stale marker (a special kind of sample that marks that time series as stale) is inserted when either the originating target disappears from the discovery mechanism, or if they are not present in the scrape after the last successful one where they existed. A time series with a stale marker as its last sample will not be returned when using instant vector selectors.

Every example in the *Label Matchers* section was an instant vector selector, and so every result was an instant vector.

Range vectors

A range vector selector is similar to an instant vector selector, but it returns a set of samples for a given time range, for each time series that matches it. Keep in mind that a timestamp of a given value might not be completely aligned with the scrape time for different targets since Prometheus spreads the scrapes across their defined intervals, reducing overlapping scrapes in the same instant.

To define a range vector selector query, you have to set an instant vector selector and append a range using square brackets `[ ]`.

The following table details the available time units for defining a range:

Abbreviation	Unit
s	Seconds
m	Minutes
h	Hours
d	Days
w	Weeks
y	Years

Like durations, as explained in `Chapter 5`, *Running a Prometheus Server*, a time range is always an integer value with a single unit. For example, 1.5d and 1d12h are considered errors and should be represented as 36h. Durations ignore leap seconds and leap days: a week is always is always exactly 7 days long, and a year 365 days.

Let's put this into practice. Using the *Hey* application as our case example, we're going to inspect the samples that were collected in the last two minutes for HTTP code `200`:

```
http_requests_total{code="200"}[2m]
```

Following is the output for the preceding code:

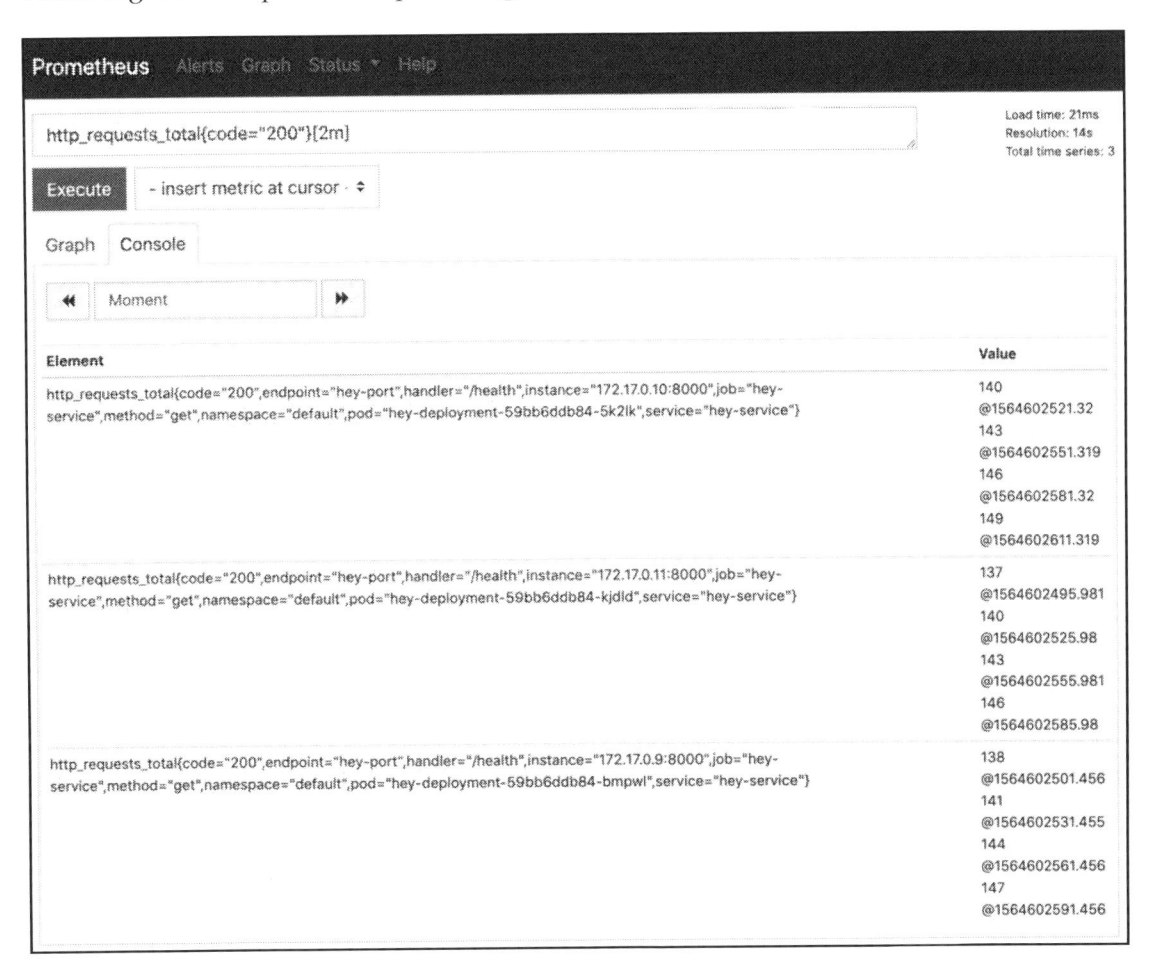

Figure 7.7: Two minutes of samples of the http_requests_total metric for the HTTP code 200

As we can see in the preceding screenshot, there are four samples available (defined by the 30s scrape interval) for each instance of the *Hey* application that are returned by our range vector selector.

The offset modifier

The `offset` modifier allows you to query data in the past. This means that we can offset the query time of an instant or range vector selector relative to the current time. It is applied on a per-selector basis, which means that offsetting one selector but not another effectively unlocks the ability to compare current behavior with past behavior for each of the matched time series. To use this modifier, we need to specify it right after the selector and add the offset time; for example:

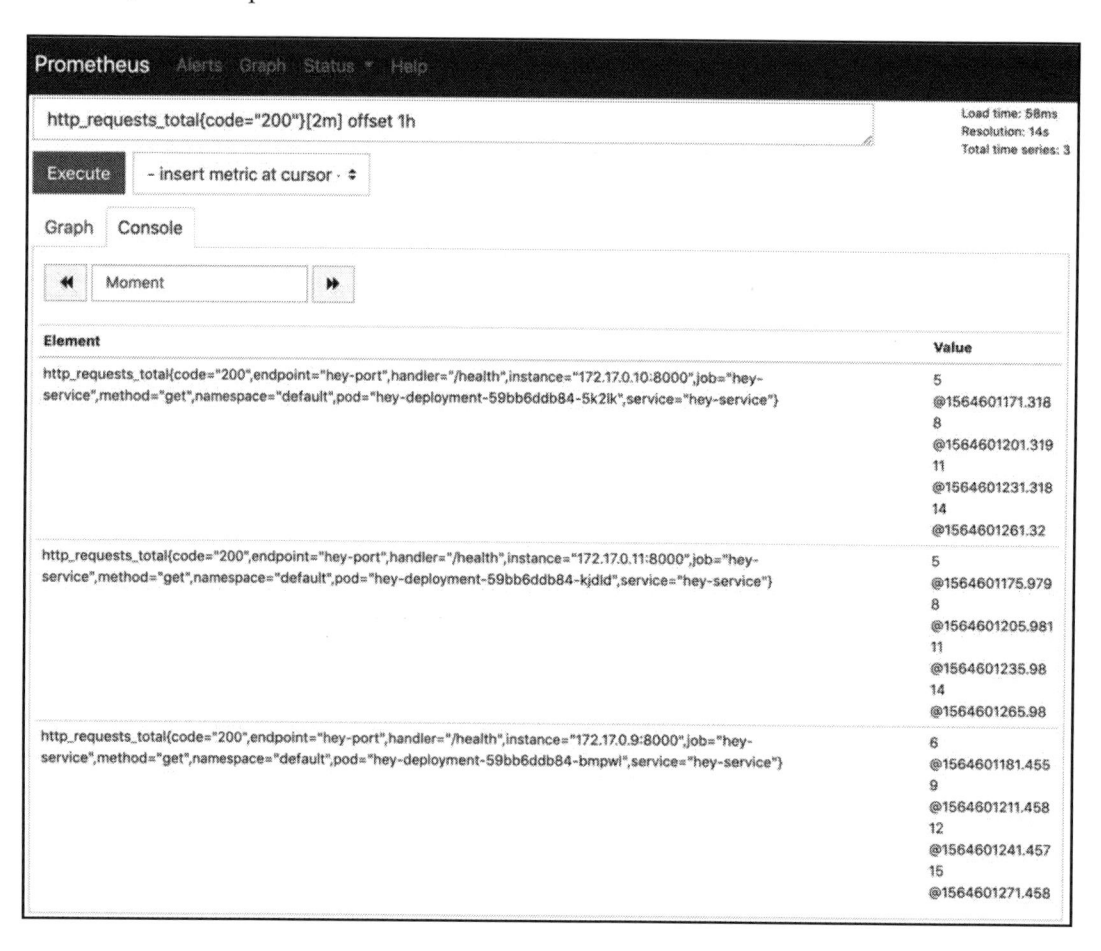

Figure 7.8: Two minutes of samples of the http_requests_total metric of the past hour for the HTTP code 200

Chapter 7

> **TIP:** Despite not being directly related to PromQL, it's important to be aware of the moment feature of the Prometheus expression browser. This feature changes the query moment as if we went back to a specific date and time. The main difference between the moment picker and using offset is that the former is absolute while the latter is relative time shifting.

Subqueries

Before the introduction of the subquery selector in Prometheus 2.7.0, there wasn't a direct way to feed the output of functions that returned instant vectors to range vector functions. In order to do that, you would have recorded the expression that produced the desired instant vector as a new time series, also called a recording rule – which we'll go into in depth in Chapter 9, *Defining Alerting and Recording Rules* – waited for it to have enough data, and then used the appropriate range vector selector to feed the recorded series into the range vector function. The subquery selector simplifies this process by allowing the evaluation of functions that return instant vectors over time and return the result as a range vector, without needing to wait for recording rules to capture sufficient data. Subquery syntax is similar to range vectors, with the added detail of being able to specify the frequency in which samples should be captured, as we'll see soon.

We'll be using the following query example to explain its syntax:

```
max_over_time(rate(http_requests_total{handler="/health",
instance="172.17.0.9:8000"}[5m])[1h:1m])
```

Splitting the query into its components, we can see the following:

Component	Description
`rate(http_requests_total{handler="/health", instance="172.17.0.9:8000"}[5m])`	The inner query to be run, which in this case is aggregating five minutes' worth of data into an instant vector.
`[1h`	Just like a range vector selector, this defines the size of the range relative to the query evaluation time.
`:1m]`	The resolution step to use. If not defined, it defaults to the global evaluation interval.
`max_over_time`	The subquery returns a range vector, which is now able to become the argument of this aggregation operation over time.

This is a common use case, as it is good practice to expose counters wherever possible (with the obvious exception of things that are gauges by nature, such as current memory occupation) and then rate them to be resilient to failed scrapes, but most interesting functions take ranges of gauges.

Subqueries are fairly expensive to evaluate, so it is strongly discouraged to use them for dashboarding, as recording rules would produce the same result given enough time. Similarly, they should not be used in recording rules for the same reason. Subqueries are best suited for exploratory querying, where it is not known in advance which aggregations are needed to be looked at over time.

Operators

PromQL allows the use of binary, vector matching, and aggregation operators. In the following sections, we'll go over each one, providing examples on how and when to use them.

Binary operators

Apart from instant and range vectors, Prometheus also supports values of the scalar type, which consist of single numbers without any dimensionality.

In the following subsections, we will explore each of the binary operators: the arithmetic and the comparison operators.

Arithmetic

The arithmetic operators provide basic math between two operands.

There are three available combinations of operands. The simplest is between two scalars, which will return a scalar after applying the chosen arithmetic operator. We can also combine an instant vector and a scalar, which will apply the chosen arithmetic operator between the scalar and each sample of the instant vector, effectively returning the same instant vector with updated samples. The last combination we can have is between two instant vectors. In this case, the arithmetic operator is applied between the vector from the left-hand side and the matching element from the right-hand side vector, while the metric name is dropped. If no match is present, those samples will not be part of the result. This case will be explained further in the *Vector matching* section.

For reference, the available arithmetic operators are as follows:

Operator	Description
+	Addition
-	Subtraction
*	Multiplication
/	Division
%	Modulo
^	Power

Comparison

The comparison operators, as shown in the following table, are useful for filtering results:

Operator	Description
==	Equal
!=	Not equal
>	Greater than
<	Less than
>=	Greater or equal
<=	Less or equal

Say, for example, we have the following instant vector:

```
process_open_fds{instance="172.17.0.10:8000", job="hey-service"} 8
process_open_fds{instance="172.17.0.11:8000", job="hey-service"} 23
```

To that, we apply a comparison operator such as the following:

```
process_open_fds{job="hey-service"} > 10
```

The result will be as follows:

```
process_open_fds{instance="172.17.0.11:8000", job="hey-service"} 23
```

This operation shows that we have effectively filtered the results of the instant vector, which is fundamental for alerting, as we'll discuss later, in Chapter 9, *Defining Alerting and Recording Rules*.

Moreover, we can use the `bool` modifier to not only return all matched time series but also modify each returned sample to become 1 or 0, depending on whether the sample would be kept or dropped by the comparison operator.

> Using the bool modifier is the only way to compare scalars; for example, `42 == bool 42`.

Therefore, we can apply the same query with the `bool` modifier to our previous example:

```
process_open_fds{job="hey-service"} > bool 10
```

This would return the following:

```
process_open_fds{instance="172.17.0.10:8000", job="hey-service"} 0
process_open_fds{instance="172.17.0.11:8000", job="hey-service"} 1
```

Vector matching

Vector matching, as the name implies, is an operation only available between vectors. So far, we have learned that when we have a scalar and an instant vector, the scalar gets applied to each sample of the instant vector. However, when we have two instant vectors, how can we match their samples? We'll be tackling this question in the following sub-sections.

One-to-one

Since binary operators require two operands, as we described previously, when vectors of the same size and label set are located on each side of one operator, that is, one-to-one, samples with the exact same label/value pairs are matched together, while the metric name and all non-matching elements are dropped.

Let's consider an example. We'll start by using the following instant vectors:

```
node_filesystem_avail_bytes{instance="172.17.0.13:9100", job="node-exporter-service", mountpoint="/Users"} 100397019136
node_filesystem_avail_bytes{instance="172.17.0.13:9100", job="node-exporter-service", mountpoint="/data"} 14120038400
node_filesystem_size_bytes{instance="172.17.0.13:9100", job="node-exporter-service", mountpoint="/Users"} 250685575168
node_filesystem_size_bytes{instance="172.17.0.13:9100", job="node-exporter-service", mountpoint="/data"} 17293533184
```

We'll then apply the following operation:

```
node_filesystem_avail_bytes{} / node_filesystem_size_bytes{} * 100
```

This will return the resulting instant vector:

```
{instance="172.17.0.13:9100", job="node-exporter-service",
mountpoint="/Users"} 40.0489813060515
{instance="172.17.0.13:9100", job="node-exporter-service",
mountpoint="/data"} 81.64923991971679
```

It might be useful to aggregate vectors with mismatching labels. In those situations, you can apply the `ignoring` keyword right after the binary operator to ignore the specified labels. Additionally, it is also possible to restrict which labels from both sides should be used in matching by using the `on` keyword after the binary operator.

Many-to-one and one-to-many

Occasionally, you are required to perform operations where the element of one side is matched with several elements on the other side of the operation. When this happens, you are required to provide Prometheus with the means to interpret such operations. If the higher cardinality is on the left-hand side of the operation, you can use the `group_left` modifier after either `on` or `ignoring`; if it's on the right-hand side, then `group_right` should be applied. The `group_left` operation is commonly used for its ability to copy labels over from the right side of the expression, as will be seen on some practical examples later in this chapter.

Logical operators

Logical operators are most easily understood as their set theory counterparts, as shown in the following table. These operators are the only ones in PromQL that work many-to-many. There are three logical operators that can be used between expressions:

Operator	Description
and	Intersection
or	Union
unless	Complement

The `and` logical operator works by only returning the matches from the left-hand side if the expression on the right-hand side has results with matching label key/value pairs. All other time series from the left-hand side that do not have a match on the right-hand side are dropped. The resulting time series will keep the name from the left operand. This is why it is also called the **intersection** operator. The `and` operator is often used like an `if` statement: by using the expression on the right as the condition to return the one on the left.

Using the following instant vector as an example, we'll validate the previous statement:

```
node_filesystem_avail_bytes{instance="172.17.0.13:9100", job="node-exporter-service", mountpoint="/Users"} 1003970
node_filesystem_avail_bytes{instance="172.17.0.13:9100", job="node-exporter-service", mountpoint="/data"} 141200
node_filesystem_size_bytes{instance="172.17.0.13:9100", job="node-exporter-service", mountpoint="/Users"} 2506855
node_filesystem_size_bytes{instance="172.17.0.13:9100", job="node-exporter-service", mountpoint="/data"} 172935
```

We'll be applying the following expression:

```
node_filesystem_size_bytes > 100000 and node_filesystem_size_bytes < 200000
```

This will return the following:

```
node_filesystem_avail_bytes{instance="172.17.0.13:9100", job="node-exporter-service", mountpoint="/data"} 141200
node_filesystem_size_bytes{instance="172.17.0.13:9100", job="node-exporter-service", mountpoint="/data"} 172935
```

The union logical operator, `or`, works by returning the elements from the left-hand side, except if there are no matches, it will return the elements from the right-hand side. Again, both sides need to have matching label names/values.

We can reuse the previous data sample and apply the following expression:

```
node_filesystem_avail_bytes > 200000 or node_filesystem_avail_bytes < 2500000
```

The result will be as follows:

```
node_filesystem_avail_bytes{instance="172.17.0.13:9100", job="node-exporter-service", mountpoint="/Users"} 1003970
```

Finally, the `unless` logical operator will return the elements from the first expression that do not match the label name/value pairs from the second. In set theory, this is called a complement. Practically speaking, this operator works in the opposite way to `and`, which means it can also be used as an `if not` statement.

Once again, we'll be using the same sample data that we used previously while applying the following expression:

```
node_filesystem_avail_bytes unless node_filesystem_avail_bytes < 200000
```

This, in turn, provides us with the following result:

```
node_filesystem_avail_bytes{instance="172.17.0.13:9100", job="node-exporter-service", mountpoint="/Users"} 1003970
node_filesystem_size_bytes{instance="172.17.0.13:9100", job="node-exporter-service", mountpoint="/Users"} 2506855
```

Aggregation operators

By employing aggregation operators, we can take an instant vector and aggregate its elements, resulting in a new instant vector, usually with fewer elements. Every aggregation of an instant vector such as this works in the ways that we described in the *Vertical aggregation* section of `Chapter 4`, *Prometheus Metrics Fundamentals*.

The available aggregation operators are as follows:

Operator	Description	Requirements
sum	Sums the elements	
min	Selects the minimum element	
max	Selects the maximum element	
avg	Calculates the average of the elements	
stddev	Calculates the standard deviation of the elements	
stdvar	Calculates the standard variance of the elements	
count	Counts the number of elements	
count_values	Counts the number of elements with the same value	
bottomk	The lower k elements by sample	Requires the number of elements (k) as a scalar
topk	The higher k elements by sample value	Requires the number of elements (k) as a scalar
quantile	Calculates the quantile of the elements	Requires the quantile ($0 \leq \varphi \leq 1$) definition as a scalar

Prometheus Query Language - PromQL

The operators that require a parameter (such as `count_values`, `bottomk`, `topk`, and `quantile`) need to specify it before the vector expression. There are two available modifiers to use in conjunction with aggregation operators that take a list of label names: `without` allows you to define which labels to aggregate away, effectively dropping those labels from the resulting vector, while `by` does exactly the opposite; that is, it allows you to specify which labels to keep from being aggregated. Only a single modifier can be used per aggregation operator. These modifiers will influence which dimensions will be aggregated by the operators.

For example, let's say that we use some sample data from the following query:

```
rate(http_requests_total[5m])
```

This would generate something like the following snippet:

```
{code="200",endpoint="hey-port",handler="/",instance="172.17.0.10:8000",job="hey-service",method="get"} 5.891716069444445

{code="200",endpoint="hey-port",handler="/",instance="172.17.0.11:8000",job="hey-service",method="get"} 5.966988444444445

{code="200",endpoint="hey-port",handler="/",instance="172.17.0.9:8000",job="hey-service",method="get"} 11.1336484826487

{code="200",endpoint="hey-port",handler="/health",instance="172.17.0.10:8000",job="hey-service",method="get"} 0.1

{code="200",endpoint="hey-port",handler="/health",instance="172.17.0.11:8000",job="hey-service",method="get"} 0.1

{code="200",endpoint="hey-port",handler="/health",instance="172.17.0.9:8000",job="hey-service",method="get"} 0.1000003703717421
```

If we want to know the aggregate of all requests, we can apply the following expression:

```
sum(rate(http_requests_total[5m]))
```

This will return the following:

```
{} 23.292353366909335
```

Now, if we add the `by` operator, we can aggregate by the handler endpoint:

```
sum by (handler) (rate(http_requests_total[5m]))
```

This would, in turn, return the following:

```
{handler="/"} 22.99235299653759
{handler="/health"} 0.3000003703717421
```

This simple example demonstrates how you can easily aggregate data.

Binary operator precedence

When a PromQL query is evaluated, the order in which binary operators are applied is dictated by the operator precedence. The following table shows the precedence order, from higher to lower:

Precedence	Operator	Description
1	^	Evaluated right to left, for example, 1 ^ 2 ^ 3 is evaluated as 1 ^ (2 ^ 3)
2	*, /, %	Evaluated left to right, for example, 1 / 2 * 3 is evaluated as (1 / 2) * 3
3	+, -	Evaluated left to right
4	==, !=, <=, <, >=, >	Evaluated left to right
5	and, unless	Evaluated left to right
6	or	Evaluated left to right

Functions

PromQL has almost 50 different functions for a variety of use cases, such as math; sorting; counter, gauge and histogram manipulation; label transformations; aggregations over time; type conversions; and finally, date and time functions. In the following sections, we'll cover some of the most commonly used ones and provide examples on why they are so relevant.

> A comprehensive overview of all functions is available at `https://prometheus.io/docs/prometheus/latest/querying/functions/`.

absent()

The `absent()` function takes an instant vector as an argument and returns the following:

- An empty vector if the argument has results
- 1-element vector with the sample value equal to 1, containing the labels from the specified argument in the case of non-conflicting equality matchers

This function is quite useful for alerting on, as the name suggests, absent time series.

For example, say that the instant vector exists and we execute the following expression:

```
absent(http_requests_total{method="get"})
```

This will return the following:

```
no data
```

Let's say we use an expression with a label matcher using a nonexistent label value, like in the following example:

```
absent(http_requests_total{method="nonexistent_dummy_label"})
```

This will produce an instant vector with the nonexistent label value:

```
{method="nonexistent_dummy_label"} 1
```

Let's apply `absent` to a nonexistent metric, as shown in this snippet:

```
absent(nonexistent_dummy_name)
```

This will translate into the following output:

```
{} 1
```

Finally, let's say we use `absent` on a nonexistent metric and a nonexistent label/value pair, as shown in the following snippet:

```
absent(nonexistent_dummy_name{method="nonexistent_dummy_label"})
```

The result can be seen in the following snippet:

```
{method="nonexistent_dummy_label"} 1
```

label_join() and label_replace()

These functions are used to manipulate labels—they allow you to join labels to other ones, extract parts of label values, and even drop labels (though that particular operation is easier and more ergonomic to do with standard aggregation operators). In both functions, if the defined target label is a new one, it will get added to the label set; if it's an existing label, it will get replaced.

When using `label_join`, you're required to provide an instant vector, define a resulting label, identify the separator of the resulting concatenation, and establish the labels to join, as exemplified in the following syntax:

```
label_join(<vector>, <resulting_label>, <separator>, source_label1, source_labelN)
```

For example, say that we use the following sample data:

```
http_requests_total{code="200",endpoint="hey-port",
handler="/",instance="172.17.0.10:8000",job="hey-service",method="get"}
1366
http_requests_total{code="200",endpoint="hey-port",
handler="/health",instance="172.17.0.10:8000",job="hey-service",method="get"} 942
```

We then apply the following expression:

```
label_join(http_requests_total{instance="172.17.0.10:8000"}, "url", "",
"instance", "handler")
```

We end up with the following instant vector:

```
http_requests_total{code="200",endpoint="hey-port",
handler="/",instance="172.17.0.10:8000",job="hey-service",
method="get",url="172.17.0.10:8000/"} 1366
http_requests_total{code="200",endpoint="hey-port",
handler="/health",instance="172.17.0.10:8000",job="hey-service",
method="get",url="172.17.0.10:8000/health"} 942
```

When you need to arbitrarily manipulate labels, `label_replace` is the function to use. The way it works is by applying a regular expression to the value of a chosen source label and storing the matched capture groups on the destination label. Both source and destination can be the same label, effectively replacing its value. This sounds complex, but it really isn't; let's have a look at the syntax of `label_replace`:

```
label_replace(<vector>, <destination_label>, <regex_match_result>,
<source_label>, <regex>)
```

Say that we take the preceding sample data and apply the following expression:

```
label_replace(http_requests_total{instance="172.17.0.10:8000"}, "port",
"$1", "instance", ".*:(.*)")
```

The result will then be the matching elements with the new label, called **port**:

```
http_requests_total{code="200",endpoint="hey-port",handler="/",
instance="172.17.0.10:8000", job="hey-service",method="get",port="8000"}
1366
http_requests_total{code="200",endpoint="hey-port",handler="/health",
instance="172.17.0.10:8000", job="hey-service",method="get",port="8000"}
942
```

When using `label_replace`, if the regular expression doesn't match the label value, the originating time series will be returned unchanged.

predict_linear()

This function receives a range vector and a scalar time value as arguments. It extrapolates the value of each matched time series from the query evaluation time to the specified number of seconds in the future, given the trend in the data from the range vector. It uses linear regression to achieve such a prediction, which means there is no complex algorithmic forecasting happening in the background. It should only be used with gauges.

We'll apply the following expression, which employs `predict_linear` using a range of one hour of data, and extrapolate the sample value four hours in the future (60 (seconds) * 60 (minutes) * 4):

```
predict_linear(node_filesystem_free_bytes{mountpoint="/data"}[1h], 60 * 60
* 4)

{device="/dev/sda1", endpoint="node-
exporter",fstype="ext4",instance="10.0.2.15:9100", job="node-exporter-
service",mountpoint="/data", namespace="monitoring", pod="node-exporter-
r88r6", service="node-exporter-service"} 15578514805.533087
```

rate() and irate()

These two functions allow you to calculate the rate of increase of the given counters. Both automatically adjust for counter resets and take a range vector as an argument.

Chapter 7

While the `rate()` function provides the per second *average rate of change* over the specified interval by using the first and last values in the range scaled to fit the range window, the `irate()` function uses the last two values in the range for the calculation, which produces the instant rate of change.

It's important to understand in what scenarios the usage of one is more suitable than the other. For example, when creating visualizations such as dashboards, we might want to increase the awareness of possible spikes; `irate` fits this criteria. Note that as `irate()` uses the last two values in a range, it is sensible to step downsampling, and so it can only be used when fully zoomed in. When building alerting expressions, we are more interested in obtaining smoother trends, so that spurious spikes don't reset the `for` timer (as we'll see in Chapter 9, *Defining Alerting and Recording Rules*); in this case, `rate` is the more appropriate function to apply. Always ensure there are at least four samples in the range vector so that `rate()` can work reliably.

To show the differences between these two functions, the following screenshot illustrate the same metric, at the same timeframe, one using `rate()` and the other using `irate()`:

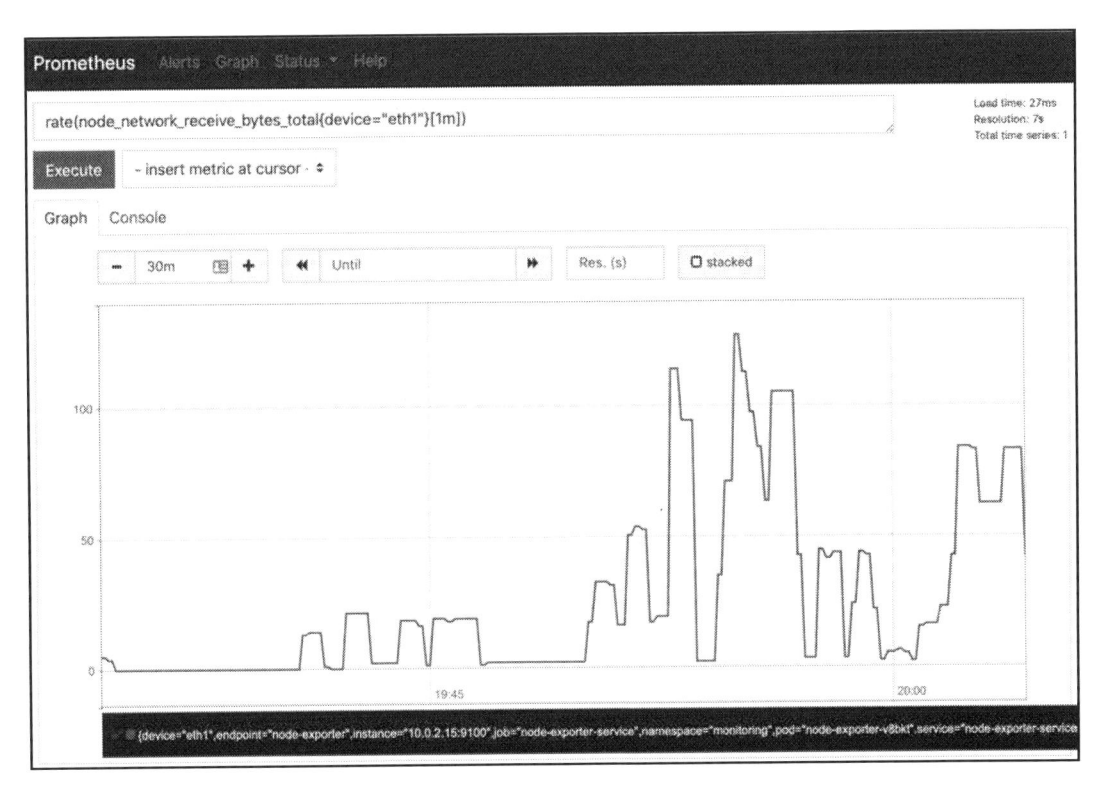

Figure 7.9: rate() of node_network_receive_bytes_total with 1m range

Prometheus Query Language - PromQL

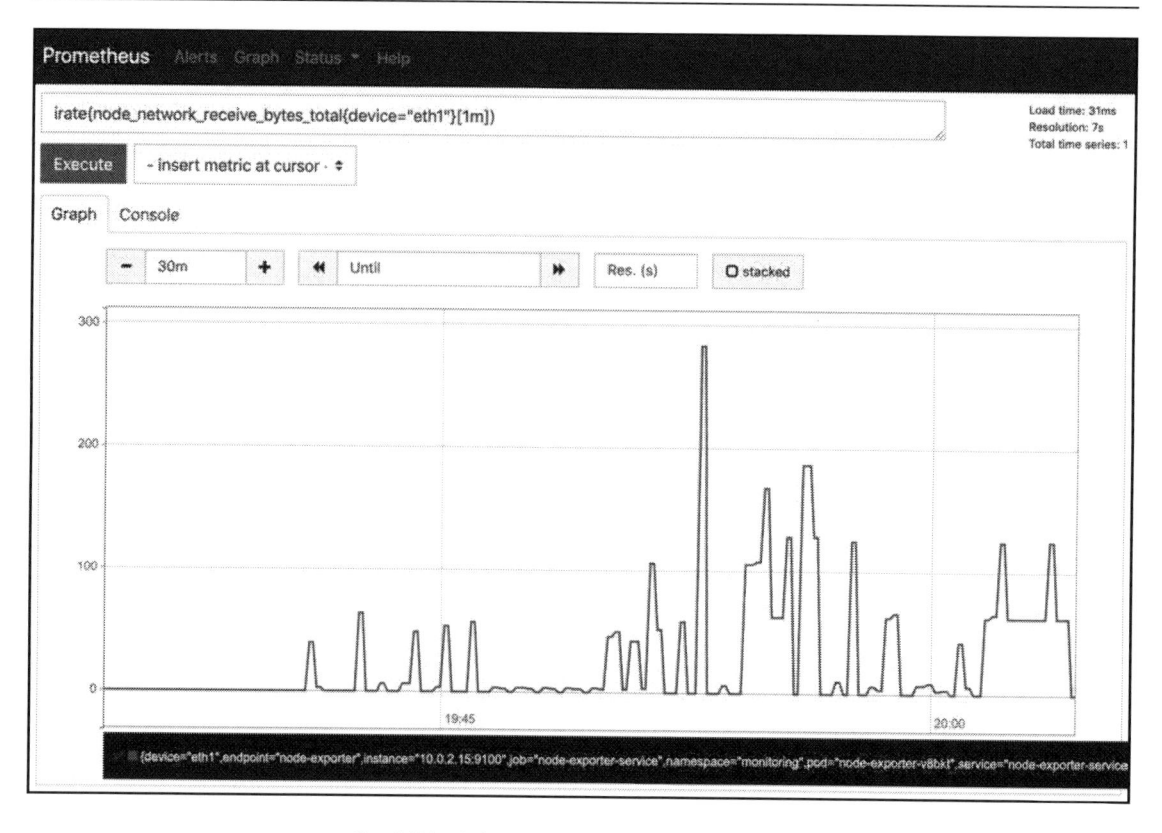

Figure 7.10: irate() of node_network_receive_bytes_total with 1m range

As we can see, `irate` is a lot more sensitive to variations in the underlying counters, while `rate` generally produces more smoothed-out values.

histogram_quantile()

This function takes a float, which defines the required quantile ($0 \leq \varphi \leq 1$), and an instant vector of the gauge type as arguments. Each time series must have a `le` label (which means less than or equal to) to represent the upper bound of a bucket. This function also expects one of the selected time series to have a bucket named such as `+Inf`, which works as the catch-all, the last bucket of the cumulative histogram. Since histograms that are generated by Prometheus client libraries use counters for each bucket, `rate()` needs to be applied to convert them into gauges for this function to do its work. The time that's range selected for the range vector will then correspond to the window for the quantile calculation. Although rare, some histograms produced by third-party software might not use counters for their buckets, so they can be used directly in `histogram_quantile` as long as they fulfil the label requirements.

For example, lets execute the following expression:

```
histogram_quantile(0.75,
sum(rate(prometheus_http_request_duration_seconds_bucket[5m])) by (handler,
le)) > 0
```

We'll be presented with a result similar to the following:

```
{handler="/"} 0.07500000000000001
{handler="/api/v1/label/:name/values"} 0.07500000000000001
{handler="/static/*filepath"} 0.07500000000000001
{handler="/-/healthy"} 0.07500000000000001
{handler="/api/v1/query"} 0.07500000000000001
{handler="/graph"} 0.07500000000000001
{handler="/-/ready"} 0.07500000000000001
{handler="/targets"} 0.7028607713983935
{handler="/metrics"} 0.07500000000000001
```

This provides an example of the output of an internal Prometheus histogram.

sort() and sort_desc()

As their names suggest, `sort` receives a vector and sorts it in ascending order by the sample values, while `sort_desc` does the same function but in descending order.

> **TIP:** The `topk` and `bottomk` aggregation operators sort their results by default.

vector()

The `vector()` function receives a scalar value as a parameter and returns a vector with no labels with the value of the specified scalar argument.

For example, query the following expression:

```
vector(42)
```

It will return the following:

```
{} 42
```

This is normally used as a way of ensuring an expression always has at least one result, by combining a vector expression with it, like in the following code:

```
http_requests_total{handler="/"} or vector(0)
```

Since the `or` operator returns both sides, a sample with the value 0 will always be present.

Aggregation operations over time

The aggregation operations we discussed earlier are always applied to instant vectors. When we need to perform those aggregations on range vectors, PromQL provides the `*_over_time` family of functions, which work as described in the *Horizontal aggregation* section of Chapter 4, *Prometheus Metrics Fundamentals*. All of them take a range vector and output an instant vector. Following is the description of the operations:

Operation	Description
avg_over_time()	Average value of all samples in the range.
count_over_time()	Count of all samples in the range.
max_over_time()	Maximum value of all samples in the range.

`min_over_time()`	Minimum value of all samples in the range.
`quantile_over_time()`	The quantile of all samples in the range. It requires two arguments, the definition of the desired quantile, φ, as a scalar, where $0 \leq \varphi \leq 1$, as a first argument and then a range-vector.
`stddev_over_time()`	The standard deviation of the sample's value in the range.
`stdvar_over_time()`	The standard variance of the sample's value in the range.
`sum_over_time()`	The sum of all sample values in the range.

Time functions

Prometheus supplies a number of functions to help manipulating time data. These are useful for a couple of scenarios, such as checking how long ago was a process or batch job last seen, only triggering alerts at certain times, or not triggering them at all on certain days. Every time function in Prometheus assumes Universal Coordinated Time (UTC).

The `time` function returns an instant vector with the current time in the UNIX epoch format (commonly known as a UNIX timestamp): the number of seconds that have elapsed since January 1st, 1970 UTC.

The `timestamp` function returns an instant vector with the UNIX timestamps of the samples returned by the supplied selector.

The `minute`, `hour`, `month` and `year` functions all work the same way: they receive an instant vector with one or more timestamps, and return an instant vector with the corresponding time component they represent. These functions' default input is the `time` function so, if they're used without an argument, they will return the current minute, hour, month or year, respectively.

The `days_in_month` function receives an instant vector with timestamps as argument and returns the number of days in the month for each of those timestamps. As with the previous functions, the default input argument is the `time` function. The result will obviously range from 28 to 31.

Lastly, and similarly to the previous function, the `day_of_week` and `day_of_month` functions expect an instant vector with timestamps as input and returns the corresponding day of the week (Sunday as 0, Monday as 1, and so on) and day of the month (from 1 to 31), respectively. The default input is the `time` function.

Info and enum

There are two metric types yet to be mentioned, info and enum. They are quite recent, but the convenience they bring is very much appreciated. Metrics of the type info have their names end with `_info` and are regular gauges with one possible value, 1. This special kind of metric was designed to be a place where labels whose values might change over time are stored, such as versions (for example, exporter version, language version, and kernel version), assigned roles, or VM metadata information; if those labels were to be exported in every time series, were they to change, a break in continuity would happen as the metric identity (the combination of the metric name and label set) would also change. This would also pollute the labels of all the time series that were affected, since these new labels would be present in every metric. To use this type of metric, we need to combine it with the metrics we wish to augment by using the multiplication operator—since the info metric value is 1, the multiplication won't change the value of the other metric—and the `group_left`/`group_right` modifiers allow us to enrich of the resulting vector with the labels we might require.

Here's an example of a query using an info metric:

```
node_uname_info{instance="10.0.2.15:9100"}
```

We can see the previous query result in the following snippet:

```
node_uname_info{domainname=" (none) ",endpoint="node-exporter",
instance="10.0.2.15:9100",job="node-exporter-service",machine="x86_64",
namespace="monitoring",nodename="minikube",pod="node-exporter-r88r6",
release="4.15.0",service="node-exporter-service",sysname="Linux",
version="#1 SMP Fri Dec 21 23:51:58 UTC 2018"} 1
```

The enum metric type is also a gauge, just like info. Its objective is to provide a way to expose anything that might need state tracking, such as the current state of a state machine. The most common use case for this type of metric is exposing the state of daemons (start, starting, stop, stopping, failed, and so on). This tracking is done by maintaining state information on a label, appropriately named state, and setting the metric value to 1 for the current state and 0 otherwise.

Here's an example of an instant vector selector query using an enum metric:

```
node_systemd_unit_state{name="kubelet.service"}
```

The previous query results in the following snippet:

```
node_systemd_unit_state{endpoint="node-
exporter",instance="10.0.2.15:9100",job="node-exporter-
service",name="kubelet.service", namespace="monitoring",pod="node-exporter-
jx2c2", state="activating"} 0
node_systemd_unit_state{endpoint="node-
exporter",instance="10.0.2.15:9100",job="node-exporter-
service",name="kubelet.service", namespace="monitoring",pod="node-exporter-
jx2c2", state="active"} 1
node_systemd_unit_state{endpoint="node-
exporter",instance="10.0.2.15:9100",job="node-exporter-
service",name="kubelet.service", namespace="monitoring",pod="node-exporter-
jx2c2", state="deactivating"} 0
node_systemd_unit_state{endpoint="node-
exporter",instance="10.0.2.15:9100",job="node-exporter-
service",name="kubelet.service", namespace="monitoring",pod="node-exporter-
jx2c2", state="failed"} 0
node_systemd_unit_state{endpoint="node-
exporter",instance="10.0.2.15:9100",job="node-exporter-
service",name="kubelet.service", namespace="monitoring",pod="node-exporter-
jx2c2"", state="inactive"} 0
```

Now that we know the basics of PromQL, let's dive into some common patterns and avoidable pitfalls when writing expressions.

Common patterns and pitfalls

With such a powerful language at your disposal, it's easy to become overwhelmed with so many options. In the following sections, we'll provide some common patterns and pitfalls to ensure the intended use of PromQL for each situation described, and in this way, further enforcing the knowledge that we have provided you with so far.

Patterns

While the power and flexibility of PromQL allows for a world of possibilities in terms of information extraction, there are a few query patterns that make a set of common problems much easier to understand and help increase the level of insight into the monitored services. In the following topics, we'll be covering a few of our favorites, in the hope they become as useful for you as they currently are for us.

Service-level indicators

In Chapter 1, *Monitoring Fundamentals*, we introduced the notion of *What to measure*, discussing *Google's Four Golden Signals*, as well as the USE and RED methodologies. Building upon that knowledge, we can start to define **service-level indicators** (**SLIs**), which reflect a given service's performance and availability. Constructing queries to generate SLIs is a common pattern of PromQL usage and one of the most useful.

Let's look at an example of an SLI: the typical definition of one is the number of good events over the number of valid events; in this case, we want to understand whether the percentage of requests being served by Prometheus is at or below 100 ms, which makes it a latency SLI. First we need to gather information about how many requests are being served under that threshold; thankfully, we can rely on an already available histogram-typed metric called `prometheus_http_request_duration_seconds_bucket`. As we already know, this type of metric has buckets represented by the `le` label (less or equal), so we just match the elements under 100 ms (0.1 s), like so:

```
prometheus_http_request_duration_seconds_bucket{le="0.1"}
```

While ratios are typically the base unit in these type of calculations, for this example, we want a percentage, and so we must divide the matched elements by the total number of requests made (`prometheus_http_request_duration_seconds_count`) and multiply that result by 100. These two instant vectors can't to be divided directly due to the mismatch of the `le` label, so we must ignore it, as follows:

```
prometheus_http_request_duration_seconds_bucket{le="0.1"} / ignoring (le)
prometheus_http_request_duration_seconds_count * 100
```

This gives us an instant vector with information per endpoint and per instance, setting the sample value to the percentage of requests answered below 100 ms since the service started on each instance (remember that `_bucket` is a counter). That's a good start, but not quite what we're after, as we want the SLI for the service as a whole, not for each instance or for each endpoint. It's also more useful to calculate it on a rolling window instead of averaging an indeterminate amount of data; as more data is collected, the average becomes smoother and harder to move. So, to fix these issues, we need to rate the counters over a time window to get a fixed rolling average, and then aggregate away instances and endpoints using `sum()`. This way, we don't need to ignore the `le` label either, as it is also discarded during aggregation. Let's put it all together:

```
sum by (job, namespace, service) (
  rate(prometheus_http_request_duration_seconds_bucket{le="0.1"}[5m])
) /
sum by (job, namespace, service) (
  rate(prometheus_http_request_duration_seconds_count[5m])
) * 100
```

Building a **service-level objective** (**SLO**) for our service now becomes trivial as we are just required to specify the percentage we're aiming to achieve using a comparison operator. This makes for an excellent condition to be defined as an alert.

Percentiles

We just learned how to extract the percentage of requests being served under a given latency, but what if we need to understand the latency of a given percentile of requests?

To obtain, for example, the 95th percentile, we can use the `histogram_quantile` function by defining the quantile (in this case, `0.95`), and then feed it the query expression that represents the set of data we're interested in—the average rate of increase for each of the buckets in the request duration histogram during a rolling time window. If we want the global latency of the service, instead of per instance/pod/handler, we need to apply the `sum()` aggregation:

```
histogram_quantile(0.95, sum without (instance, pod, handler)
(rate(prometheus_http_request_duration_seconds_bucket[5m])))
```

This expression will produce a value that represents that 95% of requests will be at or under said value.

The health of scrape jobs

For each defined scrape job, Prometheus will produce an automatic metric named `up`, which reflects the health of the job in question – 1 for a successful scrape and 0 for a failed one. We can use this metric to quickly visualize the current health state of the entire infrastructure of exporters and/or applications being scraped.

Let's get an overview of all the successful jobs being scraped:

```
sum by (job) (up)

{job="hey-service"} 3
{job="cadvisor-service"} 1
{job="kube-state-metrics"} 2
{job="node-exporter-service"} 1
{job="prometheus-service"} 2
```

Pitfalls

The power and flexibility of PromQL can enable some impressive slicing and dicing of time series data, but can also be a source of frustration, unexpected results, and even severe performance issues. While recent releases of Prometheus have been steadily introducing features to address some of these pitfalls, understanding these issues can help you get the most out of PromQL, while saving you time and computing resources.

Choosing the right functions for the data type

The most common pitfall when starting out with PromQL is not choosing the right function for the data type (such as counters, gauges, or histograms) or vector type. Even though this information is pointed out in the Prometheus documentation, there can still be some confusion as there are conceptually similar named functions and aggregators: `rate` and `deriv`, `increase` and `delta`, `quantile` and `histogram_quantile`, `sum` and `sum_over_time`, among others. Fortunately, in cases where there is a mismatch of vector types, the expression evaluation will fail and let you know what is wrong; for a mismatch in data types, such as providing a counter to a function that expects a gauge, the expression might evaluate successfully but return incorrect or deceptive results.

Sum-of-rates versus rate-of-sums

The previous point might seem obvious, but when the complexity of the queries built starts to increase, it's easy to make mistakes. A common example of this is trying to rate a sum of counters instead of summing rates. The `rate` function expects a counter, but a sum of counters is actually a gauge, as it can go down when one of the counters resets; this would translate into seemingly random spikes when graphed, because `rate` would consider any decrease a counter reset, but the total sum of the other counters would be considered a huge delta between zero and the current value. In the following diagram, we can see this in action: two counters (**G1**, **G2**), one of which had a reset (**G2**); **G3** shows the expected aggregate result that's produced by summing the rate of each counter; **G4** shows what the sum of counters 1 and 2 looks like; **G5** represents how the rate function would interpret **G4** as a counter (the sudden increase being the difference between 0 and the point where the decrease happened); and finally, **G6** shows what rating the sum of counters would look like, with the erroneous spike appearing where **G2**'s counter reset happened:

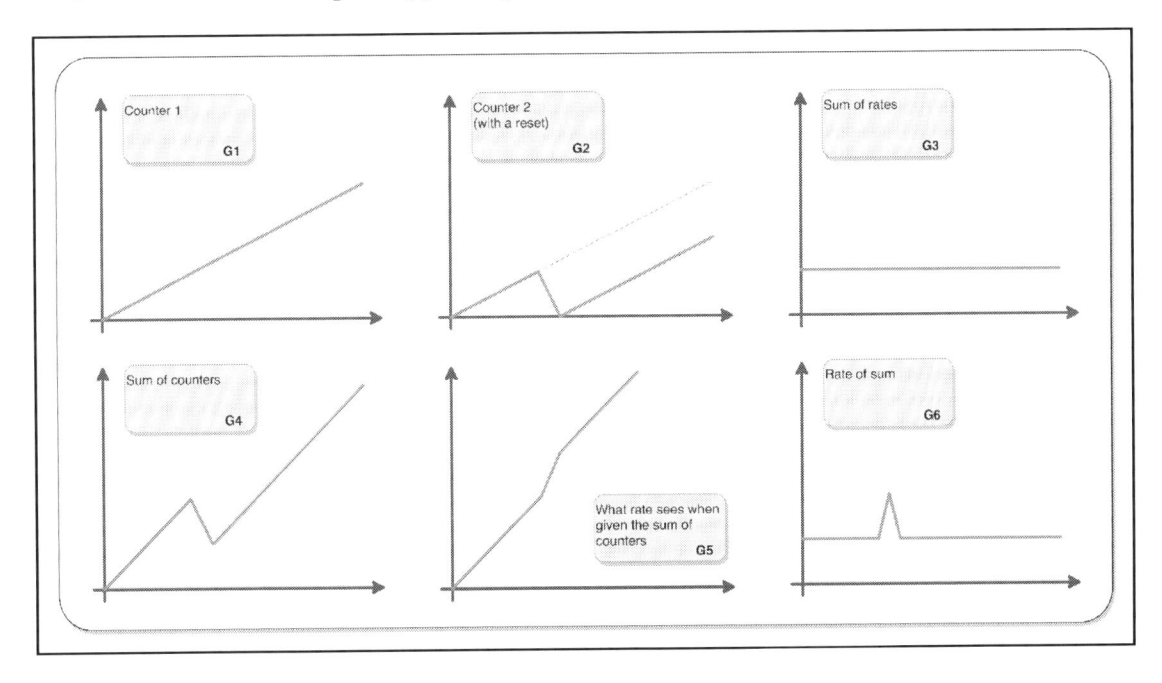

Figure 7.11: Approximation of what rate of sums and sum of rates look like

An example of how to properly do this in PromQL might be:

```
sum(rate(http_requests_total[5m]))
```

Making this mistake was a bit harder in past versions of Prometheus, because to give `rate` a range vector of sums, we would either need a recording rule or a manual sum of range vectors. Unfortunately, as of Prometheus 2.7.0, it is now possible to ask for the sum of counters over a time window, effectively creating a range vector from that result. This is an error and should not be done. So, in short, always apply aggregations after taking rates, never the other way around.

Having enough data to work with

The rate group of functions (`rate`, `irate`, `increase`, `deriv`, `delta`, and `idelta`) need at least two samples in the supplied range vector to work properly. This means that time ranges that are close to `scrape_interval` might fail to produce the desired results as a single failed scrape or window alignment issues (scrapes don't happen at exact intervals and might be delayed) will make the range contain only one sample. It is therefore recommended to use 4 (or more) times the `scrape_interval` to make sure that enough samples are returned for the calculation to work. Following diagram shows failed scrape changing the trend of samples for a given range:

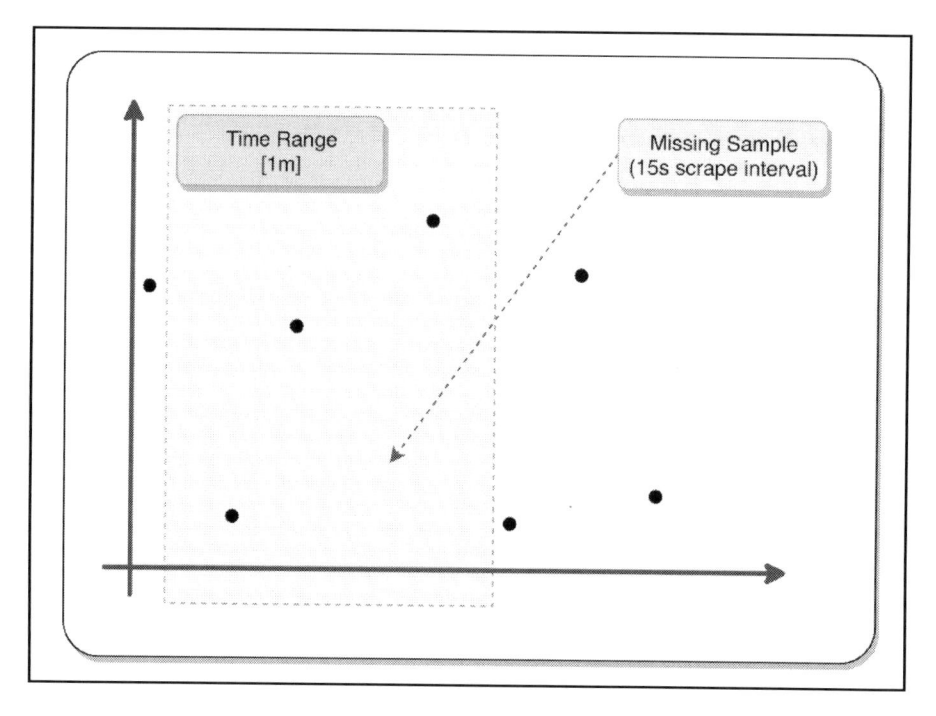

Figure 7.12: A failed scrape changing the trend of samples for a given range

Unexpected results when using increase

On a related subject, a common point of confusion is why functions such as `increase` and `delta` produce non-integer results. This point is briefly explained in the documentation, but is worth expanding upon. Since Prometheus collects data on a regular basis (defined in the `scrape_interval` configuration), when a query asks for a range of samples, the window limits for that range usually don't neatly align with the timestamps of the returned data. These functions extrapolate what the result would be like if the data points matched the time window. They do this by calculating the precise result with the samples provided, and then multiplying that result by the ratio of the time window over the interval between the first and last data point, effectively scaling the result to the requested range.

Not using enough matchers to select a time series

Another common pitfall when writing PromQL expressions, whether for dashboarding or alerting, is not using enough matchers to make sure that the returned samples are from the expected time series. It is considered an anti-pattern in the Prometheus community to namespace metric names to applications when the metric in question is not specific to that particular software, and even if it is, there might be cases where naming collisions occur; this is why it is good practice to scope selectors so that `job` is always explicitly selected when trying to extract information about a particular software. As an example, we can look at the `go_goroutines` metric, which is collected by the first-party Prometheus Go client library: as a sizeable chunk of the Prometheus ecosystem is written in Go and uses this client library for instrumentation, it is usual for this metric to be present in many scrape jobs. This means that, if we were to investigate the aggregate go-routine behavior of a particular software, we would get incorrect results if the selectors that were used weren't sufficiently narrow for the instances we were interested in.

Losing statistical significance

A mistake not specifically related to PromQL, but easy to make due to the flexibility of the language, is to apply transformations to aggregate values, thus losing their statistical significance. As an example, you might be tempted to average pre-computed quantiles in summaries from a group of instances to get a feel for the cluster, but they can't be further manipulated from a statistical standpoint – the result from that operation would not resemble the corresponding quantiles of the cluster as a whole. This, however, can be done with histograms, since buckets from each instance can be summed cluster-wide before calculating the approximate quantile. Another common example of this is averaging averages.

Knowing what to expect when constructing complex queries

An interesting detail to be mindful of when using PromQL is that, when using comparison operators between vectors, the returned result will be from the left-hand side of the comparison. This means that, when doing comparisons between a current value and a threshold, you should do them in that order (for example,`current_value < threshold`) as you probably want the returned value to be the current value and not the threshold:

```
node_filesystem_avail_bytes < node_filesystem_size_bytes * 0.2
```

Furthermore, when chaining different comparisons using `and`, the result will still be the left-hand side from the first comparison. The following example returns the percentage of space left in a filesystem, which is under 20%, and is predicted to be full within 4 hours given the fill rate of the last 6 hours. Note that it's not in read-only mode:

```
node_filesystem_avail_bytes/node_filesystem_size_bytes * 100 < 20
and
predict_linear(node_filesystem_avail_bytes[6h], 4*60*60) <= 0
and
node_filesystem_readonly == 0
```

Switching the first comparison with the second would produce the same number of results, but would also present the predicted bytes available 4 hours from now. This result would be less useful as knowing exactly the amount of negative bytes predicted just conveys the fact that they will be 0 in reality. Both expressions would be viable for alerting, though, as the resulting value of the expression is not sent in the alert notification.

The query of death

Lastly, care should be taken when crafting queries with overly broad selectors and memory-intensive aggregations. While Prometheus has default checks and bounds implemented to avoid unlimited memory usage (as discussed in Chapter 5, *Running a Prometheus Server*), it is still possible to run up against a memory limit that is not large enough—either a container limit or even the actual system RAM, which would make the OS unceremoniously terminate the Prometheus server. Compounding the problem, pinpointing which queries are using the most resources is hard, especially in environments where you have little control over what queries are sent to the server; there is no slow query log functionality built in as making it work would involve some trade-offs that would impact performance and manageability. In practice, though, constant improvements to capping resource utilization (especially on the memory front) have made it much harder for this particular issue to happen in well-dimensioned environments.

Moving on to more complex queries

With the information that's provided so far, we can move on to more complex queries, understand how they are built, and what to expect from them. In the following sections, we'll go over some intricate scenarios that demand the use of PromQL to explore and solidify the concepts we've covered so far.

In which node is Node Exporter running?

This scenario is designed to assist your understanding of concepts such as `info` metrics and the `group_left` modifier.

Scenario rationale

When running on Kubernetes, you might need to troubleshoot a Node Exporter pod, and for that you're required to know on which host it's running. Node Exporter metrics see the pod and not the host, so you don't have the hostname available in the metrics that produced. In this scenario, we are required to add the missing information to metrics that didn't have that label originally. Another alternative to this scenario would be to make the required information available in the instance labels via relabeling.

PromQL approach

The following query allows us to augment the `node_exporter_build_info` metric with yet another label, called `nodename`, which has information regarding the hostname running your Node Exporter pod.

In this example, we have the following instant vector:

```
node_exporter_build_info
```

This produces the following result:

```
node_exporter_build_info{branch="HEAD",endpoint="node-
exporter",goversion="go1.11.2", instance="10.0.2.15:9100",job="node-
exporter-service",namespace="monitoring", pod="node-exporter-
r88r6",revision="f6f6194a436b9a63d0439abc585c76b19a206b21", service="node-
exporter-service",version="0.17.0"} 1
```

We also have `node_uname_info`, which has the `nodename` label:

```
node_uname_info
```

This translates into the following code:

```
node_uname_info{domainname="(none)",endpoint="node-exporter",
instance="10.0.2.15:9100",job="node-exporter-service",machine="x86_64",
namespace="monitoring",nodename="minikube",pod="node-exporter-r88r6",
release="4.15.0",service="node-exporter-service",sysname="Linux",
version="#1 SMP Fri Dec 21 23:51:58 UTC 2018"} 1
```

With the help of an info metric, as we described previously, we'll use the following expression to add the `nodename` label from the `node_uname_info` info type metric to the `node_exporter_build_info` metric using `group_left`:

```
node_exporter_build_info * on (pod, namespace) group_left (nodename)
node_uname_info
```

The result can be inspected in the following snippet:

```
{branch="HEAD",endpoint="node-exporter",goversion="go1.11.2",
instance="10.0.2.15:9100",job="node-exporter-
service",namespace="monitoring", nodename="minikube",pod="node-exporter-
r88r6", revision="f6f6194a436b9a63d0439abc585c76b19a206b21", service="node-
exporter-service",version="0.17.0"} 1
```

Comparing CPU usage across different versions

This scenario is similar to the previous one, but takes it a step further by combining metrics from different sources and making them all work together.

Scenario rationale

You might want to observe how different software versions behave in terms of throughput or resource usage. This might be easier to analyze by graphing the patterns before and after the upgrade in clear terms. In this specific example, we are going to look at container CPU usage for `node_exporter` before and after an upgrade.

Keep in mind a couple of considerations: for the sake of this example, `node_exporter` is running as a container, which is ill-advised in a real-world scenario. Furthermore, we'll be using `container_cpu_usage_seconds_total` from cAdvisor instead of `process_cpu_seconds_total`, which is collected directly from natively instrumented applications, so that this method can be applied to any kind of containerized process, consolidating the use of cAdvisor metrics along the way.

PromQL approach

The `container_cpu_usage_seconds_total` metric gives us the amount of CPU seconds spent running each container, and comes from the `cadvisor` exporter. The `node_exporter` version can be found in the `node_exporter_build_info` metric. To make things a bit harder, since the container metrics come from `cadvisor`, the container and pod registered in those metrics are the `cadvisor` ones and not from the target pods; however, we can find the original container names and pod names in the `container_label_io_kubernetes_container_name` and `container_label_io_kubernetes_pod_name` labels, respectively.

The first thing we need to do is get the average number of CPU seconds per second each pod is using on a rolling window of one minute:

```
sum by (container_label_io_kubernetes_pod_name) (
rate(container_cpu_usage_seconds_total{container_label_io_kubernetes_container_name="node-exporter"}[1m])
```

Next, we need to create a new label in `node_exporter_build_info` so that matching works as intended. For this use case, we can use either `label_join` or `label_replace`, as we're just reading one label and writing its contents verbatim in another:

```
label_join(node_exporter_build_info,
"container_label_io_kubernetes_pod_name", "", "pod")
```

Alternatively, we can use the following code:

```
label_replace(node_exporter_build_info,
"container_label_io_kubernetes_pod_name", "$1", "pod", "(.+)")
```

Finally, we just need to match both metrics through their common label, `container_label_io_kubernetes_pod_name`, by using `on()` and then ask for the version label to be joined to the CPU expression's label set by using `group_left()`. Let's put that all together:

```
sum by (container_label_io_kubernetes_pod_name) (
rate(container_cpu_usage_seconds_total{container_label_io_kubernetes_container_name="node-exporter"}[1m])
)
* on (container_label_io_kubernetes_pod_name)
 group_left (version)
 label_replace(node_exporter_build_info,
"container_label_io_kubernetes_pod_name", "$1", "pod", "(.+)")
```

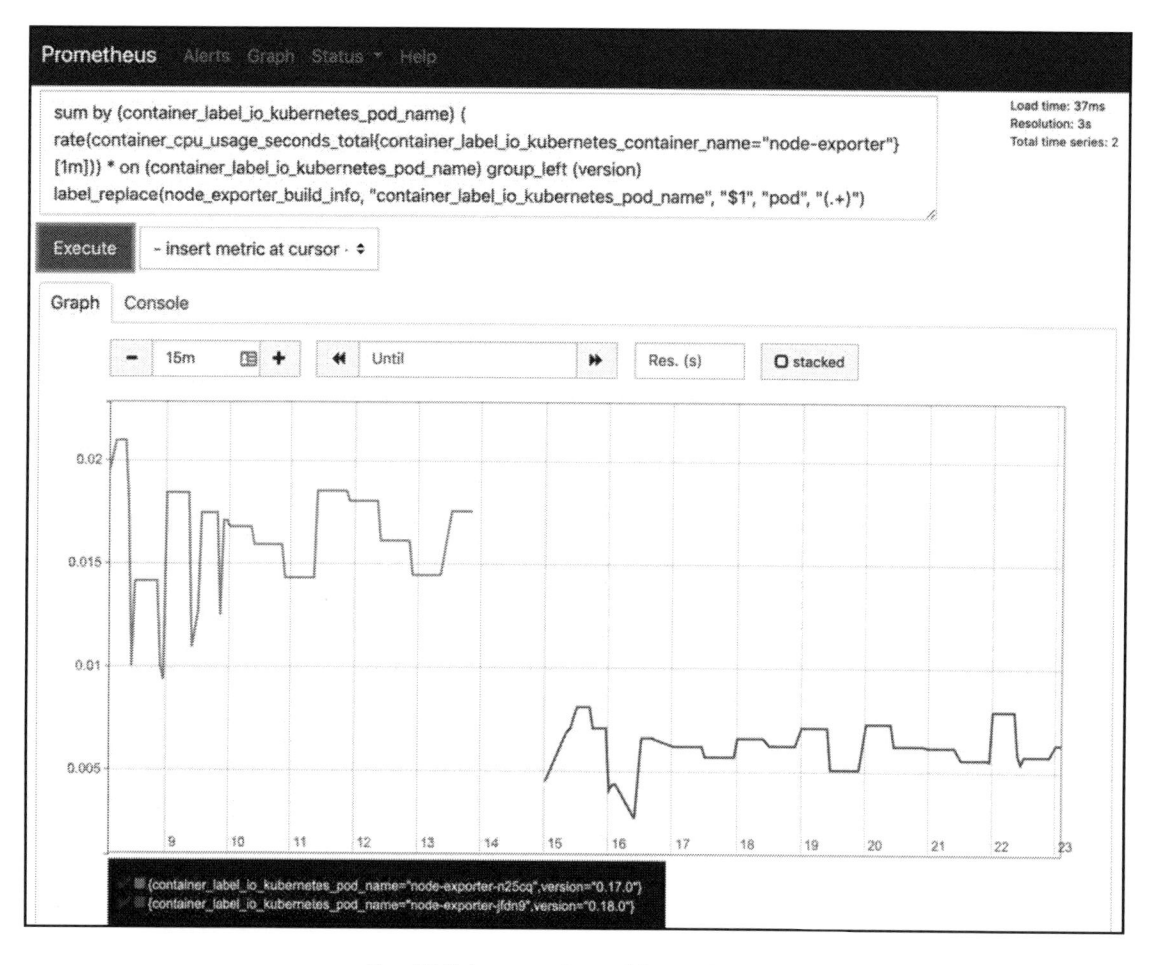

Figure 7.13: Node exporter version upgrade impact on CPU usage

Summary

In this chapter, we learned about the basics of PromQL, from selectors to functions, covering concepts such as binary operators, vector matching, and aggregations. Going through the common patterns and pitfalls, we were introduced to how this language allows much more than simple querying and how it has become an essential infrastructure tool, helping with the design and management of SLIs and SLOs. We also demonstrated several scenarios where PromQL shines, and how seemingly complex queries are not that complex after all.

In the next chapter, `Chapter 8`, *Troubleshooting and Validation*, we'll delve into how to validate a healthy Prometheus setup and learn how to troubleshoot issues quickly, ensuring the stability of the monitoring stack.

Questions

1. What are the six available comparison operators in PromQL?
2. When should a `group_right` modifier be used instead of a `group_left` one?
3. Why shouldn't you use the `sort()` function when applying the `topk` aggregation operator?
4. What is the major difference between `rate()` and `irate()`?
5. Which type of metric has an `_info` suffix and what is its purpose?
6. Should you sum and then rate or rate and then sum?
7. How can you get the average CPU usage for the last five minutes in a percentage?

Further reading

- **Querying Prometheus**: https://prometheus.io/docs/prometheus/latest/querying/basics/
- **SRE Book - Service Level Objectives**: https://landing.google.com/sre/sre-book/chapters/service-level-objectives/

Troubleshooting and Validation

Troubleshooting is, in itself, an art and, in this chapter, we will provide some useful guidelines on how to quickly detect and fix problems. You will discover useful endpoints that expose critical information, learn about promtool, Prometheus' command-line interface and validation tool, and how to integrate it into your daily workflow. Finally, we'll look into the Prometheus database and collect insightful information regarding its usage.

In brief, the following topics will be covered in this chapter:

- The test environment for this chapter
- Exploring promtool
- Logs and endpoint validation
- Analyzing the time series database

The test environment for this chapter

In this chapter, we'll be focusing on the Prometheus server and will be deploying a new instance so that we can apply the concepts covered in this chapter using a new test environment.

Deployment

To create a new instance of Prometheus, move into the correct repository path:

```
cd chapter08/
```

Ensure that no other test environments are running and spin up this chapter's environment:

```
vagrant global-status
vagrant up
```

Troubleshooting and Validation

You can validate the successful deployment of the test environment using the following:

`vagrant status`

This should output the following:

```
Current machine states:

prometheus running (virtualbox)

The VM is running. To stop this VM, you can run `vagrant halt` to shut it
down forcefully, or you can run `vagrant suspend` to simply suspend the
virtual machine. In either case, to restart it again, simply run `vagrant
up`.
```

The new instance will be available for inspection and the Prometheus web interface is accessible at http://192.168.42.10:9090.

You can now access the Prometheus instance by executing the following command:

`vagrant ssh prometheus`

Now that you're connected to the Prometheus instance, you can validate the instructions described in this chapter.

Cleanup

When you finish testing, just make sure you're inside chapter08/ and execute the following:

`vagrant destroy -f`

Don't worry too much – you can easily spin up the environment again if you so require.

Exploring promtool

Prometheus ships with a very useful supporting command-line tool called promtool. This small Golang binary can be used to quickly perform several troubleshooting actions and is packed with helpful subcommands.

The features available can be divided into four categories, which we'll be covering next.

Chapter 8

Checks

The subcommands that belong to this category provide the user with the ability to check and validate several configuration aspects of the Prometheus server and metric standards compliance. The following sections depict their usage.

check config

There are several types of checks presented by `promtool`. One of the most valuable is the check for the main configuration file for the Prometheus server.

`check config` expects a path to the Prometheus main configuration file and outputs its assessment of the validity of the configuration. When something is amiss, this subcommand can tell the user what the problem is: if it's a non-breaking issue, such as an empty discovery file, it will output a warning but permit `promtool` to exit with success; when it encounters breaking errors, such as incorrect syntax, it will output an error and will mark the check as a failure. Using the exit code returned by the tool – `0` for success and `1` for failure – is a great way to ensure configuration changes won't break Prometheus upon restart and should be used as a pre-flight check. Besides the main configuration file, this option also recursively checks any referenced file, such as rules files.

The following example illustrates its usage:

```
vagrant@prometheus:~$ promtool check config /etc/prometheus/prometheus.yml
Checking /etc/prometheus/prometheus.yml
  SUCCESS: 1 rule files found

Checking /etc/prometheus/first_rules.yml
  SUCCESS: 1 rules found
```

check rules

`check rules` analyzes and pinpoints misconfigurations in rule configuration files. It allows the targeting of specific rules files directly, which lets you test files that aren't yet referenced in the main Prometheus configuration. This ability can be handy in both the development cycle of rule files and for validating automatic changes in said files when using configuration management. We'll be covering these concepts in depth in `Chapter 9`, *Defining Alerting and Recording Rules*.

[193]

Here's the expected output when checking a rule file:

```
vagrant@prometheus:~$ promtool check rules /etc/prometheus/first_rules.yml
Checking /etc/prometheus/first_rules.yml
  SUCCESS: 1 rules found
```

check metrics

The `check metrics` subcommand validates whether the metrics passed to it follow the Prometheus guidelines in terms of consistency and correctness. This can be useful in the development cycle to make sure new instrumentation conforms to the standard, as well as using it in automation if you have some control over whether new jobs follow the same rules. It expects the metrics payload as input via `STDIN`, so you can pipe either a file or, the output of `curl` directly into it. For the sake of this example, we are exposing an issue that occurred in Prometheus prior to version `2.8.0`:

```
~$ curl -s http://prometheus:9090/metrics | promtool check metrics
prometheus_tsdb_storage_blocks_bytes_total non-counter metrics should not have "_total" suffix
```

As you can see, there appears to be an issue with the `prometheus_tsdb_storage_blocks_bytes_total` metric. Let's have a look at this particular metric to troubleshoot the error:

```
~$ curl -s http://prometheus:9090/metrics | grep prometheus_tsdb_storage_blocks_bytes_total
# HELP prometheus_tsdb_storage_blocks_bytes_total The number of bytes that are currently used for local storage by all blocks.
# TYPE prometheus_tsdb_storage_blocks_bytes_total gauge
prometheus_tsdb_storage_blocks_bytes_total 0
```

In these older versions of Prometheus, it appears the metric is declared as a gauge but has the `_total` suffix, which should only be used in counters.

Queries

The subcommands that belong to this category enable the execution of PromQL expressions directly from the command line. These queries rely on the Prometheus public HTTP API. The following topics demonstrate how to use them.

query instant

The `query instant` subcommand allows the querying of the Prometheus server directly via the command line based on the current time. For it to work, a Prometheus server URL must be supplied as an argument, as well as the query to execute, like so:

```
vagrant@prometheus:~$ promtool query instant 'http://prometheus:9090' 'up == 1'
up{instance="prometheus:9090", job="prometheus"} => 1 @[1550609854.042]
up{instance="prometheus:9100", job="node"} => 1 @[1550609854.042]
```

query range

Similar to the previous subcommand, `query range` enables the results to be displayed for a specified time range. As such, we must provide the start and end Unix-formatted timestamps, as well as the query and Prometheus server endpoint.

As an example, we'll be using the `date` command to define the start and end timestamps, generating a Unix-formatted timestamp for five minutes ago and another for now. We may also specify the resolution of our query using the `--step` flag, which in our example is one minute. Finally, we place the PromQL expression to be executed, ending up with an instruction similar to the following:

```
vagrant@prometheus:~$ promtool query range --start=$(date -d '5 minutes ago' +'%s') --end=$(date -d 'now' +'%s') --step=1m 'http://prometheus:9090' 'node_network_transmit_bytes_total{device="eth0",instance="prometheus:9100",job="node"}'
node_network_transmit_bytes_total{device="eth0", instance="prometheus:9100", job="node"} =>
139109 @[1551019990]
139251 @[1551020050]
139401 @[1551020110]
139543 @[1551020170]
139693 @[1551020230]
140571 @[1551020290]
```

> **TIP:** The `date` command available inside our test environment is from GNU `coreutils`, which differs from the BSD-based one available on macOS. The syntax might not be directly compatible between the two.

query series

With the `query series` subcommand, you can search all of the time series that match a set of metric names and labels. Here's how to use it:

```
vagrant@prometheus:~$ promtool query series 'http://prometheus:9090' --match='up' --match='go_info{job="prometheus"}'
{__name__="go_info", instance="prometheus:9090", job="prometheus", version="go1.11.5"}
{__name__="up", instance="prometheus:9090", job="prometheus"}
{__name__="up", instance="prometheus:9100", job="node"}
```

query labels

Using `query labels`, you can search for a specific label across all the available metrics and return all the possible values attached to it; for example:

```
vagrant@prometheus:~$ promtool query labels 'http://prometheus:9090' 'mountpoint'
/
/run
/run/lock
/run/user/1000
/vagrant
/var/lib/lxcfs
```

Debug

The subcommands that belong to this category allow the extraction of debug data from the running Prometheus server so it can be analyzed. We'll be demonstrating how to use them next.

debug pprof

The Prometheus server, like most serious software written in Go, is instrumented using a package from the standard library named `pprof`, which provides runtime profiling information using a specific format. The files produced in this format can then be read by a command-line tool with the same name (`pprof`), which uses them to generate reports and visualizations of the profiling data. `promtool` offers the `debug pprof` subcommand, which we can see in action in the following snippet:

```
vagrant@prometheus:~$ promtool debug pprof 'http://prometheus:9090'
collecting: http://prometheus:9090/debug/pprof/profile?seconds=30
collecting: http://prometheus:9090/debug/pprof/block
collecting: http://prometheus:9090/debug/pprof/goroutine
collecting: http://prometheus:9090/debug/pprof/heap
collecting: http://prometheus:9090/debug/pprof/mutex
collecting: http://prometheus:9090/debug/pprof/threadcreate
collecting: http://prometheus:9090/debug/pprof/trace?seconds=30
Compiling debug information complete, all files written in "debug.tar.gz".
```

When we extract the archive generated by the previous command, we can see a few files:

```
vagrant@prometheus:~$ tar xzvf debug.tar.gz
cpu.pb
block.pb
goroutine.pb
heap.pb
mutex.pb
threadcreate.pb
trace.pb
```

Using `pprof`, we can generate an image of the dump, as we can observe in the next snippet:

```
vagrant@prometheus:~$ pprof -svg heap.pb > /vagrant/cache/heap.svg
```

> The test environment comes with the `pprof` command-line tool ready to be used. More information on how to build and deploy it is available at https://github.com/google/pprof.

Troubleshooting and Validation

On your host machine, inside the code repository under the `./cache/` path (relative to the repository root), you should now have a scalable vector graphics file named `heap.svg`, which can be opened by your browser for inspection. The following screenshot shows what you might see when looking at the file produced by the preceding example:

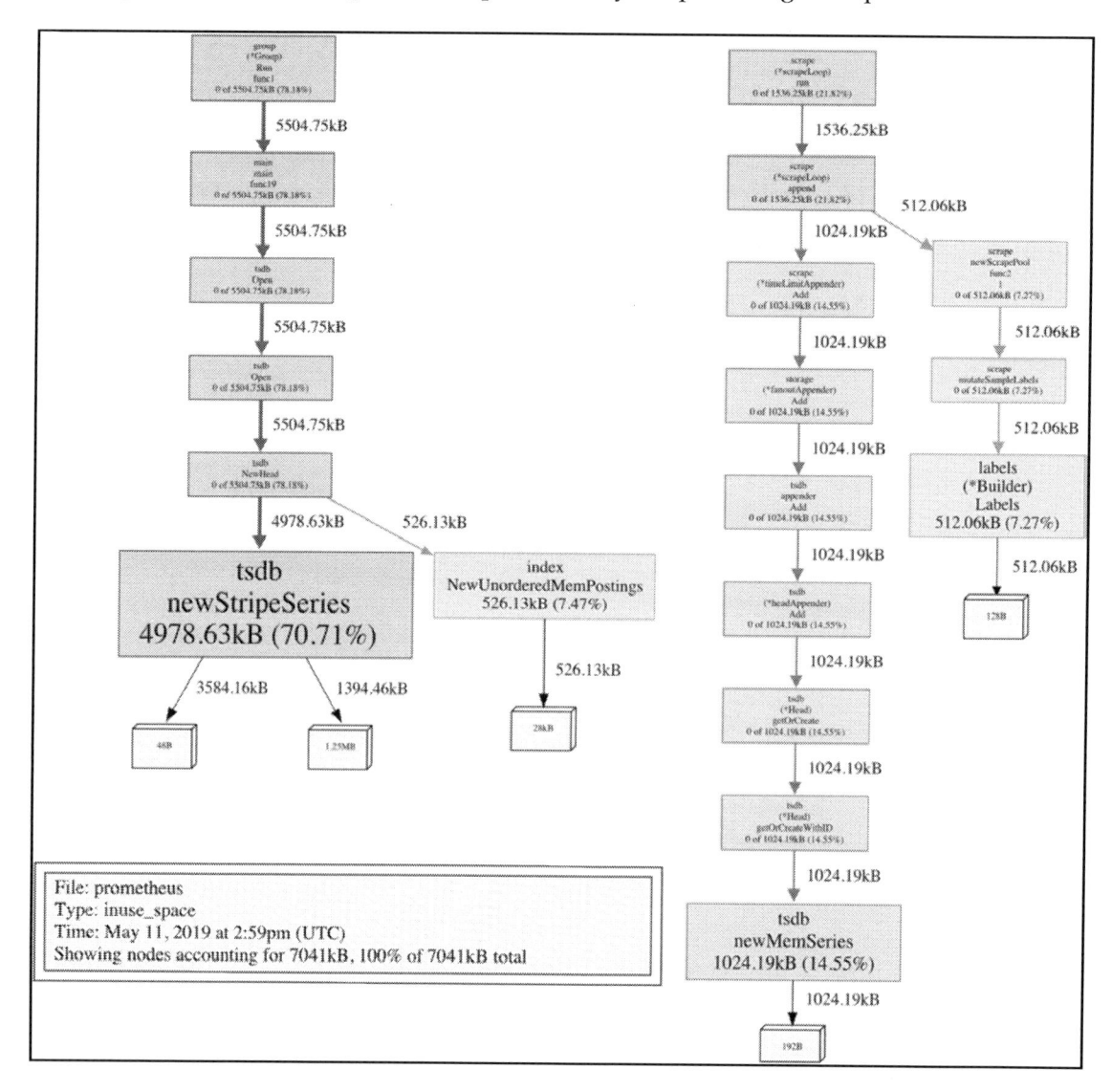

Figure 8.1: Example of a heap map generated by pprof

debug metrics

This subcommand downloads the metrics exposed by the supplied Prometheus instance in a compressed archive. `debug metrics` is not commonly used as the /metrics Prometheus endpoint is available to anyone able to run this command; it exists so that it is easier to provide the current state of a Prometheus instance to external assistance (such as the Prometheus maintainers) when asked to. This subcommand can be used as follows:

```
vagrant@prometheus:~$ promtool debug metrics 'http://prometheus:9090'
collecting: http://prometheus:9090/metrics
Compiling debug information complete, all files written in "debug.tar.gz".

vagrant@prometheus:~$ tar xzvf debug.tar.gz
metrics.txt

vagrant@prometheus:~$ tail -n 5 metrics.txt
# HELP promhttp_metric_handler_requests_total Total number of scrapes by HTTP status code.
# TYPE promhttp_metric_handler_requests_total counter
promhttp_metric_handler_requests_total{code="200"} 284
promhttp_metric_handler_requests_total{code="500"} 0
promhttp_metric_handler_requests_total{code="503"} 0
```

debug all

This option aggregates the previous debug subcommands into a single instruction, as we can see in the following example:

```
vagrant@prometheus:~$ promtool debug all 'http://prometheus:9090'
collecting: http://prometheus:9090/debug/pprof/threadcreate
collecting: http://prometheus:9090/debug/pprof/profile?seconds=30
collecting: http://prometheus:9090/debug/pprof/block
collecting: http://prometheus:9090/debug/pprof/goroutine
collecting: http://prometheus:9090/debug/pprof/heap
collecting: http://prometheus:9090/debug/pprof/mutex
collecting: http://prometheus:9090/debug/pprof/trace?seconds=30
collecting: http://prometheus:9090/metrics
Compiling debug information complete, all files written in "debug.tar.gz".
```

Tests

`promtool` has recently gained the ability to run unit tests against defined recording and alerting rules. This feature is very useful in situations where you might need to check whether an expression matches certain conditions that have never happened before, thus making it difficult to be sure they will work when the time comes. This subcommand is called `test rules` and takes one or more test files as arguments. We're going to provide a deep dive of this feature later on, when we tackle how to best take advantage of rules in `Chapter 9`, *Defining Alerting and Recording Rules*.

Logs and endpoint validation

In the next sections, we go through several useful HTTP endpoints and service logs that can be fundamental to troubleshoot issues with a Prometheus instance.

Endpoints

Checking whether Prometheus is up and running is usually very simple, as it follows the conventions most cloud-native applications use for service health: one endpoint to check whether the service is healthy and another to check whether it is ready to start handling incoming requests. For those who use or have used Kubernetes in the past, these might sound familiar; in fact, Kubernetes also uses these conventions to assess whether a container needs to be restarted (for example, if the application deadlocks and stops responding to health probes) and whether it can start sending traffic to the container. In Prometheus, these are the `/-/healthy` and `/-/ready` endpoints.

You can try these endpoints yourself by running the following commands in the test environment and checking their output, as well as their HTTP status code:

```
vagrant@prometheus:~$ curl -w "%{http_code}\n" http://localhost:9090/-/healthy
Prometheus is Healthy.
200

vagrant@prometheus:~$ curl -w "%{http_code}\n" http://localhost:9090/-/ready
Prometheus is Ready.
200
```

> In traditional infrastructure, it is usual to use the readiness endpoint as the backend health probe when using load balancers in front of a set of Prometheus instances, as only one health check can be configured. By using the readiness endpoint, traffic is only routed to an instance ready to accept it.

Additionally, Prometheus exposes a `/debug/pprof/` endpoint, which is used by the `promtool debug pprof` command, as was shown in the previous section. This endpoint also exposes a navigable web UI where `pprof` debug information can be consulted, such as current goroutines and their stack traces, heap allocations, memory allocations, and more:

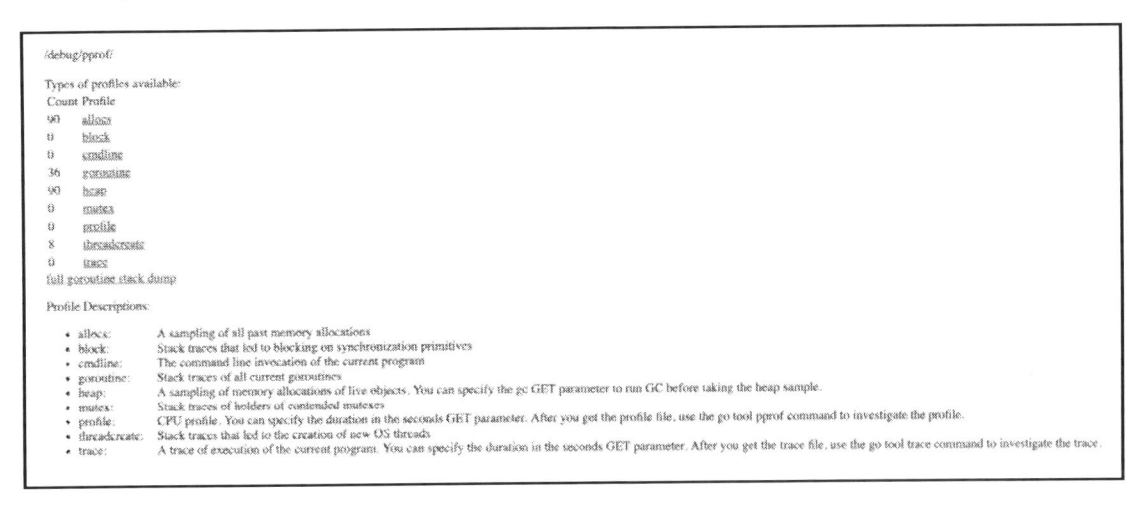

```
/debug/pprof/

Types of profiles available:
Count  Profile
90     allocs
0      block
0      cmdline
36     goroutine
90     heap
0      mutex
0      profile
8      threadcreate
0      trace
full goroutine stack dump

Profile Descriptions:
  • allocs:       A sampling of all past memory allocations
  • block:        Stack traces that led to blocking on synchronization primitives
  • cmdline:      The command line invocation of the current program
  • goroutine:    Stack traces of all current goroutines
  • heap:         A sampling of memory allocations of live objects. You can specify the gc GET parameter to run GC before taking the heap sample.
  • mutex:        Stack traces of holders of contended mutexes
  • profile:      CPU profile. You can specify the duration in the seconds GET parameter. After you get the profile file, use the go tool pprof command to investigate the profile.
  • threadcreate: Stack traces that led to the creation of new OS threads
  • trace:        A trace of execution of the current program. You can specify the duration in the seconds GET parameter. After you get the trace file, use the go tool trace command to investigate the trace.
```

Figure 8.2: Information available on the Prometheus server /debug/pprof endpoint

Logs

Prometheus logging is very terse when compared with most current software. This is a very conscious effort from the part of the Prometheus maintainers, as extraneous logging can lead to performance issues. Additionally, supporting different log streams (such as application logs, access logs, and slow query logs) without just writing it all to standard output - and thus spamming the application log with other types of logs - would force Prometheus to explicitly support writing to files, which is undesirable in cloud-native environments. Having said that, you can configure Prometheus to increase application log verbosity by setting the `--log.level` flag. As an example, failed scrapes are considered normal operating behavior and, as such, do not show up in the logs; however, they can be recorded by increasing the log verbosity to the `debug` log level.

Troubleshooting and Validation

The Prometheus instance in the test environment for this chapter is already configured with the log level set to debug. You can confirm this by running the following:

```
vagrant@prometheus:~$ sudo systemctl cat prometheus.service
```

The relevant section should have the following flags set:

```
ExecStart=/usr/bin/prometheus \
    --log.level=debug \
    --config.file=/etc/prometheus/prometheus.yml \
    --storage.tsdb.path=/var/lib/prometheus/data \
    --web.console.templates=/usr/share/prometheus/consoles \
    --web.console.libraries=/usr/share/prometheus/console_libraries
```

So, now we can see what happens when a scrape fails. To make this happen, we can stop the `node_exporter` service on the test environment and have a look at the Prometheus logs:

```
vagrant@prometheus:~$ sudo service node-exporter stop
vagrant@prometheus:~$ sudo journalctl -fu prometheus | grep debug
Feb 23 15:28:14 prometheus prometheus[1438]: level=debug ts=2019-02-23T15:28:14.44856006Z caller=scrape.go:825 component="scrape manager" scrape_pool=node target=http://prometheus:9100/metrics msg="Scrape failed" err="Get http://prometheus:9100/metrics: dial tcp 192.168.42.10:9100: connect: connection refused"
Feb 23 15:28:29 prometheus prometheus[1438]: level=debug ts=2019-02-23T15:28:29.448826505Z caller=scrape.go:825 component="scrape manager" scrape_pool=node target=http://prometheus:9100/metrics msg="Scrape failed" err="Get http://prometheus:9100/metrics: dial tcp 192.168.42.10:9100: connect: connection refused"
```

Analyzing the time series database

A critical component of the Prometheus server is its time series database. Being able to analyze the usage of this database is essential to detect series churn and cardinality problems. Churn, in this context, refers to time series that become stale (for example, from the origin target stop being collected or the series disappearing from one scrape to the next), and a new series with slightly different identity starts being collected next. A usual example of churn is related to Kubernetes application deploys, where the pod instance IP address changes making the previous time series obsolete, and replacing it with a new one. This impacts performance when querying, as samples with – possibly – no relevance are returned.

Thankfully, there's an obscure tool within the source code for the Prometheus database that allows analyzing its data, and is appropriately named tsdb.

> You can find the source code for the tsdb tool at https://github.com/prometheus/tsdb/. It can easily be built by running go get github.com/prometheus/tsdb/cmd/tsdb on a system with the proper Go toolchain installed.

Using the tsdb tool

The tsdb tool can run against Prometheus' entire database or just a particular block of data, and outputs useful information about the health of that data. To run this tool, we must ensure the Prometheus server is stopped:

```
vagrant@prometheus:~$ sudo systemctl stop prometheus
```

We'll be running the tsdb tool targeting the Prometheus database path. For the sake of brevity, we'll limit the output to three entries per section. If no block name is specified as an argument, the last available one will be used:

```
vagrant@prometheus:~$ sudo tsdb analyze --limit=3 /var/lib/prometheus/data/
```

The output is split into a couple of sections. In the heading, we can find a summary for the block, including the following:

- Its full path location
- The block duration span, which, in standard Prometheus deployments defaults to two hours
- The number of series and label names contained in the block
- Statistics regarding the number of index entries

Here, we can see the output generated by the previous instruction:

```
Block path: /var/lib/prometheus/data/01D48RFXXF27F91FVNGZ107JCK
Duration: 2h0m0s
Series: 819
Label names: 40
Postings (unique label pairs): 592
Postings entries (total label pairs): 3164
```

Troubleshooting and Validation

While churn isn't really an issue in our test environment, we can see what label pairs were detected with the highest involvement in producing churn:

```
Label pairs most involved in churning:
112 job=node
112 instance=prometheus:9100
111 instance=prometheus:9090
```

Next, we can find the label names with the highest churn:

```
Label names most involved in churning:
224 instance
224 __name__
224 job
```

Right after the label names churn, we are presented with the most common label pairs:

```
Most common label pairs:
413 job=node
413 instance=prometheus:9100
406 instance=prometheus:9090
```

Finally, we reach the high cardinality sections, starting with labels:

```
Highest cardinality labels:
394 __name__
66 le
30 collector
```

> __name__ is the internal label that stores the metric name, so it's normal in a healthy Prometheus system for it to be considered the label with the highest cardinality. Keep in mind that this doesn't mean a metric name can't be wrongly used as a label (for example, suffixing metric names with IDs), so it's important to keep an eye out for sudden increases in cardinality.

Finally, we find statistics regarding metric names:

```
Highest cardinality metric names:
30 node_scrape_collector_duration_seconds
30 node_scrape_collector_success
20 prometheus_http_request_duration_seconds_bucket
```

> **TIP**
> The preceding statistics are collected from a two hour block. This, however, can also be queried for a given moment via the expression browser using a query similar to `topk(3, count({__name__=~".+"}) by (__name__))`.

[204]

As stated before, you can choose a different block to analyze:

```
vagrant@prometheus:~$ ls -l /var/lib/prometheus/data/
total 28
drwxr-xr-x 3 prometheus prometheus 4096 Feb 21 21:15
01D45Z3QCP8D6135QNS4MEPJEK/
drwxr-xr-x 3 prometheus prometheus 4096 Feb 21 21:15
01D486GRJTNYJH1RM0F2F4Q9TR/
drwxr-xr-x 4 prometheus prometheus 4096 Feb 21 21:15
01D48942G83N129W5FKQ5B3XCH/
drwxr-xr-x 4 prometheus prometheus 4096 Feb 21 21:15
01D48G04625Y6AKQ3Z63YJVNTQ/
drwxr-xr-x 3 prometheus prometheus 4096 Feb 21 21:15
01D48G048ECAR9GZ7QY1Q8SQ6Z/
drwxr-xr-x 4 prometheus prometheus 4096 Feb 21 21:15
01D48RFXXF27F91FVNGZ107JCK/
-rw-r--r-- 1 prometheus prometheus    0 Feb 19 23:16 lock
drwxr-xr-x 2 prometheus prometheus 4096 Feb 19 23:16 wal/

vagrant@prometheus:~$ sudo tsdb analyze /var/lib/prometheus/data
01D486GRJTNYJH1RM0F2F4Q9TR
```

The benefit of the `tsdb` report is that it provides a deeper understanding of how metrics and labels are being used, and pinpoints good candidates to be explored and validated against their targets.

Summary

In this chapter, we had the opportunity to experiment with a couple of useful tools to troubleshoot and analyze Prometheus configuration issues and performance. We started with `promtool` and went through all its available options; then, we used several endpoints and logs to ensure everything was working as expected. Finally, we described the `tsdb` tool and how it can be used to troubleshoot and pinpoint problems with cardinality and the churn of metrics and labels in our Prometheus database.

We can now step into recording and alerting rules, which will be covered in the next chapter.

Questions

1. How can you validate whether the main Prometheus configuration file has an issue?
2. How can you assess whether metrics exposed by a target are up to Prometheus standards?
3. Using `promtool`, how would you perform an instant query?
4. How can you find all the label values being used?
5. How do you enable debug logs on the Prometheus server?
6. What's the difference between ready and healthy endpoints?
7. How can you find the churn of labels on an old block of Prometheus data?

Further reading

- **Golang pprof**: https://golang.org/pkg/runtime/pprof/

Section 3: Dashboards and Alerts

After this section, the reader will be able to create meaningful alerting and recording rules in Prometheus, take the most out of Grafana, and set up complex alert routing in Alertmanager.

The following chapters are included in this section:

- Chapter 9, *Defining Alerting and Recording Rules*
- Chapter 10, *Discovering and Creating Grafana Dashboards*
- Chapter 11, *Understanding and Extending Alertmanager*

9
Defining Alerting and Recording Rules

Recording rules are a useful concept of Prometheus. They allow you to speed up heavy queries and enable subqueries in PromQL that otherwise would be very expensive. Alerting rules are similar to recording rules, but with alert-specific semantics. As testing is a fundamental part of any system, you'll have the opportunity in this chapter to learn how to ensure that recording and alerting rules behave as expected before being deployed. Understanding these constructs will help make Prometheus faster and more robust, as well as enabling its alerting capabilities.

The following topics will be covered in this chapter:

- Creating the test environment
- How does rule evaluation work?
- Setting up alerting in Prometheus
- Testing your rules

Creating the test environment

In this chapter, we'll be focusing on the Prometheus server and we'll be deploying a new instance so that we can apply the concepts covered.

Defining Alerting and Recording Rules

Deployment

Let's begin by creating a new instance of Prometheus and deploying it to the server:

1. To create a new instance of Prometheus, move into the correct repository path:

   cd chapter09/

2. Ensure that no other test environments are running and spin up this chapter's environment:

   vagrant global-status
   vagrant up

3. Validate the successful deployment of the test environment using the following code:

   vagrant status

   This will output the following:

   ```
   Current machine states:

   prometheus                running (virtualbox)

   The VM is running. To stop this VM, you can run `vagrant halt` to
   shut it down forcefully, or you can run `vagrant suspend` to simply
   suspend the virtual machine. In either case, to restart it again,
   simply run `vagrant up`.
   ```

The new instance will be available for inspection and the Prometheus web interface will be accessible at http://192.168.42.10:9090.

You can now access the prometheus instance by executing the following command:

vagrant ssh prometheus

Now that you're connected to the prometheus instance, you can validate the instructions described in this chapter.

Cleanup

When you've finished testing, make sure that you're inside `chapter09/` and execute the following command:

```
vagrant destroy -f
```

Don't worry too much; you can easily spin up the environment again if you so require.

Understanding how rule evaluation works

Prometheus allows the periodic evaluation of PromQL expressions and the storage of the time series generated by them; these are called **rules**. There are two types of rules, as we'll see in this chapter. These rules are *recording* and *alerting* rules. They share the same evaluation engine, but have some variation in purpose, which we'll go into next.

The recording rules' evaluation results are saved into the Prometheus database as samples for the time series specified in the configuration. This type of rule can help take the load off of heavy dashboards by pre-computing expensive queries, aggregating raw data into a time series that can then be exported to external systems (such as higher-level Prometheus instances through federation, as described in `Chapter 13`, *Scaling and Federating Prometheus*), and can help to create compound range vector queries (while recording rules were the only way to do this in the past, the new subquery syntax enabled exploratory use cases for these).

Alerting rules trigger when an evaluated PromQL expression in a rule produces a non-empty result. They are the mechanism by which alerting over time series is done in Prometheus. Alerting rules also produce new time series when they trigger, but don't use the evaluation result as a sample; instead, they create an `ALERTS` metric with the alert name and state as labels, as well as any additional labels defined in the configuration. This will be further analyzed in the next section.

Using recording rules

Rules are defined separately from the main Prometheus configuration file, and are included by the latter through the `rule_files` top-level configuration key. They are evaluated periodically, and that interval can be defined globally with `evaluation_interval` inside `global` (defaults to one minute).

Defining Alerting and Recording Rules

We can see this by looking at the configuration provided with the test environment:

```
vagrant@prometheus:~$ cat /etc/prometheus/prometheus.yml
global:
...
  evaluation_interval: 1m
...

rule_files:
  - "recording_rules.yml"
...
```

`rule_files` takes a list of paths, which can be relative to the main Prometheus configuration or absolute paths. Additionally, globs can be used to match filenames (not directories); for example, `/etc/prometheus/rules/*.yml`. Changes in rule files are not automatically picked up by Prometheus, so a reload is needed (as described in Chapter 5, *Running a Prometheus Server*). Prometheus will fail to reload if any error are found in rule files, and will keep running using the previous configuration. However, if the server is restarted, it will fail to start. To make sure that this does not happen, `promtool` can be used to test for errors in advance (as explained in Chapter 8, *Troubleshooting and Validation*) – this is strongly recommended when using automation to deploy rules.

Just like the `prometheus.yml` configuration file, the `rules` files are also defined in are YAML format. The actual format is very easy to understand:

```
groups:
- name:  <group_name_1>
  interval:  <evaluation_interval>
  rules:
  - record:  <rule_name_1>
    expr:  <promql_expression_1>
    labels:
  <label_name> :  <label_value>
  ...
  - record:  <rule_name_N>
    expr:  <promql_expression_N>
...
- name:  <group_name_N>
  ...
```

Each file defines one or more rule groups under the `groups` key. Each group has a `name`, an optional evaluation `interval` (which defaults to the global evaluation interval defined in the main Prometheus configuration file), and a list of `rules`. Each rule instructs Prometheus to record the result of evaluating the PromQL expression defined in `expr` into the specified metric name, optionally adding or overriding the series label set before storing the result by setting them in `labels`. The rules in each group are evaluated sequentially in the order they are declared, which means that a time series generated by a rule can safely be used in subsequent rules within the same group. Samples generated by rules will have the timestamp corresponding to the rule group evaluation time. The next figure illustrates the process previously mentioned:

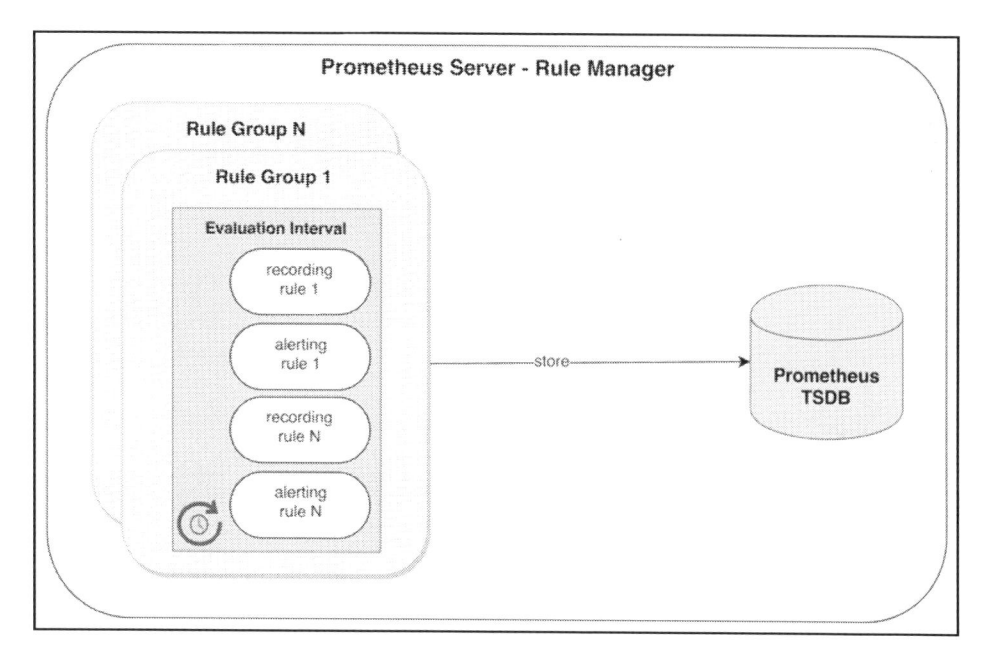

Figure 9.1: The Rule Manager is the Prometheus internal subsystem responsible for the periodic evaluation of rules according to their group's evaluation interval, as well as managing the alerting life cycle

Let's have a look at the recording rules available in the test environment for this chapter:

```
vagrant@prometheus:~$ cat /etc/prometheus/recording_rules.yml
```

Defining Alerting and Recording Rules

This file has two rule groups, named `recording_rules` and `different_eval_interval`:

```
...
- name: recording_rules
  rules:
  - record: instance:node_cpu:count
    expr: count without (cpu) (count without (mode)
(node_cpu_seconds_total))
...
```

The first rule group is composed of a single recording rule, which is using the global evaluation interval, taking the `node_cpu_seconds_total` metric from the Node Exporter to count the number of CPU cores available in the **virtual machine** (**VM**), and recording that result into a new time series named `instance:node_cpu:count`.

The second rule group is busier; it shows a custom evaluation interval for the group and a recording rule using the time series generated by previous rules in the group. We won't go into exactly what these rules are doing, as they will serve as examples for the following rule naming conventions section, but the evaluation interval can be seen here:

```
...
- name: different_eval_interval
  interval: 5s
...
```

By declaring an evaluation interval in this second rule group, we are overriding the configuration set in the `global` section of `prometheus.yml`—the rules in this group will produce samples at the specified frequency. This was done for demonstration purposes only; setting different intervals is usually discouraged, for the same reasons as in scrape jobs: queries might produce erroneous results when using a series with different sampling rates, and having to periodically keep track of what series have what becomes unmanageable.

Prometheus provides a status page in the web **user interface** (**UI**) where a user can check the loaded rule groups along with their enclosed recording rules, their recording state, how long the last evaluation took for each, and how long ago they were run. You can find this page by going into **Status | Rules** on the top bar:

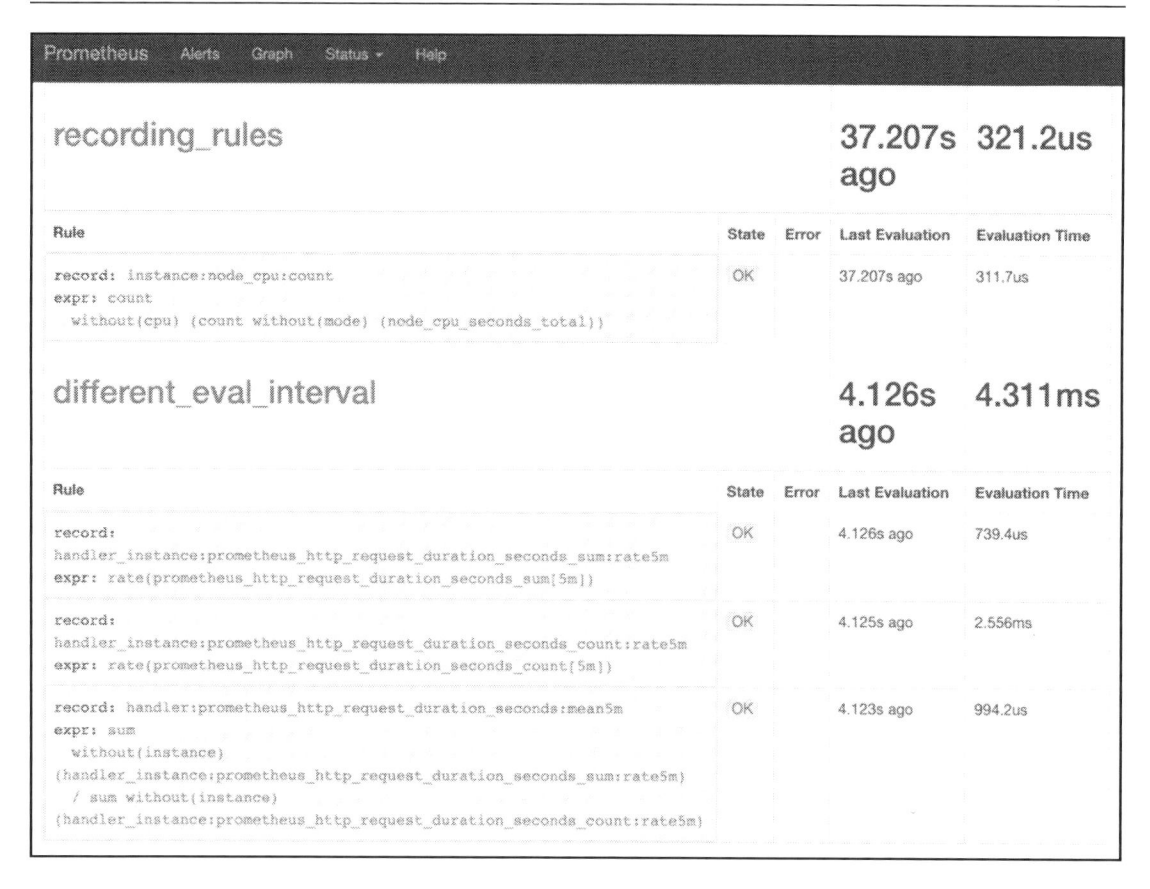

Figure 9.2: Prometheus web interface showing the /rules endpoint

With this information, we have now the fundamentals on how to create recording rules. Next, we'll explore the naming convention that the Prometheus community has agreed upon for recording rules.

Naming convention for recording rules

Recording rule name validation abides by the same regular expression as metric names, and so rules can technically be named the same as any other metric. However, having clear standards when naming recording rules can make it easier to identify them among scraped metrics, know from which metrics they were derived, and understand what aggregations were applied to them.

Defining Alerting and Recording Rules

The Prometheus community has gravitated toward a well-defined naming convention for recording rules. This is based on years of experience running Prometheus at scale. This enables all of the aforementioned advantages when used correctly.

The recommended convention for recording rule naming is composed of three sections, separated by colons, and takes the following form: `level:metric:operations`. The first section represents the aggregation level of the rule, which means that it will list the labels/dimensions that are present and relevant (usually separated by underscores); the second section is the metric name that was the basis for the rule; and the third section lists the aggregation operations that were applied to the metric.

The recording rules presented in this chapter all follow this convention, so let's have a look at the second rule group available in the test environment:

```
- record:
  handler_instance:prometheus_http_request_duration_seconds_sum:rate5m
    expr: >
      rate(prometheus_http_request_duration_seconds_sum[5m])

- record:
  handler_instance:prometheus_http_request_duration_seconds_count:rate5m
    expr: >
      rate(prometheus_http_request_duration_seconds_count[5m])

- record: handler:prometheus_http_request_duration_seconds:mean5m
    expr: >
      sum without (instance) (
        handler_instance:prometheus_http_request_duration_seconds_sum:rate5m
      )
      /
      sum without (instance) (
        handler_instance:prometheus_http_request_duration_seconds_count:rate5m
      )
```

Looking at the naming of the first rule, we can easily understand that the rule is based on the `prometheus_http_request_duration_seconds_sum` metric; `rate5m` indicates that `rate()` is being applied to a range vector of five minutes, and the interesting labels present are `handler` and `instance`.

The same logic is applied to the second rule, but this time using the `prometheus_http_request_duration_seconds_count` metric. The third rule, however, is a bit more nuanced; as it is dividing _sum by the _count of latency events, it effectively represents the five-minute latency average of, in this case, HTTP requests served by Prometheus. As we aggregated the `instance` label away, the `level` section reflects this by only having `handler` as the relevant dimension. The last thing to note is that the metric name for this rule is now `prometheus_http_request_duration_seconds`, as it neither represents the sum nor the count, but it still makes it possible to clearly understand which metrics this rule is based on.

Naming recording rules can be a hard task, a balancing act between precisely representing all the factors at play and being concise enough for metric names to be manageable. When you find yourself in a situation where it isn't immediately clear how to name a recording rule given its expression, a good rule of thumb to follow is to make sure another person that is aware of this naming convention can tie the rule back to the metric used, what labels/dimensions should be present, and what transformations were applied.

Setting up alerting in Prometheus

So far, we have covered how PromQL can be invaluable in querying the collected data, but when we require an expression to be continuously evaluated so that an event is triggered when a defined condition is met, we're promptly stepping into alerting. We explained how alerting is one of the components of monitoring in `Chapter 1`, *Monitoring Fundamentals*. To be clear, Prometheus is not responsible for issuing email, Slack, or any other forms of notification; that is the responsibility of another service. This service is typically Alertmanager, which we'll go over in `Chapter 11`, *Understanding and Extending Alertmanager*. Prometheus leverages the power of alerting rules to push alerts, which we'll be covering next.

What is an alerting rule?

An alerting rule is much like a recording rule with some additional definitions; they can even share the same rule group without any issues. The biggest difference is that, when firing, they are sent to an external endpoint via an HTTP POST with a JSON payload for further processing. Expanding on the term active, in this context, we are talking about when the current state differs from the desired state, which boils down to when an expression returns one or more samples.

Defining Alerting and Recording Rules

Alerting rules, such as recording rules, rely on PromQL expressions that are evaluated on a defined interval. This interval can be a globally configured one or can be local to the specific rule group. In each of the interval iterations, triggered alerts are validated to ensure that they're still active; if not, they're considered to be resolved.

For every sample returned by our expression, it will trigger an alert. This is important to keep in mind, because a relaxed PromQL expression can generate a deluge of alerts, so keep them as aggregated as possible.

Configuring alerting rules

To demonstrate how to create and understand alerting rules, we'll guide you through the entire process. This will touch not only on the main Prometheus configuration file, but also on rule files and how the web interface of the server behaves with regard to alerts.

Prometheus server configuration file

Inside this chapter's test environment, we can find the following Prometheus configuration:

```
vagrant@prometheus:~$ cat /etc/prometheus/prometheus.yml
global:
...
 evaluation_interval: 1m
...
rule_files:
 - "recording_rules.yml"
 - "alerting_rules.yml"
alerting:
 alertmanagers:
 - static_configs:
 - targets:
 - "prometheus:5001"
...
```

In this configuration, there are three components to be aware of:

- `evaluation_interval`: This is responsible for defining the global evaluation interval for recording and alerting rules, which can be overridden at the rule group level using the `interval` keyword.
- `rule_files`: This is the file location where Prometheus can read the configured recording and/or alerting rules.

- **alerting**: This is the endpoint(s) where Prometheus sends alerts for further processing.

In the alerting section, we've configured "`prometheus:5001`". Behind this endpoint, there is nothing more than a small service, called **alertdump**, that is listening on port `5001` for the HTTP POST requests and is simply dumping their payload onto a log file. This will help dissect what Prometheus sends when an alert is firing.

Rule file configuration

Previously, we took a look at the Prometheus configuration file; we'll now move onto the provided alerting rules example, which we can see in the following snippet:

```
vagrant@prometheus:~$ cat /etc/prometheus/alerting_rules.yml
groups:
- name: alerting_rules
  rules:
  - alert: NodeExporterDown
    expr: up{job="node"} != 1
    for: 1m
    labels:
      severity: "critical"
    annotations:
      description: "Node exporter {{ $labels.instance }} is down."
      link: "https://example.com"
```

Let's look at the `NodeExporterDown` alert definition more closely. We can split the configuration into five distinct sections: `alert`, `expr`, `for`, `labels`, and `annotations`. We'll now go over each one of these in the next table:

Section	Description	Mandatory
alert	The alert name to use	Yes
expr	The PromQL expression to evaluate	Yes
for	The time to ensure that the alert is being triggered before sending the alert, defaults to 0	No
labels	User-defined key-value pairs	No
annotations	User-defined key-value pairs	No

> **TIP**: The Prometheus community typically uses CamelCase for alert naming.

Defining Alerting and Recording Rules

> Prometheus does not carry out validation to check whether an alert name is already in use, so it is possible for two or more alerts to share the same name but evaluate different expressions. This might cause issues, such as tracking which specific alert is triggering, or writing tests for alerts.

The `NodeExporterDown` rule will only trigger when the `up` metric with the `job="node"` selector is not 1 for more than one minute, which we'll now test by stopping the Node Exporter service:

```
vagrant@prometheus:~$ sudo systemctl stop node-exporter
vagrant@prometheus:~$ sudo systemctl status node-exporter
...
Mar 05 20:49:40 prometheus systemd[1]: Stopping Node Exporter...
Mar 05 20:49:40 prometheus systemd[1]: Stopped Node Exporter.
```

We're now forcing an alert to become active. This will force the alert to go through three different states:

Order	State	Description
1	Inactive	Not yet pending or firing
2	Pending	Not yet active long enough to become firing
3	Firing	Active `for` more than the defined `for` clause threshold

Going to the `/alerts` endpoint on the Prometheus server web interface, we can visualize the three different states for the `NodeExporterDown` alert. First, the alert is inactive, as we can see in the following figure:

Figure 9.3: The NodeExporterDown alert is inactive

Then, we can see the alert in a pending state. This means that, while the alert condition has been triggered, Prometheus will continue to check whether that condition keeps being triggered for each evaluation cycle until the `for` duration has passed. The next figure illustrates the pending state; notice that the **Show annotations** tick box is selected, which expands the alert annotations:

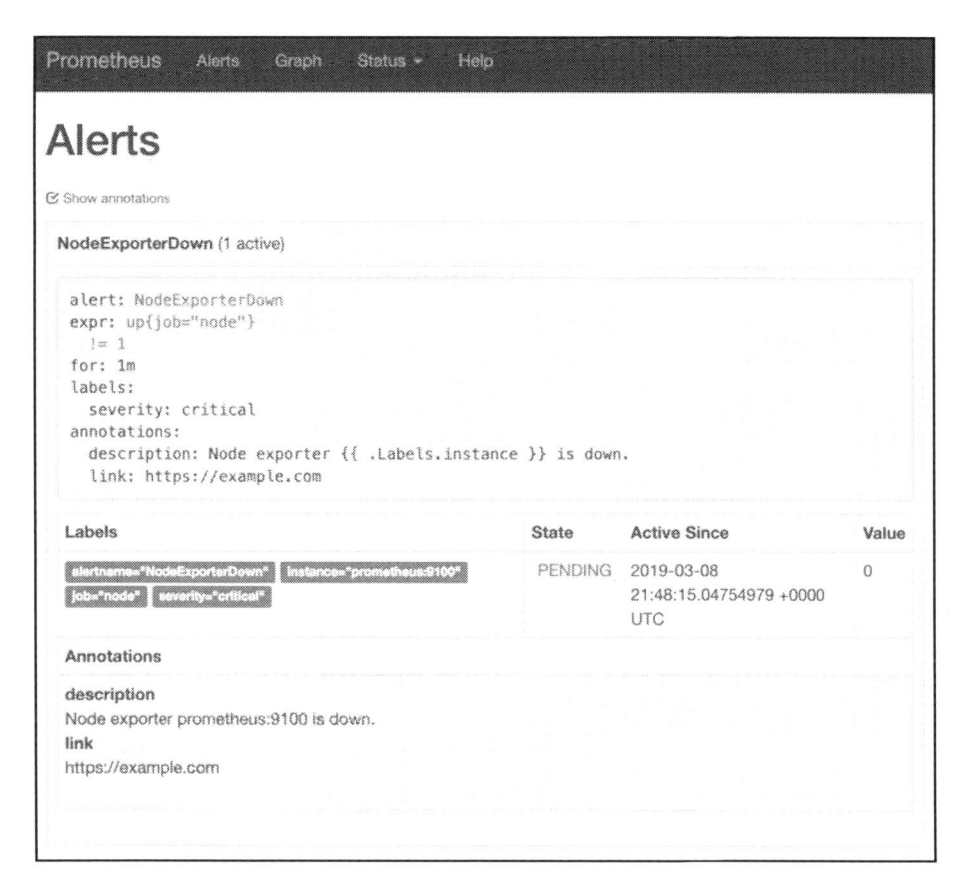

Figure 9.4: The NodeExporterDown alert is pending

Defining Alerting and Recording Rules

Finally, we can see the alert turn to firing. This means that the alert is active for more than the duration defined by the `for` clause – in this case, 1 minute:

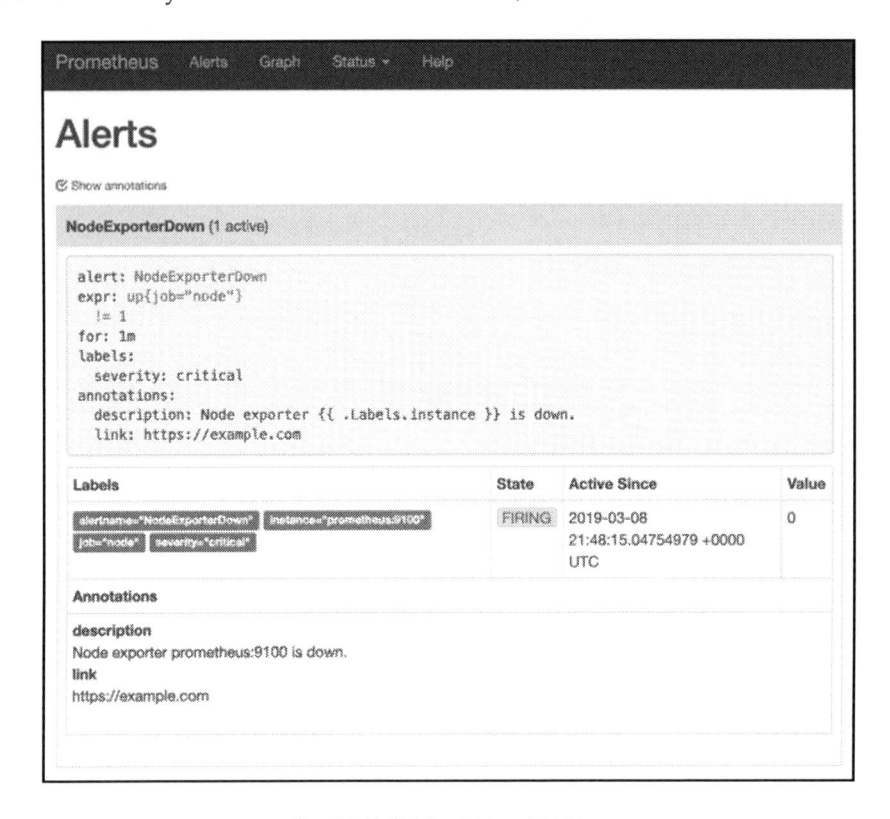

Figure 9.5: The NodeExporterDown alert is firing

When an alert becomes firing, Prometheus sends a JSON payload to the configured alerting service endpoint, which, in our case, is the alertdump service, which is configured to log to the `/vagrant/cache/alerting.log` file. This makes it very easy to understand what kind of information is being sent and can be validated as follows:

```
vagrant@prometheus:~$ cat /vagrant/cache/alerting.log
[
    {
        "labels": {
            "alertname": "NodeExporterDown",
            "dc": "dc1",
            "instance": "prometheus:9100",
            "job": "node",
            "prom": "prom1",
```

```
            "severity": "critical"
        },
        "annotations": {
            "description": "Node exporter prometheus:9100 is down.",
            "link": "https://example.com"
        },
        "startsAt": "2019-03-04T21:51:15.04754979Z",
        "endsAt": "2019-03-04T21:58:15.04754979Z",
        "generatorURL":
"http://prometheus:9090/graph?g0.expr=up%7Bjob%3D%22node%22%7D+%21%3D+1&g0.tab=1"
    }
]
```

Now that we've seen how to configure some alerting rules and validated what Prometheus is sending to the configured alerting system, let's explore how to enrich those alerts with contextual information by using labels and annotations.

Labels and annotations

In the alert rule definition, there were two optional sections: labels and annotations. Labels define the identity of an alert and they can change according to the evaluation cycle they're in; if they do this, it will alter the alert identity. To demonstrate this point, we'll introduce the `ALERTS` metric, which tracks all active alerts and their labels. As we can see in the following figure, we have a label called `alertstate`, which tracks the alert state and transitions from `pending` to `firing`:

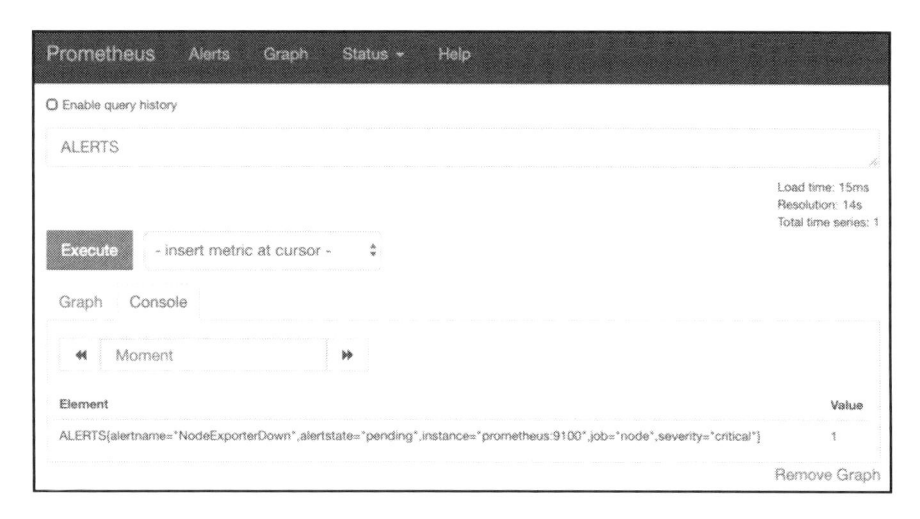

Figure 9.6: The ALERTS metric

Something to keep in mind is the issue of using a sample value in a label. Although it is technically possible, it's also a very bad idea. Doing so will change the alert identity every time the value changes, and, as such, will always be restarting the defined `for` countdown, resulting in an alert that will never enter the `firing` state.

On the other hand, annotations do not belong to the identity of an alert, and, as such, are not stored in the `ALERTS` metric. These are useful to enrich the alert with more context and information. Annotations are also templated using the Go templating language, as we saw in our example. By using the `{{ .Labels.instance }}` template syntax, we are accessing the available alert labels, selecting the `instance` label, and using its value in the annotation `description` field. The value of the firing sample is available by using `{{ .Value }}`, if required.

> **TIP**: The Golang template `.Labels` and `.Value` variables are also available as `$labels` and `$value` for convenience.

The following snippet shows the alert rule in our example:

```
annotations:
  description: "Node exporter {{ .Labels.instance }} is down."
  link: "https://example.com"
```

This will produce the following rendered result when `firing`:

```
"annotations": {
    "description": "Node exporter prometheus:9100 is down.",
    "link": "https://example.com"
},
```

> **TIP**: You can find more information regarding Golang templating at https://golang.org/pkg/text/template/.

Delays on alerting

In the previous topics, we talked about the three states that an alert goes through; but there's more to it when calculating the total time required for an alert to become firing. First, there's the scrape interval (which, in our example, is 30 seconds, although generally the scrape and evaluation intervals should be the same for clarity), we then have the rule evaluation interval (in our case, it was globally defined as 1 minute), and, finally, there's the 1 minute defined in the alert rule's `for` clause. If we put all of these variables together, the time for this alert to be considered as `firing` can take up to 2 minutes and 30 seconds in the worst-case scenario. The next figure illustrates this example situation:

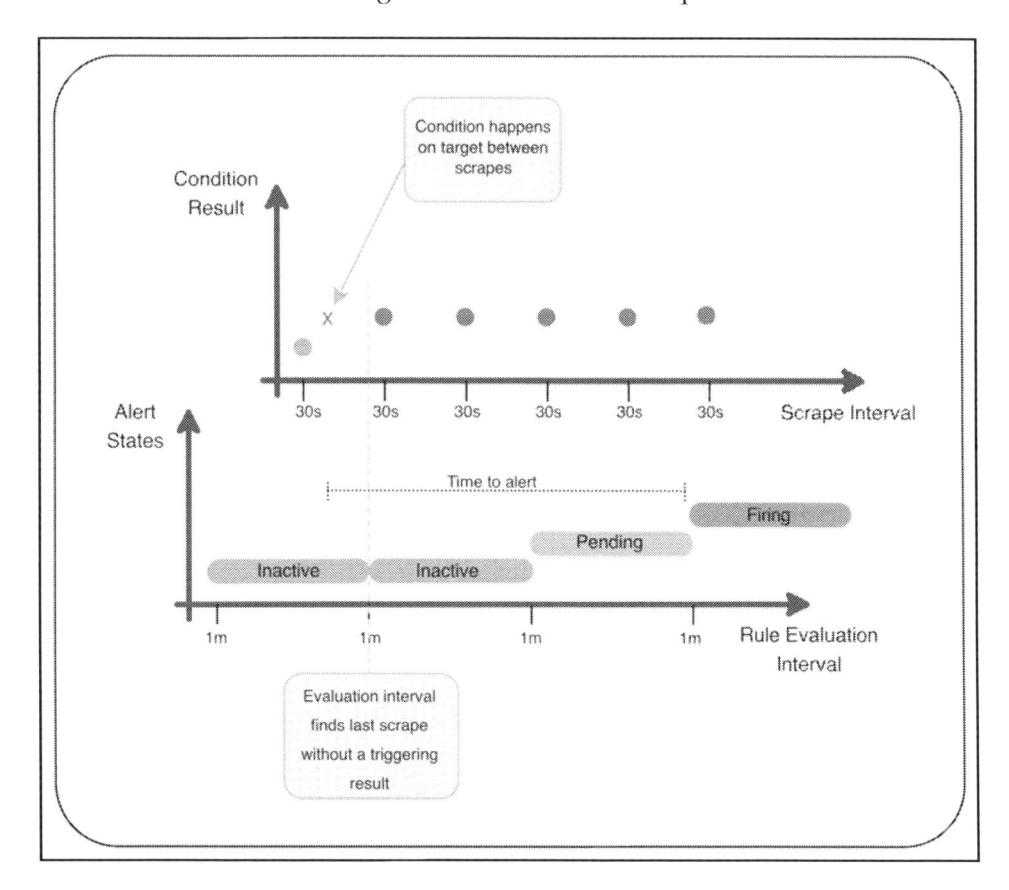

Figure 9.7: Alert delay visualized

All these delays are just on the Prometheus side. The external service processing the alert sent may have other constraints, which can make the global delay until a notification is sent even longer.

Defining Alerting and Recording Rules

> Before Prometheus 2.4.0, the `pending` and `firing` states were not persistent across restarts, which could extend the delay for alerting even further. This was solved by implementing a new metric, called `ALERTS_FOR_STATE`, which stores the alert states. You can find the release notes for Prometheus 2.4.0 at https://github.com/prometheus/prometheus/releases/tag/v2.4.0.

Testing your rules

In Chapter 8, *Troubleshooting and Validation*, we went through the features that `promtool` has to offer, with the exception of testing. The `test rules` subcommand can simulate the periodic ingestion of samples for several time series, use those series to evaluate recording and alerting rules, and then test whether the recorded series match what was configured as the expected results. Now that we understand recording and alerting rules, we'll look at how to ensure that they behave as expected, by creating unit tests and using `promtool` to validate our rules.

Recording rules tests

The `promtool` tool included in the Prometheus binary distribution allows us to define test cases to validate that the rules we write behave as expected. The test environment for this chapter also comes with a suite of pre-built tests for the rules we've explored so far. You can have a look at the configuration here:

```
vagrant@prometheus:~$ cat /etc/prometheus/tests.yml
```

This file has tests for all recording and alerting rules presented in this chapter. Although you don't need to define every test in a single file (it is, in fact, tidier to do a test file per rule group to keep things organized), this was done in this case for simplicity. For now, let's analyze only the recording rules, as they are simpler to grasp. The top-level configuration keys for the test file defines which rule files to load and the default evaluation interval for the tests, which governs the periodicity of recording and alerting rule evaluation when they don't explicitly state their own:

```
rule_files:
  - /etc/prometheus/recording_rules.yml
...
evaluation_interval: 1m
```

Chapter 9

> ℹ️ While the `rule_files` configuration key in the test files might look the same as in the main Prometheus configuration file, it does not support globing (using filename wildcards).

Following these global configurations comes the definition of the test cases, under the `tests` key. You can define multiple test packs, each with their own simulated scrape intervals, collected series, and rules under test. Let's have a look at the first test defined in the file, to which we added some comment to make it easier to understand:

```
tests:
```

`interval` sets the time that interval samples are generated in our simulated time series:

```
- interval: 15s
```

The list of `input_series` define what time series to generate and what values to produce in each iteration of the simulated collection interval:

```
    input_series:
      - series:
'node_cpu_seconds_total{cpu="0",instance="prometheus:9100",job="node",mode="user"}'
        values: '1 1 1 1 1 1 1 1 1'
      - series:
'node_cpu_seconds_total{cpu="1",instance="prometheus:9100",job="node",mode="user"}'
        values: '1 1 1 1 1 1 1 1 1'
      - series:
'node_cpu_seconds_total{cpu="0",instance="example:9100",job="node",mode="idle"}'
        values: '1 1 1 1 1 1 1 1 1'
      - series:
'node_cpu_seconds_total{cpu="0",instance="example:9100",job="node",mode="system"}'
        values: '1 1 1 1 1 1 1 1 1'
```

The list of PromQL expressions to test is defined as `promql_expr_test`:

```
promql_expr_test:
```

Each `expr` defines a particular expression:

```
- expr: instance:node_cpu:count
```

[227]

Defining Alerting and Recording Rules

The point in time at which this expression will be run is set by setting `eval_time`, and the expected samples should be returned by running that expression as `exp_samples`:

```
eval_time: 1m
exp_samples:
    - labels: 'instance:node_cpu:count{instance="prometheus:9100",
job="node"}'
      value: 2
    - labels: 'instance:node_cpu:count{instance="example:9100",
job="node"}'
      value: 1
```

In this test pack, we can see four time series being generated every 15 seconds for the same metric, `node_cpu_seconds_total`. As the actual value of these series isn't relevant for this recording rule (it only counts the number of CPUs per instance), a value of 1 was set for every sample. Do note the variation of labels present, namely that the `prometheus:9100` instance is reporting metrics for two CPUs and `example:9100` for one. The actual test is just validating that, when the `instance:node_cpu:count` expression is evaluated at `t=1m` (as if 1 minute had passed after the generated collection started), the returned samples should show the correct count of CPUs for each instance.

We are now ready to execute the tests using the following instruction:

```
vagrant@prometheus:/etc/prometheus$ promtool test rules tests.yml
Unit Testing: tests.yml
  SUCCESS
```

This ensures that the recording rule configured behaves the way we were expecting. You can try breaking the test by removing one of the input series from the `prometheus:9100` instance in the `instance:node_cpu:count` test pack. When you run the tests again, the following will be displayed, as one of the tests is now failing:

```
vagrant@prometheus:/etc/prometheus$ promtool test rules tests.yml
Unit Testing: tests.yml
  FAILED:
    expr:'instance:node_cpu:count', time:1m0s,
        exp:"{__name__=\"instance:node_cpu:count\",
instance=\"example:9100\", job=\"node\"} 1E+00,
{__name__=\"instance:node_cpu:count\", instance=\"example:9100\",
job=\"node\"} 1E+00, {__name__=\"instance:node_cpu:count\",
instance=\"prometheus:9100\", job=\"node\"} 2E+00",
        got:"{__name__=\"instance:node_cpu:count\",
instance=\"example:9100\", job=\"node\"} 1E+00,
{__name__=\"instance:node_cpu:count\", instance=\"example:9100\",
job=\"node\"} 1E+00, {__name__=\"instance:node_cpu:count\",
instance=\"prometheus:9100\", job=\"node\"} 1E+00"
```

What this output tells us is that `promtool` was expecting the defined set of samples, but a different set of samples was returned. You can see that, just as we configured, the recording rule now only reports one CPU for the `prometheus:9100` instance. This gives us confidence that the rule is behaving exactly as we wanted.

The tests for the second recording rule group are mostly the same, but they showcase a powerful notation for generating a richer input series:

```
    - interval: 5s
      input_series:
        - series:
'prometheus_http_request_duration_seconds_count{handler="/",instance="local
host:9090",job="prometheus"}'
          values: '0+5x60'
        - series:
'prometheus_http_request_duration_seconds_sum{handler="/",instance="localho
st:9090",job="prometheus"}'
          values: '0+1x60'
```

This is called an **expanding notation**. This is a compact way of declaring a formula for the generation of time series values over time. It takes the form of either A+BxC or A-BxC, where A is the starting value, B is the amount of increase (when preceded by +) or decrease (when preceded by -) the series value should have in each iteration, and C is how many iterations this increase or decrease should be applied for.

Coming back to our example, `0+5x60` will expand to the following series:

```
0 5 10 15 20 ... 290 295 300
```

You can mix and match literal values with expanding notation when declaring the values for an input time series. This allows you to create complex behavior with ease. Take the following example:

```
0 1 1 0 1+0x3 0 1 1 0 1 1 0 0 0 1 1 0+0x3 1
```

This will be expanded into the following:

```
0 1 1 0 1 1 1 1 0 1 1 0 1 1 0 0 0 1 1 0 0 0 0 1
```

Testing is fundamental to avoid unforeseen problems and, with the information covered so far, you're now able to generate your own unit tests for recording rules. Next, we'll continue tackling unit tests, but this time specifically related to alerting rules.

Alerting rules tests

Unit tests for alerting rules are quite similar to the ones used for recording rules. We'll be using the example alert provided earlier in this chapter to perform a walkthrough on how to configure alerting tests and how to validate them. As mentioned before, the test environment for this chapter comes with a suite of tests for the rules presented here, including the alert rule we're interested in. Once again, you can have a look at the test file using the following command:

```
vagrant@prometheus:~$ cat /etc/prometheus/tests.yml
```

Focusing solely on the alerting component, we can see that we first define where the alerting rules are located:

```
rule_files:
  - /etc/prometheus/alerting_rules.yml
```

The default rule evaluation interval is shared between recording and alerting rules in the same file:

```
evaluation_interval: 1m
```

The alerting test is conveniently in its own test group, so let's have a look at its full definition:

```
- interval: 1m
  input_series:
    - series: 'up{job="node",instance="prometheus:9100"}'
      values: '1 1 1 0 0 0 0 0 0 0'
    - series: 'up{job="prometheus",instance="prometheus:9090"}'
      values: '1 0 1 1 0 1 1 1 1'
```

The test group definition is the same as explained previously, with the exception of the `alert_rule_test` section, which is where we define alerting tests. A thing to note in this example is that the second input series should never be picked up by our testing rule, as the defined alert is specifically matching `job="node"`:

```
alert_rule_test:
  - alertname: NodeExporterDown
    eval_time: 3m
  - alertname: NodeExporterDown
    eval_time: 4m
    exp_alerts:
      - exp_labels:
          instance: "prometheus:9100"
          job: "node"
```

```
            severity: "critical"
        exp_annotations:
          description: "Node exporter prometheus:9100 is down."
          link: "https://example.com"
```

> **TIP**: It's not mandatory to have `alert_rule_test` and `promql_expr_test` in separate test blocks; you may have both in the same test group when you have recording and alerting rules using the same input time series and with the same evaluation interval.

The `alert_rule_test` section lists what alerts should be evaluated (`alertname`) at what time relative to the simulated start of the test run (`eval_time`). If the alert is expected to be firing at that time, an additional `exp_alerts` section should be defined listing what set of expected labels (`exp_labels`) and annotations (`exp_annotations`) should be present for each instance of the alert. Leaving the `exp_alerts` section empty means that the alert is not expected to be firing at the given time.

The first alerting test will be executed at the third minute, and, as the matching series we provided previously returns the value 1 at that moment, the alert expression defined at `alerting_rules.yml` will not trigger – this means that no data is returned by the expression defined in the alert.

The second alerting rule will be executed at the fourth minute and will return data, as the matching series we provided has the sample value 0 at that specific moment. All the labels returned by the alerting rule needs to be explicitly checked. The test must also check all the descriptions returned by the alert, with any templated variable fully expanded.

We can now run the test using the following instruction:

```
vagrant@prometheus:~$ promtool test rules /etc/prometheus/tests.yml
Unit Testing: /etc/prometheus/tests.yml
  SUCCESS
```

As an extra step, try changing the description of the second alert from `prometheus:9100` to something like `prometheus:9999` and run the test again. You should get the following output:

```
vagrant@prometheus:~$ promtool test rules /etc/prometheus/tests.yml
Unit Testing: /etc/prometheus/tests.yml
  FAILED:
    alertname:NodeExporterDown, time:4m0s,
        exp:"[Labels:{alertname=\"NodeExporterDown\",
instance=\"prometheus:9100\", job=\"node\", severity=\"critical\"}
Annotations:{description=\"Node exporter prometheus:9999 is down.\",
link=\"https://example.com\"}]",
```

Defining Alerting and Recording Rules

```
         got:"[Labels:{alertname=\"NodeExporterDown\",
instance=\"prometheus:9100\", job=\"node\", severity=\"critical\"}
Annotations:{description=\"Node exporter prometheus:9100 is down.\",
link=\"https://example.com\"}]"
```

While this alert is very simple and easy for determining in which conditions it will fire, tests for alerting rules provide you with the assurance that alerts will trigger when conditions that you can't reasonably reproduce in your environment happen.

Summary

In this chapter, we had the opportunity to observe a different way to produce a derivative time series. Recording rules help improve monitoring system stability and performance when recurrent heavy queries are required by pre-computing them into new time series that are comparatively cheap to consult. Alerting rules bring the power and flexibility of PromQL to alerts; they enable triggering alerts for complex and dynamic thresholds as well as targeting multiple instances or even different applications using a single alert rule. Having a good grasp on how delays are introduced in alerts will now help you tailor them to your needs, but remember, a little delay is better than noisy alerts. Finally, we explored how to create unit tests for our rules and validate them even before a Prometheus server is running.

The next chapter will step into another component of monitoring: visualization. We'll be diving into Grafana, the community-preferred choice for Prometheus-powered dashboards.

Questions

1. What are the primary uses for recording rules?
2. Why should you avoid setting different evaluation intervals in rule groups?
3. If you were presented with the `instance_job:latency_seconds_bucket:rate30s` metric, what labels would you expect to find and what would be the expression used to record it?
4. Why is using the sample value of an alert in the alert labels a bad idea?
5. What is the pending state of an alert?
6. How long would an alert wait between being triggered and transitioning to the `firing` state when the `for` clause is not specified?
7. How can you test your rules without using Prometheus?

Further reading

- **Prometheus recording rules**: https://prometheus.io/docs/prometheus/latest/configuration/recording_rules/
- **Rule naming best practices**: https://prometheus.io/docs/practices/rules/
- **Prometheus alerting rules**: https://prometheus.io/docs/prometheus/latest/configuration/alerting_rules/
- **Prometheus unit testing**: https://prometheus.io/docs/prometheus/latest/configuration/unit_testing_rules/

10
Discovering and Creating Grafana Dashboards

The Prometheus expression browser is great for performing exploratory queries, but sometimes we require prebuilt visualizations to assist us when we want to quickly debug issues. In this chapter, we'll dive into Grafana, the tool recommended by the Prometheus project for building dashboards. The Grafana community keeps growing and thriving, in part by hosting a multitude of ready-to-use dashboards, making it easy to reuse them and contribute to the community and thus improve the ecosystem. In this chapter, we will learn how to find and use dashboards from the community, as well as how to write our own and give something back to the community. Finally, we'll also provide a cursory look at consoles, the dashboarding solution built into Prometheus for advanced use cases.

In brief, the following topics will be covered in this chapter:

- Test environment for this chapter
- How to use Grafana with Prometheus
- Building your own dashboards
- Discovering ready-made dashboards
- Default Prometheus visualizations

Test environment for this chapter

To provide a hands-on approach, we'll be creating a new test environment for this chapter. The setup we'll be using resembles the following diagram:

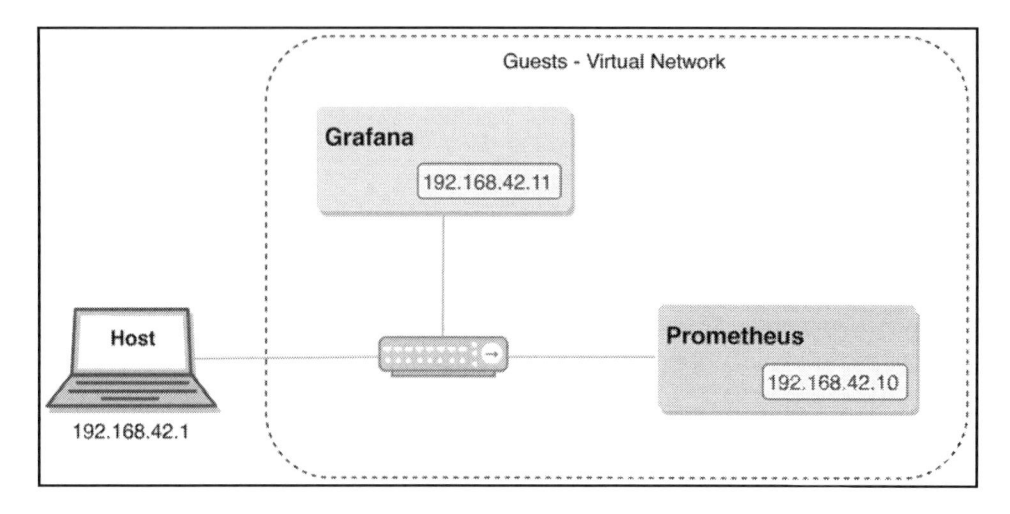

Figure 10.1: Test environment network

Deployment

To generate this chapter's **virtual machine** (**VM**) based test environment, go to the correct repository path, relative to the code repository root:

```
cd ./chapter10/
```

Ensure that no other test environments are running and spin up this chapter's environment, as follows:

```
vagrant global-status
vagrant up
```

You can validate the successful deployment of the test environment using the following code:

```
vagrant status
```

This will give the following output:

```
Current machine states:

prometheus                running (virtualbox)
grafana                   running (virtualbox)

This environment represents multiple VMs. The VMs are all listed above with
their current state. For more information about a specific VM, run `vagrant
status NAME`.
```

When the deployment tasks end, you'll be able to validate the following endpoints on your host machine using your favorite JavaScript-enabled web browser:

Service	Endpoint
Prometheus	`http://192.168.42.10:9090`
Grafana	`http://192.168.42.11:3000`

You should be able to access the desired instance by using one of the following commands:

Instance	Command
Prometheus	`vagrant ssh prometheus`
Grafana	`vagrant ssh grafana`

Cleanup

When you've finished testing, just make sure you're inside `chapter10/` and execute the following command:

```
vagrant destroy -f
```

Don't worry too much—you can easily spin up the environment again if you need to.

How to use Grafana with Prometheus

Grafana is the most recognized open source project for dashboarding. It has the concept of data sources, which are nothing more than integrations with data backends. At the time of writing, the following are the available data sources:

- Prometheus
- Graphite
- InfluxDB
- Elasticsearch
- Google Stackdriver
- AWS CloudWatch
- Azure Monitor
- Loki (logging visualization)
- MySQL
- PostgreSQL
- Microsoft SQL Server
- OpenTSDB
- TestData (useful for generating fake data for testing)

Several efforts have been made to improve the integration of Prometheus into Grafana—for example, PromQL autocompletion. Currently, Grafana is the go-to dashboarding solution for anyone interested in visualizing Prometheus data. The previous sentence isn't completely true, because we know that for exploratory queries, there's nothing like the Prometheus expression browser. Recently, though, after the release of version 6.0.0, a feature called Explore was introduced in Grafana as an alternative expression browser.

> You can find the installation files for several operating systems and distributions at `https://grafana.com/grafana/download`.

Grafana is built and preconfigured with automation in mind. In the following examples, we will demonstrate how you can pretty much set up an environment without touching the main configuration file. A noteworthy benefit is that Grafana comes natively instrumented with Prometheus metrics.

Login screen

With the test environment running, you can access Grafana using the `http://192.168.42.11:3000` URL. The user is greeted with a simple login screen, as follows:

Figure 10.2: Grafana login screen

The default authentication credentials are as follows:

Username	Password
`admin`	`admin`

After a successful login, we're welcomed to the Grafana homepage, which displays a setup wizard. Next, we're going to explain each one of the configuration steps that are presented. The following screenshot shows the wizard with some steps already configured:

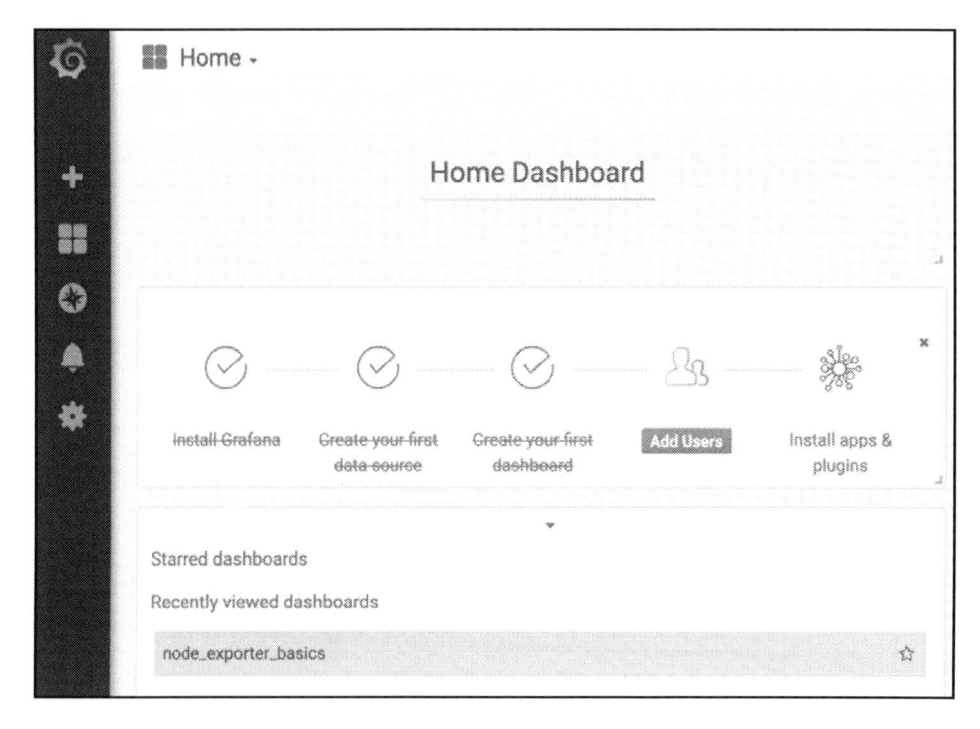

Figure 10.3: Grafana home screen

For the sake of readability, we've changed the default Grafana theme to **Light** instead of **Dark**. This is easily configured in the **Preferences** menu in the **Configuration** tab (the small gear icon on the left).

Data source

To have data to query, we must configure a data source. In our case, we'll add our Prometheus instance as the default data source. To do this, we need to indicate where the data source is located, any authentication/authorization details that are needed, and any additional data source-specific configuration.

There are two ways to configure a data source. One way is by adding a YAML file with the required configuration in the Grafana provisioning path, which is picked up by the service when starting up and is configured automatically. This is what we are doing in the test environment for this chapter, as it is the better solution for automated deployments. When connecting to the `grafana` instance in the test environment, you can see the configuration we are using by looking at the default provisioning path, shown as follows:

```
vagrant@grafana:~$ cat
/etc/grafana/provisioning/datasources/prometheus.yaml
apiVersion: 1

datasources:
- name: prometheus
  type: prometheus
  access: proxy
  orgId: 1
  url: http://prometheus:9090
  isDefault: True
  version: 1
  editable: True
```

The other option is using the web interface by going into **Configuration** (the small gear icon on the left) | **Data Sources** and adding the options for the setup manually. When clicking on **Save & Test**, Grafana will validate the settings and let you know if anything went wrong. Grafana provides two options for accessing data sources that provide HTTP-based APIs (such as Prometheus): with or without proxying requests. When proxying requests, every single query that's made from a dashboard panel or through the Explore expression browser will be proxied through the Grafana backend to the data source. Although this has the advantages of being able to manage data source credentials centrally and to close off direct network access to those data sources from everywhere except trusted clients, it creates additional load on the Grafana instances as a lot more traffic needs to pass through them. Not proxying requests means that the client browser will hit the data source directly for each request. This configuration expects that the user accessing Grafana also has direct access to the data source being used, and that security settings for that data source allow requests from different origins. In all of our examples, Grafana will be set to proxy queries.

Discovering and Creating Grafana Dashboards

The following screenshot shows the configuration that's being used in our test environment:

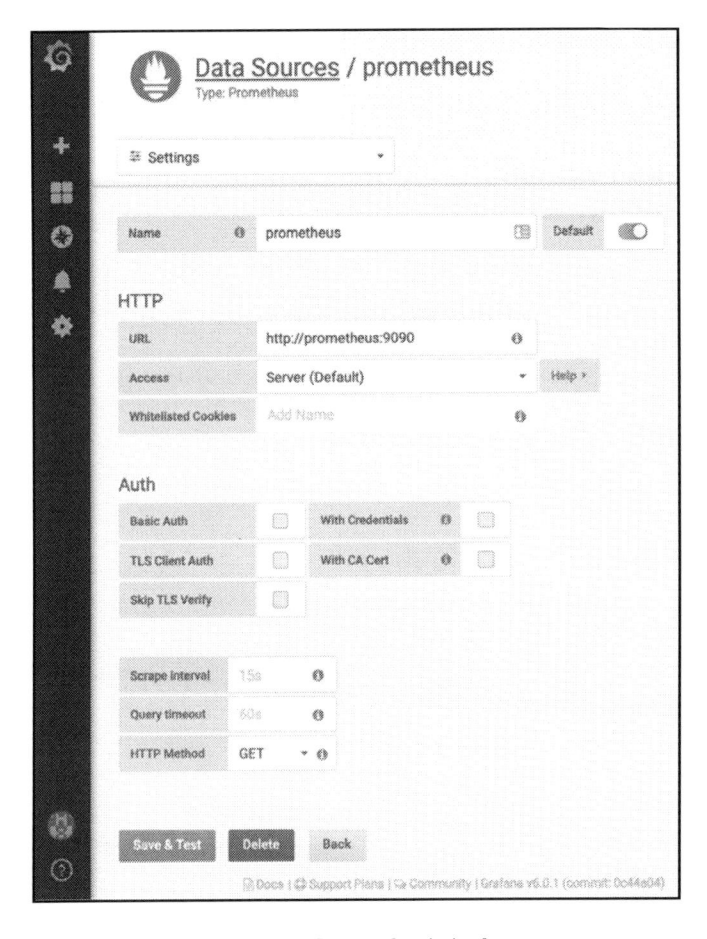

Figure 10.4: Data Sources configuration interface

Note that the **Access** option is set as **Server (Default)**. This means that all the requests for the data source will be proxied through the Grafana instance.

Explore

This feature was introduced in Grafana 6 and its developers continue to improve its tight integration with Prometheus. Before Explore, every single time you wanted to perform an exploratory query, you were required to jump to the Prometheus expression browser.

Besides this convenience, there are also some noteworthy features that make Explore unique, as shown in the following list:

- **Metrics list**: In the top-left corner, we can find a combo box called **Metrics**. This lists metrics in a hierarchical form, grouped by their prefix, and even detects and groups recording rules when they follow the double-colon naming convention.
- **Query field**: Besides suggesting and autocompleting metrics, the query field also displays useful tooltips about PromQL functions and can even expand recording rules that are detected in their originating expression.
- **Context menus**: You can choose to open the query from any dashboard panel directly in the Explore page.

The following screenshot illustrates the **Explore** interface while also displaying a tooltip for the PromQL function that is being used:

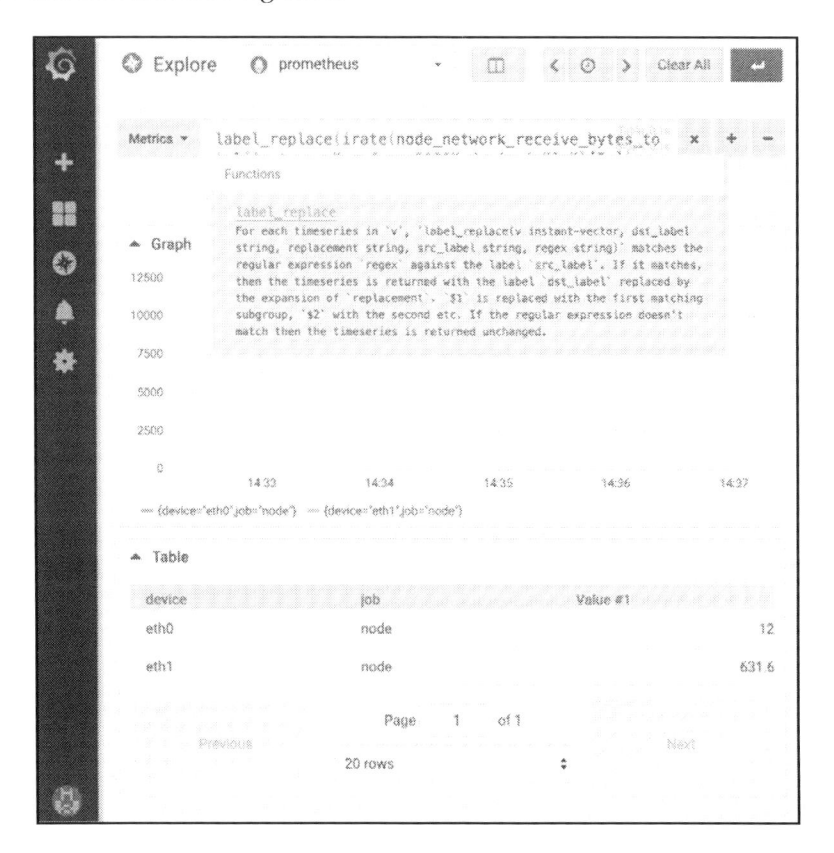

Figure 10.5: Grafana Explore page depicting the tooltip for the label_replace function

Explore can normally be found by clicking the small compass icon on the left.

Dashboards

Similar to managing data sources, there are several ways that you can add dashboards, listed as follows:

- By manually building your own
- By importing `grafana.com` community-driven dashboards
- By automatically provisioning previously stored dashboards

We'll be tackling the last way right now since the test environment is using this approach. We will focus on the other two methods in the following sections.

A dashboard file is a declarative representation of a dashboard, with all the required settings specified, and uses the JSON format. If you place it in the expected provisioning path, the Grafana service will pick it up at the start. In our example, we used the default path, as we can see in the following snippet:

```
vagrant@grafana:~$ ls /etc/grafana/dashboards/
node_exporter_basics.json
```

You can find this dashboard by going into the **Home** menu on the top left of the page and then selecting `node_exporter_basics`. This translates visually into the following screenshot:

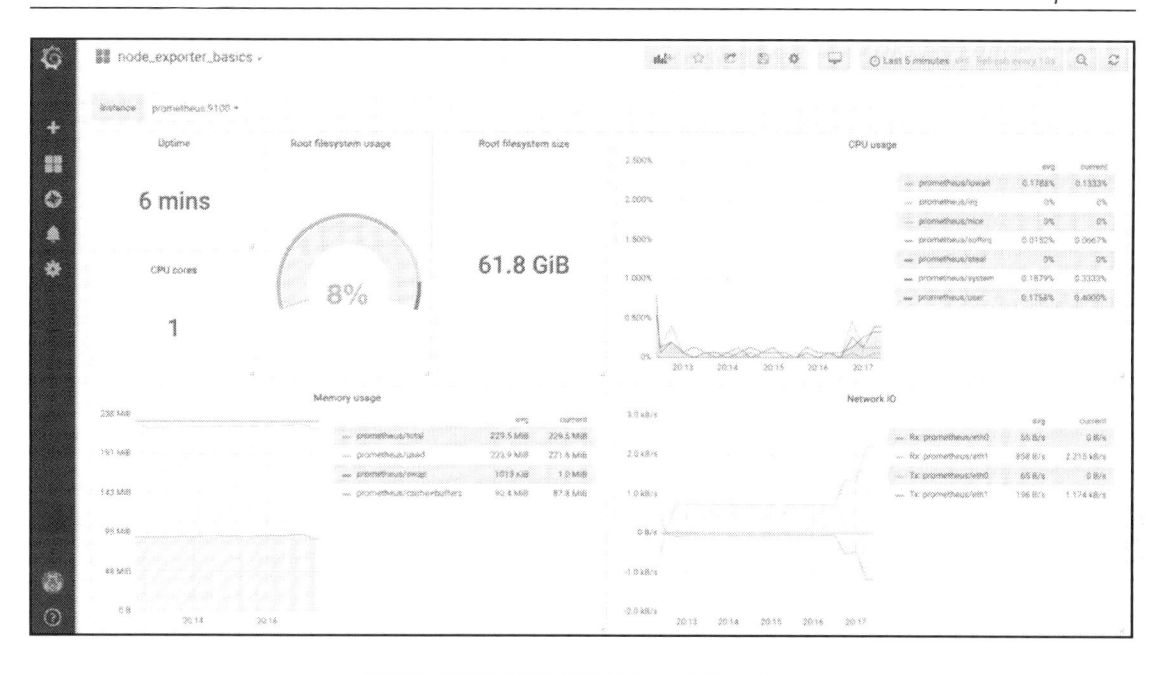

Figure 10.6: Example dashboard that's been automatically provisioned

Grafana running on Kubernetes

Deploying Grafana on Kubernetes involves mostly the same method as deploying it in VMs, so we're just going to focus on some of the finer points that an operator should be aware of. The Kubernetes manifests for getting Grafana and Prometheus up and running in our Kubernetes test environment can be found, relative to the code repository root path, at the following path:

```
cd ./chapter10/provision/kubernetes/
```

Since the Kubernetes deployment procedure is the same as in previous chapters (bootstrapping the Prometheus Operator, deploying Prometheus using the Operator, and deploying exporters and their respective ServiceMonitors), this won't be covered in length again here. If you need additional context, feel free to have a look at the test environment walkthroughs in the previous chapters, such as Chapter 7, *Prometheus Query Language – PromQL*.

The following steps will ensure the creation of a new Kubernetes environment with all the required software provisioned so that we can focus on the Grafana component.

1. Validate that no other environment is running:

   ```
   minikube status
   minikube delete
   ```

2. Start an empty Kubernetes environment, by using the following command:

   ```
   minikube start \
     --cpus=2 \
     --memory=3072 \
     --kubernetes-version="v1.14.0" \
     --vm-driver=virtualbox
   ```

3. Add the Prometheus Operator components and follow its deployment, as follows:

   ```
   kubectl apply -f ./bootstrap/
   kubectl rollout status deployment/prometheus-operator -n monitoring
   ```

4. Add the new Prometheus cluster, ensuring that it's successful, by using the following command:

   ```
   kubectl apply -f ./prometheus/
   kubectl rollout status statefulset/prometheus-k8s -n monitoring
   ```

5. Add all the targets to Prometheus and list them using the following command:

   ```
   kubectl apply -f ./services/
   kubectl get servicemonitors --all-namespaces
   ```

Now that the Kubernetes environment is running, we can proceed with Grafana-specific configurations. Similar to the VM-focused test environment, we'll require the provisioning of not only Grafana itself, but also the data source and dashboards.

For the data source, since we might want to add sensitive information such as authentication in the future, we are going to use a Kubernetes secret. This also implies that there should be a ServiceAccount for accessing that secret.

We can create the ServiceAccount by applying the following manifest:

```
kubectl apply -f ./grafana/grafana-serviceaccount.yaml
```

Since we're using a secret, the data source configuration needs to be encoded into base64. As for the provisioning configuration itself, it is the same as in the VM deployment, but we will be substituting the Prometheus URL with the Kubernetes equivalent that is managed by the service. Here's a snippet before encoding:

```
...
datasources:
- name: prometheus
...
  url: http://prometheus-service.monitoring.svc:9090
...
```

After applying the following manifest, a new secret with the desired Grafana data source will be available:

```
kubectl apply -f ./grafana/grafana-datasources-provision.yaml
```

Now, it's time to add our example dashboard to Grafana. To achieve this, we need to provide Grafana with a provisioning configuration that tells it where to look for dashboard definitions and then put our example dashboard definition in that path. These are going to be available to the Grafana deployment as ConfigMaps. The relevant snippet that shows the dashboard location provisioning configuration is as follows:

```
...
data:
  dashboards.yaml: |-
    {
        "apiVersion": 1,
        "providers": [{
           "folder": "",
           "name": "default",
           "options": {
              "path": "/etc/grafana/dashboards"
           },
           "orgId": 1,
           "type": "file"
        }]
    }
kind: ConfigMap
...
```

The other `ConfigMap` contains our example dashboard, shown as follows:

```
...
data:
  node_exporter_basics.json: |-
    {
...
    }
kind: ConfigMap
...
```

Both manifests can be deployed in the Kubernetes test environment using the following commands:

```
kubectl apply -f ./grafana/grafana-dashboards-provision.yaml

kubectl apply -f ./grafana/grafana-dashboards.yaml
```

It's now time to deploy Grafana and take advantage of all the preceding configurations, as follows:

```
kubectl apply -f ./grafana/grafana-deployment.yaml
```

This deployment brings everything together: it mounts the data source's secret, and the dashboard provision and dashboards ConfigMaps at the same locations as the VM test environment, as follows:

```
...
        volumeMounts:
        - name: grafana-datasources-provision
          mountPath: /etc/grafana/provisioning/datasources
        - name: grafana-dashboards-provision
          mountPath: /etc/grafana/provisioning/dashboards
        - name: grafana-dashboards
          mountPath: /etc/grafana/dashboards
...
```

You may follow the deployment status using the following instruction:

```
kubectl rollout status deployment/grafana -n monitoring
```

Finally, we can add a service so that we can access the newly launched Grafana instance, and a ServiceMonitor so that the Prometheus Operator configures Prometheus to collect metrics:

```
kubectl apply -f ./grafana/grafana-service.yaml

kubectl apply -f ./grafana/grafana-servicemonitor.yaml
```

You can now access the Grafana interface using the following command:

```
minikube service grafana -n monitoring
```

When you're finished testing, you can delete this Kubernetes-based test environment by issuing the following command:

```
minikube delete
```

This setup gives you a quick overview of how to integrate Grafana with Prometheus on Kubernetes. It's not awfully different from the VM test environment, but the details that were shown here will hopefully prevent you from having to search for information on how to accomplish it elsewhere.

Building your own dashboards

Inside the provided VM test environment, you had the opportunity to try out the bundled dashboard. Now, it's time to learn how to build your own, but for that, you will need to grasp some concepts. In this section, we'll walk you through the process of creating a dashboard.

Dashboard fundamentals

A dashboard is composed of several components. We'll go over the most important concepts in the following sections, including panels, the visualizations they support, how to template variables, and changing the time range of the displayed data.

Panels

A panel is a rectangular-shaped slot in the visualization area of a dashboard. An example is shown in the following screenshot. It can be rearranged and resized as necessary by dragging and dropping its various dimensions. You can also put a set of panels inside a row, which is nothing more than a logical grouping of those panels. Rows can be expanded or collapsed to show or hide the panels within them:

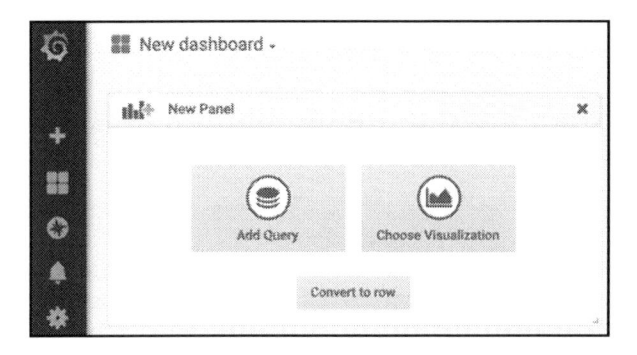

Figure 10.7: New panel

A panel, besides having the ability to query the chosen data source, also provides multiple visualization options to choose from. These visualization options allow you to present data in a variety of ways, such as simple single-value panels, bar graphs, line graphs, tables, all the way to heatmaps. The following screenshot illustrates the available built-in visualizations:

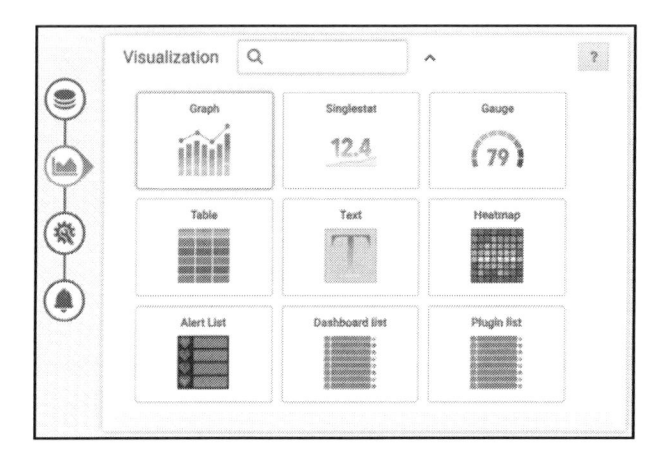

Figure 10.8: Built-in visualization options

In the preceding screenshot, we can see several panel types. Four of the most used ones are as follows:

- **Graph**: This the main Grafana panel. It provides the tools to create rich two-dimensional graphs backed by one or more PromQL expressions.
- **Singlestat**: This is a multipurpose single-value display. As such, the PromQL query must return an instant vector with one sample only.
- **Gauge**: Using thresholds, this represents the position the current value is at in relation to the defined higher and lower bounds. Like the Singlestat visualization, this option requires a single instant vector with only one sample.
- **Table**: This displays the result of a PromQL expression in a table format, with each label in its own column, along with the value and the timestamp.

For each one of the available visualizations, there are numerous options that allow for the extraordinary level of customization of each panel's appearance. The official Grafana documentation explains every option in detail, so we will focus on the most relevant ones here.

Variables

The variables feature is extremely powerful. It allows a dashboard to configure placeholders that can be used in expressions, and those placeholders can be filled with values from either a static or dynamic list, which are usually presented to the dashboard user in the form of a drop-down menu. Whenever the selected value changes, Grafana will automatically update the queries in panels that use that particular variable. In our example dashboard, we're using this feature to allow the user to choose which node instance to present. Besides being commonly used in queries, they're also available, for example, in panel titles.

This feature is available in the **Dashboard settings**, which can be found by clicking the top-right cog icon, which in turn is available inside any dashboard. The following screenshot depicts the **Variables** option from the **node_exporter_basics** dashboard in the **Settings** menu:

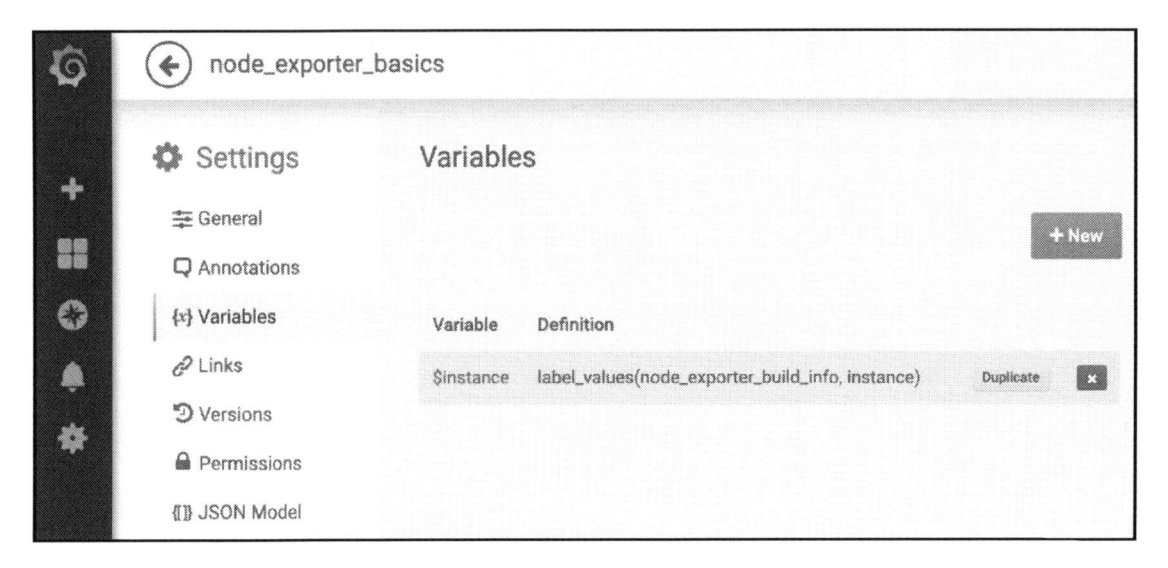

Figure 10.9: Dashboard variables

As you can see, we're using a PromQL query to dynamically fetch the possible values for the $instance variable.

> **TIP**
> When the viewport is not large enough, the responsive design of Grafana will hide some of the top-right icons.

Time picker

The time picker feature is available in any dashboard in the top-right corner as a button containing the clock icon. The interface is split into two major blocks: **Quick ranges** of predefined time ranges (most of them relative to the current time) or a **Custom range**, which allows you to specify the exact time span to use in all the dashboard panels. As the name suggests, the **Refreshing every:** option will make the dashboard panels automatically reload at the interval specified. This is useful to see new data coming in when used in conjunction with a relative time range.

The following screenshot shows a series of quick ranges:

Figure 10.10: Time picker

Creating a basic dashboard

We are going to get hands-on with Grafana by guiding you through the creation process of a bare-bones dashboard. You can start by clicking the left plus sign logo | **Dashboard**. This will open a new empty dashboard with a new panel, ready to be edited. Since we want a dynamic dashboard, we're going to create a new variable, which will expand into a list of the available Node Exporter instances in our Prometheus server.

> Using the *Shift* + *?* key combination will display a helpful tooltip of all the available shortcuts.

Discovering and Creating Grafana Dashboards

To achieve our goal, we must click the top-right cog icon, open the **Dashboard settings**, then select **Variables**. The following screenshot illustrates the options that are available when creating such a variable:

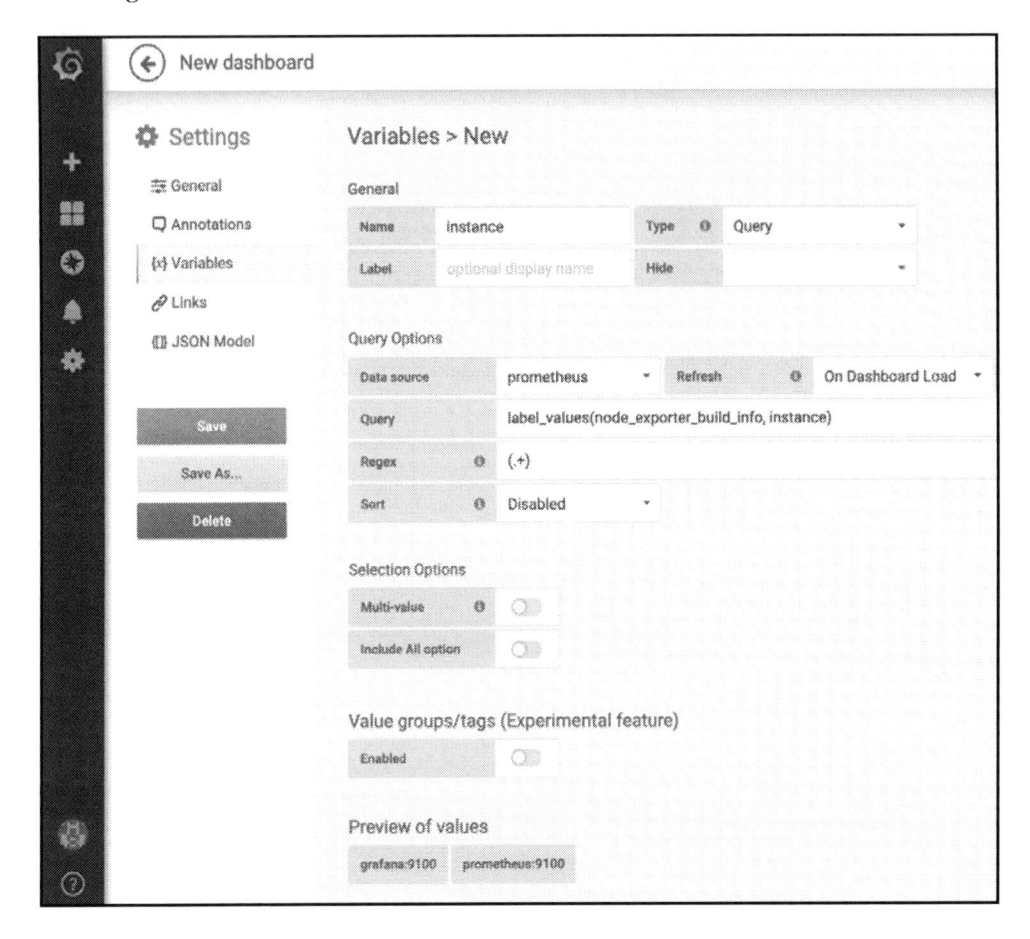

Figure 10.11: Variables interface

> **TIP**
> The preview values depicted in the preceding screenshot show the Node Exporter targets from the VM-based test environment. You will get a different preview if you are following along using the Kubernetes test environment.

In this example, we're creating a variable named `instance` using the **Query** type, which means it will populate its values from the results of the query to the data source. We're specifying the data source as `prometheus`, the identifier we gave during provisioning, and that we want to refresh that variable only when the dashboards get loaded.

Now comes the interesting part: since we are interested in collecting Node Exporter instances, we use a metric in the **Query** field that is guaranteed to return the instances we require, `node_exporter_build_info`. The `label_values()` function isn't actually valid PromQL, but is provided by the Prometheus data source plugin in Grafana to use in this field to facilitate these kind of expressions.

The **Regex** field is used to match the parts of the query result we want to use to populate the variable. In our example, we want the full content of the instance label, so we match everything inside a regular expression capture group, `(.+)`. We can see that the matching is working in the **Preview of values** section at the bottom of the screen. After clicking **Add** and saving this dashboard using the name `example`, we can now see the following dropdown menu with the values of the `instance` variable:

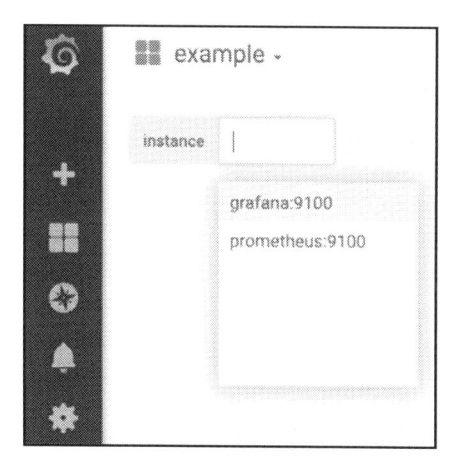

Figure 10.11: Instance values

Discovering and Creating Grafana Dashboards

It's time to create our first panel. Click on the top-right graph logo, and in the new panel, click **Add Query**. The following screenshot illustrates the query interface:

Figure 10.12: Query interface

Here, we can specify the PromQL queries (one or more, depending on the visualization type) to perform on the desired data source. In our example, we'll be creating a graph of CPU usage per mode, and we want to template the query so that it uses the `instance` variable we created earlier. Note the `$instance`, which will be replaced at query time with the selected value in the `instance` combo box. The full expression is as follows:

```
label_replace(avg by (mode, instance)
(irate(node_cpu_seconds_total{instance="$instance", mode!="idle"}[5m])),
"instance", "$1", "instance", "([^:]+):.+")
```

Chapter 10

The `label_replace()` function allows us to remove the port from the instance value, which we'll use in the **Legend** field. This field allows the substitution of {{ }} template markers with the values of the metric labels set within it. This will, in turn, reflect on the graph legend preceding the **Query** menu. In the following screenshot, we can see several visual options that have been applied to our dashboard, and we'll go over each one:

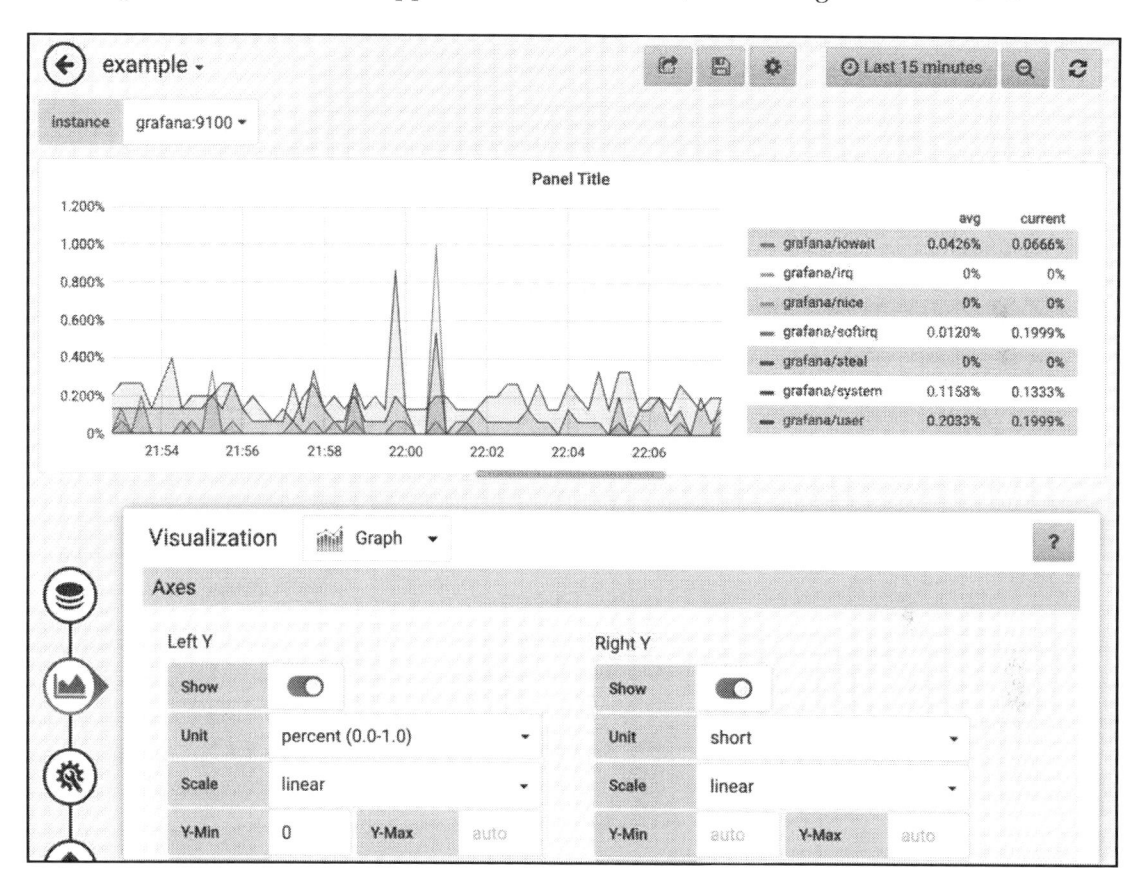

Figure 10.13: Visualization interface

In the **Axes** section, we select which of the graph axes to enable; the **Right Y** configuration options do not produce any change, as that axis is not used. In the **Left Y** configuration, we can specify the **Unit**. In our case, we want a percentage; we could simply multiply our expression by 100, but not doing so exposes one of the handy features Grafana has to offer. As we already know, our value range is from 0 to 1; this **Unit** type will take the values in the 0-1 range and automatically transform them into percentages (from 0 to 100). We're also ensuring that **Y-min** is set to, so that the graph becomes easier to understand visually, as without it the graph would have the *y* axis scale adapted to start near the lowest *Y* value in the query result. Additionally, for the sake of this example, we want three decimal places in the values of the *y* scale, and so we set that using the **Decimals** field. On the **X-Axis**, we didn't change anything, as we want the time.

In the **Legend** section, we control how we want the graph legend to look and where it's placed inside the panel. In our case, we want it as a table, placed on the right-hand side of the graph, and we want it to present the average and current value of *Y*.

To finish our panel, we need to step into the **General** menu, as shown in the following screenshot, where we can name our panel and add a description. The description will be available as a small **i** icon in the top-left corner of the panel:

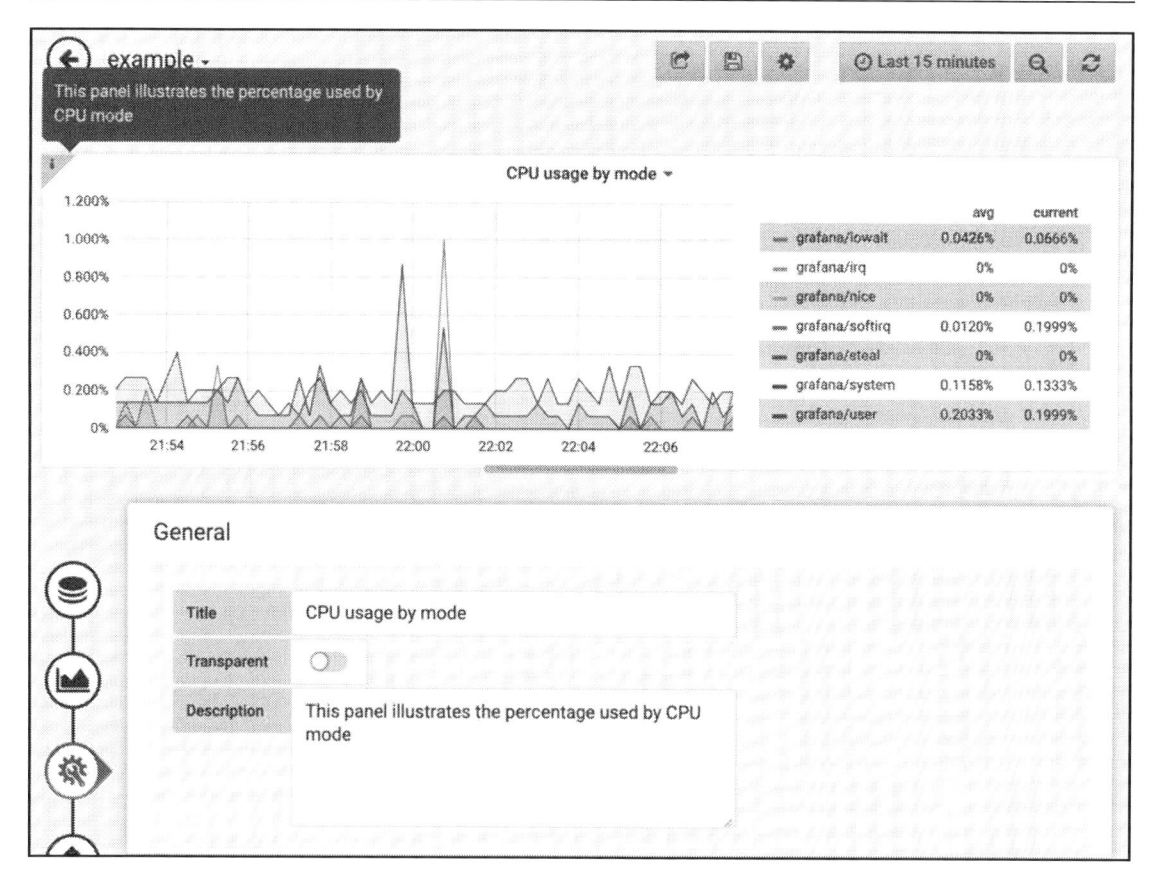

Figure 10.14: The general menu of the panel

To save your new dashboard, just click the small floppy disk icon in the top-right corner. You have now created a simple dashboard from scratch! You can continue adding panels and visualizations, but the main concepts are pretty much the same. You can explore the provided dashboard in the test environment for more examples on how to use different visualizations options.

Something to keep in mind when creating a dashboard is to avoid unnecessary clutter. It is usual to see dashboards with dozens of panels, with a multitude of data on display. Try to have the right amount of information so that, for example, troubleshooting issues is quick and painless. Focus is the key word here: if there are panels that are not related to each other inside a dashboard, perhaps it would be a good idea to split them into their own dashboard.

Exporting dashboards

Grafana makes it easy to export dashboards. To proceed, just open the dashboard you intend to export and press the small **square with arrow** icon in the top-right panel, near the floppy disk icon.

The following form will open:

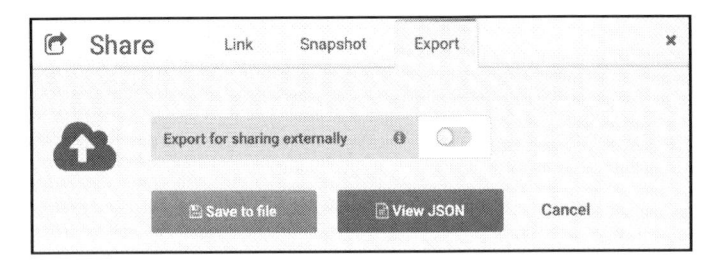

Figure 10.15: Grafana dashboard export

Here, you're presented with several options:

- **Export for sharing externally**: Enables the templating of the data source names, which is helpful for sharing the dashboard publicly. This is mandatory in order to publish the dashboard on the `grafana.com` website.
- **View JSON**: Allows you to visualize the code of the dashboard.
- **Save to file**: Downloads the dashboard as a JSON file.

Next, we're going to see how we can download dashboards from the Grafana dashboard gallery, and how to contribute our own to it.

Discovering ready-made dashboards

Since Grafana is widely used and has a huge community behind it, it's logical that a huge number of dashboards are being created by that community. The folks at Grafana provide a service where registered users are able to publish their dashboards onto a gallery, and anyone can download and install them on their own Grafana instances. In the following sections, we'll be providing an overview of both actions, not only using community-made dashboards, but also how to publish your own.

Grafana dashboards gallery

Both community-driven and official dashboards are available at `https://grafana.com/dashboards` and, as expected, there are a lot to choose from. Since we're interested in Prometheus-specific dashboards when searching the site, we should restrict the search results to that data source. By applying additional filters, we keep restricting results to exactly what we're after, as you can see in the following screenshot:

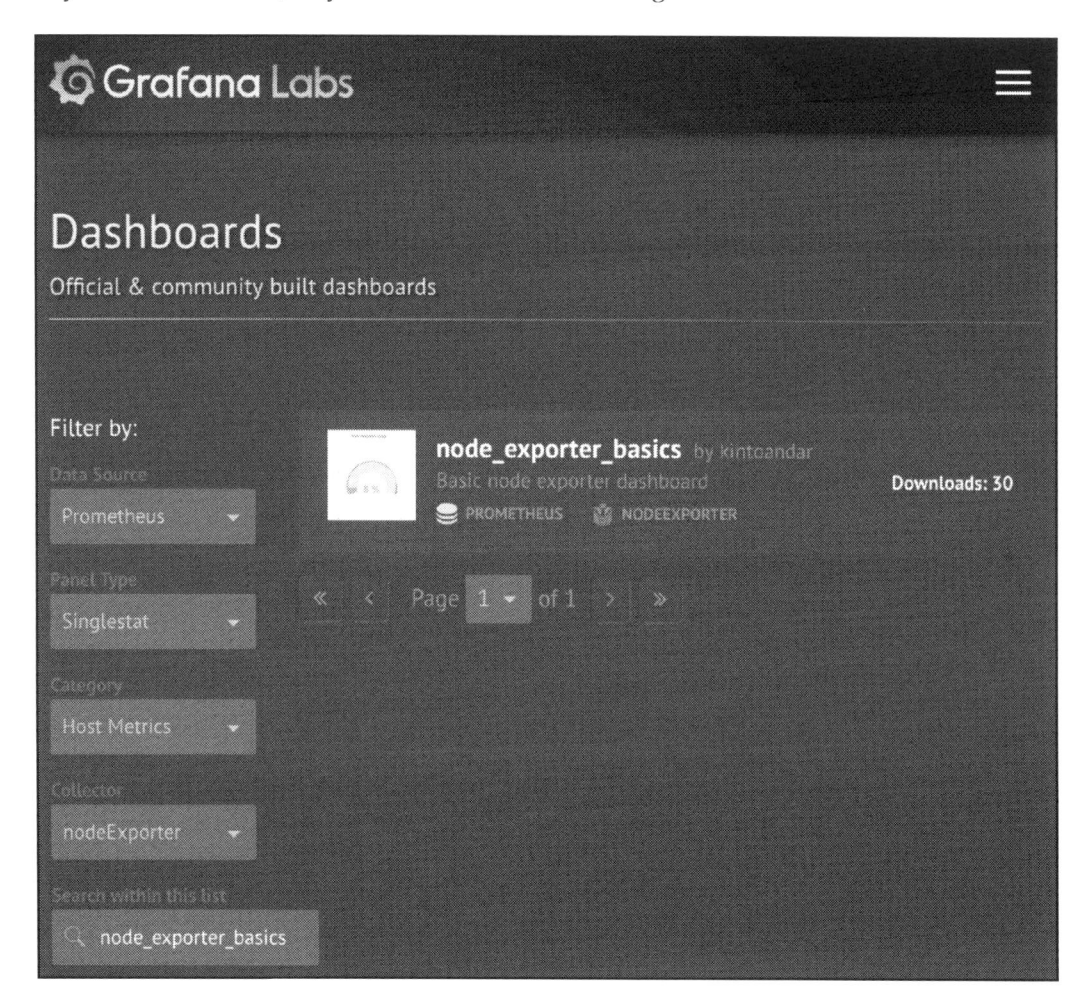

10.16: Grafana.com filtered dashboards result

Discovering and Creating Grafana Dashboards

We can then select the dashboard we're interested in, which will in turn open a screen, as shown in the following screenshot:

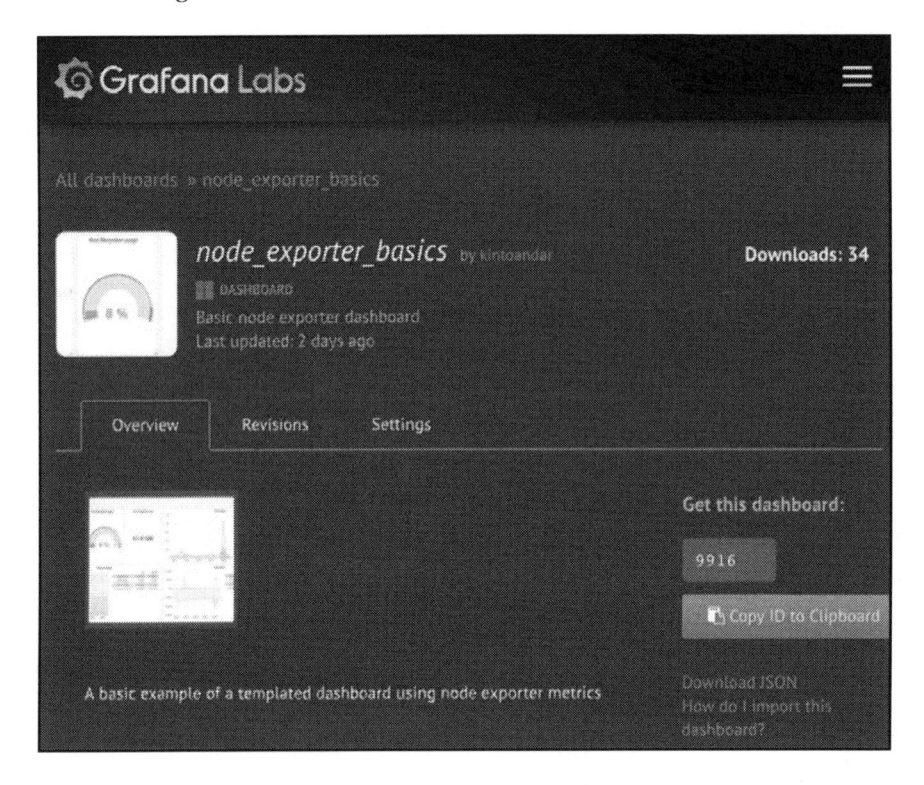

Figure 10.17: Grafana.com selected dashboard information

Here, we can see some information regarding the dashboard and a screenshot of it. Notice the ID **9916** on the right; it's a unique identifier in the Grafana gallery for this particular dashboard. We can use it by going into a Grafana instance, such as the one in our test environment, clicking on the plus sign in the main menu on the left-hand side, selecting **Import** from the submenu, and pasting it in the appropriate text field, as shown in the following screenshot:

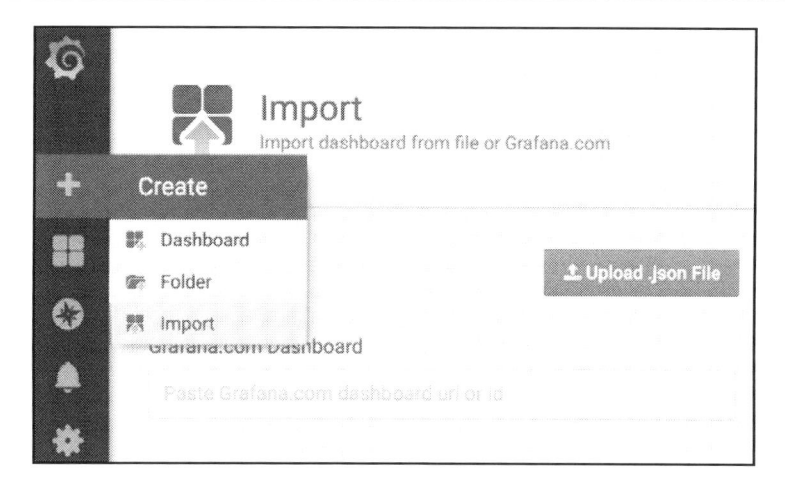

Figure 10.18: Import dashboard interface

After pasting in the ID, a new menu will pop up, asking for the name we want to give to this dashboard, in which folder it should be placed, and what data source it should use. If there are any conflicts with pre-existing dashboards (such as dashboards with the same name), you will be asked to resolve them before you will be able to finish the import process.

Publishing your dashboards

Publishing a newly created dashboard is quite easy. First, ensure that you have an account for the Grafana website by using the registration form located at `https://grafana.com/signup`. After a successful registration, go into your profile via **Personal** | **My Dashboards** or use the `https://grafana.com/orgs/<user>/dashboards` link, replacing `<user>` with your Grafana username.

Inside **My Dashboards**, you can now click the **Upload Dashboard** button. This action will open an upload form, requesting the dashboard to be uploaded. Remember, this will only accept dashboards that are exported with the **Export for sharing externally** option toggled on:

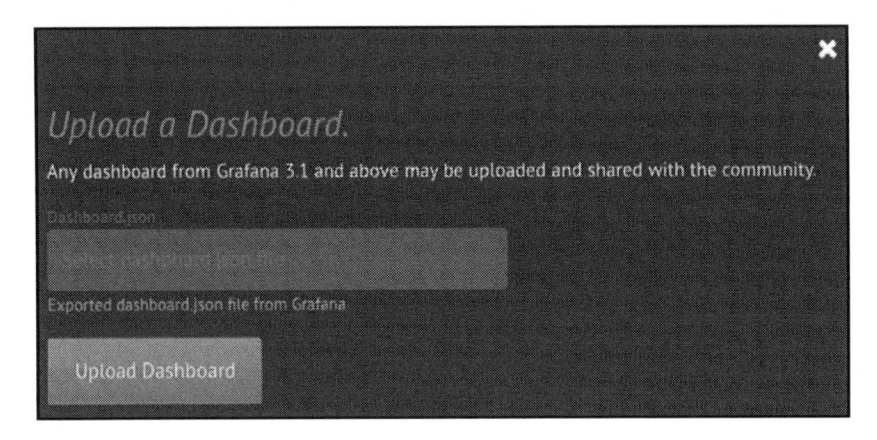

Figure 10.19: Dashboard upload form

And you're done! You'll now obtain a numeric ID for your dashboard and you can start using it or sharing it across the globe. You can update the published dashboard if you want to, as this will not alter the generated ID. Instead, it will create another revision of the published dashboard, and users will always download the latest revision that's available.

Default Prometheus visualizations

Historically, Prometheus maintained its own tool to create dashboards, called PromDash. Over time, since Grafana improved its native support for Prometheus as a data source, the community began gravitating toward using Grafana as its primary visualization solution—so much so that PromDash was deprecated by the people who maintained Prometheus in favor of Grafana.

> You can find the source code for PromDash at `https://github.com/prometheus-junkyard/promdash`.

Even though Grafana is the recommended visualization solution for most people, Prometheus also ships with an internal dashboarding feature called **console templates**. These console templates are written in raw HTML/CSS/JavaScript and leverage the power of the Go templating language to generate dashboards (called consoles) that are served by the Prometheus server itself. This makes them blazingly fast and endlessly customizable. Console templates are as powerful as they are complex. We are going to introduce this feature by giving you a small overview of how to use and build console templates in the next section.

Out-of-the-box console templates

When you unpack the Prometheus release archive, besides the binaries for the server and promtool, there are also a few console templates readily available. To make this clear, we can look inside our test environment where we unpacked these templates into system paths, shown as follows:

```
vagrant@prometheus:/usr/share/prometheus$ systemctl cat prometheus
...
ExecStart=/usr/bin/prometheus \
    --config.file=/etc/prometheus/prometheus.yml \
    --storage.tsdb.path=/var/lib/prometheus/data \
    --web.console.templates=/usr/share/prometheus/consoles \
    --web.console.libraries=/usr/share/prometheus/console_libraries
...
```

Both directories need to be properly configured for consoles to work. Console libraries define helper functions that are then used in console templates so that repetition is kept to a minimum. We are going to have a closer look at these libraries in the next section when we build our own template.

For now, here are the console templates that ship with Prometheus:

```
vagrant@prometheus:~$ ls -lh /usr/share/prometheus/consoles
total 36K
-rw-r--r-- 1 root root  623 Mar 10 16:28 index.html.example
-rw-r--r-- 1 root root 2.7K Mar 10 16:28 node-cpu.html
-rw-r--r-- 1 root root 3.5K Mar 10 16:28 node-disk.html
-rw-r--r-- 1 root root 1.5K Mar 10 16:28 node.html
-rw-r--r-- 1 root root 5.7K Mar 10 16:28 node-overview.html
-rw-r--r-- 1 root root 1.4K Mar 10 16:28 prometheus.html
-rw-r--r-- 1 root root 4.1K Mar 10 16:28 prometheus-overview.html
```

As you can see in `index.html.example`, these templates expect the scrape jobs for Prometheus and Node Exporter to be named `prometheus` and `node` respectively, so they might not work for your Prometheus configuration out of the box.

We can access it by using the web interface URL at `http://192.168.42.10:9090/consoles/index.html.example` and exploring the available consoles. The following screenshot depicts the console for the node CPU of the Prometheus instance:

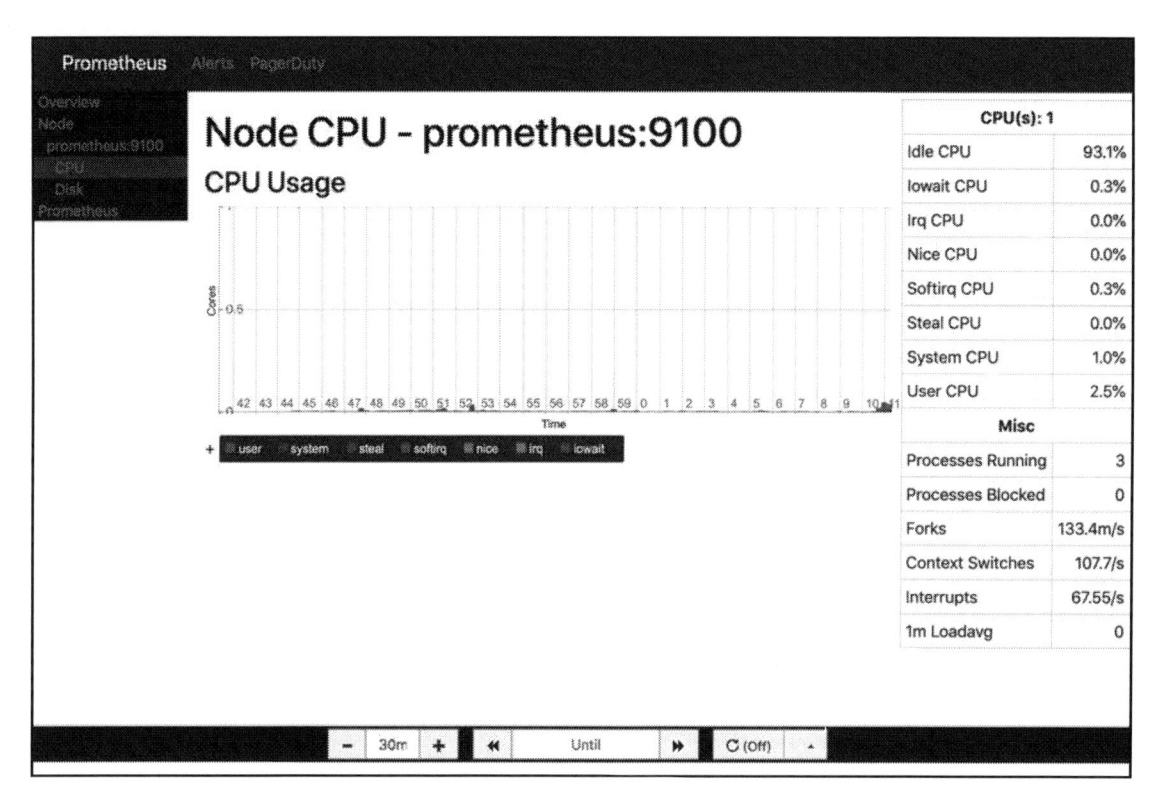

Figure 10.20: Node CPU for Prometheus

Console template basics

Creating console templates from scratch has a steep learning curve. Unlike in Grafana, console templates are crafted directly in HTML and JavaScript, with a fair dose of Go templating in the mix. This means that consoles can technically take any form, but for simplicity, we will stick to the structure provided by the built-in console libraries.

The libraries that power the example console templates define the scaffold for the consoles. They take care of things such as constructing the HTML structure, including the necessary CSS and JavaScript and modeling the four sections around the main console content: the navigation bar at the top, the menu on the left, the console time controls at the bottom, and a table to show summary statistics on the right. Let's see how we could use them to construct a simple console template by looking at the following code:

```
{{template "head" .}}

{{template "prom_content_head" .}}
```

The `head` template expands to HTML that defines the inclusion of CSS and JavaScript, the top navbar, and the menu; the `prom_content_head` template on the other hand, defines the time controls, as shown in the following code:

```
<h1>Grafana</h1>

<h3>Requests by endpoint</h3>
<div id="queryGraph"></div>
<script>
new PromConsole.Graph({
  node: document.querySelector("#queryGraph"),
  expr: "sum(rate(http_request_total{job='grafana'}[5m])) by (handler)",
  name: '[[ handler ]]',
  yAxisFormatter: PromConsole.NumberFormatter.humanizeNoSmallPrefix,
  yHoverFormatter: PromConsole.NumberFormatter.humanizeNoSmallPrefix,
  yUnits: "/s",
  yTitle: "Requests"
})
</script>
```

This section defines the console itself. The `queryGraph` element is used as the placeholder that the graphing JavaScript library will use to generate the graph. The JavaScript snippet, on the other hand, configures the graph with the selector that is to be used (`node`), what expression to graph (`expr`), what to use in the legend (`name`), and several *y*-axis configurations, as shown in the following code:

```
{{template "prom_content_tail" .}}

{{template "tail"}}
```

The last two templates close the sections that the first opened. They are needed so that the generated HTML is well formed.

Discovering and Creating Grafana Dashboards

The resulting console is available in the test environment for this chapter, and can be checked out at `http://192.168.42.10:9090/consoles/grafana.html`. Here is a screenshot of how it should look:

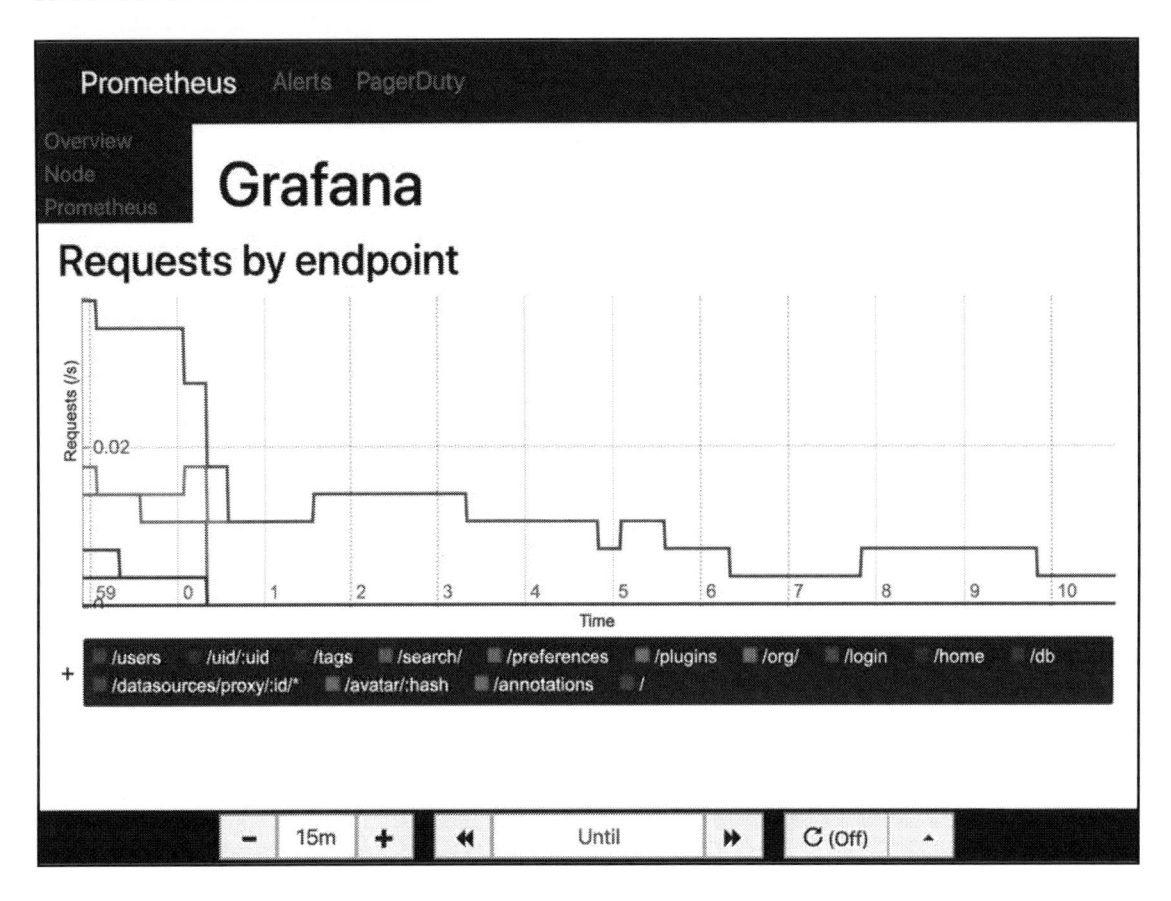

Figure 10.21: Example console for Grafana requests per second

Note that the menu on the left-hand side does not have a link to our newly created console template. This is because the included `menu.lib` only supports the example console templates that ship with Prometheus. When deploying actual custom console templates, you would need to replace this library with your own. This would allow you to add links to other internal systems in the navbar at the top and list which consoles should be available on the navigation menu on the left. By leveraging the fact that you can perform PromQL queries in templates, you should be able to find out which jobs are scraped by that Prometheus instance and generate links to similarly named consoles.

Summary

In this chapter, we explored the standard visualization tool for Prometheus: Grafana. We've learned how to provision not only data sources, but dashboards as well. After learning about the building blocks of a dashboard, we created a simple dashboard from scratch, learning all that it entails step by step. We also learned how to take advantage of the thriving community-built dashboard gallery. Giving back to the community is always important, so we've gone through the process of exporting and publishing dashboards. Finally, we were introduced to the Prometheus default visualizations—the consoles—which, even though they have a steep learning curve, are extremely powerful.

In the next chapter, we'll be exploring the Alertmanager, how to best take advantage of its functionalities, and how to integrate it with Prometheus.

Questions

1. How can you provision a data source automatically in Grafana?
2. What are the steps to import a dashboard from the Grafana gallery?
3. How do Grafana dashboard variables work?
4. What's the building block of a dashboard?
5. When you update a dashboard that's published to `grafana.com`, does it change its ID?
6. In Prometheus terms, what is a console?
7. Why would you use Prometheus console templates?

Further reading

- **Grafana Explore**: http://docs.grafana.org/features/explore/
- **Grafana templating**: http://docs.grafana.org/reference/templating/
- **Grafana time range**: http://docs.grafana.org/reference/timerange/
- **Console templates official documentation**: https://prometheus.io/docs/visualization/consoles/
- **Console templates best practices**: https://prometheus.io/docs/practices/consoles/

11
Understanding and Extending Alertmanager

Alerting is a critical component in any monitoring stack. In the Prometheus ecosystem, alerts and their subsequent notifications are decoupled. Alertmanager is the component that handles these alerts. In this chapter, we'll be focusing on converting alerts into useful notifications using Alertmanager. From reliability to customization, we'll delve into the inner workings of the Alertmanager service, providing the required knowledge to configure, troubleshoot, and customize all the options available. We'll make sure that concepts such as alert routing, silencing, and inhibition are clear so that you can decide how to implement them in your own stack.

Since Alertmanager is a critical component, high availability will also be explored, and we will also explain the relationship between Prometheus and Alertmanager. We will customize notifications and learn how to build and use reusable templates so that notifications are appropriate and carry accurate information when they reach their destination. We will finish this chapter by learning how to monitor the monitoring system and, more importantly, learning how to be alerted when the system is partially or completely down.

We will explore the following topics in this chapter:

- Test environment for this chapter.
- Alertmanager fundamentals.
- Alertmanager configuration.
- Common Alertmanager notification integrations.
- Customizing your alert notifications.
- Who watches the Watchmen?

Setting up the test environment

To work with Alertmanager, we'll be three new instances to simulate a highly available setup. This approach will allow us to not only expose the required configurations, but also validate how everything works together.

The setup we'll be using resembles the following diagram:

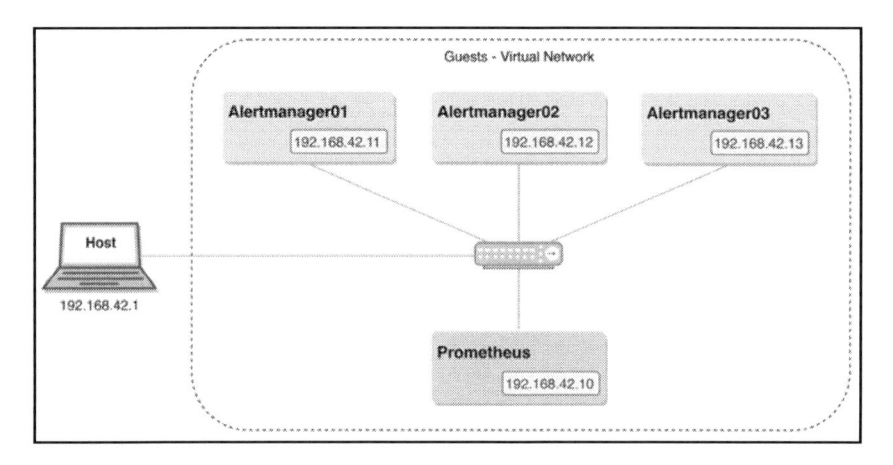

Figure 11.1: Test environment

Deployment

Let's begin by deploying the Alertmanager test environment:

1. To launch a new test environment, move into this chapter's path, relative to the repository root:

    ```
    cd ./chapter11/
    ```

2. Ensure that no other test environments are running and spin up this chapter's environment:

    ```
    vagrant global-status
    vagrant up
    ```

3. You can validate the successful deployment of the test environment using the following command:

    ```
    vagrant status
    ```

You will receive the following output:

```
Current machine states:

prometheus       running (virtualbox)
alertmanager01   running (virtualbox)
alertmanager02   running (virtualbox)
alertmanager03   running (virtualbox)

This environment represents multiple VMs. The VMs are all listed
above with their current state. For more information about a
specific
VM, run `vagrant status NAME`.
```

When the deployment tasks end, you'll be able to validate the following endpoints on your host machine using your favorite JavaScript-enabled web browser:

Service	Endpoint
Prometheus	`http://192.168.42.10:9090`
Alertmanager01	`http://192.168.42.11:9093`
Alertmanager02	`http://192.168.42.12:9093`
Alertmanager03	`http://192.168.42.13:9093`

You should be able to access the desired instance by using one of the following commands:

Instance	Command
Prometheus	`vagrant ssh prometheus`
Alertmanager01	`vagrant ssh alertmanager01`
Alertmanager02	`vagrant ssh alertmanager02`
Alertmanager03	`vagrant ssh alertmanager03`

Cleanup

When you've finished testing, just make sure you're inside `./chapter11/` and execute the following:

```
vagrant destroy -f
```

Don't worry too much – you can easily spin up the environment again if you need to.

Alertmanager fundamentals

We covered how alerting rules work in Prometheus in `Chapter 9`, *Defining Alerting and Recording Rules*, but those, by themselves, aren't all that useful. As we mentioned previously, Prometheus delegates notification handling and routing to external systems through a Webhook-style HTTP interface. This is where Alertmanager comes in.

Alertmanager is responsible for accepting the alerts generated from Prometheus alerting rules and converting them into notifications. The latter can take any form, such as email messages, chat messages, pages, or even Webhooks that will then trigger custom actions, such as logging alerts to a data store or creating/updating tickets. Alertmanager is also the only component in the official stack that distributes its state across instances so that it can keep track of things such as which alerts were already sent and which ones are silenced.

The notification pipeline

The following diagram, inspired by the architecture diagram of Alertmanager, provides an overview of the steps an alert goes through until it's successfully sent as a notification:

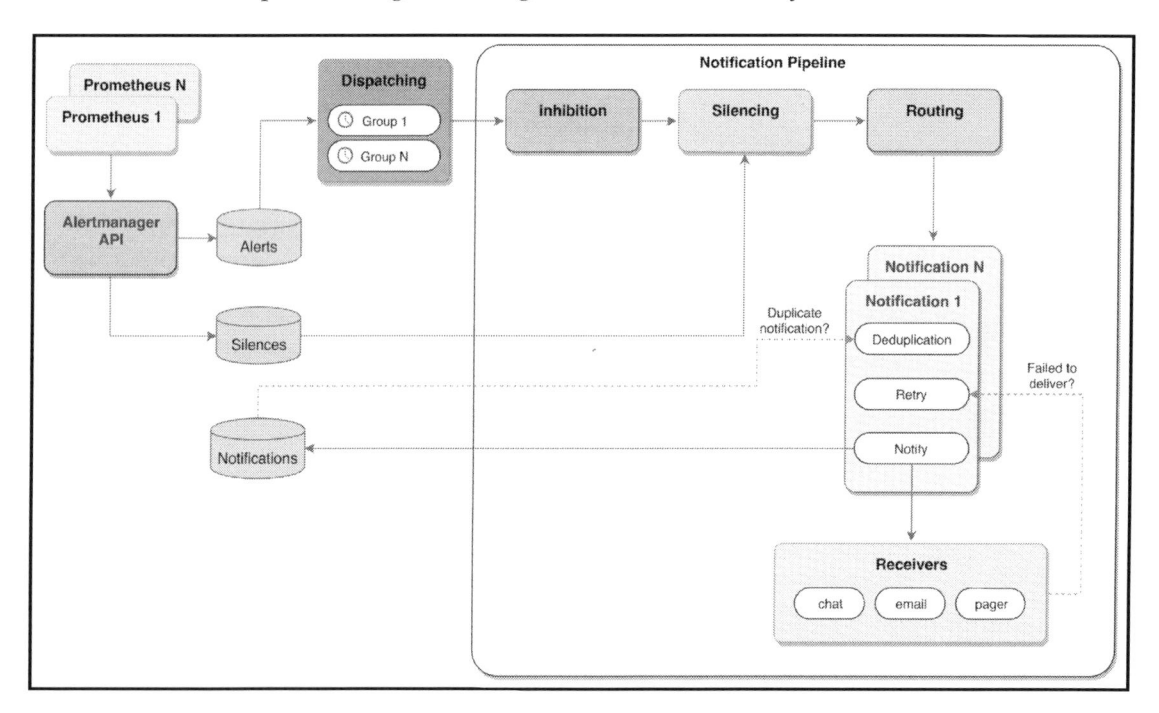

Figure 11.2: Notification pipeline overview

The preceding diagram has a lot to unpack, so we're going to go through each of these steps in the next few sections. Knowing how the alert pipeline works will help you understand the various configuration options, how to troubleshoot missing alerts, and generally take full advantage of everything Alertmanager has to offer.

Dispatching alert groups to the notification pipeline

Whenever an alerting rule is triggered, Prometheus will send an alert in the form of a JSON payload to the Alertmanager API, and it will keep sending updates at each evaluation interval of that rule or every minute (configurable through the `--rules.alert.resend-delay` flag), whichever is longer. When alerts are received by Alertmanager, they go through the dispatching step, where they will be grouped using one or more of the alert labels, such as `alertname`. We're going to discuss more about this in the *Alertmanager configuration* section, later in this chapter. This allows you to sort alerts into categories, which can reduce the number of notifications that are sent as multiple alerts in the same category and are grouped together in a single notification, which will then trigger the notification pipeline:

Figure 11.3: Alertmanager interface grouping alerts by alertname

When running multiple Prometheus instances with the same configuration (a common setup when pursuing high availability/redundancy), alerting rules for the same condition won't necessarily trigger at the exact same time. Alertmanager accounts for this situation by having a configurable time interval. It will wait before doing anything else so that similar alerts can be grouped together and thus avoid sending multiple notifications for a single type of problem.

This grouping is done in parallel across all the user-specified criteria. Each group will then trigger the notification pipeline, which we'll cover next.

Inhibition

A good example to help us understand what alert inhibition is imagining a server rack and what happens if the top-of-rack switch fails. In this scenario, all the servers and services in that rack will start triggering alerts because they suddenly became unreachable. To avoid this problem, we can use the alert for the top-of-rack switch which, if triggered, will prevent the notifications for all the other alerts in that rack from going out. This helps the operator become more focused on the real problem and avoid a flood of unactionable alerts.

So, in a nutshell, inhibition allows you to map dependencies between alerts, and therefore prevents notifications for dependent alerts from going any further in the notification pipeline. This is set up in the Alertmanager configuration file, which means inhibitions require a service reload if changed.

If the alert is not matched in the inhibition phase, it will then step into the silencer step.

Silencing

Silencing is a common concept in monitoring/alerting systems; it is how you can avoid alert notifications from going out in a time-capped way. It is often used to disable notifications during maintenance windows, or to temporarily suppress alerts of lower importance during incidents. Alertmanager takes this concept and supercharges it by taking advantage of the fact that alerts coming in usually have one or more differentiating labels: ones from the originating alerting rule expression, the alertname, the alert's label fields, from `alert_relabel_configs`, as well as the ones from the Prometheus `external_labels`. This means that any one of these labels (or a combination of them) can be used to temporarily disable notifications through either direct matching or through regular expression matching:

New Silence

Start
2019-04-03T21:25:38.137Z

Duration
2h

End
2019-04-03T23:25:38.137Z

Matchers Alerts affected by this silence.

Name
alertname

Value
NodeExporterDown

☐ Regex

+

Creator
Marvin

Comment
Creating an example of a silence.

Affected alerts: 2

21:09:00, 2019-04-03 (UTC) + Info ⎘ Source

| alertname=NodeExporterDown | base_instance=alertmanager02 | dc=dc1 | instance=alertmanager02:9100 | job=node | prom=prom1 | severity=slack |

21:09:00, 2019-04-03 (UTC) + Info ⎘ Source

| alertname=NodeExporterDown | base_instance=alertmanager01 | dc=dc1 | instance=alertmanager01:9100 | job=node | prom=prom1 | severity=slack |

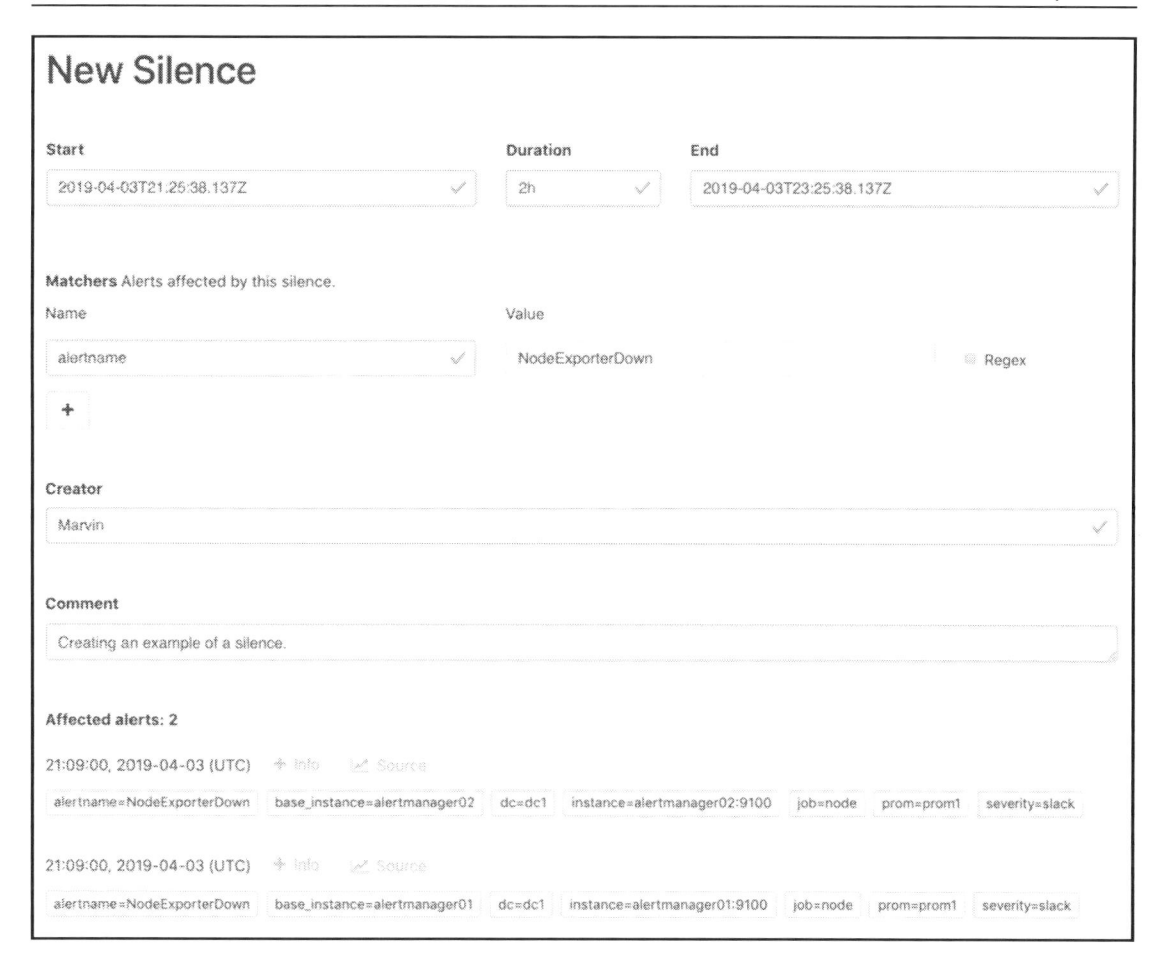

Figure 11.4: Creating a silence matching alertname=NodeExporterDown

> **TIP**: You should be careful with regex matching as you can accidentally silence more than you expect. The Alertmanager web UI can help prevent this as it shows a preview of which firing alerts will be suppressed when creating new silences.

Silences are defined at runtime. They can be set using the Alertmanager web interface, `amtool` (the Alertmanager command-line interface, which is going to be presented shortly), or directly through the API. They can be set while an alert is firing, such as during an incident, or in advance so that planned maintenance doesn't spam the people doing on-call. It is not supposed to be a permanent solution for a firing alert, only a temporary measure; this is why creating a silence requires that you set an expiration date for it, and why the web UI only recognizes durations up to days.

Since the silencing step comes after inhibition, if you silence an alert that is triggering inhibition rules, it will continue to inhibit other alerts.

If the alert didn't match any of the silences, it will go through to the next step in the notification pipeline, which is the routing phase.

Routing

When an alert batch reaches this phase, Alertmanager needs to decide where to send it. Since the most common use cases are to have different people interested in different alerts, different notification methods for different alert severities, or even a combination of both, this step enables just that by way of a routing tree. It is composed of routes (if any), each of which specifies a match criteria for one or more labels and a receiver, and a root node, which defines a catch-all receiver in case none of the sub-routes have a match for the alert groups passing through. Sub-routes can have their own routes, making it a multi-level tree. Matching is done in the order the routes are declared in, going into defined sub-routes first when a route matches, and the highest depth match will define which receiver will be used. This will become clearer when we put it in action using the Alertmanager configuration.

Receivers and notifiers work similar in concept to address book contacts. Receivers are named contacts that can have one or more notifiers, which are like contact information. Alertmanager supports a lot of different notifiers that generally fall into one of the following categories: email, chat (Slack, WeChat, HipChat), and page (PagerDuty, Opsgenie, VictorOps, Pushover). Additionally, it also supports the Webhook notifier, which is a generic integration point that can be used to support every other notification system that is not built into Alertmanager.

After this routing stage connects an alert batch with a receiver, Alertmanager will then run a notification job for each notifier specified in that receiver. This job takes care of deduplicating, sending, and retrying notifications. For deduplication, it first checks the notification log (which will be discussed later in this chapter) to make sure that this particular notification hasn't been sent yet; if is already there, no further action is taken. Next, it will try to send the notification and, if it succeeds, that will be recorded in the notification log. If a notification fails to go through (for example, API error, connection timeout, and so on), the job will try again.

Now that we know the basics of the notification pipeline, let's have a look at what happens when there are several Alertmanager instances and how the alert state is shared among them.

Alertmanager clustering

The overview of the notification pipeline does not touch on the high availability component of Alertmanager. The way high availability is achieved is by relying on gossip (based on the HashiCorp memberlist, `https://github.com/hashicorp/memberlist`), instead of using a consensus-based protocol; this means there's no real reason for choosing an odd number of instances in a cluster. Using gossip, the cluster shares the **notification log (nflog)** between all Alertmanager instances, which in turn will be aware of the collective state of the cluster regarding notifications. In the case of a network partition, there will be notifications being sent from each side of the partition, since logically it's better to receive more notifications than failing to notify altogether.

As we now know, inhibition is set at the configuration file level, so it should be the same across all Alertmanager instances. However, silences also need to be gossiped across the cluster as they are set at runtime on a single Alertmanager instance. This is a good way to validate if the clustering is working as expected – confirming whether the configured silences show up in all instances.

The Alertmanager `/#/status` page shows the status of the gossip cluster, along with the known peers. You can check out this endpoint in our test environment by opening up, for example, `http://192.168.42.11:9093/#/status`:

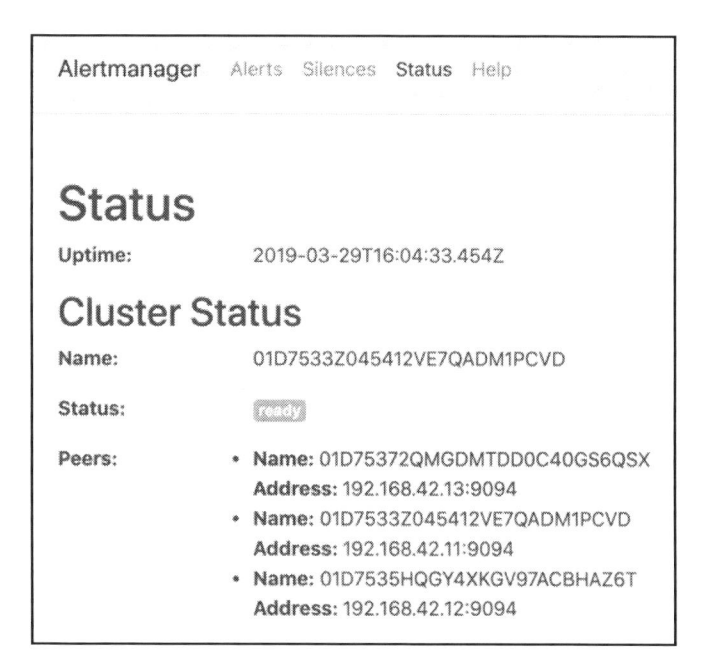

Figure 11.5: Alertmanager cluster status

The way clustering works in Alertmanager is like so: every Prometheus instance sends alerts to all the Alertmanager instances they know about. Those instances, assuming they are all in the same HA cluster, order themselves, and the one that becomes the first will handle alert notifications. That instance will distribute the notification log through gossip, which will list the notifications that were successfully sent. Each of the remaining Alertmanager instances will have an increasing amount of delay, according to their respective position in the ordering, to wait for the notification log updates. Alerts in the notification log will not be sent again by these instances – if the notification log does not state that a given notification was taken care of by the time the gossip delay is done, then the second Alertmanager will take care of it, and so on:

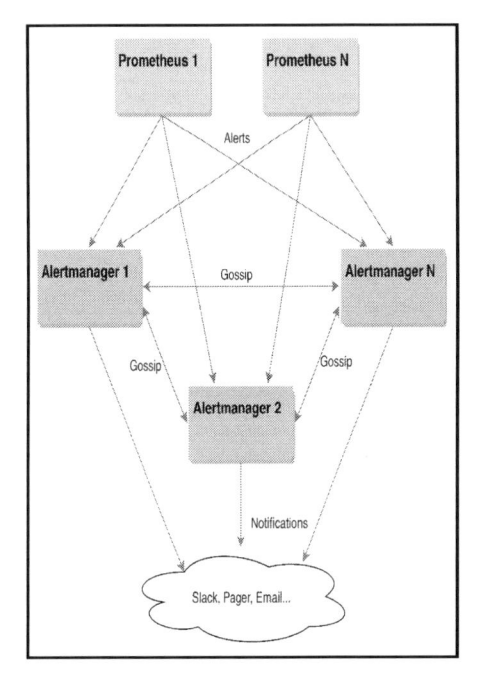

Figure 11.6: Alertmanager clustering overview

> **TIP**: Prometheus instances talk directly to all Alertmanager instances, since the cluster members will take care of deduplication between themselves. This means that no load balancers should be placed between Prometheus and Alertmanager.

Alertmanager clustering assumes that every instance is running with the same configuration file. However, failing to do so should only impact its ability to deduplicate notifications.

Alertmanager configuration

In Chapter 9, *Defining Alerting and Recording Rules*, we discussed how Prometheus generates and pushes out alerts. Having also made clear the distinction between an alert and a notification, it's now time to use Alertmanager to handle the alerts that are sent by Prometheus and turn them into notifications.

Next, we'll go through the configuration required on Prometheus, along with the configuration options available in Alertmanager, so that we have notifications going out from our monitoring stack.

Prometheus configuration

There are a couple of configurations that need to be done in Prometheus so that we can start using Alertmanager. The first thing to do is configure the external labels, which are labels that are added to time series data (if it doesn't already have them) when communicating with external systems, including but not limited to Alertmanager. These are labels that uniquely identify the origin of the metrics, such as region, datacenter, or environment. As a rule of thumb, if you feel tempted to add the same label name/value to every single scrape and recording rule, that label would probably make more sense as an external label as it introduces no dimension to metrics locally in your Prometheus instance, but would most likely be useful in higher-level systems (such as with federation or long-term metric storage), as we will also see in the next few chapters. As we'll see in the following example, external labels are configured inside the top-level global key in the Prometheus main configuration file.

The second thing to do is configure Prometheus so that it can send alerts to Alertmanager. As we discussed previously, in the *Alertmanager clustering* section, Prometheus instances are required so that you can find out about and send alerts to all the Alertmanager cluster members individually. This configuration is set on the Prometheus configuration file in a top-level section called alerting. An example of this configuration can be found in our test environment, as follows:

```
vagrant@prometheus:~$ cat /etc/prometheus/prometheus.yml
global:
  external_labels:
    dc: dc1
alerting:
  alertmanagers:
  - static_configs:
    - targets:
      - alertmanager01:9093
```

```
      - alertmanager02:9093
      - alertmanager03:9093
...
```

In this `alerting` section, we can also use `alert_relabel_configs`, which has the same configuration syntax as `relabel_configs` and `metric_relabel_configs`, as explained in Chapter 5, *Running a Prometheus Server*, but in this case, it applies only to alerts going out. Using relabeling here can be useful to prevent certain alerts from reaching Alertmanager altogether, altering or dropping labels to ease grouping, or even adding alert-specific labels that for, some reason, don't make sense in `external_labels`. Since `alert_relabel_configs` is run right before we send out alerts, external labels are present in those alerts and as such are available for manipulation. Here's an example of preventing alerts with a label called `environment` and matching value of `development` from being pushed to Alertmanager:

```
alert_relabel_configs:
- source_labels: [environment]
  regex: development
  action: drop
```

While the preceding example illustrates how to drop alerts, it should not be used as a permanent solution as the better solution would probably be to not create these alerts at all.

Next, we're going to go through the Alertmanager configuration file, and its main areas, and point out some useful information that will help you get started with it.

Configuration file overview

Alertmanager is configured through a single configuration file, and can reload it at runtime without restarting the same way Prometheus does: either sending a `SIGHUP` to the process or sending an HTTP POST request to the `/-/reload` endpoint. Such as Prometheus, a malformed configuration will not be applied – an error message will be logged and the `alertmanager_config_last_reload_successful` metric that's found in its `/metrics` endpoint will be set to `0`.

The configuration file is divided into five top-level sections: `global`, `route`, `inhibit_rules`, `receivers`, and `templates`. In the following sections, we'll be exploring each one of them.

global

The global section gathers all the configuration options that are valid in other sections of the file, and act as default settings for those options. Since those parameters may be overridden in other sections, using them is a good way to keep the configuration file as clean as possible, avoiding repetition. Among all the available parameters in this section, most of them are related to credentials and tokens as notifiers. There's a noteworthy one called `resolve_timeout`. Prometheus will send alerts that are produced by triggering alerting rules on every evaluation interval, updating the `EndTime` field in JSON payload. When those get resolved, it notify Alertmanager of those resolutions by updating the `EndTime`. If, for some reason, an alert stops getting updated periodically (for example, the Prometheus instance sending that alert crashed and is still in the recovery process), Alertmanager will use the last received `EndTime` to resolve the alert.

The `resolve_timeout` configuration is used to resolve alerts created by non-Prometheus systems, that don't use `EndTime`. To be clear, this is not a setting you should be changing as it pertains to the Prometheus-Alertmanager alert protocol; it is being explained here for completeness.

As an example, the global section of the Alertmanager configuration in our test environment looks as follows:

```
global:
  smtp_smarthost: 'mail.example.com:25'
  smtp_from: 'example@example.com'
...
```

This example configuration sets the default email `smarthost` and the `from` address for every receiver that uses the email (SMTP) notifier.

route

This is ostensibly the most important configuration section of Alertmanager. In this section, we will define how to group alerts based on their labels (`group_by`), how long to wait for new alerts before sending additional notifications (`group_interval`), and how long to repeat them (`repeat_interval`), but most importantly, which receivers should be triggered for each alert batch (`receiver`). Since each route can have its own child routes, this forms a routing tree. The top-level route can't have any matching rules as it works like a catch-all for any alert that doesn't match any of its sub-routes. Each setting, except `continue`, made on a route is carried over to its child routes in a cascading fashion. Although the default behavior is to stop searching for a receiver when the most specific match possible is found, it is possible to set `continue` to `true`, making the matching process keep going, thereby allowing you to trigger multiple receivers.

You can find the following example route configuration in our test environment:

```
route:
  receiver: operations
  group_by: ['alertname', 'job']
  group_wait: 30s
  group_interval: 5m
  repeat_interval: 4h

  routes:
  - match_re:
      job: (checkoutService|paymentService)
    receiver: yellow-squad-email
    routes:
    - match:
        severity: pager
      receiver: yellow-squad-pager
...
```

The main route in the preceding example does the following:

- Defines the `operations` receiver as the default route when no other sub-routes match
- Groups incoming alerts by `alertname` and `job`
- Waits 30 seconds for more alerts to arrive before sending the first notification to reduce the number of notifications for the same problem
- Waits five minutes before sending additional notifications when new alerts are added to a batch
- Resends a notification every four hours for each alert batch with the currently firing alerts

Additionally, it sets a sub-route for alerts whose `job` label matches either `checkoutService` or `paymentService` with its own receiver, `yellow-squad-email`. That sub-route, in turn, define its own child route that, if the severity label matches `pager`, should use the `yellow-squad-pager receiver` instead.

> **TIP:** The official Prometheus website offers a routing tree editor and visualizer at https://prometheus.io/webtools/alerting/routing-tree-editor/.

[284]

The `group_by` clause can also take the sole value of `...`, which will signal Alertmanager to not do any grouping for incoming alerts. This is very rarely used, as the purpose of grouping is to tune down the number of notifications so that the signal-to-noise ratio is high. One possible usage of this feature is to send every alert as-is to another system where alerts get processed.

inhibit_rules

In this section, we will add rules to inhibit alerts. The way this works is by matching source alerts and muting target ones by using matchers on both. The only requirement is that the labels on the target and source match in terms of both label name and value, for example:

```
inhibit_rules:
  - source_match:
      job: 'icmp'
    target_match_re:
      alertname: (AlertmanagerDown|NodeExporterDown)
    equal: ['base_instance']
```

In this example, we can read the following: if there's an alert with the `job` label set to `icmp`, mute all other alerts with an `alertname` that matches `AlertmanagerDown` or `NodeExporterDown` when `base_instance` is the same across all matched alerts. In other words, if the instance that is running Alertmanager and Node Exporter is down, skip sending alerts about those services and just send the one about the instance itself, allowing the operator to focus on the real problem.

> **TIP**: If any label in the equal clause does not exist in both source and target alerts, it will be considered matched and thus inhibition will be enabled.

> If an alert matches both source and target in the inhibit rule definition, that alert will not be inhibited – this is to prevent an alert from inhibiting itself.

Understanding and Extending Alertmanager

We can see the interface of Alertmanager when this occurs in the following screenshot:

![Alertmanager interface screenshot showing InstanceDown and deadmanswitch alerts]

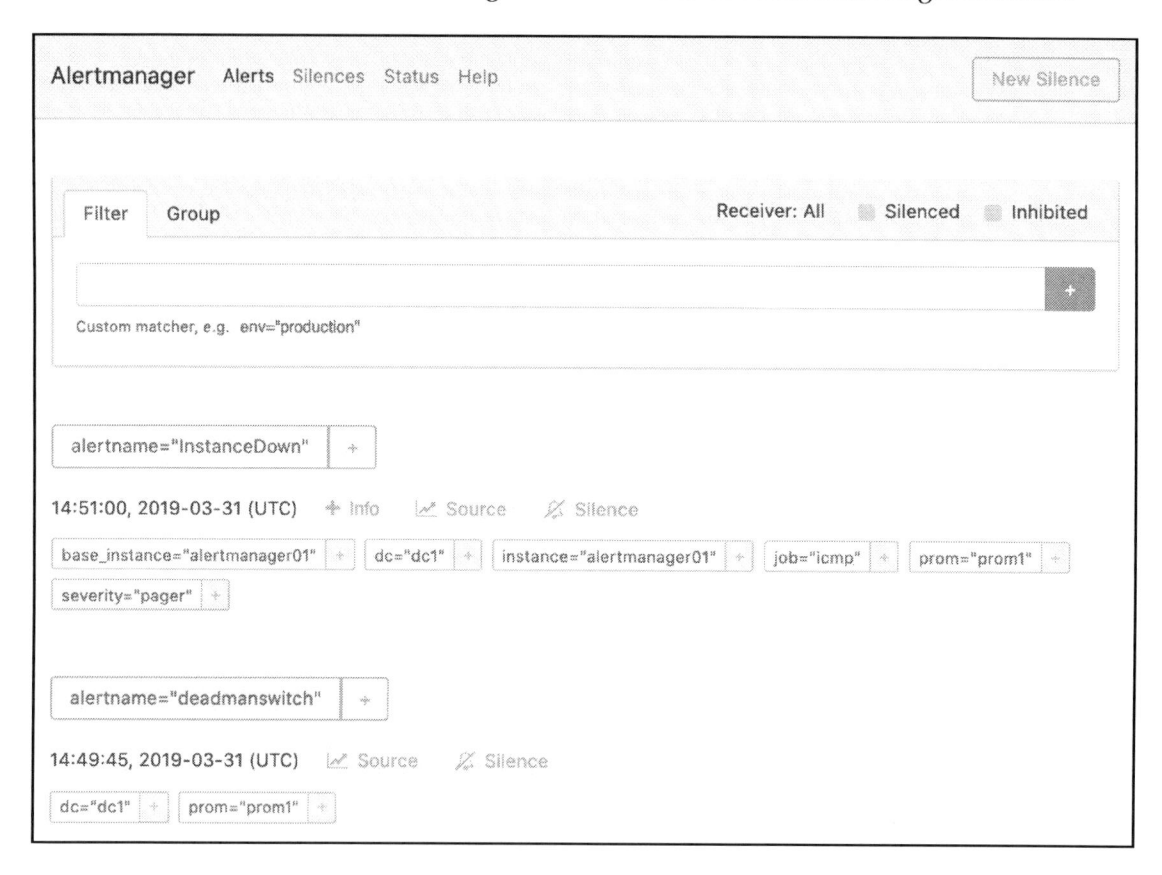

Figure 11.7: Alertmanager interface showing only firing notifications

In the following screenshot, we can see all the inhibited alerts that weren't present in the preceding screenshot by selecting the **Inhibited** option in the top-right corner:

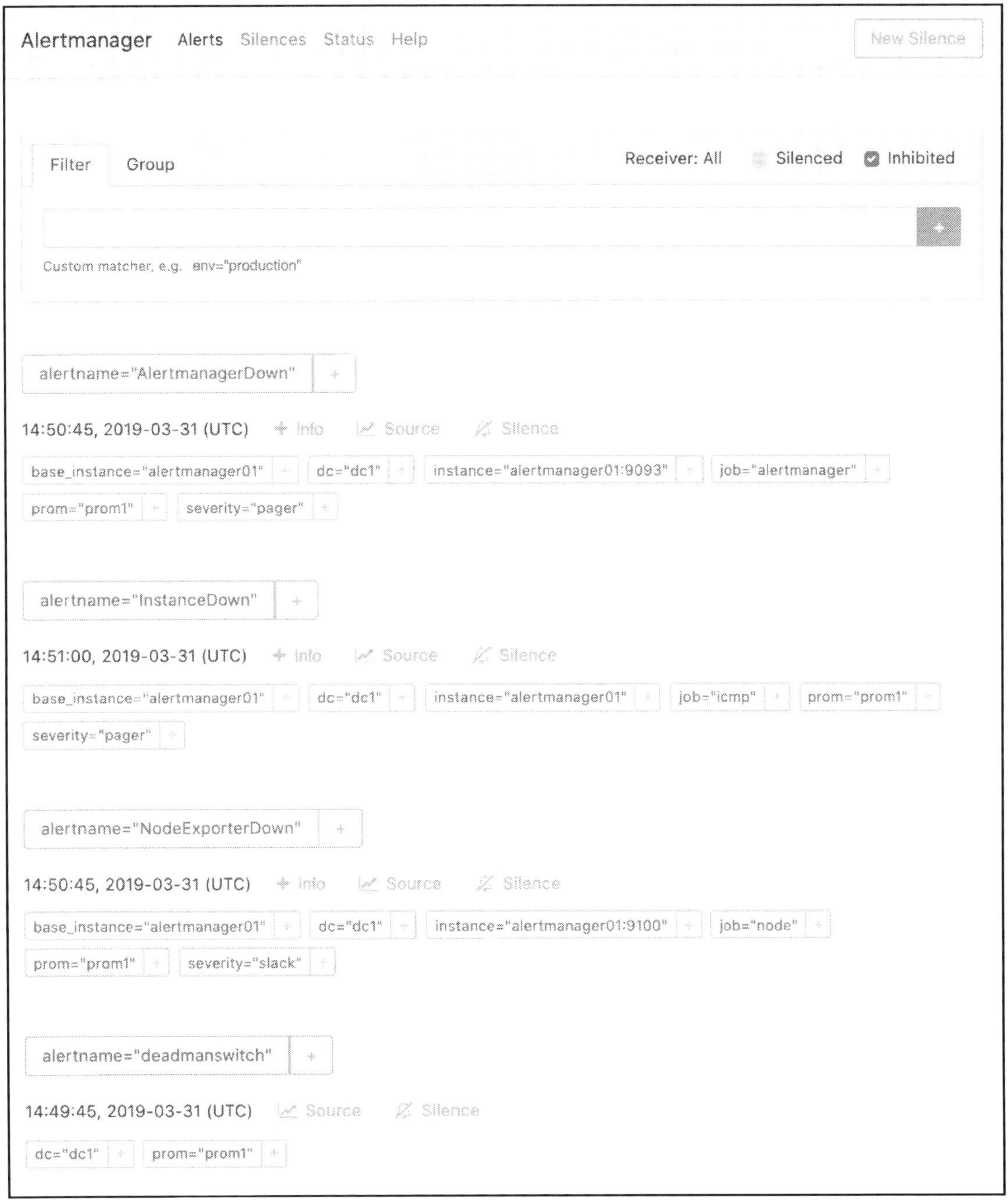

Figure 11.8: Alertmanager interface showing notifications, including the inhibited ones

The Alertmanager interface allows you to have a bird's-eye view of all alerts, not only the ones that are active but also the ones that are inhibited. The default is to not show inhibited alerts in order to reduce visual clutter; however, as we can see in the preceding screenshot, you can easily enable showing them by selecting the **Inhibited** checkmark in the top-right corner of the **Filter/Group** box.

receiver

When a route is matched, it will invoke a receiver. A receiver contains notifiers, which we'll be exploring more deeply in the following sections. Basically, the receiver is a named configuration for the available integrations.

In our test environment, we can find an example of a receiver by using the Webhook notifier, as follows:

```
route:
  receiver: operations
...
receivers:
- name: 'operations'
  webhook_configs:
  - url: 'http://127.0.0.1:5001'
...
```

The top-level route, also known as the catch-all or fallback route, will trigger the receiver named `operations` when incoming alerts aren't matched in other sub-routes. The `operations` receiver is configured using a single notifier, which is the Webhook notifier. This means that alerts that go to this receiver are sent to the URL specified in the `url` configuration key. The Webhook notifier will be further dissected later in this chapter.

templates

This section is where a list of paths that point to custom notification templates for the several notifiers that are available can be defined. Similar to other file path configurations in Prometheus, each path definition allows globing on the last component and can be defined as follows:

```
templates:
  - /etc/alertmanager/templates/*.tmpl
```

We'll be using this section to define our custom templates in the *Customizing your alert notifications* section.

The amtool command-line tool

Similar to `promtool`, `amtool` is an easy-to-use command-line tool backed by the Alertmanager HTTP API. Besides being useful for validating the correctness of the Alertmanager configuration file, it also allows you to query the server for currently triggering alerts, and to execute actions such as silencing alerts or creating new ones. The `amtool` sub-commands are split into four groups – `alert`, `silence`, `check-config`, and `config` – and we'll provide an overview of each one using the test environment.

To follow the examples in this section, make sure that you connect to one of the Alertmanager instances. Since they are clustered, any one of them will do, for example:

```
vagrant ssh alertmanager02
```

After logging in, you can run `amtool` as the default user, as no administrative permissions are required to interact with the Alertmanager API. Additionally, you can even use `amtool` to connect to any of the Alertmanager instances, not just the local instance, as most commands that interact with the HTTP API require that you specify the instance URL.

alert

This sub-command allows you to query the Alertmanager cluster for currently firing alerts, which can be achieved as follows:

```
vagrant@alertmanager02:~$ amtool alert --alertmanager.url http://alertmanager02:9093
Alertname      Starts At             Summary
deadmanswitch  2019-03-31 14:49:45 UTC
InstanceDown   2019-03-31 15:48:30 UTC
```

> The `alert` sub-command default action is `query`. The equivalent command to the previous example would be `amtool alert query --alertmanager.url http://alertmanager02:9093`.

Another feature this sub-command has is the ability to create alerts on demand. This can come in useful for testing purposes. For example, let's create a new alert named `ExampleAlert` with the label `example="amtool"`:

```
vagrant@alertmanager02:~$ amtool alert add alertname="ExampleAlert" example="amtool" --alertmanager.url http://alertmanager02:9093
```

The `add` action expects one label name/value pair per command argument, as we can see in the preceding code. This action will also consider the first argument since the alertname has no label name. An alert can be created without a name if we omit the `alertname` label, which can cause some weirdness in both `amtool` and the Alertmanager web UI, so some caution regarding this is advised.

We can check that it was added correctly by waiting a bit (the defined `group_wait` in the test environment is 30 seconds) and then querying the current alerts again:

```
vagrant@alertmanager02:~$ amtool alert --alertmanager.url
http://alertmanager02:9093
Alertname     Starts At              Summary
deadmanswitch 2019-03-31 14:49:45 UTC
InstanceDown  2019-03-31 15:48:30 UTC
ExampleAlert  2019-03-31 15:55:00 UTC
```

This action also allows you to specify other alert fields, such as end time, generator URL, and annotations. You can consult the `add` action command-line interface (arguments and options) by using the `help` flag:

```
vagrant@alertmanager01:~$ amtool alert add --help
```

Keep in mind that this newly created alert will be considered resolved after five minutes of inactivity (the default value for `resolve_timeout`), so be sure to add new instances of this alert (by running the `add` action) to keep it going if you need more time to test.

We'll be using this new alert next as a target for silencing.

silence

With this sub-command, we can manage silences. First, we can try to query the available silences in the cluster by using the following instruction:

```
vagrant@alertmanager02:~$ amtool silence --alertmanager.url
http://alertmanager02:9093
ID Matchers Ends At Created By Comment
```

> The `silence` sub-command default action is `query`. The equivalent command to the previous example would be `amtool silence query --alertmanager.url http://alertmanager02:9093`.

[290]

As we can see, no silence is currently being enforced. Let's create a new one for the previous generated alert by matching its label, `example="amtool"`, and checking the silences again:

```
vagrant@alertmanager02:~$ amtool silence add 'example="amtool"' --comment "ups" --alertmanager.url http://alertmanager02:9093
1afa55af-306a-408e-b85c-95b1af0d7169

vagrant@alertmanager02:~$ amtool silence --alertmanager.url http://alertmanager02:9093
ID Matchers Ends At Created By Comment
1afa55af-306a-408e-b85c-95b1af0d7169 example=amtool 2019-03-31 16:58:08 UTC vagrant ups
```

We can now see that the new silence has been added. To verify that it's already in effect, we can use the `alert` sub-command and check that the `ExampleAlert` has disappeared from the list of current alerts:

```
vagrant@alertmanager02:~$ amtool alert --alertmanager.url http://alertmanager02:9093
Alertname Starts At Summary
deadmanswitch 2019-03-31 14:49:45 UTC
InstanceDown 2019-03-31 15:48:30 UTC
```

Let's remove the silence we just created by using the `expire` action. For this, we need the silence identifier, which can be seen in the `ID` column when we listed the current silences:

```
vagrant@alertmanager02:~$ amtool silence expire 1afa55af-306a-408e-b85c-95b1af0d7169 --alertmanager.url http://alertmanager02:9093

vagrant@alertmanager02:~$ amtool silence --alertmanager.url http://alertmanager02:9093
ID Matchers Ends At Created By Comment
```

If we query the list of current alerts again, we will see our `ExampleAlert` there again.

These are the most common use cases for the silence feature. There are also other actions available, such as batch importing of silences (useful when migrating to a new cluster) or even updating an existing one if you ever so desire. As usual, the `--help` flag will provide you with guidance on how to use these actions.

Understanding and Extending Alertmanager

check-config

This is probably the most useful feature of `amtool`: the ability to validate the syntax and schema of our Alertmanager configuration file and referenced template files. You can test the `check-config` sub-command by following this example:

```
vagrant@alertmanager02:~$ amtool check-config
/etc/alertmanager/alertmanager.yml
Checking '/etc/alertmanager/alertmanager.yml'  SUCCESS
Found:
 - global config
 - route
 - 1 inhibit rules
 - 8 receivers
 - 1 templates
  SUCCESS
```

This type of validation is quite easy to automate and should be done after any configuration change, but before reloading the Alertmanager instance, thereby preventing most types of configuration issues.

config

With the `config` sub-command, we can consult the internal configuration of a running Alertmanager instance, which includes all configurable fields, even ones not explicitly listed in the configuration file. You can check this by issuing the following command:

```
vagrant@alertmanager02:~$ amtool config --alertmanager.url
http://alertmanager02:9093
global:
  resolve_timeout: 5m
  http_config: {}
  smtp_from: example@example.com
  smtp_hello: localhost
  smtp_smarthost: example.com:25
  smtp_require_tls: true
  slack_api_url: <secret>
...
```

Configuration fields that were not specified in the configuration file will show with their default values, and fields that deal with secrets (such as passwords and tokens) will be automatically redacted.

> The `config` sub-command default action is shown. The equivalent command to the previous example would be `amtool config show --alertmanager.url http://alertmanager02:9093`.

The next sub-command action, `routes`, generates a text visualization of the configured routing tree. This command can be run against a running Alertmanager instance or a local configuration file. The syntax and output is as follows:

```
vagrant@alertmanager02:~$ amtool config routes --alertmanager.url http://alertmanager02:9093
Routing tree:
.
└── default-route  receiver: operations
    ├── {job=~"^(?:^(?:(checkoutService|paymentService))$)$"}  receiver: yellow-squad-email
    │   └── {severity="pager"}  receiver: yellow-squad-pager
    ├── {job="firewall"}  receiver: purple-squad-email
    │   ├── {severity="slack"}  receiver: purple-squad-slack
    │   └── {severity="pager"}  receiver: purple-squad-pager
    └── {alertname=~"^(?:^(?:(AlertmanagerDown|NodeExporterDown))$)$"}  receiver: violet-squad-slack
        └── {severity="pager"}  receiver: violet-squad-pager
```

You can even validate the routing tree by providing labels to the `routes test` action and checking which route would be triggered. We can see this in action in the following example, where we're validating whether the triggered receiver is in fact `yellow-squad-email` when an alert comes in with the `job="checkoutService"` label:

```
vagrant@alertmanager02:~$ amtool config routes test 'job="checkoutService"' --config.file /etc/alertmanager/alertmanager.yml
yellow-squad-email
```

Having this command-line tool around can help you streamline the development of complex routing rules and validate produced configurations without even needing an Alertmanager instance running locally.

Kubernetes Prometheus Operator and Alertmanager

In Chapter 5, *Running a Prometheus Server*, we had the opportunity to experiment with the Prometheus Operator. Since Alertmanager is a fundamental component of the Prometheus stack, the Operator is also able to manage its instances. Besides taking care of an Alertmanager cluster, the Operator is also responsible for managing the configuration of recording and alerting rules.

To provide some insight into how to use the Operator to manage an Alertmanager cluster, we will provide, as an example, a full setup for you to try out. The Kubernetes manifests for getting Alertmanager and Prometheus up and running in our Kubernetes test environment can be found, relative to the repository root path, at the following path:

```
cd ./chapter11/provision/kubernetes/
```

The following steps will ensure that a new Kubernetes environment with all the required software has been provisioned so that we can then focus on the Alertmanager component:

1. Validate that no other Kubernetes environment is running:

    ```
    minikube status
    minikube delete
    ```

2. Start an empty Kubernetes environment:

    ```
    minikube start \
      --cpus=2 \
      --memory=3072 \
      --kubernetes-version="v1.14.0" \
      --vm-driver=virtualbox
    ```

3. Add the Prometheus Operator components and follow its deployment:

    ```
    kubectl apply -f ./bootstrap/
    ```

    ```
    kubectl rollout status deployment/prometheus-operator -n monitoring
    ```

4. Add the new Prometheus cluster, ensuring that it's successful:

    ```
    kubectl apply -f ./prometheus/
    ```

    ```
    kubectl rollout status statefulset/prometheus-k8s -n monitoring
    ```

5. Add all the targets to Prometheus and list them:

   `kubectl apply -f ./services/`

   `kubectl get servicemonitors --all-namespaces`

After the Kubernetes test environment is running, we can proceed with Alertmanager-specific configurations. Similar to the virtual machine-based test environment, we'll require the provisioning of not only Alertmanager itself, but also the alerting rules for Prometheus.

For the Alertmanager configuration, since we might want to add sensitive information such as email credentials or a pager token, we are going to use a Kubernetes secret. This also implies that there should be a ServiceAccount for accessing that secret.

We can create the ServiceAccount by applying the following manifest:

`kubectl apply -f ./alertmanager/alertmanager-serviceaccount.yaml`

Since we're using a secret, the Alertmanager configuration needs to be encoded into base64. A minimal configuration is provided and can be deployed by issuing the following command:

`kubectl apply -f ./alertmanager/alertmanager-configuration.yaml`

For reference, the minimal configuration that is encoded in the secret is the following:

```
global:

route:
  receiver: "null"
  group_by:
    - job
  group_interval: 3m
  repeat_interval: 3h
  routes:
    - match:
        alertname: deadmanswitch
      receiver: "null"

receivers:
  - name: "null"
```

Now, we can proceed with the deployment and get the Operator to do the heavy lifting for us. It will abstract the creation of a StatefulSet and get the cluster up and running. For this, we're required to apply the following manifest:

```
kubectl apply -f ./alertmanager/alertmanager-deploy.yaml
```

The important bit of the previous manifest can be seen in the following snippet:

```
...
kind: Alertmanager
...
spec:
  baseImage: quay.io/prometheus/alertmanager
...
  replicas: 3
...
```

We can follow the state of the deployment by issuing the following instruction:

```
kubectl rollout status statefulset/alertmanager-k8s -n monitoring
```

To ensure that the Prometheus instances can collect metrics from the newly created Alertmanagers, we'll add a new Service and ServiceMonitor. For this, we need to apply the following manifests:

```
kubectl apply -f ./alertmanager/alertmanager-service.yaml
```

```
kubectl apply -f ./alertmanager/alertmanager-servicemonitor.yaml
```

It's now time to add the alerting rules. To do this, you're just required to apply the following manifest:

```
kubectl apply -f ./alertmanager/alerting-rules.yaml
```

If you open the previous manifest, you will see several rules. The following snippet illustrates the first one:

```
...
kind: PrometheusRule
...
spec:
  groups:
  - name: exporter-down
    rules:
    - alert: AlertmanagerDown
      annotations:
        description: Alertmanager is not being scraped.
        troubleshooting:
```

```
https://github.com/kubernetes-monitoring/kubernetes-mixin/blob/master/runbo
ok.md
      expr: |
        absent(up{job="alertmanager-service",namespace="monitoring"} == 1)
      for: 5m
      labels:
        severity: page
...
```

These rules will be added to the Prometheus instances, and the Operator will take care of reloading their configuration without causing any downtime of the service.

Finally, you can access the web interface of Prometheus and Alertmanager and validate all the configurations you've made so far by issuing the following instructions, which will open a couple of browser tabs:

```
minikube service alertmanager-service -n monitoring

minikube service prometheus-service -n monitoring
```

When you're finished testing, you can delete this Kubernetes-based environment by issuing the following command:

```
minikube delete
```

This setup gives you a quick overview of how to integrate Alertmanager with Prometheus on Kubernetes. Once again, the Prometheus Operator abstracts most of the complexity and allows you to focus on what matters most.

Common Alertmanager notification integrations

Users and/or organizations have different requirements regarding notification methods; some might be using HipChat as a means of communication, while others rely on email, on-call usually demands a pager system such as PagerDuty or VictorOps, and so on. Thankfully, Alertmanager provides several integration options out of the box and covers most of the notification needs you might have. If not, there's always the Webhook notifier, which allows integration with custom notification methods. Next, we'll be exploring the most common integrations and how to configure them, as well as providing basic examples to get you started.

Understanding and Extending Alertmanager

Something to keep in mind when considering integrating with chat systems is that they're designed for humans, and the use of a ticketing system is advised when thinking about low-priority alerting. When the process of creating alerts is easy and self-service, managing them can quickly get out of control. Tickets ensure accountability: Some of the major advantages of using tickets over alerting on chat channels is that they allow tracking, prioritization, and proper follow-up to ensure that the alerted problem does not happen again. This method also implicitly ensures ownership of notifications and stops the usual *who's the owner of this alert?* question from arising. Ownership empowers service maintainers to curate the alerts they receive and, as a side effect, also helps reduce alert fatigue.

> **TIP:** If you happen to be using JIRA for task tracking, there's a custom integration that relies on the Webhook notifier called JIRAlert, available at `https://github.com/free/jiralert`.

There is a configuration key that is common to all notifiers, and is called `send_resolved`. It takes a Boolean (true or false) and declares whether a notification should be sent when an alert is resolved. This is enabled by default for PagerDuty, Opsgenie, VictorOps, Pushover, and the Webhook integration, but disabled for the remaining notifiers, and is the main reason why you should prevent unnecessary spam.

Email

Email is the standard communication method in most organizations, so it should be no surprise that it's supported by Alertmanager. Configuration-wise, it's quite straightforward to set up; however, since Alertmanager doesn't send emails directly, it needs to use an actual email relay. Let's use a real-world example that should be helpful for quick tests and low-budget setups, which is using the SMTP of an email provider (in this case, Google's Gmail):

```
global:
  smtp_smarthost: 'smtp.gmail.com:587'
  smtp_from: 'alertmanager@example.com'
  smtp_auth_username: 'alertmanager@example.com'
  smtp_auth_identity: 'alertmanager@example.com'
  smtp_auth_password: '<generated_token>'

route:
  receiver: 'default'

receivers:
- name: 'default'
```

```
        email_configs:
        - to: 'squad@example.com'
```

In this particular example, since it's a bad idea in terms of online security to use your main Gmail password directly, you'll need an account with two-factor authentication enabled, and then generate an app password to use in the `smtp_auth_password` field.

> **TIP**
> You can find out how to generate app passwords for a Gmail account on the *Sign in using App Passwords* support page, located at `https://support.google.com/accounts/answer/185833`.

Chat

At the time of writing, there are integrations for three chat services: Slack, WeChat, and HipChat. The following example represents the configuration for the Slack integration; later in this chapter, we'll provide a more in-depth customization overview for this kind of integration:

```
global:
  slack_api_url: 'https://hooks.slack.com/services/TOKEN'

route:
  receiver: 'default'

receivers:
- name: 'default'
  slack_configs:
  - channel: '#alerting'
```

The `slack_api_url` should point to a *Slack Incoming Webhooks* URL. You can find out more by going to their documentation about this subject at `https://api.slack.com/incoming-webhooks`. Since `slack_configs` is a list, you can specify multiple channels on a single receiver.

Pager

Being on-call is generally synonymous with carrying a pager, physical or otherwise. Alertmanager, at the time of writing, supports four pager-style service integrations: PagerDuty, Opsgenie, VictorOps, and Pushover. The configuration for each of these services is fairly simple to get started, as they mostly revolve around API URLs and authentication tokens. However, they also support deeper levels of customization, such as adding images, and links, and configuring service-specific fields, such as severity. These advanced configuration options are described in Alertmanager's official documentation, so they won't be replicated here. The following example demonstrates a basic configuration for PagerDuty:

```
global:
  pagerduty_url: 'https://events.pagerduty.com/v2/enqueue'

route:
  receiver: 'default'

receivers:
- name: 'default'
  pagerduty_configs:
  - service_key: 'PAGERDUTYSQUADTOKENEXAMPLE'
```

Just like in the previous notifier, since the `pagerduty_configs` configuration is a list, you can trigger multiple service routes in a single receiver. You can find out more about PagerDuty's integration with Alertmanager here: https://www.pagerduty.com/docs/guides/prometheus-integration-guide/.

Webhook

The Webhook integration opens up a world of possibilities for custom integrations. This feature allows Alertmanager to issue an HTTP POST request with the JSON payload of the notification to an endpoint of your choosing. Keep in mind that the URL is not templateable and the destination endpoint must be designed to handle the JSON payload. It can be used, for example, to push all notifications into a logging system such as Elasticsearch so that you can perform reporting and statistical analysis of the alert being generated. If your team uses IRC, this could also be a solution to integrate with it. One last example is the alertdump tool we've created for this book. It was previously used in Chapter 9, *Defining Alerting and Recording Rules*, to show what Prometheus sends out when alerting rules trigger, but it can also be used to demonstrate the notification payloads being sent by Alertmanager.

A simple configuration can be seen in the following code:

```
global:

route:
  receiver: 'default'

receivers:
- name: 'default'
  webhook_configs:
  - url: 'http://127.0.0.1:5001'
```

This configuration will send every alert that's received by Alertmanager as-is to alertdump, which in turn will then append the payload to a log file named after the host that alertdump is running on. This log file is located in a path that's accessible both inside each virtual machine from our test environment (`/vagrant/cache/alertmanager*.log`), and outside it (`./cache/alertmanager*.log`, relative to the repository root).

null

This is not a notifier per se, but a pattern commonly used to drop notifications. The way it's configured is by specifying a receiver without a notifier, which causes the notification to be dropped. The following example ensures that no notification will ever be sent:

```
global:

route:
  receiver: 'null'

receivers:
- name: 'null'
```

This is sometimes useful for demonstrative purposes, but not much else; alerts that aren't supposed to trigger notifications should be dropped at their source and not in Alertmanager, with the exception of alerts being used as source for inhibitions.

> Something to always keep an eye on is the `alertmanager_notifications_failed_total` Alertmanager metric, as it tracks all the failed attempts to deliver notifications per integration.

Now that we know the basics of Alertmanager notifiers, we can proceed to learn how to customize alert notifications so that the most important information is properly surfaced.

Customizing your alert notifications

For each of the available integrations, Alertmanager already includes built-in templates for their notifications. However, these can be tailored to the specific needs of the user and/or organization. Similar to the alerting rule annotations we explored in Chapter 9, *Defining Alerting and Recording Rules*, alert notifications are templated using the Go templating language. Let's use the Slack integration as an example and understand how the messages are constructed so that they are tailored to your needs.

Default message format

To have an idea of what a notification without any customization looks like, we're going to use a very simple example. Take the following alerting rule, which we defined in our Prometheus instance:

```
- alert: deadmanswitch
  expr: vector(42)
```

As soon as this alert starts firing, an alert payload will be sent to Alertmanager. The following snippet demonstrates the payload being sent. Note the labels that are present, which include the `alertname` and the `external_labels` from the Prometheus instance:

```
{
    "labels": {
        "alertname": "deadmanswitch",
        "dc": "dc1"
    },
    "annotations": {},
    "startsAt": "2019-04-02T19:11:30.04754979Z",
    "endsAt": "2019-04-02T19:14:30.04754979Z",
    "generatorURL":
"http://prometheus:9090/graph?g0.expr=vector%2842%29&g0.tab=1"
}
```

On the Alertmanager side, we will have this minimal configuration, just so that we can send a Slack notification (substituting `TOKEN` with an actual Slack token):

```
global:
  slack_api_url: 'https://hooks.slack.com/services/TOKEN'

route:
  receiver: 'default'

receivers:
```

```
  - name: 'default'
    slack_configs:
    - channel: '#alerting'
```

The end result would be a Slack message like the following:

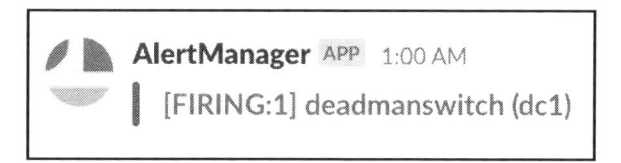

Figure 11.9: Slack default notification format

As we can see, the default notification format has a lot of information in it. But the question remains, *how was this generated*? To answer this question, we can have a look into the runtime configuration of the `default` receiver that was generated from our basic Alertmanager configuration, which the following snippet illustrates:

```
...
receivers:
- name: default
  slack_configs:
  - send_resolved: false
    http_config: {}
    api_url: <secret>
    channel: '#alerting'
    username: '{{ template "slack.default.username" . }}'
    color: '{{ if eq .Status "firing" }}danger{{ else }}good{{ end }}'
    title: '{{ template "slack.default.title" . }}'
    title_link: '{{ template "slack.default.titlelink" . }}'
    pretext: '{{ template "slack.default.pretext" . }}'
    text: '{{ template "slack.default.text" . }}'
...
```

> **TIP**: The Alertmanager runtime configuration can be inspected by using `amtool config` or by accessing the `/#/status` endpoint of an Alertmanager web interface.

As we can see, each of the customizable fields is configured using Go templating. We will take the `username` field to exemplify how the username in the Slack message gets generated, as it's a fairly straightforward template. All other templates being used follow the same logic, with varying levels of complexity.

The default templates used by Alertmanager can't be consulted locally on the test environment instances, as they are compiled and shipped within the Alertmanager binary. However, we can consult all the default templates for all the notification integrations provided by Alertmanager by looking at the `templates/default.tmpl` file in the Alertmanager code base. At the time of writing, the current version is 0.16.2 so, for convenience, we're linking to the referenced file here: https://github.com/prometheus/alertmanager/blob/v0.16.2/template/default.tmpl.

If we have a look at the `default.tmpl` file, we will find the definition of the `slack.default.username` template:

```
{{ define "slack.default.username" }}{{ template "__alertmanager" . }}{{ end }}
```

As we can see, the template uses another template as its definition. So, if we look for the definition of the `__alertmanager` template, we'll find the following:

```
{{ define "__alertmanager" }}AlertManager{{ end }}
```

Now, you understand how the name `AlertManager` appears in the Slack notification. The tracing of each of the other templates is left as an exercise for you. In the next section, we're going to learn how to create our own templates, and then use them to customize our alert notifications.

Creating a new template

Before we dive into creating a template, we must first realize what kind of data structures are sent to the notification templates. The following table depicts the available variables that can be used:

Variable	Description
`Alerts`	A list of Alert structures, each one with its own Status, Labels, Annotations, StartsAt, EndsAt, and GeneratorURL
`CommonAnnotations`	The annotations that are common to all alerts
`CommonLabels`	The labels that are common to all alerts
`ExternalURL`	The URL for the Alertmanager that sent the alert
`GroupLabels`	The labels that are used in the grouping of alerts
`receiver`	The receiver that will handle the notification
`status`	This will be firing as long as there's an alert in that state, or it will become resolved

> A comprehensive reference of all available data structures and functions is available at https://prometheus.io/docs/alerting/notifications/.

The best way to demonstrate how we can build a template is to provide an example. We've built the following template, which is available in the test environment, exactly with that intent. We will explain each part in detail while stripping the Alertmanager configurations down to only the important bits.

The end result we aim to create can be seen in the following screenshot:

Figure 11.10: Example Slack notification template

Now, we're going to dissect the example configuration, which will generate notifications that look like the ones shown in the preceding screenshot:

```
route:
  group_by: [alertname, job]
  receiver: null
  routes:
  - match:
      severity: slack
    receiver: purple-squad-slack
```

Understanding and Extending Alertmanager

For the sake of this example, we're grouping alerts by `alertname` and `job`. This is important, because it will influence the `CommonAnnotations` and `CommonLabels`, as we'll see soon:

```
receivers:
- name: null
- name: purple-squad-slack
  slack_configs:
  - api_url: 'https://hooks.slack.com/TOKEN'
    channel: '#alerting'
    title: >
      [{{ .Alerts | len }}x ALERT{{ if gt (len .Alerts.Firing) 1 }}S{{end}}] {{ .CommonLabels.alertname }}
```

As we saw in the previous table, `.Alerts` is a list of all the alerts, so we want the length (`len`) of that list to create a title for the message, starting with the number of firing alerts. Note the `if` clause, which ensures the use of plurals if there is more than one alert. Finally, since we're grouping the alerts by `alertname`, we print the `alertname` after the square brackets:

```
    text: >
      :link: <{{ .CommonAnnotations.troubleshooting }}/{{ .CommonLabels.alertname }}|Troubleshooting Guide>
```

For the message body, we want to generate a link to the troubleshooting guide for this particular kind of alert. Our alerts are sending an annotation called `troubleshooting` with a base URL. If we rely on convention so that the guide name matches the alertname, we can easily generate the link using both fields.

To provide more context about the firing alerts, we'll add all the available alert labels to the message. To achieve this goal, we must go through every alert in the list:

```
      {{ range .Alerts }}
```

For every alert, we'll print the description that's available as an annotation of that alert:

```
        *Description:* {{ .Annotations.description }}
        *Details:*
```

We'll print each alert label/value pair as well. To do that, we'll be ranging over the result of `SortedPairs`, which returns a sorted list of label/value pairs:

```
{{- range .Labels.SortedPairs }}
```

> **TIP**
> The `{{-` code trims all trailing whitespace from the preceding text. More information on this is available at https://tip.golang.org/pkg/text/template/#hdr-Text_and_spaces.

We're using the severity label as a routing key in order to choose the notifier (pager, email, or slack), so we don't want to expose it in the alert message. We can do that by adding an `if` clause so that we don't print that particular label/value:

```
       {{- if ne .Name "severity"}}
     • *{{ .Name }}:* `{{ .Value }}`
       {{- end}}
{{- end }}
{{ end }}
```

And that's it. You can even make this more manageable by getting this template out of the Alertmanager configuration and into its own template file. We've done this in the test environment, where the receiver configuration is just the following:

```
- name: violet-squad-slack
  slack_configs:
  - channel: '#violet-squad-alerts'
    title: '{{ template "slack.example.title" . }}'
    text: '{{ template "slack.example.text" . }}'
```

All the template definitions are available in the Alertmanager instances at the following path:

```
/etc/alertmanager/templates/example.tmpl
```

> **TIP:** Notification templating is quite hard to understand and build at first. Luckily, a tool was created by Julius Volz, one of Prometheus' co-founders and core maintainer, that allows you to quickly iterate on Slack notification templates. It's by far the best way to understand how they work and how to generate them. You can find it at `https://juliusv.com/promslack/`.

Who watches the Watchmen?

The monitoring system is a critical component of any infrastructure. We rely on it to keep watch over everything – from servers and network devices to services and applications – and expect to be notified whenever there's a problem. However, when the problem is on the monitoring stack itself, or even on a notification provider so that alerts are generated but don't reach us, how will we, as operators, know?

Guaranteeing that the monitoring stack is up and running, and that notifications are able to reach recipients, is a commonly overlooked task. In this section, we will go into what can be done to mitigate risk factors and improve overall confidence in the monitoring system.

Meta-monitoring and cross-monitoring

In broad terms, you can't have your monitoring system monitor itself; if the system suffers a serious failure, it won't be able to send a notification about it. Although it is common practice to have Prometheus scrape itself (you may see this in most tutorials), you obviously can't rely on it to alert on itself. This is where meta-monitoring comes in: it is the process by which the monitoring system is monitored.

The first option you should consider to mitigate this issue is to have a set of Prometheus instances that monitor every other Prometheus instance in their datacenter/zone. Since Prometheus generates relatively few metrics of its own, this would translate to a fairly light scrape job for the ones doing the meta-monitoring; they wouldn't even need to be solely dedicated to this:

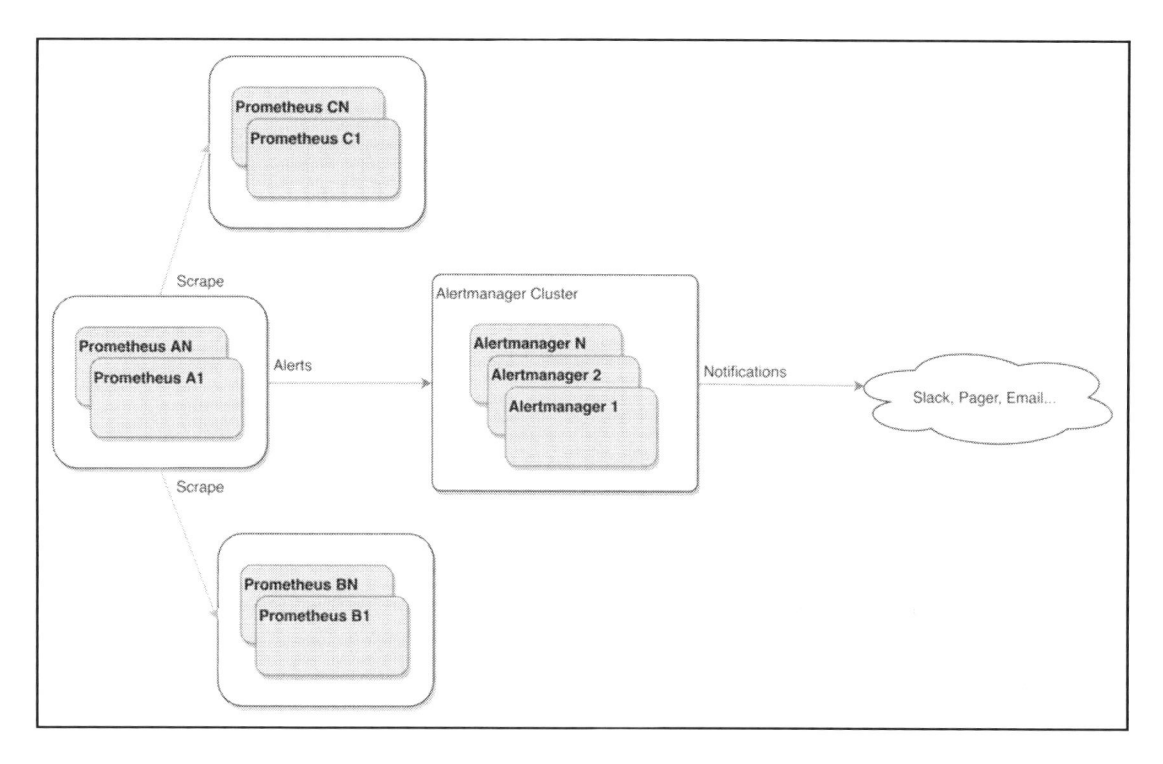

Figure 11.11: Meta-monitoring – Prometheus group monitoring every other group

However, you may be wondering how this set of instances would be monitored. We could keep adding progressively higher-level instances to do meta-monitoring in a hierarchical fashion – at the datacenter level, then at the regional level, then at the global level – but we would still be left with a set of servers that aren't being monitored.

Understanding and Extending Alertmanager

A complementary technique to mitigate this shortcoming is known as cross-monitoring. This method involves having Prometheus instances on the same responsibility level monitor as their peers. This way, every instance will have at least one other Prometheus watching over it and generating alerts if it fails:

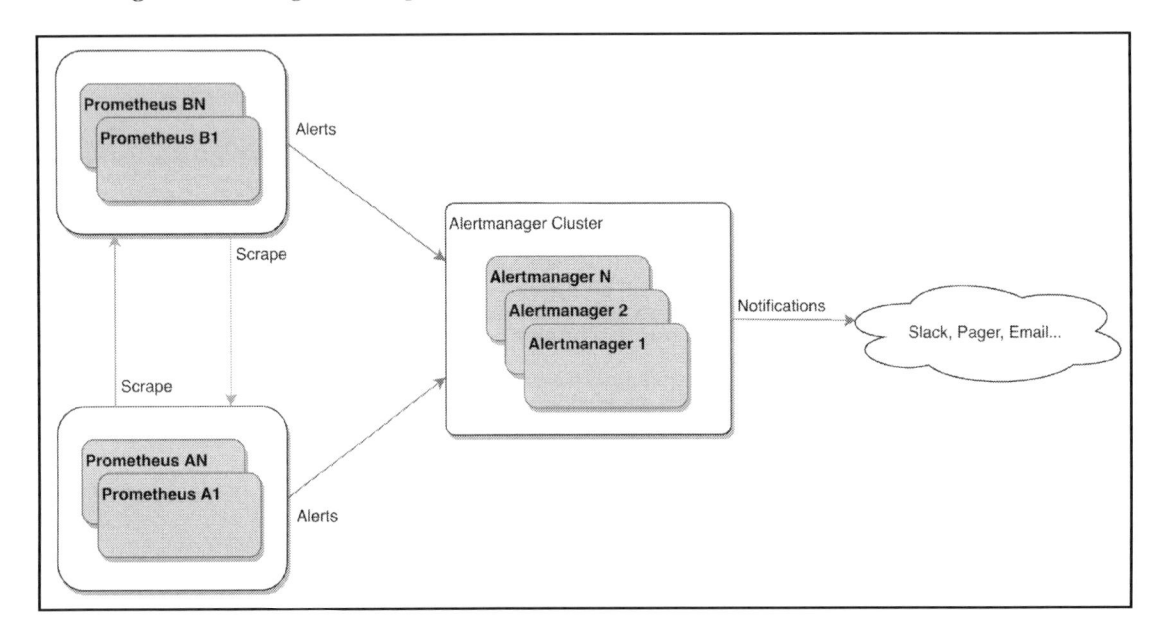

Figure 11.12: Prometheus groups monitoring themselves

But what happens if the problem is in the Alertmanager cluster? Or if external connectivity prevents notifications from reaching the notification provider? Or even if the notification provider itself is suffering an outage? In the next section, we'll provide possible solutions to these questions.

Dead man's switch alerts

Imagine that you have a set of Prometheus instances using an Alertmanager cluster for alerting. For some reason, a network partition happens between these two services. Even though each Prometheus instance detects that it can no longer reach any of the Alertmanager instances, they will have no means to send notifications.

In this situation, no alerts about the issue will ever be sent:

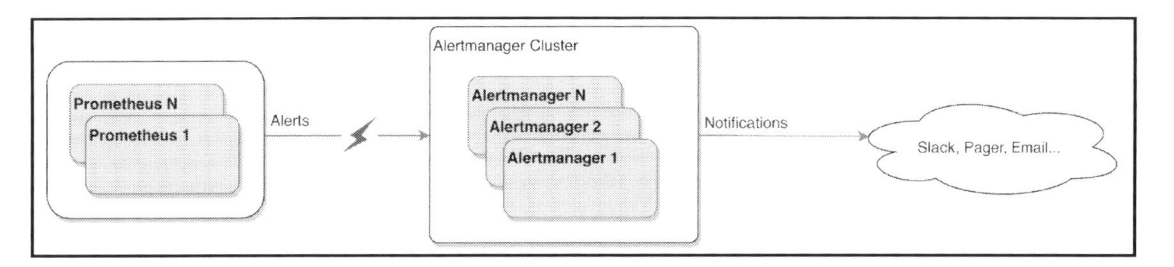

Figure 11.13: Network partition between Prometheus and Alertmanager

The original concept of a dead man's switch refers to a mechanism that activates if it stops being triggered/pressed. This concept has been adopted in the software world in several ways; for our purpose, we can achieve this by creating an alert that should always be firing – thereby constantly sending out notifications – and then checking if it ever stops. This way, we can exercise the full alerting path from Prometheus, through Alertmanager, to the notification provider, and ultimately to the recipient of the notifications so that we can ensure end-to-end connectivity and service availability. This, of course, goes against all we know about alert fatigue and we wouldn't want to be constantly receiving pages or emails about an always-firing alert. You can implement your own custom service implementing watchdog timers, but then you'll be in a situation where you need to monitor that as well. Ideally, you should leverage a third party so that you mitigate the risk of this service suffering from the same outage that is preventing notifications from going out.

For this, there's a service built around the dead man's switch type of alert, and it's curiously named *Dead Man's Snitch* (`deadmanssnitch.com`). This is a third-party provider, outside of your infrastructure, that's responsible for receiving your always-firing notification via email or Webhook and will, in turn, issue a page, Slack message, or Webhook if that notification stops being received for more than a configurable amount of time. This setup mitigates the problems we presented previously – even if the entire datacenter goes up in flames, you'll still be paged!

> The full configuration guide for integrating Dead Man's Snitch with VictorOps and PagerDuty can be found at `https://help.victorops.com/knowledge-base/victorops-dead-mans-snitch-integration/` and `https://www.pagerduty.com/docs/guides/dead-mans-snitch-integration-guide/`, respectively.

Summary

In this chapter, we dived into the alerting component of the Prometheus stack, Alertmanager. This service was designed with availability in mind, and we had the opportunity to understand how it works, from generating better notifications to avoiding being flooded by useless ones. The notification pipeline is a very good starting point to grok the inner workings of Alertmanager, but we also went through its configuration, while providing examples to better solidify that knowledge. We were introduced to `amtool` and all the features it provides, such as adding, removing, and updating silences directly from the command line.

Alertmanager has several notification integrations available and we went through all of them, so you can pick and choose the ones you're interested in. Since we all want better notifications, we delved into how to customize the default notifications, using Slack as our example. A hard problem to solve is how to monitor the monitoring system; in this chapter, we learned how to make sure we are alerted when notifications aren't getting out.

In an always-changing infrastructure, it's not trivial to keep track of what's running and where it's running. In the next chapter, we'll be providing more insight into how Prometheus tackles service discovery and automates these tasks for you.

Questions

1. What happens to the notifications if there's a network partition between Alertmanager instances in the same cluster?
2. Can an alert trigger multiple receivers? What is required for that to happen?
3. What's the difference between `group_interval` and `repeat_interval`?
4. What happens if an alert does not match any of the configured routes?
5. If the notification provider you require is not supported natively by Alertmanager, how can you use it?
6. When writing custom notifications, how are `CommonLabels` and `CommonAnnotations` populated?
7. What can you do to ensure that the full alerting path is working from end to end?

Further reading

- **Official Alertmanager page**: `https://prometheus.io/docs/alerting/alertmanager/`
- **Alertmanager notification guide**: `https://prometheus.io/docs/alerting/notifications/`
- **Alertmanager configuration specifics**: `https://prometheus.io/docs/alerting/configuration/`

Section 4: Scalability, Resilience, and Maintainability

Great things start off small but after a while, they can quickly get out of hand. This section will go through several options for handling scale by setting targets dynamically, sharding and federation.

The following chapters are included in this section:

- `Chapter 12`, *Choosing the Right Service Discovery*
- `Chapter 13`, *Scaling and Federating Prometheus*
- `Chapter 14`, *Integrating Long-Term Storage with Prometheus*

12
Choosing the Right Service Discovery

When tackling dynamic environments, manually maintaining a file of targets is not an option. Service discovery handles the complexity of an ever-changing infrastructure for you, making sure that no service or host slips through the cracks. This chapter focuses on how to take advantage of Prometheus service discovery to decrease the infrastructure management toil regarding coping with constant change.

In brief, the following topics will be covered in this chapter:

- Test environment for this chapter
- Running through the service discovery options
- Using a built-in service discovery
- Building a custom service discovery

Test environment for this chapter

In this chapter, we'll be focusing on service discovery. For this, we'll be deploying two new instances to simulate a scenario where Prometheus generates targets dynamically using a popular service discovery software. This approach will allow us to not only expose the required configurations, but also validate how everything works together.

The setup we'll be using resembles the following diagram:

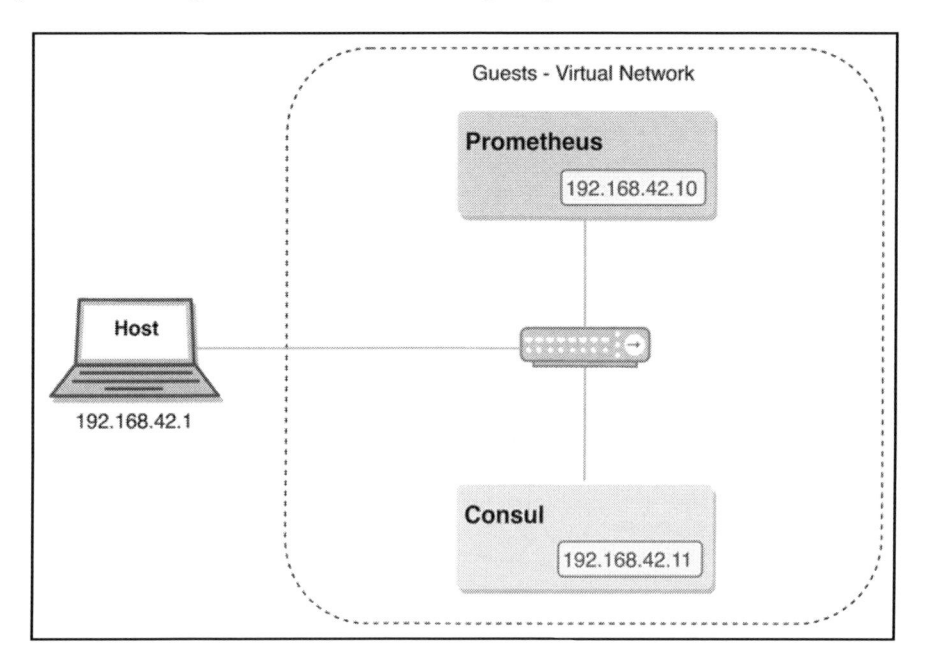

Figure 12.1: Test environment for this chapter

The usual deployment pattern for Consul is to have an agent running in client mode on every node in the infrastructure, which will then contact Consul instances running in server mode. Furthermore, client instances act as API proxies, so it is common practice for Prometheus Consul service discovery to be configured using the localhost. However, to make their different responsibilities clear, we've opted to just have a Prometheus instance in one VM and a Consul running as a server in another in our test environment.

In the next section, we will explain how to get the test environment up and running.

Deployment

To launch a new test environment, move into this chapter's path, relative to the repository root:

```
cd ./chapter12/
```

Ensure that no other test environments are running and spin up this chapter's environment:

```
vagrant global-status
vagrant up
```

You can validate the successful deployment of the test environment using the following command:

```
vagrant status
```

This will provide you with the following output:

```
Current machine states:

prometheus                running (virtualbox)
consul                    running (virtualbox)

This environment represents multiple VMs. The VMs are all listed above with
their current state. For more information about a specific VM, run `vagrant
status NAME`.
```

When the deployment tasks end, you'll be able to validate the following endpoints on your host machine using your favorite JavaScript-enabled web browser:

Service	Endpoint
Prometheus	http://192.168.42.10:9090
Consul	http://192.168.42.11:8500

You should be able to access the desired instance by using one of the following commands:

Instance	Command
Prometheus	vagrant ssh prometheus
Consul	vagrant ssh consul

Cleanup

When you've finish testing, just make sure you're inside `./chapter12/` and execute the following:

```
vagrant destroy -f
```

Don't worry too much – you can easily spin up the environment again if you need to.

Running through the service discovery options

Prometheus comes with several discovery integrations available out of the box. These cover most of the mainstream data sources for application and machine inventories, such as public and private cloud compute APIs, VM and container orchestration systems, standalone service registration and discovery systems, among others. For those discovery mechanisms that aren't directly supported by Prometheus, integration can be done through a generic discovery system using the filesystem and some glue code, as we'll see later in this chapter.

Every integration works in the same way – by setting all the discovered addresses as targets and their associated metadata as temporary labels (not persisted without some relabeling to keep them). For each discovered target, the `__address__` label is usually set to the service address and port. This is relevant, because this label is the one Prometheus uses to connect to the scrape target; the `instance` label defaults to use the `__address__` value when not explicitly defined, but it can be set to anything else that makes it easier to identify the target.

Metadata labels provided by service discovery integrations follow the pattern of `__meta_<service discovery name>_<key>`. There are also some labels added by Prometheus, such as `__scheme__` and `__metrics_path__`, which define whether the scrape should be performed using HTTP or HTTPS and the configured endpoint to scrape, respectively.

> **TIP**: URL parameters are not supported in the `metrics_path` scrape configuration. Instead, these need to be set in the `params` configuration. This is covered in `Chapter 5`, *Running a Prometheus Server*.

The following sections provide an overview of the available discovery options, and also present some examples on how to configure them, accompanied by screenshots of their generated data.

Cloud providers

With the rise of cloud infrastructure, it is increasingly common to have workloads running in these environments. This brings new sets of challenges; for example, ephemeral and highly dynamic infrastructure provisioning. The ease of scalability is also something to keep in mind: in the past, it might have taken months to negotiate, agree on support contracts, buy, deploy, and configure new hardware; nowadays, it's a matter of seconds to have a new fleet of instances up and running. With technology such as auto-scaling, which deploys new instances without you even knowing, change is hard to keep up with. To ease the burden of keeping tabs on this cloud-native dynamic infrastructure, Prometheus integrates out of the box with some of the big players in the **Infrastructure as a Service (IaaS)** market, such as Amazon Web Services, Microsoft Azure Cloud, Google Cloud Platform, OpenStack, and Joyent.

Using Amazon **Elastic Compute (EC2)** as an example for virtual machine discovery, the scrape job configuration can be as simple as the following:

```
scrape_configs:
  - job_name: ec2_sd
    ec2_sd_configs:
      - region: eu-west-1
        access_key: ACCESSKEYTOKEN
        secret_key: 'SecREtKeySecREtKey+SecREtKey+SecREtKey'
```

Choosing the Right Service Discovery

Other cloud providers will have different settings, but the logic is pretty much the same. Basically, we need to set the appropriate level of credentials to query the cloud provider API so that Prometheus discovery integration can consume all the data required to produce our targets, as well as their associated metadata. The following screenshot illustrates how a configuration similar to the one listed previously but with actual credentials translates into a set of targets:

Service Discovery

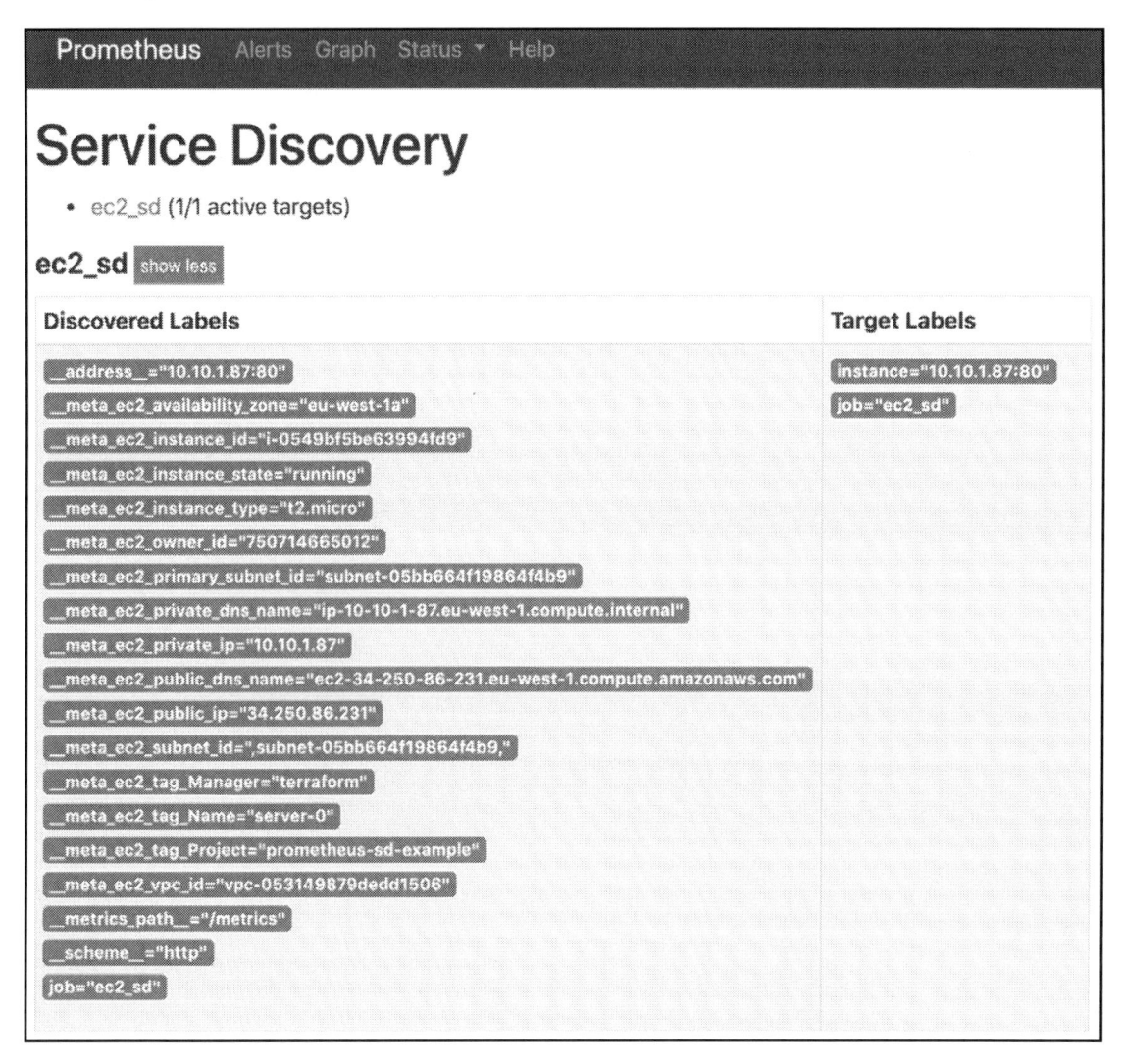

- ec2_sd (1/1 active targets)

ec2_sd show less

Discovered Labels	Target Labels
__address__="10.10.1.87:80"	instance="10.10.1.87:80"
__meta_ec2_availability_zone="eu-west-1a"	job="ec2_sd"
__meta_ec2_instance_id="i-0549bf5be63994fd9"	
__meta_ec2_instance_state="running"	
__meta_ec2_instance_type="t2.micro"	
__meta_ec2_owner_id="750714665012"	
__meta_ec2_primary_subnet_id="subnet-05bb664f19864f4b9"	
__meta_ec2_private_dns_name="ip-10-10-1-87.eu-west-1.compute.internal"	
__meta_ec2_private_ip="10.10.1.87"	
__meta_ec2_public_dns_name="ec2-34-250-86-231.eu-west-1.compute.amazonaws.com"	
__meta_ec2_public_ip="34.250.86.231"	
__meta_ec2_subnet_id=",subnet-05bb664f19864f4b9,"	
__meta_ec2_tag_Manager="terraform"	
__meta_ec2_tag_Name="server-0"	
__meta_ec2_tag_Project="prometheus-sd-example"	
__meta_ec2_vpc_id="vpc-053149879dedd1506"	
__metrics_path__="/metrics"	
__scheme__="http"	
job="ec2_sd"	

Figure 12.2: Prometheus /service-discovery endpoint depicting ec2_sd data

As we can see in the preceding screenshot, EC2 discovery attaches a fair amount of metadata labels to each discovered target. These are available during the relabeling phase so that you can use them to only scrape targets that are running, change scraping from the private IP address to the public one, or rename the instance label to a friendlier name.

This information, which is collected from the discovery process, is either periodically refreshed (the refresh interval is configurable at the service discovery level) or, automatically refreshed via watches, allowing Prometheus to become aware of targets being created or deleted.

Container orchestrators

Container orchestrators are a perfect place to extract what services are running and where, as it's their job to manage exactly that information. As such, the Prometheus discovery mechanism supports some of the most widely used container orchestration platforms, such as Kubernetes and Marathon, the container orchestration platform for Mesos and DC/OS. Since we've been using Kubernetes for most of our examples throughout this book, we're going to focus on this platform to explain how these types of systems work.

Like Prometheus, Kubernetes is a graduated project from the **Cloud Native Computing Foundation** (**CNCF**). While that doesn't mean one was created specifically to work with the other, the connection between the two is undeniable. Borg and Borgmon, Google's container orchestration and monitoring systems, are definitely the inspiration for Kubernetes and Prometheus, respectively. To tackle the monitoring of cloud-native platforms such as Kubernetes, where the rate of change is almost overwhelming, a special set of features is required. Prometheus fits these requirements, such as efficiently handling the ephemeral nature of containers.

The Prometheus service discovery integration retrieves all the required data via the Kubernetes API, keeping up to date with the state of the cluster. Due to the number of API objects available to query, the discovery configuration for Prometheus has the concept of role, which can be either `node`, `service`, `pod`, `endpoint`, or `ingress`. While explaining Kubernetes core concepts is out of scope for this book, we can quickly go through what each of these roles is used to discover: `node` is used to collect the actual nodes that form the Kubernetes cluster (for example, the VMs that run the kubelet agent), and thus can be used to monitor the cluster itself, as well as its underlying infrastructure; the service object in Kubernetes acts like a load balancer, and `service` will give you just that – a single endpoint per port of each configured service, whether it is backed by one or several application instances – and is only used for blackbox monitoring; `pod` is used to discover individual pods, independently of whether they belong to a service or not; `endpoint` discovers the main process in a pod that is backing a given service; and finally, `ingress`, similar to `service`, returns the external-facing load balancer for a set of application instances and thus should only be used for end-to-end probing.

The following code snippet provides an example of how to query pods, matching the ones that have a label, `app`, that matches the value `hey`:

```
scrape_configs:
  - job_name: kubernetes_sd
    kubernetes_sd_configs:
      - role: pod
    relabel_configs:
      - action: keep
        regex: hey
        source_labels:
          - __meta_kubernetes_pod_label_app
```

The preceding configuration generates the data depicted in the following screenshot, where we can see all the metadata that was gathered via the Kubernetes API:

Chapter 12

Service Discovery

- kubernetes_sd (1/16 active targets)

kubernetes_sd show less

Discovered Labels

- __address__="172.17.0.6:8000"
- __meta_kubernetes_namespace="default"
- __meta_kubernetes_pod_container_name="hey"
- __meta_kubernetes_pod_container_port_name="hey-port"
- __meta_kubernetes_pod_container_port_number="8000"
- __meta_kubernetes_pod_container_port_protocol="TCP"
- __meta_kubernetes_pod_controller_kind="ReplicaSet"
- __meta_kubernetes_pod_controller_name="hey-deployment-888ccddbc"
- __meta_kubernetes_pod_host_ip="10.0.2.15"
- __meta_kubernetes_pod_ip="172.17.0.6"
- __meta_kubernetes_pod_label_app="hey"
- __meta_kubernetes_pod_label_pod_template_hash="888ccddbc"
- __meta_kubernetes_pod_name="hey-deployment-888ccddbc-jxp6l"
- __meta_kubernetes_pod_node_name="minikube"
- __meta_kubernetes_pod_phase="Running"
- __meta_kubernetes_pod_ready="true"
- __meta_kubernetes_pod_uid="2a28df81-5bba-11e9-86a3-080027b799d7"
- __metrics_path__="/metrics"
- __scheme__="http"
- job="kubernetes_sd"

Target Labels

- instance="172.17.0.6:8000"
- job="kubernetes_sd"

Figure 12.3: Prometheus /service-discovery endpoint depicting kubernetes_sd data

This is a very small example of what can be done. Configurations that use the Kubernetes service discovery usually make extensive use of `relabel_configs` to filter targets, rewrite the `job` label to match container names, and to generally do clever auto-configuration based on conventions around Kubernetes annotations.

Service discovery systems

As the number of services grows, it becomes harder and harder to tie everything together – both in terms of services being correctly configured to contact each other, as well as operators having visibility of how the system is behaving. A common solution to these problems is to implement a service discovery system that acts as registry and that can then be consulted by software clients, as well as the monitoring system.

Prometheus integrates seamlessly with a few mainstream service discovery systems and currently supports Consul, Nerve, and ServerSets. Integrating directly with discovery services allows Prometheus to always have an up-to-date view of what is running and where, allowing service instances to be monitored automatically as soon as they are created, up until they are destroyed.

Consul is by far the most popular, as it provides a full set of features to implement service discovery and powerful yet simple-to-use command-line tools and APIs, and is easy to scale. Let's use the following for our example:

```
scrape_configs:
  - job_name: 'consul_sd'
    consul_sd_configs:
      - server: http://consul.prom.inet:8500
        datacenter: dc1
    relabel_configs:
      - source_labels: [__meta_consul_service]
        target_label: job
      - source_labels: [job, __address__]
        regex: "consul;([^:]+):.+"
        target_label: __address__
        replacement: ${1}:9107
```

The preceding example translates into the following screenshot, where we can see not only the generated labels, but also the definitions of the targets:

Chapter 12

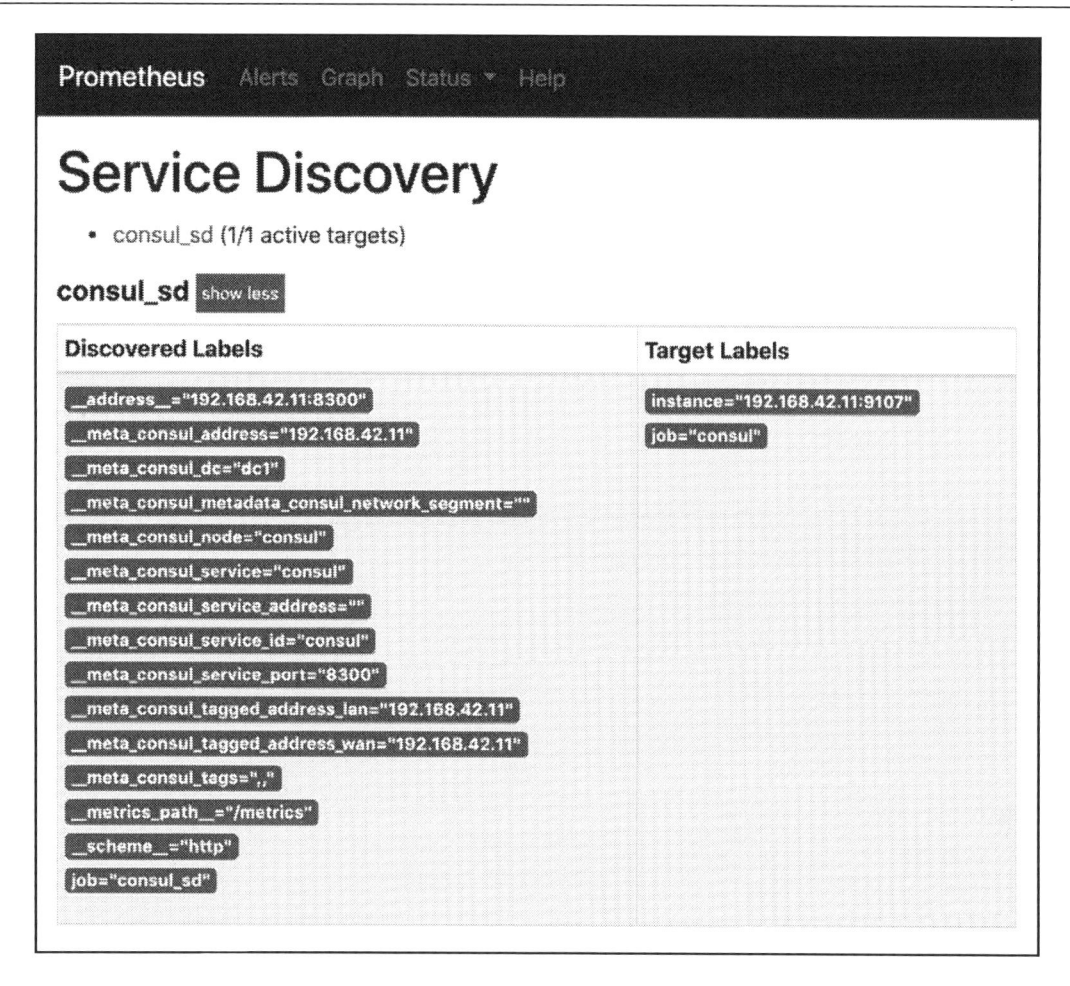

![Service Discovery screenshot showing consul_sd with 1/1 active targets. Discovered Labels include __address__="192.168.42.11:8300", __meta_consul_address="192.168.42.11", __meta_consul_dc="dc1", __meta_consul_metadata_consul_network_segment="", __meta_consul_node="consul", __meta_consul_service="consul", __meta_consul_service_address="", __meta_consul_service_id="consul", __meta_consul_service_port="8300", __meta_consul_tagged_address_lan="192.168.42.11", __meta_consul_tagged_address_wan="192.168.42.11", __meta_consul_tags=",,", __metrics_path__="/metrics", __scheme__="http", job="consul_sd". Target Labels: instance="192.168.42.11:9107", job="consul".]

Figure 12.4: Prometheus /service-discovery endpoint depicting consul_sd data

The preceding example shows a working configuration for gathering data from all the available services registered within a Consul server, using `relabel_configs` to rewrite the target's `job` label to be the service name instead of the `job_name`. This means that every application instance registered in Consul would be automatically picked up as a scrape target and correctly assigned the proper job name. Additionally, the last relabel rule changes the target port to `9107` when the service is named Consul, thus changing the target from Consul itself to an exporter for it.

DNS-based service discovery

This type of service discovery relies on DNS to gather data. It works by defining a list of domain names that will be queried regularly to obtain targets. The name servers that are used for resolution are looked up in `/etc/resolv.conf`. This discovery integration, besides supporting A and AAAA DNS records, is also able to query SRV records, which also provide the port for the service:

```
~$ dig SRV hey.service.example.inet
...
;; QUESTION SECTION:
;hey.service.example.inet.     IN      SRV

;; ANSWER SECTION:
hey.service.example.inet. 0 IN SRV 1 1 8080 server01.node.example.inet.

;; ADDITIONAL SECTION:
server01.node.example.inet. 0 IN A 192.168.42.11
server01.node.example.inet. 0 IN TXT "squad=purple"
...
```

We can see that, by querying the SRV record for `hey.service.example.inet` in this example, we get the service location `server01.node.example.inet` and port `8080`. We also get the A record with the service IP address and a TXT record with some metadata.

The following snippet illustrates a sample scrape configuration using this DNS service discovery integration. It does this by using the domain `hey.service.example.inet` from before:

```
scrape_configs:
  - job_name: 'dns_sd'
    dns_sd_configs:
      - names:
        - hey.service.example.inet
```

The returned SRV records will be converted into new targets. Prometheus doesn't support the advanced DNS-SD specified in RFC 6763, which allows metadata to be transmitted in associated TXT records (as seen in the `dig` command previously). This means that only the service address and port can be discovered using this method. We can see what discovered labels are available in the following screenshot:

Chapter 12

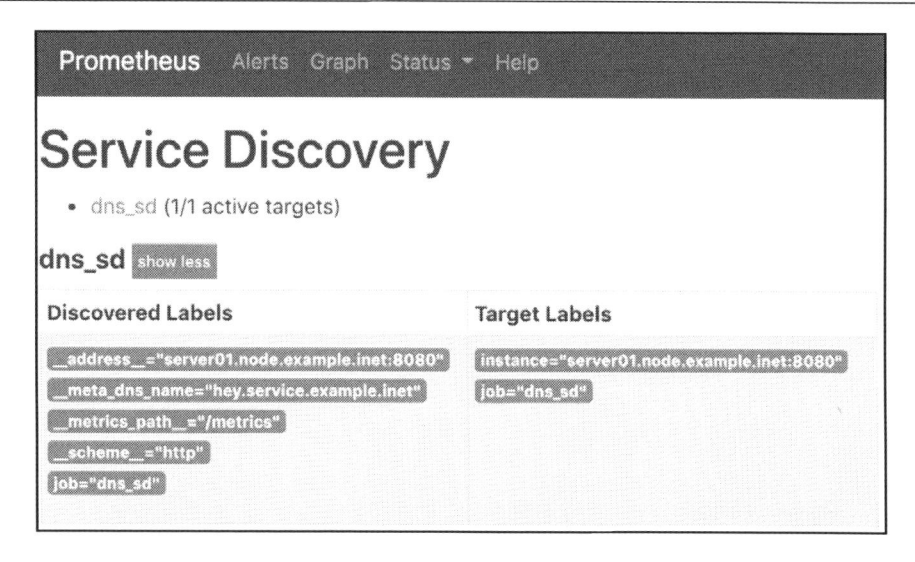

Figure 12.5: Prometheus /service-discovery endpoint depicting *dns_sd* data

From all the discovery integrations, this is the one with the lowest amount of provided metadata. Adding to that, using DNS for service discovery is hard to get right – planning for slow convergence, considering several different cache layers that may or may not respect record TTLs, among other concerns. This should only be considered for advanced cases.

File-based service discovery

Similar to the webhook notifier being the solution for integrating with unsupported notification systems (as explained in `Chapter 11`, *Understanding and Extending Alertmanager*), file-based integration provides the same type of solution for service discovery. It works by loading a list of valid JSON or YAML files, which in turn are used to generate the required targets and their labels. Reloading or restarting Prometheus after discovery files change is not necessary as they are watched for changes and automatically reread, depending on the operating system. Additionally, and as a fallback, the discovery files are also read on a schedule (every 5 minutes, by default).

The following JSON snippet shows a valid Prometheus discovery file. As we can see, there is a label list and a targets array that the labels apply to:

```
[
    {
        "labels": {
            "job": "node"
```

Choosing the Right Service Discovery

```
        },
        "targets": [
            "192.168.42.11:9100"
        ]
    }
]
```

The following scrape configuration uses the `file_sd` discovery, which loads the `file_sd.json` that has the content we showed previously:

```
scrape_configs:
  - job_name: 'file_sd'
    file_sd_configs:
      - files:
        - file_sd.json
```

> **TIP**: The `files` list also allows globing on the last element of the path, at the file level.

The discovered target from this configuration can be seen in the following screenshot, where we can check the metadata provided by our file, as well as the labels that were generated automatically by Prometheus:

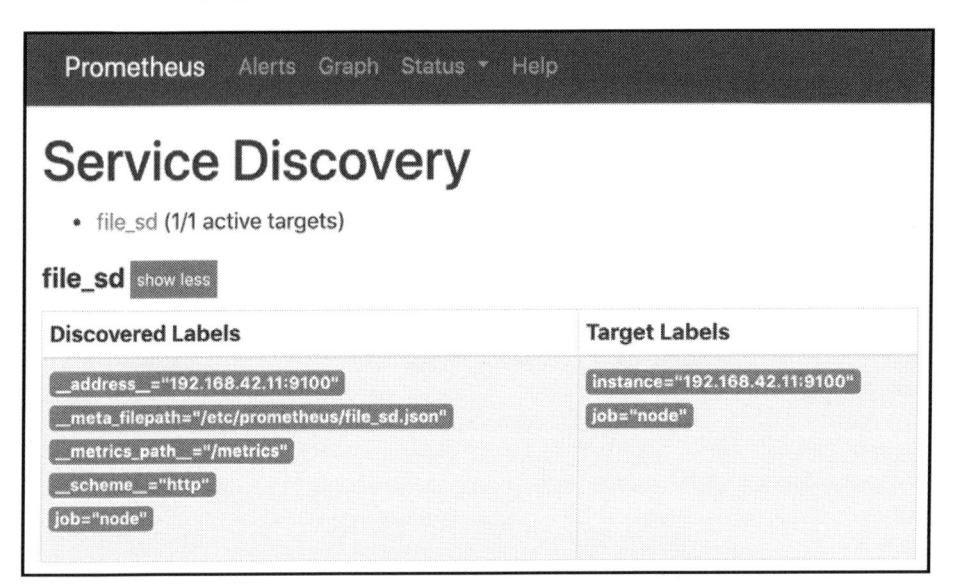

Figure 12.6: Prometheus /service-discovery endpoint depicting file_sd data

It is easy to see how this integration opens up a world of possibilities: these files can be created through a daemon that's constantly running or a cron job, using shell scripts (even a simple wget) or full-fledged programming languages, or simply put in place by configuration management. We will explore this topic later in this chapter when we discuss how to build a custom service discovery.

Using a built-in service discovery

To understand how the integration between Prometheus and a service discovery provider works, we're going to rely on our test environment. Going even further, we'll provide a working example of Prometheus running in Kubernetes, relying on its native service discovery for this platform. These hands-on examples will showcase how everything ties together, helping you figure out not only the benefits but, above all, the simplicity of these mechanics.

Using Consul service discovery

For this chapter, we configured Consul as an example service discovery system in our virtual machine-based test environment – Consul is quite simple to set up, which makes it perfect for our example. The way it works is by having an agent running in client mode in each node and an odd number of agents running in server mode that maintain the service catalog. The services that are available on the client nodes are communicated to the server nodes directly, while cluster membership is propagated using a gossip protocol (random peer-to-peer message passing) between every node in the cluster. Since our main objective is to showcase the Prometheus service discovery using Consul, we configured our test environment with an agent running in development mode, which enables an in-memory server to play around with. This, of course, has complete disregard for security, scalability, data safety, and resilience; documentation regarding how to properly configure Consul can be found at `https://learn.hashicorp.com/consul/`, and should be taken into account when deploying and maintaining Consul in production environments.

Choosing the Right Service Discovery

To poke around how this is set up in the test environment, we need to connect to the instance running Consul:

```
vagrant ssh consul
```

From here, we can start to explore how Consul is set up. For example, the following snippet shows the systemd unit file being used, where we can see the configuration flags being used – it's configured to run as an agent in development mode, and has to bind its ports to the instance's external-facing IP address:

```
vagrant@consul:~$ systemctl cat consul.service
...
[Service]
User=consul
ExecStart=/usr/bin/consul agent \
          -dev \
          -bind=192.168.42.11 \
          -client=192.168.42.11 \
          -advertise=192.168.42.11
...
```

If we run `ss` and filter its output to only show lines belonging to Consul, we can find all the ports it's using:

```
vagrant@consul:~$ sudo /bin/ss -lnp | grep consul
udp UNCONN 0 0 192.168.42.11:8301 0.0.0.0:* users:(("consul",pid=581,fd=8))
udp UNCONN 0 0 192.168.42.11:8302 0.0.0.0:* users:(("consul",pid=581,fd=6))
udp UNCONN 0 0 192.168.42.11:8600 0.0.0.0:* users:(("consul",pid=581,fd=9))
tcp LISTEN 0 128 192.168.42.11:8300 0.0.0.0:*
users:(("consul",pid=581,fd=3))
tcp LISTEN 0 128 192.168.42.11:8301 0.0.0.0:*
users:(("consul",pid=581,fd=7))
tcp LISTEN 0 128 192.168.42.11:8302 0.0.0.0:*
users:(("consul",pid=581,fd=5))
tcp LISTEN 0 128 192.168.42.11:8500 0.0.0.0:*
users:(("consul",pid=581,fd=11))
tcp LISTEN 0 128 192.168.42.11:8502 0.0.0.0:*
users:(("consul",pid=581,fd=12))
tcp LISTEN 0 128 192.168.42.11:8600 0.0.0.0:*
users:(("consul",pid=581,fd=10))
```

As we can see, Consul listens on a lot of ports, both TCP and UDP. The port we're interested in is the one serving the HTTP API, which defaults to TCP port `8500`. If we open a web browser to `http://192.168.42.11:8500`, we will see something similar to the following:

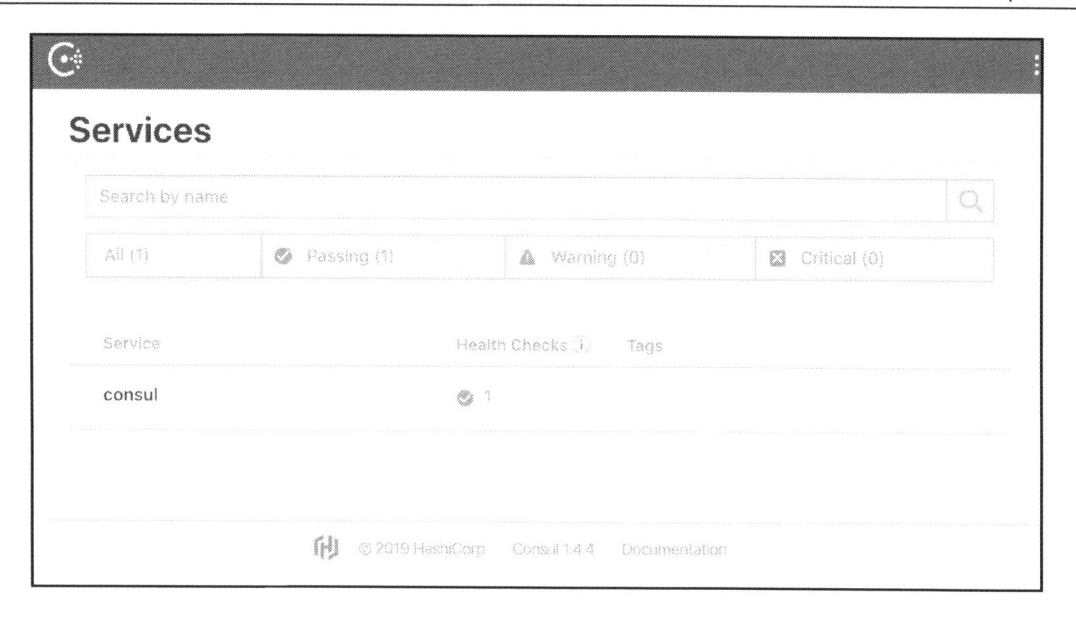

Figure 12.7: Consul web interface displaying its default configuration

There's a single service configured by default, which is the Consul service itself.

To make this example more interesting, we also have `consul_exporter` (an exporter provided by the Prometheus project) deployed in the `consul` instance. This exporter doesn't require any additional configuration on Consul's side, so it should just work. We can find the configuration used to run this service in the systemd unit file, like so:

```
vagrant@consul:~$ systemctl cat consul-exporter.service
...
[Service]
User=consul_exporter
ExecStart=/usr/bin/consul_exporter --consul.server=consul:8500
...
```

> The source code and installation files for the `consul_exporter` are available at https://github.com/prometheus/consul_exporter.

Choosing the Right Service Discovery

To validate that the exporter is correctly contacting Consul and parsing its metrics, we can run the following instruction:

```
vagrant@consul:~$ curl -qs localhost:9107/metrics | grep "^consul"
consul_catalog_service_node_healthy{node="consul",service_id="consul",service_name="consul"} 1
consul_catalog_services 1
consul_exporter_build_info{branch="HEAD",goversion="go1.10.3",revision="75f02d80bbe2191cd0af297bbf200a81cbe7aeb0",version="0.4.0"} 1
consul_health_node_status{check="serfHealth",node="consul",status="critical"} 0
consul_health_node_status{check="serfHealth",node="consul",status="maintenance"} 0
consul_health_node_status{check="serfHealth",node="consul",status="passing"} 1
consul_health_node_status{check="serfHealth",node="consul",status="warning"} 0
consul_raft_leader 1
consul_raft_peers 1
consul_serf_lan_members 1
consul_up 1
```

The exporter sets the `consul_up` metric to 1 when it can successfully connect and collect metrics from Consul. We can also see the `consul_catalog_services` metric, which is telling us that Consul knows about one service, matching what we've seen in the web interface.

We can now disconnect from the `consul` instance and connect to the `prometheus` one using the following commands:

```
exit
vagrant ssh prometheus
```

If we take a look at the Prometheus server configuration, we will find the following:

```
vagrant@prometheus:~$ cat /etc/prometheus/prometheus.yml
...
  - job_name: 'consul_sd'
    consul_sd_configs:
      - server: http://consul:8500
        datacenter: dc1
    relabel_configs:
      - source_labels: [__meta_consul_service]
        target_label: job
...
```

This configuration allows Prometheus to connect to the Consul API address (available at `http://192.168.42.11:8500`) and, by means of `relabel_configs`, rewrite the `job` label so that it matches the service name (as exposed in the `__meta_consul_service` label). If we inspect the Prometheus web interface, we can find the following information:

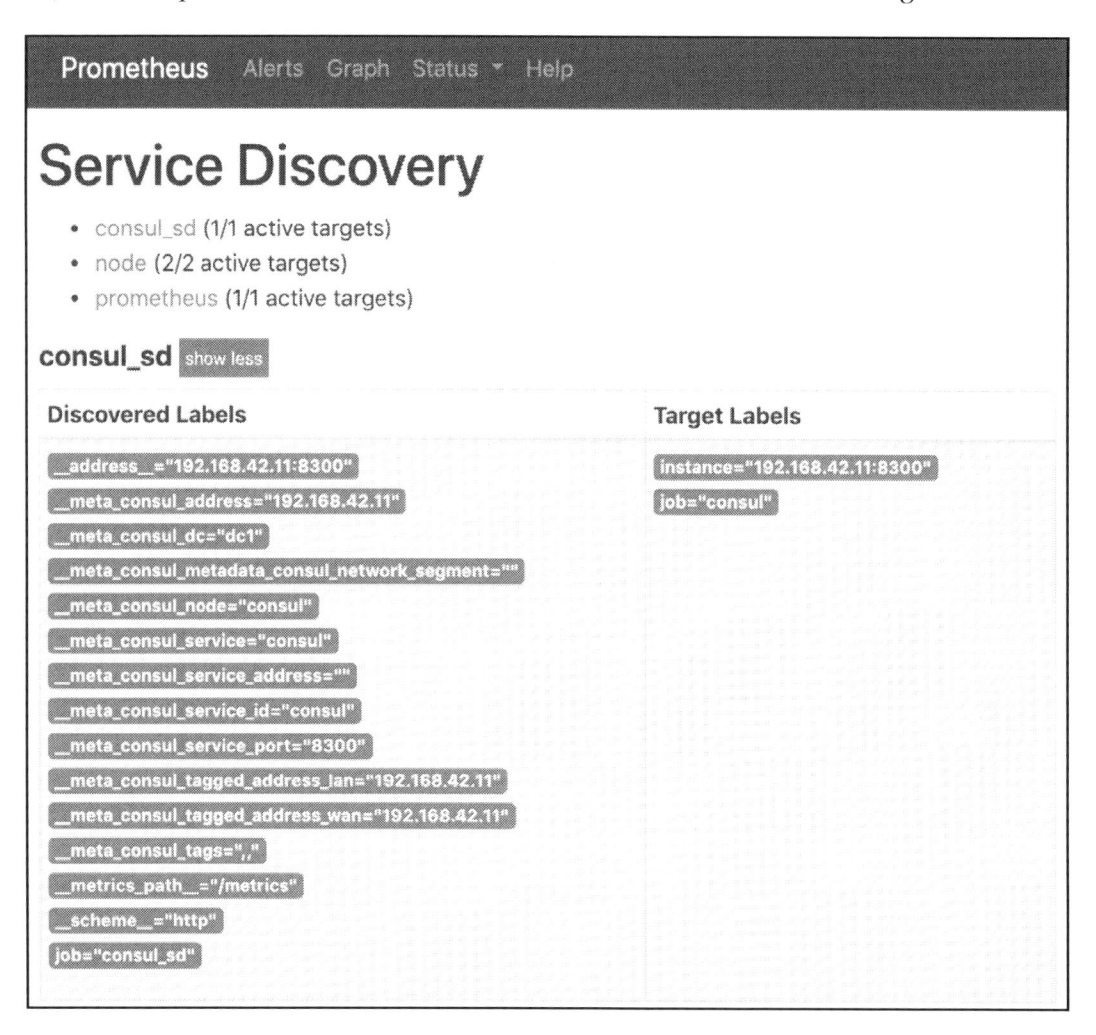

Figure 12.8: Prometheus /service-discovery endpoint showing Consul default service

Now, the fun part: let's add a scrape target for `consul_exporter` automatically by defining it as a service in Consul. A JSON payload with a Consul service configuration is provided in this chapter's resources, so we can add it via the Consul API. The payload can be found at the following path:

```
vagrant@prometheus:~$ cat
/vagrant/chapter12/configs/consul_exporter/payload.json
{
  "ID": "consul-exporter01",
  "Name": "consul-exporter",
  "Tags": [
    "consul",
    "exporter",
    "prometheus"
  ],
  "Address": "consul",
  "Port": 9107
}
```

Using the following instruction, we'll add this new service to Consul's service catalogs via the HTTP API:

```
vagrant@prometheus:~$ curl --request PUT \
--data @/vagrant/chapter12/configs/consul_exporter/payload.json \
http://consul:8500/v1/agent/service/register
```

After running this command, we can validate that the new service was added by having a look at the Consul web interface, which will show something like the following:

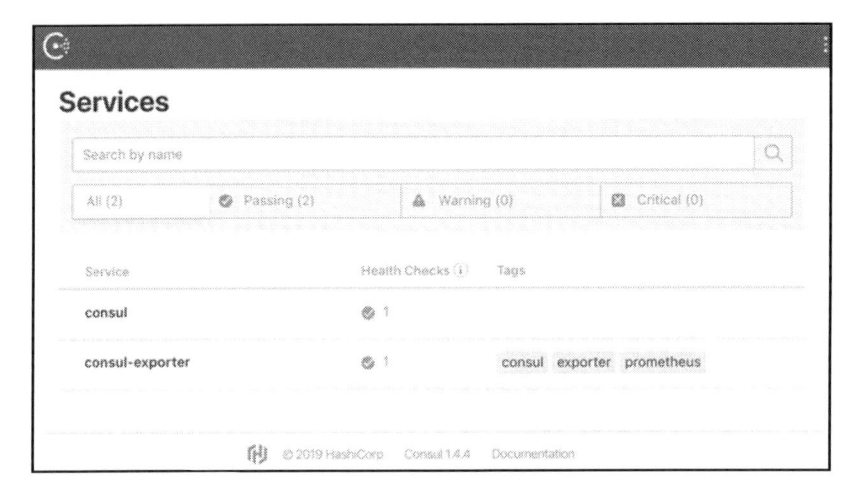

Figure 12.9: Consul web interface showing the consul-exporter service

Chapter 12

Finally, we can inspect the Prometheus `/service-discovery` endpoint and check that we have a new target, proving that the Consul service discovery is working as expected:

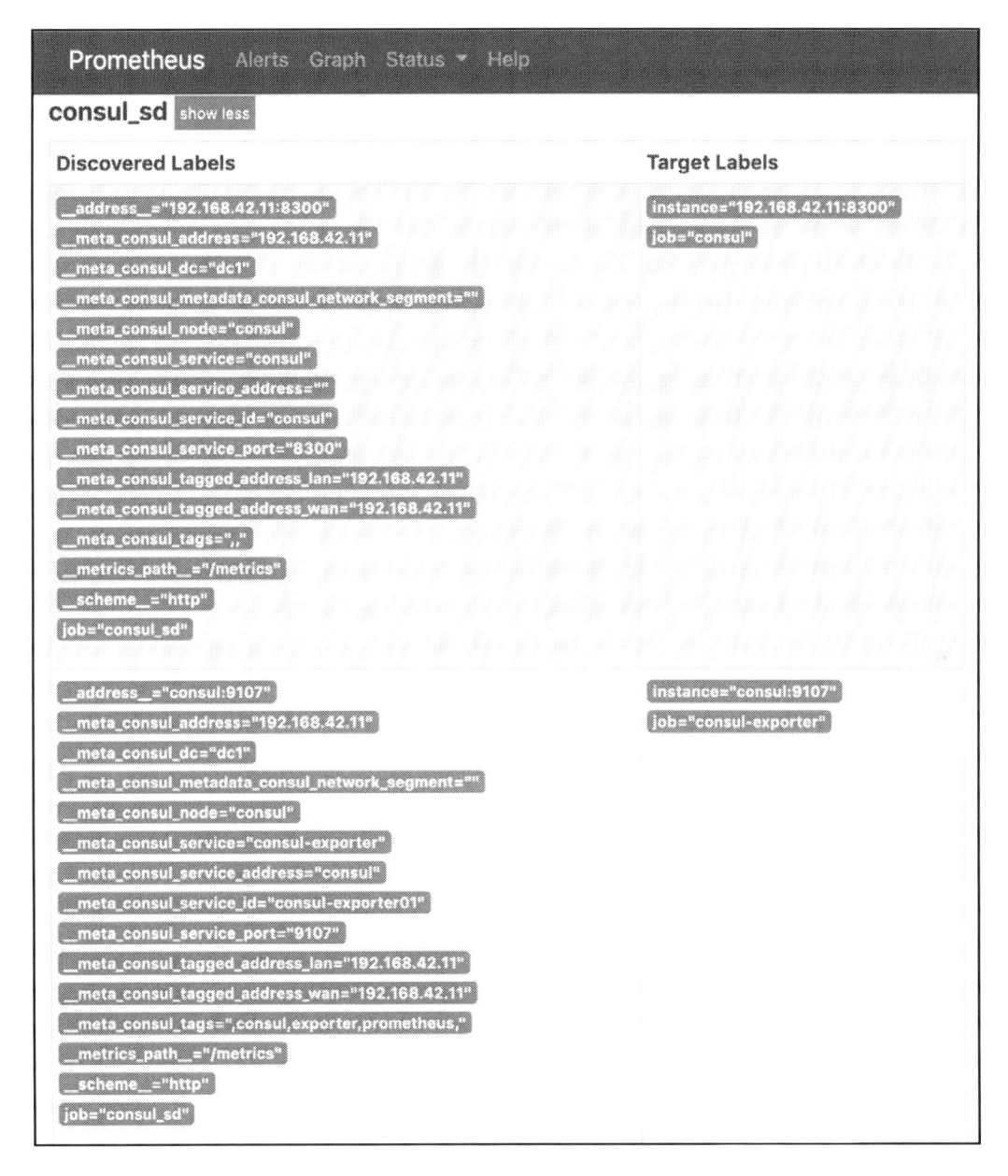

Figure 12.10: Prometheus /service-discovery endpoint showing consul-exporter target

[337]

If we consult the `consul_catalog_services` metric once again, we can see that it has changed to 2. Since we're now collecting the `consul_exporter` metrics in Prometheus, we can query its current value using `promtool`:

```
vagrant@prometheus:~$ promtool query instant http://localhost:9090 'consul_catalog_services'
consul_catalog_services{instance="consul:9107", job="consul-exporter"} => 2 @[1555252393.681]
```

Consul tags can be used to do scrape job configuration using `relabel_configs` for services that have different requirements, such as changing the metrics path when a given tag is present, or having a tag to mark whether to scrape using HTTPS. The `__meta_consul_tags` label value has the comma separator at the beginning and end to make matching easier; this way, you don't need to special-case your regular expression, depending on the position in the string of the tag you're trying to match. An example of this at work could be:

```
...
    relabel_configs:
      - source_labels: [__meta_consul_tags]
        regex: .*,exporter,.*
        action: keep
...
```

This would only keep services registered in Consul with the `exporter` tag, discarding everything else.

Using Kubernetes service discovery

In this example, we're stepping away from the Prometheus Kubernetes Operator we've been using in previous chapters so that we can focus on the Prometheus native service discovery integration for this container orchestration platform. The manifests for getting Prometheus up and running in our Kubernetes test environment can be found, relative to the code repository root path, at the following path:

```
cd ./chapter12/provision/kubernetes/
```

The following steps will ensure a new Kubernetes environment with all the required software provisioned so that we can then focus on the service discovery component.

Validate that no other environment is running:

```
minikube status
minikube delete
```

Start an empty Kubernetes environment:

```
minikube start \
  --cpus=2 \
  --memory=3072 \
  --kubernetes-version="v1.14.0" \
  --vm-driver=virtualbox \
  --extra-config=kubelet.authentication-token-webhook=true \
  --extra-config=kubelet.authorization-mode=Webhook
```

The extra configuration we're providing to minikube is needed so that Prometheus is able to interact with `kubelets` using service account tokens. When the previous command finishes, a new Kubernetes environment will be ready to be used. We can then proceed to deploy our configurations using the following instructions:

```
kubectl apply -f ./bootstrap/
kubectl rollout status deployment/prometheus-deployment -n monitoring
```

The previous command applies several manifests, which, among other things, create a namespace called `monitoring`, a ServiceAccount, and all the required RBAC configurations so that Prometheus can query the Kubernetes API. A `ConfigMap` with the Prometheus server configuration is also included, which can be found at `bootstrap/03_prometheus-configmap.yaml`. It defines several scrape jobs for Kubernetes components that are targeted through the use of service discovery, as we can see in the following snippet:

```
$ cat bootstrap/03_prometheus-configmap.yaml
...
data:
  prometheus.yml: |
    scrape_configs:
...
    - job_name: kubernetes-pods
      kubernetes_sd_configs:
      - role: pod
      relabel_configs:
      - action: keep
        regex: hey
        source_labels:
        - __meta_kubernetes_pod_label_app
...
```

We can open the Prometheus web interface by issuing the following command:

```
minikube service prometheus-service -n monitoring
```

Choosing the Right Service Discovery

By moving into the service discovery section available on the `/service-discovery` endpoint, we can see that, even though several pods were discovered, none of them matched the label value `hey` for the `app` label, and as such are being dropped:

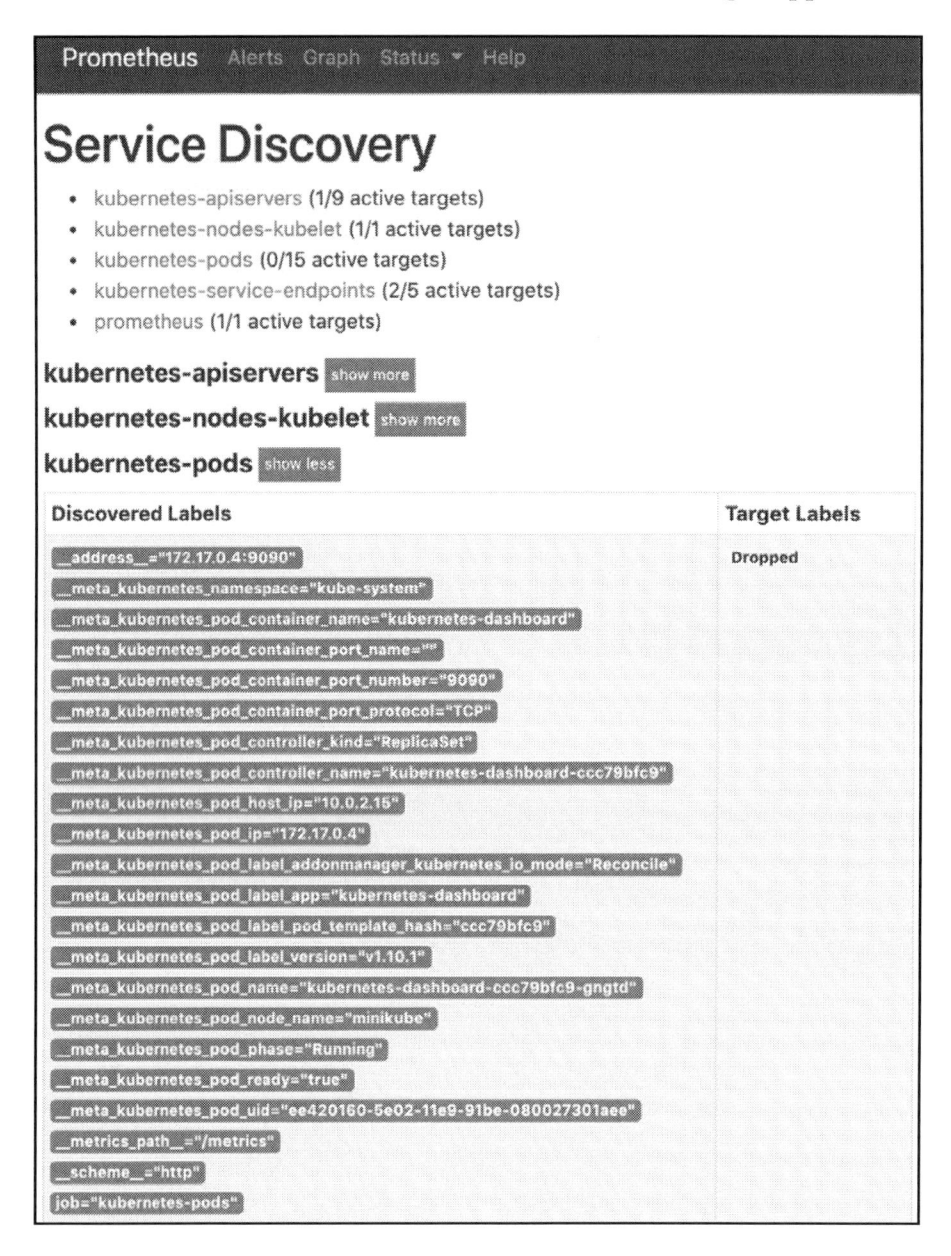

Figure 12.11: Prometheus /service-discovery endpoint showing dropped targets for the kubernetes-pods job

It's now time to add some new pods with the correct label/value pair to trigger our service discovery configuration. We can proceed by running the following commands, which will be deploying the `hey` application, and then follow the status of the deployment:

```
kubectl apply -f ./services/
kubectl rollout status deployment/hey-deployment -n default
```

After a successful deployment, we can go, once again, to the Prometheus web interface at the `/service-discovery` endpoint, where we can see that there are now three active targets in the `kubernetes-pods` scrape job. The following screenshot depicts one of those targets and all the labels provided by the Kubernetes API:

Figure 12.12: Prometheus /service-discovery endpoint showing the discovered targets for the kubernetes-pods job

When you're finished testing, you can delete this Kubernetes-based environment by issuing the following command:

```
minikube delete
```

This approach to service discovery allows us to keep track of several Kubernetes objects automatically, without forcing us to change the Prometheus configuration manually. This environment allows us to test all sorts of settings and provides the basis for tailoring the Kubernetes service discovery to our specific needs.

Building a custom service discovery

Even with all the available service discovery options, there are numerous other systems/providers that are not supported out of the box. For those cases, we've got a couple of options:

- Open a feature request for Prometheus to support that particular service discovery, and rely on the community and/or maintainers to implement it.
- Implement the service discovery integration yourself in Prometheus and either maintain a fork or contribute it back to the project.
- Figure out a way to get the targets you require into your Prometheus instances with minimal maintenance work and time cost, and without relying on the Prometheus roadmap to get the job done.

The first two options aren't great, as they are either outside of our control or are cumbersome to maintain. Furthermore, adding additional service discovery integrations to Prometheus without fairly large interest and backing communities places an undue support burden on the maintainers, who aren't currently accepting any new integrations. Luckily, there is a way to easily integrate with any type of service or instance catalog, without needing to maintain costly forks or creative hacks. In the following section, we'll be tackling how to integrate our own service discovery with Prometheus.

Custom service discovery fundamentals

The recommended way to integrate a custom service discovery is by relying on the file-based service discovery, `file_sd`. The way this integration should be implemented is to have a process (local or remote, scheduled or permanently running) query a data source (catalogue/API/database/**configuration management database** (**CMDB**)) and then write a JSON- or YAML-formatted file with all the targets and their respective labels on a path that's accessible by Prometheus. The file is then read by Prometheus either automatically through disk watches or on a schedule, which in turn allows you to dynamically update the targets that are available for scraping.

The following diagram illustrates the aforementioned workflow:

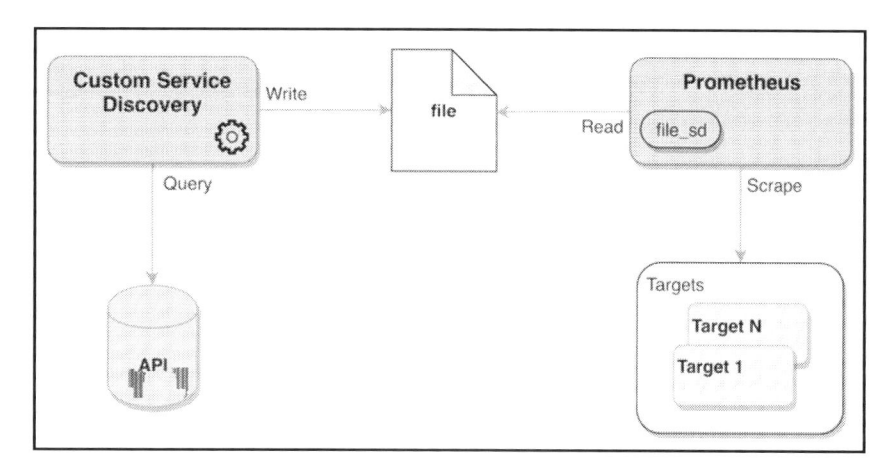

Figure 12.13: Custom service discovery flow

This type of approach is generic enough to comply with most, if not all, required use cases, making it possible to build a custom service discovery mechanism in a straightforward manner.

> Community-driven `file_sd` integrations can be found at https://prometheus.io/docs/operating/integrations/#file-service-discovery.

Now that we know how this type of integration should work, let's dive right in and start building our own.

Recommended approach

As we've explained so far, building a custom service discovery seems like a manageable enough endeavor. We're required to query something for data and write that data into a file, following a standard format. To make our lives easier, the Prometheus team made an adapter available that removes a big chunk of the boilerplate for creating a new service discovery integration. This adapter is only provided for the Go programming language, as it reuses some code from Prometheus itself. The adapter was made this way so that some less-maintained service discovery integrations could be migrated out to standalone services without too much effort, as well as easing the migration into the main Prometheus binary of external discovery integrations that are built using the adapter, all of which have proven themselves. Note that nothing prevents you from using the language of your choice to build such integrations, but for the sake of following the recommended approach, we'll be sticking with Go and the discovery adapter. Explaining how to program in Go is outside the scope of this book.

In the main Prometheus repository, we can find the code for the adapter, as well as an example using Consul, which, curiously enough, we've already set up in our test environment. As we know by now, Consul integration is supported natively in Prometheus; however, let's pretend it's not and that we need to integrate with it. In the following topics, we'll go over how to put everything together and build a custom service discovery.

> The code for the custom service discovery example is available at https://github.com/prometheus/prometheus/tree/v2.9.1/documentation/examples/custom-sd.

The service discovery adapter

As a high-level overview, the adapter takes care of launching and managing our custom service discovery code, consuming the groups of targets it produces, converting them into `file_sd` format, and ensuring that the JSON data is written to a file when required. When writing a service discovery integration using this adapter, no change is needed in its code, and so it can just be imported as a library. To give a bit more context about what the adapter is doing, we're going to explain some of the lower-level details so that its behaviors are clear when we implement our own discovery using it.

The following snippet illustrates the `Run` function of the adapter that we will need to invoke from our code. This function will take care of starting a `discovery.Manager` in its own goroutine (`a.manager.Run`), instructing it to run our discovery implementation (`a.disc`), and, finally, running the adapter itself in another goroutine (`a.runCustomSD`):

```
// Run starts a Discovery Manager and the custom service discovery
implementation.
func (a *Adapter) Run() {
    go a.manager.Run()
    a.manager.StartCustomProvider(a.ctx, a.name, a.disc)
    go a.runCustomSD(a.ctx)
}
```

After starting, the adapter consumes from a channel provided by the `Manager` that updates the target groups that our code will produce. When an update arrives, it will convert the target groups into `file_sd` format and verify whether there were any changes since the last update. If there are changes, it will store the new target groups for future comparisons and write them out as JSON to the output file. This implies that the full list of target groups should be sent in every update; groups that are not sent through the channel will get removed from the produced discovery file.

> The `file_sd` adapter source code can be found at https://github.com/prometheus/prometheus/blob/v2.9.2/documentation/examples/custom-sd/adapter/adapter.go.

Custom service discovery example

Now that we have an idea of how the adapter works, let's take a look at what we need to implement to have our custom service discovery working. As we saw previously, the adapter uses a `discovery.Manager`, so we need to provide it with an implementation of the `Discoverer` interface so that it can run our discovery. The interface looks like this:

```
type Discoverer interface {
    Run(ctx context.Context, up chan<- []*targetgroup.Group)
}
```

> The `Discoverer` interface documentation can be found at https://godoc.org/github.com/prometheus/prometheus/discovery#Discoverer.

This means that we only need to implement the `Run` function, where we will run the logic of our discovery on a loop, generating the appropriate target groups and sending them through the `up` channel to the adapter. The `ctx` context is there so that we know when we need to stop. The code we implement will then be regularly gathering all the available targets/metadata from our data source. In this example, we're using Consul, which requires us to get a list of services first and then, for each one of them, query which instances are backing it and their metadata to generate labels. If something fails, we won't be sending any updates via the channel, because it's better to serve stale data than incomplete or incorrect data.

Finally, in our `main` function, we just need to instantiate a new adapter, and feed it a background context, the name of the output file, the name of our discovery implementation, the discovery object that implements the `Discoverer` interface, and a `log.Logger` instance:

```
func main() {
...
    sdAdapter := adapter.NewAdapter(ctx, *outputFile, "exampleSD", disc, logger)
    sdAdapter.Run()
...
}
```

> The working example of this adapter implementation can be found at https://github.com/prometheus/prometheus/blob/v2.9.2/documentation/examples/custom-sd/adapter-usage/main.go.

The next step is to deploy and integrate this newly created service discovery provider with Prometheus, so that's what we'll do in the following section.

Using the custom service discovery

To see for ourselves how a custom service discovery behaves, we'll rely on our test environment. The `custom-sd` binary, which recreates the Consul discovery integration as an example of a custom service discovery, is deployed alongside Prometheus and is ready to be used. Together with the Consul deployment, we have all the required components in the test environment to see how everything fits together.

> `custom-sd` can be built on a machine with a Go development environment set up by issuing the following command: `go get github.com/prometheus/prometheus/documentation/examples/custom-sd/adapter-usage`.

First, we need to ensure that we are connected to the `prometheus` instance. We can use the following command:

```
vagrant ssh prometheus
```

We can then proceed to change the Prometheus configuration to use `file_sd` as our integration. For this, we must replace the scrape job configured to use `consul_sd` with a new one. To make things easier, we placed a configuration file with this change already made in `/etc/prometheus/`. To use it, you just need to replace the current configuration with the new one:

```
vagrant@prometheus:~$ sudo mv /etc/prometheus/prometheus_file_sd.yml /etc/prometheus/prometheus.yml
```

The scrape job we are interested in is as follows:

```yaml
- job_name: 'file_sd'
  file_sd_configs:
    - files:
      - custom_file_sd.json
```

To make Prometheus aware of these changes, we must reload it:

```
vagrant@prometheus:~$ sudo systemctl reload prometheus
```

We should also make sure that the Consul server has the configuration for `consul-exporter`, which we added previously. If, by any chance, you missed that step, you may add it now by simply running the following code:

```
vagrant@prometheus:~$ curl --request PUT \
--data @/vagrant/chapter12/configs/consul_exporter/payload.json \
http://consul:8500/v1/agent/service/register
```

If we take a look in the Prometheus web interface, we will see something similar to the following:

12.14: Prometheus /service-discovery endpoint without any file_sd targets

We're now ready to try out the `custom-sd` application. We'll need to specify the Consul API address and the path to the output file, which the Prometheus server is configured to read from. The following command will take care of that, and also ensure that the right user is creating the file, so that the Prometheus process is able to access it:

```
vagrant@prometheus:~$ sudo -u prometheus -- custom-sd --
output.file="/etc/prometheus/custom_file_sd.json" --
listen.address="consul:8500"
```

We now have the custom service discovery running. If we go back to the web interface of Prometheus in the `/service-discovery` endpoint, we'll be able to see the discovered target:

Service Discovery

- file_sd (1/1 active targets)
- node (2/2 active targets)
- prometheus (1/1 active targets)

file_sd show less

Discovered Labels	Target Labels
__address__="consul:9107"	instance="consul:9107"
__meta_consul_address="192.168.42.11"	job="file_sd"
__meta_consul_network_segment=""	
__meta_consul_node="consul"	
__meta_consul_service_address="consul"	
__meta_consul_service_id="consul-exporter01"	
__meta_consul_service_port="9107"	
__meta_consul_tags=",consul,exporter,prometheus,"	
__meta_filepath="/etc/prometheus/custom_file_sd.json"	
__metrics_path__="/metrics"	
__scheme__="http"	
job="file_sd"	

node show more
prometheus show more

12.15: Prometheus /service-discovery endpoint depicting the discovered target

We can also inspect the file that was created by our `custom-sd`, and validate its contents, as follows (the output has been made compact for brevity):

```
vagrant@prometheus:~$ sudo cat /etc/prometheus/custom_file_sd.json
[
    {
        "targets": ["consul:9107"],
        "labels": {
            "__address__": "consul:9107",
            "__meta_consul_address": "192.168.42.11",
            "__meta_consul_network_segment": "",
            "__meta_consul_node": "consul",
            "__meta_consul_service_address": "consul",
```

```
            "__meta_consul_service_id": "consul-exporter01",
            "__meta_consul_service_port": "9107",
            "__meta_consul_tags": ",consul,exporter,prometheus,"
}}]
```

And that's it! You now have a custom service discovery up and running, fully integrated with Prometheus using the file-based service discovery mechanism. A more serious deployment would have the `custom-sd` service running as a daemon. If you're more comfortable with a scripting language, you could choose to write a service discovery script that produces the discovery file and exits, in which case running it as a cron job would be an option. As a last suggestion, you could have your configuration management software produce the discovery file dynamically on a schedule.

Summary

In this chapter, we had the opportunity to understand why service discovery is essential for managing ever-growing infrastructure in a sane way. Prometheus leverages several service discovery options out of the box, which can kick-start your adoption in a very quick and friendly manner. We went through the available options Prometheus provides for service discovery, and showed you what to expect from them. We then stepped into a couple of examples using Consul and Kubernetes to materialize the concepts we exposed previously. Finally, we went through how to integrate a custom service discovery with Prometheus by using the recommended approach and relying on `file_sd`.

In the next chapter, we'll go through how to scale and federate Prometheus.

Questions

1. Why should you use a service discovery mechanism in Prometheus?
2. When you're using a cloud provider service discovery, what is the major requirement for setting the integration?
3. What are the types of records supported by the DNS-based service discovery integration?
4. What purpose does the concept of role serve in the Kubernetes service discovery integration?

5. When you're building a custom service discovery, what available integration will you be relying upon?
6. Do you need to reload Prometheus when a target file configured in `file_sd` is updated?
7. What is the recommended way of building your own custom service discovery?

Further reading

- **Prometheus service discovery configuration**: `https://prometheus.io/docs/prometheus/latest/configuration/configuration`

13
Scaling and Federating Prometheus

Prometheus was designed to be run as a single server. This approach will allow you to handle thousands of targets and millions of time series but, as you scale, you might find yourself in a situation where this just is not enough. This chapter tackles this necessity and clarifies how to scale Prometheus through sharding. However, sharding makes having a global view of the infrastructure harder. To address this, we will also go through the advantages and disadvantages of sharding, how federation comes into the picture, and, lastly, introduce Thanos, a component that was created by the Prometheus community to address some of the issues presented.

In brief, the following topics will be covered in this chapter:

- Test environment for this chapter
- Scaling with the help of sharding
- Having a global view using federation
- Using Thanos to mitigate Prometheus shortcomings at scale

Test environment for this chapter

In this chapter, we'll be focusing on scaling and federating Prometheus. For this, we'll be deploying three instances to simulate a scenario where a global Prometheus instance gathers metrics from two others. This approach will allow us not only to explore the required configurations, but also to understand how everything works together.

The setup we'll be using is illustrated in the following diagram:

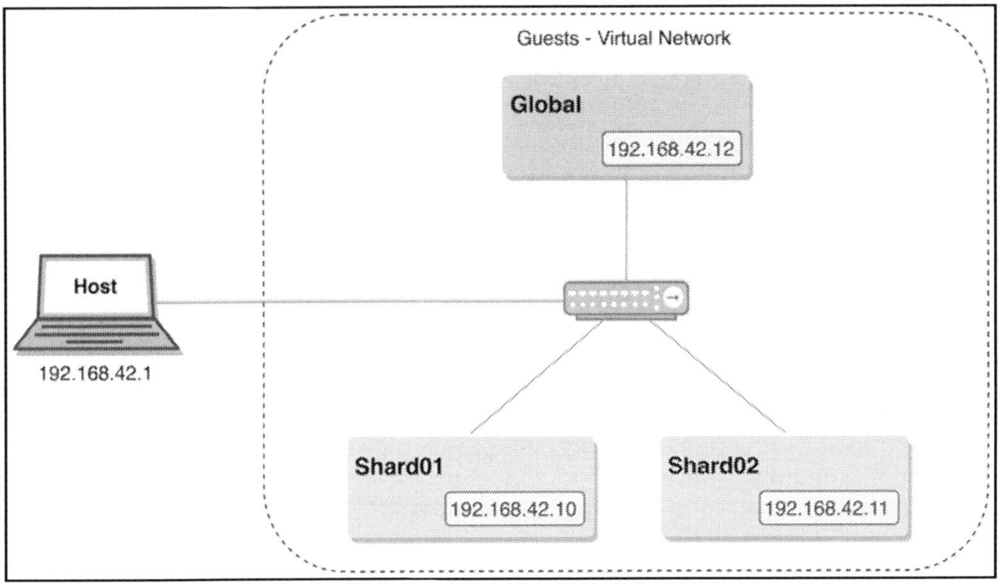

Figure 13.1: Test environment for this chapter

In the next section, we will explain how to get the test environment up and running.

Deployment

To launch a new test environment, move into the following chapter path, relative to the code repository root:

```
cd ./chapter13/
```

Ensure that no other test environments are running and spin up this chapter's environment, by using this command:

```
vagrant global-status
vagrant up
```

Chapter 13

You can validate the successful deployment of the test environment using the following command:

```
vagrant status
```

This will output the following:

```
Current machine states:

shard01                   running (virtualbox)
shard02                   running (virtualbox)
global                    running (virtualbox)

This environment represents multiple VMs. The VMs are all listed above with
their current state. For more information about a specific VM, run `vagrant
status NAME`.
```

When the deployment tasks end, you'll be able to validate the following endpoints on your host machine using your favorite JavaScript-enabled web browser:

Service	Endpoint
Shard01 Prometheus	`http://192.168.42.10:9090`
Shard02 Prometheus	`http://192.168.42.11:9090`
Global Prometheus	`http://192.168.42.12:9090`
Global Thanos querier	`http://192.168.42.12:10902`

You should be able to access each of these instances by using the respective command:

Instance	Command
Shard01	`vagrant ssh shard01`
Shard02	`vagrant ssh shard02`
Global	`vagrant ssh global`

Cleanup

When you've finished testing, just make sure that you're inside `./chapter13/` and execute the following command:

```
vagrant destroy -f
```

Don't worry too much: you can easily spin up the environment again if you need to.

[355]

Scaling with the help of sharding

With growth come more teams, more infrastructure, more applications. With time, running a single Prometheus server can start to become infeasible: changes in recording/alerting rules and scrape jobs become more frequent (thus requiring reloads which, depending on the configured scrape intervals, can take up to a couple of minutes), missed scrapes can start to happen as Prometheus becomes overwhelmed, or the person or team responsible for that instance may simply become a bottleneck in terms of organizational process. When this happens, we need to rethink the architecture of our solution so that is scales accordingly. Thankfully, this is something the community has tackled time and time again, and so there are some recommendations on how to approach this problem. These recommendations revolve around sharding.

In this context, sharding means splitting the list of scrape targets among two or more Prometheus instances. This can be accomplished in two ways: via vertical or horizontal sharding. Sharding vertically is by far the most common method, and it's done by grouping scrape jobs logically (for example, by scope, technology, organizational boundary) into different Prometheus instances, where the sharding limit is the scrape job. On the flip side, horizontal sharding is done at the level of the scrape job; it means having multiple instances of Prometheus, each scraping a subset of targets for a given job. Horizontal sharding is seldom used, as it is uncommon for a scrape job to be larger than a single Prometheus instance can handle.

Additionally, we're not considering having a Prometheus for each datacenter/environment as sharding; Prometheus is supposed to be run alongside the systems/services it monitors for reasons of bandwidth and latency, as well as resiliency (less prone to suffer from network failures).

Logical grouping of jobs

A good starting point for scaling when a single Prometheus instance isn't enough is to split scrape jobs into logical groups and then assign these groups to different Prometheus instances. This is called vertical sharding. The groups can be made around anything that makes sense to you: by architecture/scope (frontend, backend, databases), by layers (OS-level metrics, infrastructure services, applications), by internal organization vertical, by team, by network security boundary (so that scrapes don't need to cross firewalls), or even by application cluster.

The following diagram exemplifies what this type of vertical sharding looks like:

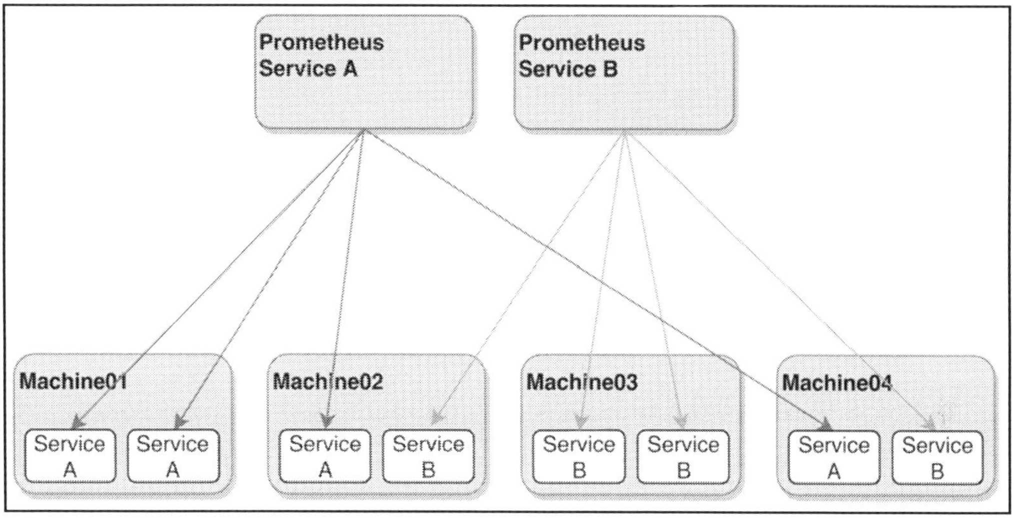

Figure 13.2: Diagram illustrating vertical sharding

This type of sharding also enables isolation between Prometheus instances, which means that a heavily used subset of metrics from a given set of targets can be split into multiple instances, possibly with more resources. This way, any negative side-effects from their heavy usage will be circumscribed, and won't affect the overall monitoring platform stability.

Additionally, doing vertical sharding for each team can have a couple of organizational benefits:

- It makes cardinality considerations more visible to the service owners.
- Teams feel both empowered and accountable for the monitoring of their services.
- It can enable more experimentation for rules and dashboards without the fear of impacting others.

The single job scale problem

We went through a couple of strategies for vertically sharding Prometheus, but there's a problem we still haven't addressed: scaling requirements tied to a single job. Imagine that you have a job with tens of thousands of scrape targets inside one datacenter, and there isn't a logical way to split it any further. In this type of scenario, your best bet is to shard horizontally, spreading the same job across multiple Prometheus servers. The following diagram provides an example of this type of sharding:

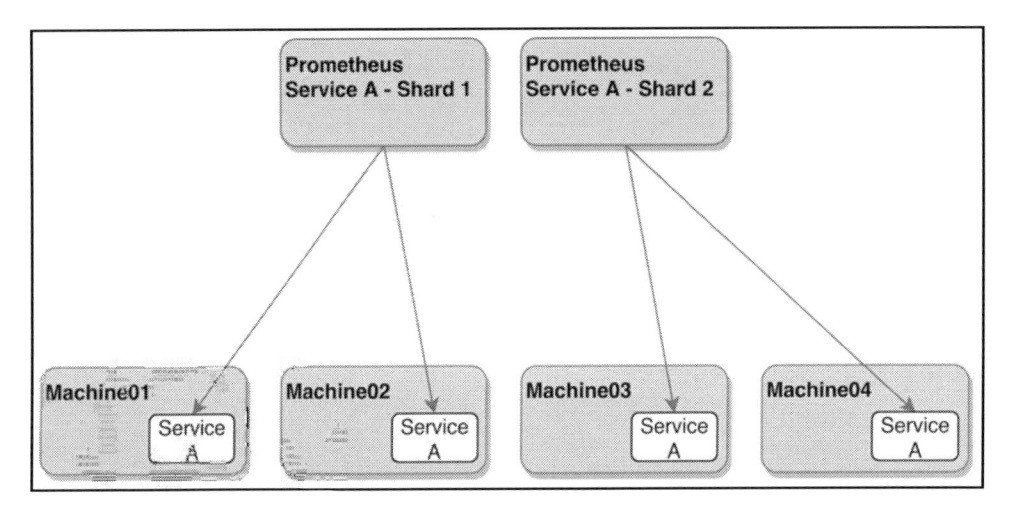

Figure 13.3: Diagram illustrating horizontal sharding

To accomplish this, we must rely on the `hashmod` relabeling action. The way `hashmod` works is by setting `target_label` to the `modulus` of a hash of the concatenated `source_labels`, which we then place in a Prometheus server. We can see this configuration in action in our test environment in both `shard01` and `shard02`, effectively sharding the node job. Let's go through the following configuration, which can be found at `/etc/prometheus/prometheus.yml`:

```
...
scrape_configs:
  - job_name: 'node'
    static_configs:
      - targets: ['shard01:9100', 'shard02:9100', 'global:9100']
    relabel_configs:
      - source_labels: [__address__]
        modulus: 2 # Because we're using 2 shards
        target_label: __tmp_shard
        action: hashmod
```

```
      - source_labels: [__tmp_shard]
        regex: 0 # Starts at 0, so this is the first
        action: keep
...
```

> **TIP**: When using temporary labels, like in the previous example, always use the `__tmp` prefix, as that prefix is guaranteed to never be used internally by Prometheus.

In the following screenshot, we can see the `/service-discovery` endpoint from the `shard01` and `shard02` Prometheus instances side by side. The result of the `hashmod` action allowed us to split the node exporter job across both instances, as shown:

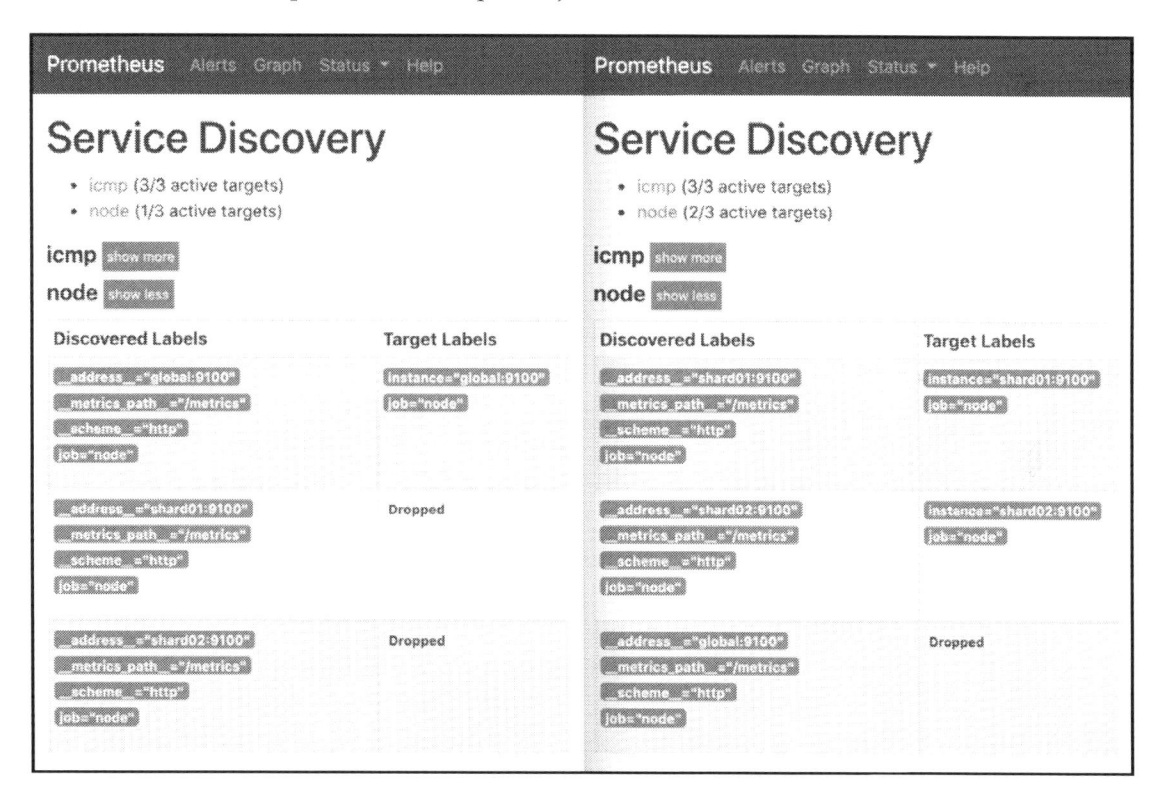

Figure 13.4: shard01 and shard02 /service-discovery endpoints showing the *hashmod* result

Few reach the scale where this type of sharding is needed, but it's great to know that Prometheus supports it out of the box.

What to consider when sharding

A sharding strategy, whether vertical or horizontal, while necessary in certain situations, shouldn't be taken lightly. The complexity in managing multiple configurations for multiple Prometheus instances quickly adds up, making your life more difficult if you didn't plan the required automation accordingly. Things such as external labels, external URLs, user consoles, and scrape jobs can be programmatically set to reduce the operational toil for the team maintaining the shards.

Having a global view also becomes a problem as each Prometheus instance will have its own subset of the data. This can make dashboarding harder as the location of the data may not be immediately clear (for example, when using multiple data sources in Grafana), and can also prevent some queries from aggregating services that are spread over many shards globally. This issue can be mitigated through a couple of techniques, which we'll explore later in this chapter.

Lastly, some recording and alerting rules might become impractical if the required time series aren't located in the same shard. As an example, let's imagine we have a shard with OS-level metrics and another with an application metrics. Alerts that need to correlate metrics from both shards are going to be a problem. This issue can be mitigated by carefully planning what goes into each shard, by using federation to make the required metrics available where they are needed, or by using a remote write to external systems that can do this outside Prometheus (as we'll see in `Chapter 14`, *Integrating Long-Term Storage with Prometheus*).

Alternatives to sharding

As mentioned at the beginning of this chapter, a single Prometheus instance will take you a long way if configured and utilized properly. Striving to avoid high cardinality metrics should be a top concern, mitigate the need to start sharding. Something that helps to protect Prometheus instances from scraping targets that produce unreasonable amounts of metrics involves defining the maximum sample ingestion per scrape job. For this, you just need to add `sample_limit` to the scrape job; if the number of samples after `metric_relabel_configs` goes over the configured limit, the scrape will be dropped entirely. An example configuration is as follows:

```
scrape_configs:
  - job_name: 'massive_job'
    sample_limit: 5000
    static_configs:
      - targets:
        - 'shard01:9999'
```

```
          - 'shard02:9999'
```

The following screenshot illustrates what happens when a scrape hits the configured `sample_limit`:

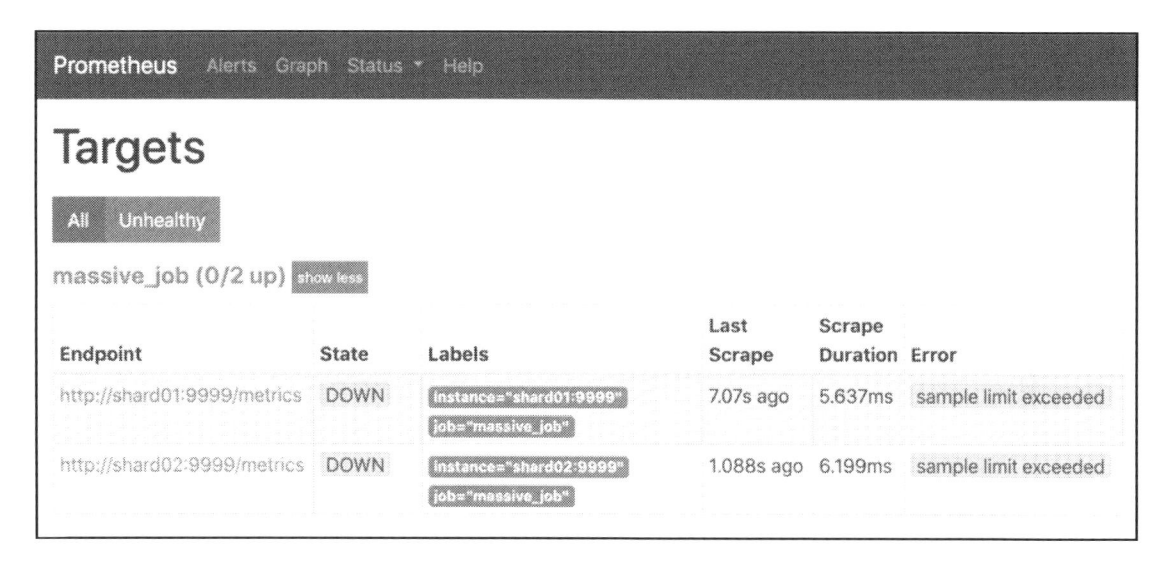

Figure 13.5: Prometheus targets endpoint showing scrape jobs being dropped due to exceeded sample limit

When using this limiter, you should keep an eye out for scrapes getting dropped using the `prometheus_target_scrapes_exceeded_sample_limit_total` metric in conjunction with the `up` metric. While the latter tells you Prometheus couldn't scrape the target, the former will give you the reason why.

If dropping scrapes is out of the question and you are able to sustain the loss of resolution, an alternative is to increase the scrape interval. Bear in mind that you shouldn't increase it over two minutes, as doing so creates the risk of metric staleness due to a single scrape failing, as we explained in `Chapter 5`, *Running a Prometheus Server*.

Having a global view using federation

When you have multiple Prometheus servers, it can become quite cumbersome to know which one to query for a certain metric. Another problem that quickly comes up is how to aggregate data from multiple instances, possibly in multiple datacenters. Here's where federation comes into the picture. Federation allows you to have a Prometheus instance scraping selected time series from other instances, effectively serving as a higher-level aggregating instance. This can happen in a hierarchical fashion, with each layer aggregating metrics from lower-level instances into larger-encompassing time series, or in a cross-service pattern, where a few metrics are selected from instances in the same level for federation so that some recording and alerting rules become possible. For example, you could collect data for service throughput or latency in each shard, and then aggregate them across all the shards to have a global value.

Let's have a look at what is needed to set up federation in Prometheus, and then go into each of the aforementioned federation patterns.

Federation configuration

A running Prometheus server exposes a special endpoint served at /federate. This endpoint allows for the retrieval of time series that match one or more instant vector selectors (which we covered in Chapter 7, *Prometheus Query Language – PromQL*). To make these mechanisms clear, we provided a very simple example in our test environment. Each one of the shard instances has a recording rule producing aggregate metrics representing the number of HTTP requests to exporters, illustrated in the following code block:

```
vagrant@shard01:~$ cat /etc/prometheus/rules.yml
groups:
  - name: recording_rules
    rules:
      - record: job:promhttp_metric_handler_requests:sum_rate1m
        expr: sum by (job) (rate(promhttp_metric_handler_requests_total[1m]))
```

To provide a global view, we can use the `global` instance in the test environment to scrape the federation endpoint of both shards, requesting only those aggregate metrics (all that start with `job:`), as can be seen in the following snippet:

```
vagrant@global:~$ cat /etc/prometheus/prometheus.yml
...
scrape_configs:
  - job_name: shards
    honor_labels: true
```

```
        metrics_path: /federate
        params:
          match[]:
            - '{__name__=~"job:.+"}'
        static_configs:
          - targets:
            - shard01:9090
            - shard02:9090
...
```

There are a couple of things to note in this snippet. Federation uses the same mechanics as regular scrape jobs, but needs the configuration of a different scrape endpoint, and a HTTP parameter to specify which metrics we want to collect. Additionally, setting `honor_labels: true` will ensure that all the original label values are kept and never overridden; this needs to be configured, as otherwise Prometheus would set labels such as `instance` and `job` to the values from the scrape job otherwise.

You can check on the status of federated targets in the aggregator Prometheus instance in our test environment at the `http://192.168.42.12:9090/targets` endpoint, as shown:

Figure 13.6: Prometheus *targets* endpoint showing the federated servers

Scaling and Federating Prometheus

We can also test the federation of metrics in the global Prometheus web interface: even though this instance is not scraping any exporter nor does it have the recording rule, we can get every time series from the `job:promhttp_metric_handler_requests:sum_rate1m` metric, which were originally produced in each shard instance. Note that the `job` label that is returned comes from the original job and not the federation scrape job. Additionally, we can see that the `shard` label we configured as an external label in our instances is present here; labels defined in the `external_labels` section are automatically added to metrics that are returned from the `/federate` endpoint, as follows:

Figure 13.7: Global Prometheus view on the aggregate metric

Now that we understand the mechanics of how federation works, we can proceed to look at common patterns and best practices for federation.

Federation patterns

The first thing to be aware of when starting to implement federation in Prometheus is that the set of federated metrics should either be pre-aggregated or hand-picked. Trying to import big chunks of data, or even every metric, from one Prometheus into another using federation is generally a bad idea, for a couple of reasons:

- Due to the massive amount of data being collected in each scrape, it will have a negative performance impact on both the instance producing the metrics and the one consuming them.
- Since scrape ingestion is atomic but not isolated, the Prometheus instance being targeted can present an incomplete snapshot of its time series due to races: it can be in the middle of processing scrape jobs and will return what is had processed at that moment. This is especially relevant for multi-series metric types such as histograms and summaries.
- Bigger scrapes are more likely to suffer from timeouts, which will in turn create gaps in the data on the Prometheus instance doing the federation scrapes.
- Trying to get all time series from a Prometheus instance into another defeats the point of federation. If it's a matter of proxying metrics, an actual proxy server would probably be a better choice. Nevertheless, the best practice is still to run Prometheus near what you're trying to monitor.

There are two main ways a Prometheus time series federation is implemented: hierarchical and cross-service. As we'll see, both patterns are complementary and can be used together.

Hierarchical

Having multiple shards, or even just more than one datacenter, means that time series data is now spread out across different Prometheus instances. Hierarchical federation aims to solve this issue by having one or more Prometheus servers collecting high-level aggregate time series from other Prometheus instances. You can have more than two levels of federation, though that would require significant scale. This allows the higher-tiered Prometheus to have a broader view over the infrastructure and its applications. However, as only aggregated metrics should be federated, those with the most context and detail will still reside on the lower tiers. The following diagram illustrates how this works:

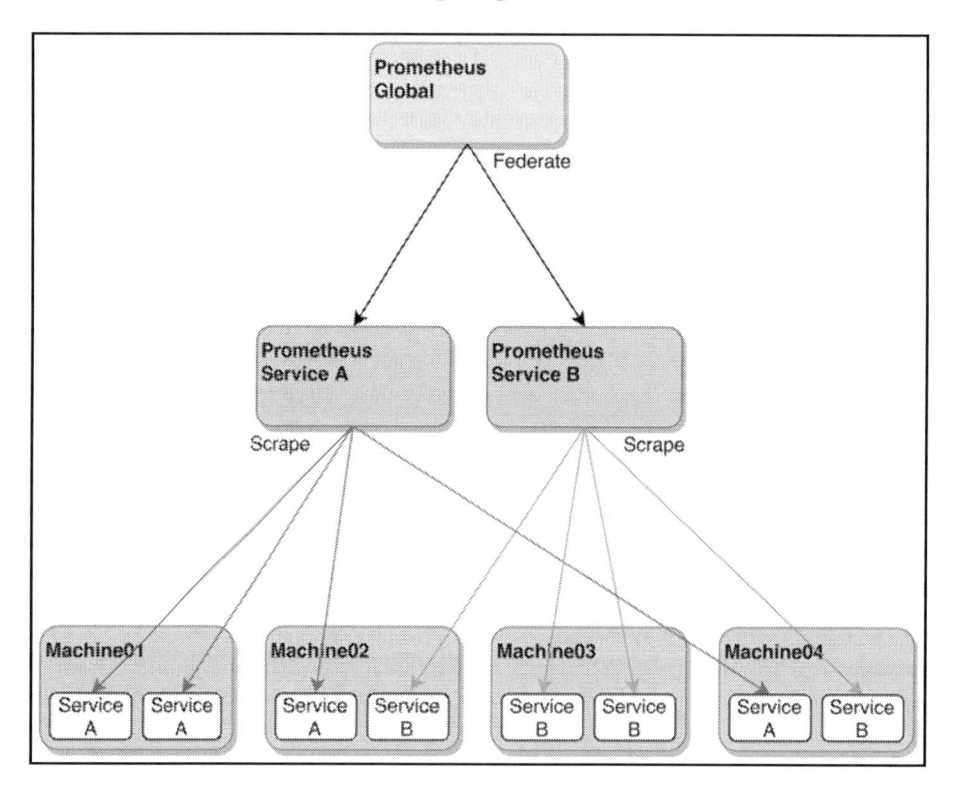

Figure 13.8: Hierarchical federation example diagram

As an example, you may want to have a view of latency across several datacenters. A three-tiered Prometheus hierarchy to fulfil that requirement could look like the following:

- A couple of vertical shards scraping several jobs
- A datacenter instance scraping those shards for time series aggregated at the job level (__name__=~"job:.+")

- A global Prometheus that scrapes the datacenter instances for time series aggregated at the datacenter level (`__name__=~"dc:.+"`)

When using a monitoring platform with this layout, it is common to start at the highest level and then drill down to the next level. This can be easily done with Grafana, as you can have each tier in the federation hierarchy configured as a data source.

Alerting rules should be run as close to the origin of the time series they use as possible, as every federation layer that needs to be crossed will introduce new points of failure in the alerting critical path. This is especially true when aggregating across datacenters, given that the scrapes might need to go through less reliable networks or even through an internet link.

Cross-service

This type of federation is useful when you need a few select time series from another Prometheus instance locally for recording or alerting rules. Going back to the example scenario where you have a Prometheus instance tasked with scraping Node Exporters and another for applications, this pattern would allow you to federate specific OS-level metrics that could then be used in applications alerts, as shown in the following diagram:

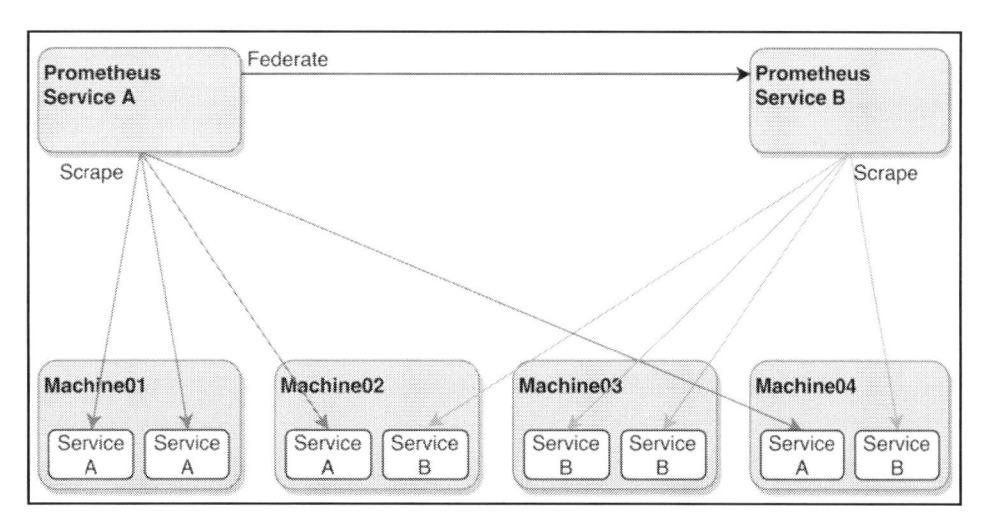

Figure 13.9: Cross-service federation example diagram

The configuration of cross-service federation looks mostly the same as the previous pattern, but in this case the scraped Prometheus is in the same logical tier and the selectors that were used should be matching specific metrics instead of aggregates.

In the next section, we're going to introduce a new component that has been gaining traction in the Prometheus community and tackles the challenge of having a global view in a new and interesting way.

Using Thanos to mitigate Prometheus shortcomings at scale

When you start to scale Prometheus, you quickly bump into the problem of cross-shard visibility. Indeed, Grafana can help, as you can add multiple datastore sources in the same dashboard panel, but this becomes harder to maintain, especially if multiple teams have different needs. Keeping track of which shard has which metric might not be trivial when there aren't clearly defined boundaries - while this might not be a problem when you have a shard per team as each team might only care about their own metrics, issues arise when there are several shards maintained by a single team and exposed as a service to the organization.

Additionally, it is common practice to run two identical Prometheus instances to prevent single points of failure (SPOF) in the alerting path - known as HA (or high-availability) pairs. This complicates dashboarding further, as each instance will have slightly different data (especially in gauge metrics), and having a load balancer distributing queries will result in inconsistent results across dashboard data refreshes.

Thankfully, a project was initiated to, among other things, tackle this exact issue – this project is called Thanos. It was developed at Improbable I/O with the collaboration of Fabian Reinartz (the author of the new storage engine/time series database in Prometheus 2.x).

Prometheus has a well-defined scope of action; for example, it was not built for clustering, and all the decisions that have been made so far have always been aimed at reliability and performance above all else. These design choices are some of the cornerstones of Prometheus' success and allowed it to scale from simple deployments handling a handful of targets to huge instances handling a million of ingested samples per second, but choices almost always come with trade-offs. While Prometheus does offer some workarounds to implement features without resorting to shared state (namely through federation, as we've seen previously), it does so with some limitations, such as having to select which metrics to federate. It is in these cases that creative solutions appear to try and overcome some of these limitations. Thanos is an elegant example of this, as we'll see later.

We'll be discussing more of Thanos' features in `Chapter 14`, *Integrating Long-Term Storage with Prometheus*, but for now our focus will be on the global querying aspect of this project.

Thanos' global view components

To attain a global view using Thanos, we must first understand some of its components. Thanos, like Prometheus, is written in Go and ships a single binary (for each platform/architecture) that behaves differently depending on the provided sub-command in its execution. In our case, we'll be expanding on sidecar and Query components.

> You can find all the source code and installation files for Thanos at `https://github.com/improbable-eng/thanos`.

Scaling and Federating Prometheus

In short, the sidecar makes data from a Prometheus instance available to other Thanos components, while the Query component is an API-compatible replacement for Prometheus that distributes queries it receives to other Thanos components, such as sidecars or even other Query instances. Conceptually, the global-view approach Thanos takes resembles the following diagram:

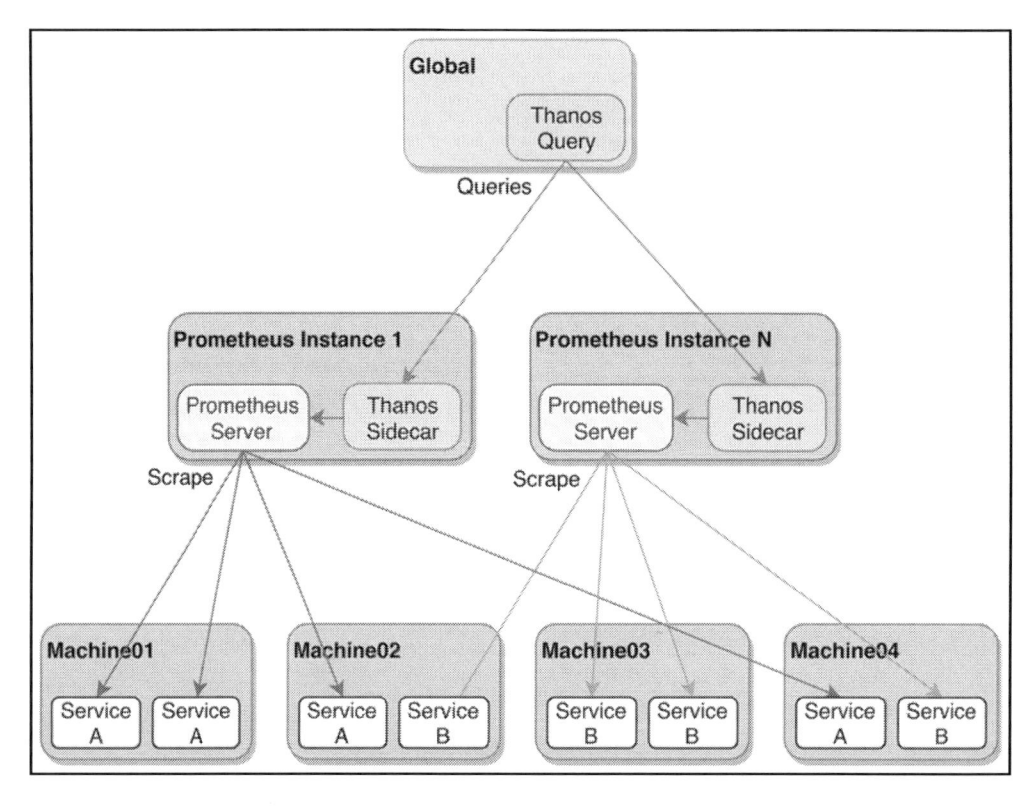

Figure 13.10: Global view with Thanos example diagram

Thanos components that can return query results implement what is called a *store API*. When a request hits a Thanos querier, it will fan out to all the store API nodes configured for it, which in our example are the Thanos sidecars that make time series available from their respective Prometheus servers. The querier will collate the responses (being able to aggregate disjointed or deduplicate data) and then perform the required PromQL query over the dataset. The deduplication feature is particularly useful when using pairs of Prometheus servers for high availability.

[370]

Now, let's take a look at each of these components, digging deeper into how they work and how to set them up.

Sidecar

The sidecar component is meant to be deployed locally alongside Prometheus and connect to it via its remote-read API. Prometheus' remote-read API allows integration with other systems so that they can access samples as if they were locally available for them to query. This obviously introduces the network in the query path, which might cause bandwidth related issues. The sidecar takes advantage of this to make data available in Prometheus to other Thanos components. It exposes the store API as a gRPC endpoint (bound to port `10901` by default), which will then be used by the Thanos query component, effectively turning the sidecar into a datastore from the querier's point of view. Sidecar also exposes an HTTP endpoint on port `10902` with a handler for `/metrics` so that you can collect its internal metrics in Prometheus.

The Prometheus instance that the sidecar is attached to must set `external_labels` so that each instance is uniquely identified. This is essential for Thanos to filter out which store APIs to query and for deduplication to work.

> **TIP**
> Unfortunately, having unique external labels will break Alertmanager deduplication when using pairs of Prometheus instances for high availability. You should use `alert_relabel_configs` in the `alerting` section to drop any label that is unique to each Prometheus instance.

In our test environment, we can find a Thanos sidecar running in each of the available shards. To quickly validate the configuration in use, we can run the following instruction in any shard instances:

```
vagrant@shard01:~$ systemctl cat thanos-sidecar
...
ExecStart=/usr/bin/thanos sidecar \
        --prometheus.url "http://localhost:9090"
...
```

The previous snippet indicates that the sidecar is connecting to the local Prometheus instance. Sidecar offers a lot more functionality, as we'll see in the next chapter, but for the purpose of implementing a global view, this configuration will suffice.

Query

The query component implements the Prometheus HTTP API, which enables PromQL expressions to run against data from all configured Thanos store APIs. It also includes a web interface for querying, which is based on Prometheus' own UI with a couple of minor changes, making users feel right at home. This component is completely stateless and can be scaled horizontally. Due to being compatible with the Prometheus API, it can be used directly in Grafana as a data source of the Prometheus type, enabling drop-in replacement of Prometheus querying for Thanos.

This Thanos component is also running in our test environment, specifically in the *global* instance, and its configuration can be viewed by running the following instruction:

```
vagrant@global:~$ systemctl cat thanos-query
...
ExecStart=/usr/bin/thanos query \
          --query.replica-label "shard" \
          --store "shard01:10901" \
          --store "shard02:10901"
...
```

As we can see in the previous snippet, we are required to specify all the components with a store API that we want to make available through the querier. Since we're using most of the default values for this component, the web interface is available on port `10902`, which we can validate by pointing our browser to `http://192.168.42.12:10902/stores`, as shown in the following screenshot:

Endpoint	Status	Announced Labels	Min Time	Max Time	Last Health Check	Last Message
shard01:10901	UP	shard="shard01"	1970-01-01T00:00:00Z	292278994-08-17T07:12:55Z	4.707s ago	
shard02:10901	UP	shard="shard02"	1970-01-01T00:00:00Z	292278994-08-17T07:12:55Z	4.707s ago	

Figure 13.11: Thanos query web interface showing the /stores endpoint

> **TIP**: The querier HTTP port also serves the `/metrics` endpoint for Prometheus metric collection.

The `--query.replica-label` flag allows for the deduplication of metrics using a specific Prometheus external label. For example, we have the exact same `icmp` job on `shard01` and `shard02`, and both have a `shard` external label to uniquely identify them. Without any deduplication, we would see two results for each of the metrics when doing queries with this job, as both sidecars have relevant data. By marking `shard` as the label that identifies a replica, the querier can select one of the results. We can toggle deduplication via Application Programming Interface (sending `dedup=true` in the `GET` parameters) or the web interface (selecting the **deduplication** option), depending on whether we want to include metrics from all the store APIs or just for single results as if only a single Prometheus instance had the data. The following screenshot exemplifies this difference:

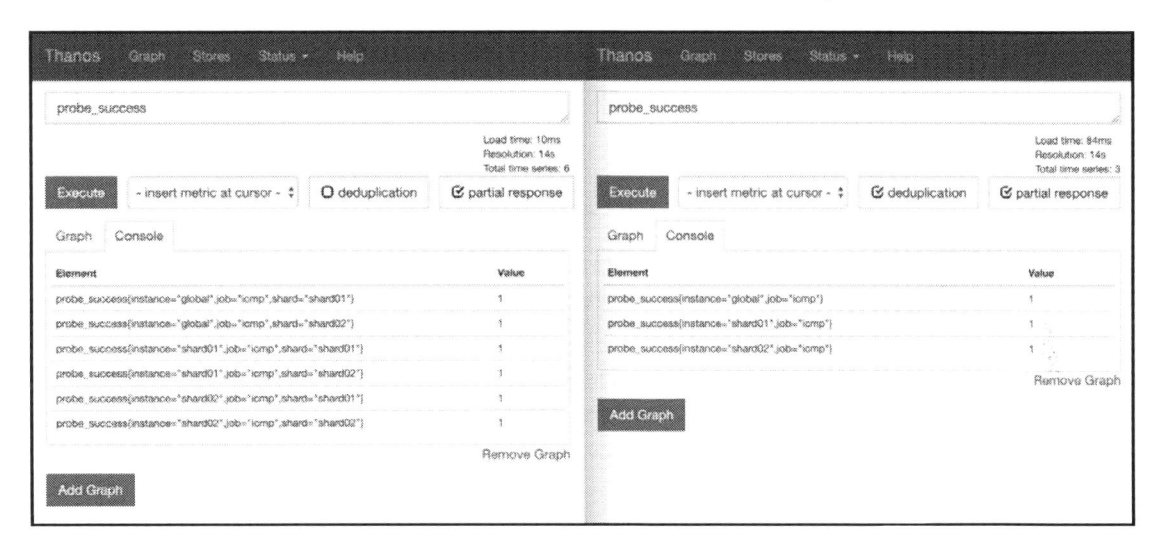

Figure 13.12: Thanos query deduplication disabled and enabled

The deduplication feature is enabled by default so that the querier can seamlessly replace Prometheus in serving queries. This way, upstream systems such as Grafana can continue functioning without even knowing that the query layer has changed.

Summary

In this chapter, we tackled issues concerning running Prometheus at scale. Even though a single Prometheus instance can get you a long way, it's a good idea to have the knowledge to grow if required. We've learned how vertical and horizontal sharding works, when to use sharding, and what benefits and concerns sharding brings. We were introduced to common patterns when federating Prometheus (hierarchical or cross-service), and how to choose between them depending on our requirements. Since, sometimes, we want more than the out-of-the-box federation, we were introduced to the Thanos project and how it solves the global view problem.

In the next chapter, we'll be tackling another common requirement and one that isn't a core concern of the Prometheus project, which is the long-term storage of time series.

Questions

1. When should you consider sharding Prometheus?
2. What's the difference between sharding vertically and horizontally?
3. Is there anything you can do before opting for a sharding strategy?
4. What type of metrics are best suited for being federated in a hierarchical pattern?
5. Why might you require cross-service federation?
6. What protocol is used between Thanos querier and sidecar?
7. If a replica label is not set in a Thanos querier that is configured with sidecars running alongside Prometheus HA pairs, what happens to the results of queries that are executed there?

Further reading

- **Scaling and Federating Prometheus**: https://www.robustperception.io/scaling-and-federating-prometheus
- **Thanos components**: https://github.com/improbable-eng/thanos/tree/master/docs/components
- **Thanos - Prometheus at scale**: https://improbable.io/blog/thanos-prometheus-at-scale

14
Integrating Long-Term Storage with Prometheus

The single-instance design of Prometheus makes it impractical to maintain large datasets of historical data, as it is limited by the amount of storage that's available locally. Having time series that span large periods allows seasonal trend analysis and capacity planning, and so, when the dataset doesn't fit into local storage, Prometheus provides this by pushing data to third-party clustered storage systems. In this chapter, we will look into remote read and write APIs, as well as shipping metrics for object storage with the help of Thanos. This will provide options on how to tackle this requirement, enabling several architecture choices.

In brief, the following topics will be covered in this chapter:

- Test environment for this chapter
- Remote write and remote read
- Options for metrics storage
- Thanos remote storage and ecosystem

Test environment for this chapter

In this chapter, we'll be focusing on clustered storage. For this, we'll be deploying three instances to help simulate a scenario where Prometheus generates metrics and then we'll go through some options regarding how to store them on an object storage solution. This approach will allow us to not only explore the required configurations but also see how everything works together.

The setup we'll be using resembles the following diagram:

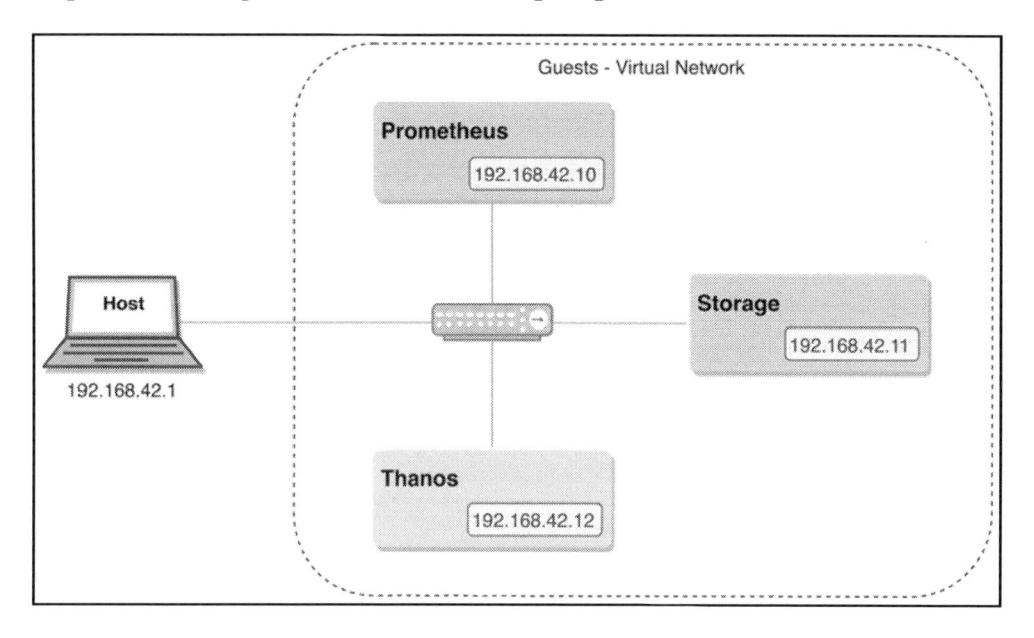

Figure 14.1: Test environment for this chapter

In the next section, we will explain how to get the test environment up and running.

Deployment

To launch a new test environment, move into this path, relative to the repository root, shown as follows:

```
cd ./chapter14/
```

Ensure that no other test environments are running and spin up this chapter's environment, shown as follows:

```
vagrant global-status
vagrant up
```

You can validate the successful deployment of the test environment using the following command:

```
vagrant status
```

This will output the following:

```
Current machine states:

prometheus                 running (virtualbox)
storage                    running (virtualbox)
thanos                     running (virtualbox)

This environment represents multiple VMs. The VMs are all listed above with
their current state. For more information about a specific VM, run `vagrant
status NAME`.
```

When the deployment tasks end, you'll be able to validate the following endpoints on your host machine using your favorite JavaScript-enabled web browser:

Service	Endpoint
Prometheus	`http://192.168.42.10:9090`
Thanos sidecar	`http://192.168.42.10:10902`

Object storage
`Access key: strongACCESSkey`
`Secret key: strongSECRETkey`
	`http://192.168.42.11:9000`

Thanos querier	`http://192.168.42.12:10902`

You should be able to access the desired instance by using one of the following commands:

Instance	Command
Prometheus	`vagrant ssh prometheus`
Storage	`vagrant ssh storage`
Thanos	`vagrant ssh thanos`

Cleanup

When you've finished testing, just make sure that you're inside `./chapter14/` and execute the following command:

```
vagrant destroy -f
```

Don't worry too much; you can easily spin up the environment again if you need to.

Remote write and remote read

Remote write and remote read allow Prometheus to push and pull samples, respectively: remote write is usually employed to implement remote storage strategies, while remote read allows PromQL queries to transparently target remote data. In the following topics, we'll go into each of these functionalities and present some examples of where they can be used.

Remote write

Remote write was a very sought after feature for Prometheus. It was first implemented as native support for sending samples in the openTSDB, InfluxDB, and Graphite data formats. However, a decision was soon made to not support each possible remote system but instead provide a generic write mechanism that's suitable for building custom adapters. This enabled custom integrations decoupled from the Prometheus roadmap, while opening up the possibility of supporting the read path in those bridges as well. The system-specific implementations of remote write were removed from the Prometheus binary and converted into a standalone adapters as an example. The logic of relying on adapters and empowering the community so that it can build whatever integration is required follows the philosophy we discussed in `Chapter 12`, *Choosing the Right Service Discovery*, for building custom service discovery integrations.

> **TIP**
> Official examples of custom remote storage adapters can be found at `https://github.com/prometheus/prometheus/tree/master/documentation/examples/remote_storage/remote_storage_adapter`.

Prometheus sends individual samples to remote write endpoints, using a very simple format which isn't tied to Prometheus internals. The system on the other end might not even be a storage system but a stream processor, such as Kafka or Riemann. This was a tough decision when defining the remote write design, as Prometheus already knew how to create efficient chunks and could just send those over the wire. Chunks would have made supporting streaming systems impractical, and sending samples is both easier to understand and easier to implement with regard to adapters.

Remote write was the target of a great enhancement with the release of Prometheus 2.8. Previously, when a metric failed to be delivered to a remote write endpoint (due to network or service issues) there was just a small buffer to store the data. If that buffer was filled, metrics would be dropped, and were permanently lost to those remote systems. Even worse, the buffer could create back-pressure and cause the Prometheus server to crash due to an **Out of Memory** (**OOM**) error. Since the remote write API started relying on the **Write-Ahead Log** (**WAL**) for bookkeeping, this doesn't happen anymore. Instead of using a buffer, the remote write now reads directly from the WAL, which has all transactions in flight and scraped samples. Using the WAL on the remote write subsystem makes Prometheus memory usage more predictable and allows it to resume from where it left off after a connectivity outage to the remote system.

Configuration-wise, the following snippet illustrates the minimal code required to set up a remote write endpoint in Prometheus:

```
remote_write:
  - url: http://example.com:8000/write
```

Since remote write is another instance of interfacing with external systems, `external_labels` are also applied to samples before being sent. This can also prevent collision of metrics on the remote side when using more than one Prometheus server to push data to the same location. Remote write also supports `write_relabel_configs` to allow you to control which metrics are sent and which are dropped. This relabeling is run after external labels are applied.

Later in this chapter, we'll talk about a fairly new (and experimental) Thanos component called **receiver** as a practical example of remote write usage.

Remote read

After the remote write feature was made available, requests for remote read started to flow. Imagine sending Prometheus data to a remote endpoint and then having to learn a new query language such as InfluxQL (the InfluxDB query language) to access the aforementioned data. The inclusion of this feature enables the transparent use of PromQL against data stored outside the Prometheus server as if it was locally available.

Integrating Long-Term Storage with Prometheus

Queries run against remote data are centrally evaluated. This means that remote endpoints just send the data for the requested matchers and time ranges, and PromQL is applied in the Prometheus instance where the query originated. Once again, choosing centralized (as opposed to distributed) query evaluation was a critical decision at the time of designing the API. Distributed evaluation could have spread the load of each query, but would force the remote system to understand and evaluate PromQL and handle numerous corner cases when data is non-disjoint, greatly increasing the implementation complexity of the aforementioned systems. Centralized evaluation also allows the remote systems to downsample the requested data, which greatly improves queries with very long time ranges.

One example where remote read can be useful is assisting migration between major versions of Prometheus, such as going from Prometheus *v1* to Prometheus *v2*. The latter can be configured to a remote read from the former, thus making the old instance read-only (no scrape jobs configured). This uses the *v1* instance as glorified remote storage until its metrics are no longer useful. A common gotcha that trips the implementer of this strategy is the fact that `external_labels` from the Prometheus instance configured with remote read need to have a match in the `external_labels` from the Prometheus instance being read.

On the flipside, an example of the remote read endpoint in Prometheus itself was seen in the previous chapter (Chapter 13, *Scaling and Federating Prometheus*): the Thanos sidecar uses the remote read API from the local Prometheus instance to get the time series data requested by the Thanos querier.

Configuration-wise, it is quite simple to set up Prometheus to do a remote read. The following snippet shows the required section of the configuration file:

```
remote_read:
  - url: http://example.com:8000/read
```

The `remote_read` section also allows you to specify a list of matchers using `required_matchers` that need to be present in a selector to query a given endpoint. This is useful for remote systems that aren't storage or when you only write a subset of your metrics to remote storage, thus needing to restrict remote reads to those metrics.

Options for metrics storage

By default, Prometheus does a great job of managing local storage of metrics using its own TSDB. But there are cases where this is not enough: local storage is limited by the amount of disk space available locally to the Prometheus instance, which isn't ideal for large retention periods, such as years, and large data volumes that go beyond the amount of disk space that is feasible to have attached to the instance. In the following sections, we'll be discussing the local storage approach, as well as the currently available options for remote storage.

Local storage

Prometheus' out-of-the-box storage solution for time series data is simply local storage. It is simpler to understand and simpler to manage: the database lives in a single directory, which is easy to back up, restore, or destroy if needed. By avoiding clustering, Prometheus ensures sane behavior when facing network partitions; you don't want your monitoring system to fail when you need it the most. High availability is commonly achieved by simply running two Prometheus instances with the same configuration, each with its own database. This storage solution, however, does not cover all uses cases, and has a few shortcomings:

- It's not durable – in a container orchestration deployment, the collected data will disappear when the container is rescheduled (as the previous data is destroyed and the current data is started afresh) if persistent volumes are not used, while in a VM deployment, the data will be as durable as the local disk.
- It's not horizontally scalable – using local storage means that your dataset can only be as big as the disk space you can make available to the instance.
- It wasn't designed for long-term retention, even though, with the right metric criteria and cardinality control, commodity storage will go a long way.

These shortcomings are the result of trade-offs that are made to ensure that small and medium deployments (which are by far the more common use cases) work great while also making advanced and large-scale use cases possible. Alerting and dashboards, in the context of day-to-day operational monitoring or troubleshooting ongoing incidents, only require a couple of weeks of data at most.

Integrating Long-Term Storage with Prometheus

Before going all out for a remote metric storage system for long-term retention, we might consider managing local storage through the use of TSDB admin API endpoints, that is, `snapshot` and `delete_series`. These endpoints help keep local storage under control. As we mentioned in Chapter 5, *Running a Prometheus Server*, the TSDB administration API is not available by default; Prometheus needs to be started with the `--web.enable-admin-api` flag so that the API is enabled.

In this chapter's test environment, you can try using these endpoints and evaluate what they aim to accomplish. By connecting to the `prometheus` instance, we can validate that the TSDB admin API has been enabled, and look up the local storage path by using the following command:

```
vagrant@prometheus:~$ systemctl cat prometheus
...
    --storage.tsdb.path=/var/lib/prometheus/data \
    --web.enable-admin-api \
...
```

Issuing an HTTP `POST` to the `/api/v1/admin/tsdb/snapshot` endpoint will trigger a new snapshot that will store the available blocks in a snapshots directory. Snapshots are made using hard links, which makes them very space-efficient as long as Prometheus still has those blocks. The following instructions illustrate how everything is processed:

```
vagrant@prometheus:~$ curl -X POST
http://localhost:9090/api/v1/admin/tsdb/snapshot
{"status":"success","data":{"name":"20190501T155805Z-55d3ca981623fa5b"}}

vagrant@prometheus:~$ ls /var/lib/prometheus/data/snapshots/
20190501T155805Z-55d3ca981623fa5b
```

You can then back up the snapshot directory, which can be used as the TSDB storage path for another Prometheus instance through `--storage.tsdb.path` when that historical data is required for querying. Note that `--storage.tsdb.retention.time` might need to be adjusted to your data duration, as Prometheus might start deleting blocks outside the retention period.

This, of course, will not prevent the growth of the TSDB. To manage this aspect, we can employ the `/api/v1/admin/tsdb/delete_series` endpoint, which is useful for weekly or even daily maintenance. It operates by means of an HTTP POST request with a set of match selectors that mark all matching time series for deletion, optionally restricting the deletion to a given time window if a time range is also sent. The following table provides an overview of the URL parameters in question:

URL parameters	Description
match[]=<selector>	One or more match selectors, for example, `match[]={__name__=~"go_.*"}` (Deletes all metrics whose name starts with `go_`)
start=<timestamp>	Start time for the deletion in the RFC 3339 or Unix format (optional, defaults to the earliest possible time)
end=<unix_timestamp>	End time for the deletion in RFC 3339 or Unix format (optional, defaults to the latest possible time)

After the POST request is performed, an HTTP 204 is returned. This will not immediately free up disk space, as it will have to wait until the next Prometheus compaction event. You can force this cleanup by requesting the `clean_tombstones` endpoint, as exemplified in the following instructions:

```
vagrant@prometheus:~$ curl -X POST -w "%{http_code}\n" --globoff
'http://localhost:9090/api/v1/admin/tsdb/delete_series?match[]={__name__=~"
go_.*"}'
204

vagrant@prometheus:~$ curl -X POST -w "%{http_code}\n"
http://localhost:9090/api/v1/admin/tsdb/clean_tombstones
204
```

This knowledge might help you keep local storage under control and avoid stepping into complex and time-consuming alternatives, when the concern is mostly around scalability.

Remote storage integrations

Opting for remote metric storage shouldn't be taken lightly as it has several implications. Some factors to consider when choosing a remote storage solution, to name but a few, are as follows:

- **Maturity**: Some storage solutions are more mature and better maintained than others.
- **Control**: There are some solutions where you run your own instances, while others are SaaS offerings.
- **Availability, reliability and scalability**: If you choose to manage the storage solution internally, you need to consider these aspects.
- **Maintainability**: Some options are truly complex to deploy and/or maintain.
- **Remote read and write**: Do you truly need both, or does write suffice for your use case?
- **Cost**: It might all come down to this; we define cost not only in the monetary sense, but also in terms of the time required to learn, test, and operate a solution.

Another critical factor to consider relates to alerting. For reliability, rules should only query local data; this prevents transient failures in the network layer to negatively affect rule evaluation. As such, data in remote storage systems shouldn't be used for critical alerting, or at least you should be able to tolerate them being missing.

If the scale you're working with demands scalable storage or if historical data is crucial for your use case, for example, for capacity planning, then there are a few options available. The official Prometheus documentation has a comprehensive list of known remote storage integrations, available at https://prometheus.io/docs/operating/integrations/#remote-endpoints-and-storage. This list has integrations for several different use cases: SaaS offerings (such as SignalFX and Splunk); a stream processing system (Kafka); different time series databases – both paid (IRONdb) and open source (InfluxDB, Cortex, TimescaleDB, M3DB, to name a few); other monitoring systems (OpenTSDB, Graphite); and even generic datastores (such as Elasticsearch and TiKV). A good portion of them support both remote read and write. Some of them deserve an entire book of their own.

Curiously, the solution we are going to explore in depth isn't in the aforementioned list at the time of writing, as it uses an entirely different approach to the problem we're dealing with. In fact, Prometheus doesn't even need to know about it because it works like an overlay. We are going to focus on the most promising long-term storage solution, which beautifully balances complexity, cost, and the feature set: Thanos.

Thanos remote storage and ecosystem

In `Chapter 13`, *Scaling and Federating Prometheus*, we were introduced to Thanos, an open source project that was created to improve upon some of the shortcomings of Prometheus at scale. Specifically, we went through how Thanos solves having a global view of several Prometheus instances using the Thanos sidecar and querier components. It's now time to meet other Thanos components and explore how they work together to enable cheap long-term retention using object storage. Keep in mind that complexity will increase when going down this path, so validate your requirements and whether the global view approach and local storage aren't enough for your particular use case.

Thanos ecosystem

Besides the Thanos querier and sidecar, which we covered previously, there are a few other components in the Thanos ecosystem. All of these components coexist in the same binary and are run by invoking different sub-commands, which we'll enumerate later:

- `query`: Commonly known as *querier*, it's a daemon that's responsible for fanning out queries and deduplicating results to configured StoreAPI endpoints
- `sidecar`: A daemon which exposes a StoreAPI endpoint for accessing the data from a local Prometheus instance and ships the aforementioned instance's TSDB blocks to object storage
- `store`: A daemon which acts as a gateway for remote storage, exposing a StoreAPI endpoint
- `compact`: Commonly known as *compactor*, this daemon is responsible for compacting blocks that are available in object storage and creating new downsampled time series
- `bucket`: A command line-tool that can verify, recover, and inspect data stored in object storage
- `receive`: Known as *receiver*, it's a daemon that accepts remote writes from Prometheus instances, exposing pushed data through a StoreAPI endpoint, and can ship blocks to object storage
- `rule`: Commonly known as *ruler*, it's a daemon that evaluates Prometheus rules (recording and alerting) against remote StoreAPI endpoints, exposes its own StoreAPI to make evaluation results available for querying, ships results to object storage, and connects to an Alertmanager cluster to send alerts

> You can find all the source code and installation files for Thanos at `https://github.com/improbable-eng/thanos`.

All of the following components work together to solve several challenges:

- **Global view**: Querying every Prometheus instance from the same place, while aggregating and deduplicating the returned time series.
- **Downsampling**: Querying months or even years of data is a problem if samples come at full resolution; by automatically creating downsampled data, queries that span large time periods become feasible.
- **Rules**: Enables the creation of global alerts and recording rules that mix metrics from different Prometheus shards.
- **Long-term retention**: By leveraging object storage, it delegates durability, reliability, and scalability concerns of storage to outside the monitoring stack.

While we'll be providing a glimpse of how these challenges are tackled with Thanos, our main focus will be on the long-term storage aspect of it.

Storage-wise, the Thanos project settled on object storage for long-term data. Most cloud providers provide this service, with the added benefit of also ensuring **service-level agreements (SLA)** for it. Object storage usually has 99.999999999% durability and 99.99% availability on any of the top cloud providers. If you have an on-premise infrastructure, there are also some options available: using Swift (the OpenStack component that provides object storage APIs), or even the MinIO project, which we use in this chapter's test environment. Most of these on-premise object storage solutions share the same characteristic: they provide APIs that are modeled to mimic the well-known AWS S3 due to so many tools supporting it. Moreover, object storage from cloud providers is typically a very cost-effective solution.

The following diagram provides a simple overview of the core components that are needed to achieve long-term retention of Prometheus time series data using Thanos:

Chapter 14

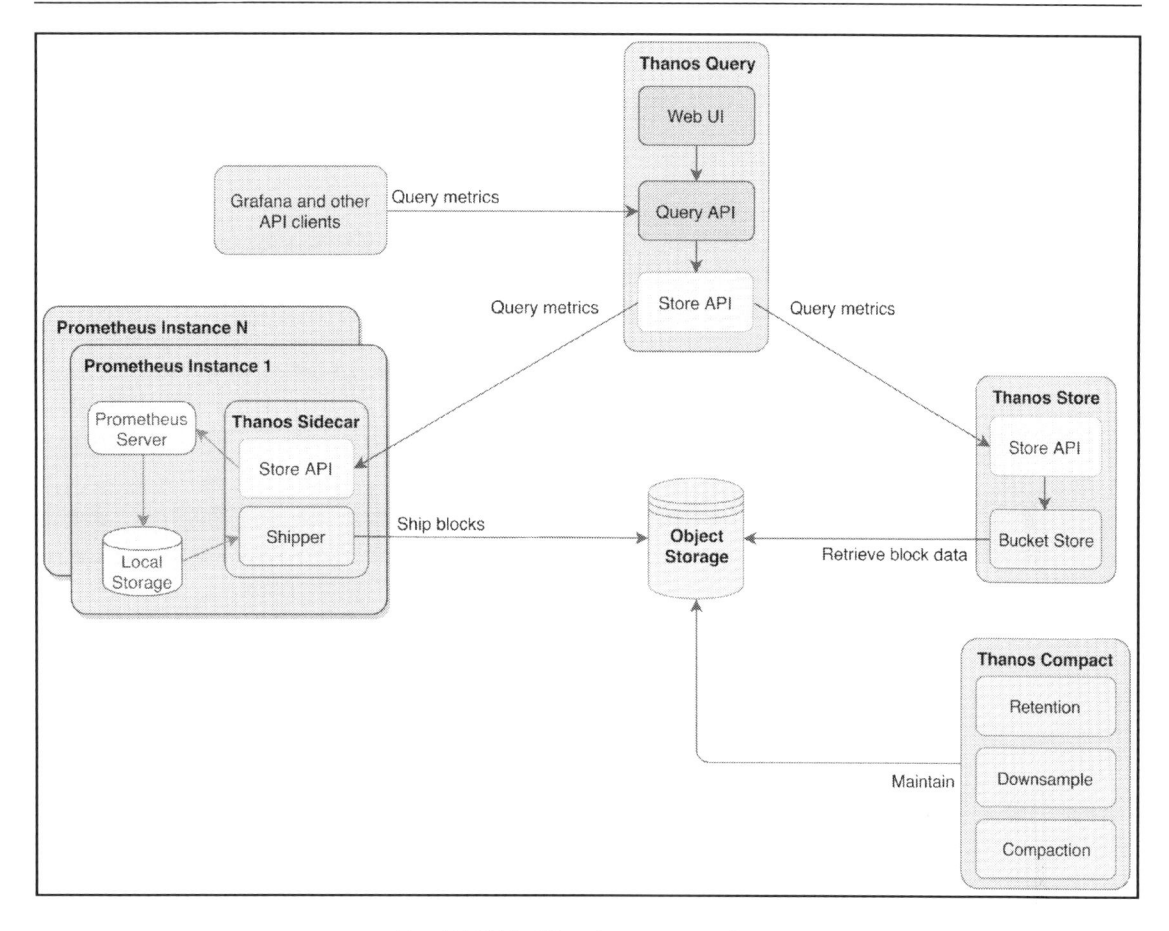

Figure 14.2: High-level Thanos long-term storage architecture

As we can see in the previous diagram, we only need some Thanos components to tackle this challenge. In the following topics, we'll go over every component and expand on its role in the overall design.

Thanos components

Now that we've seen an overview of the Thanos long-term storage architecture, it's time to meet all the available Thanos components. Besides providing an introduction to every single one of them, we'll be emphasizing those that are available in the test environment, expanding on their role in the ecosystem, and the configuration which is in place.

> **TIP**: You can find some community-driven alerts and dashboards at https://github.com/improbable-eng/thanos/tree/master/examples.

Test environment specifics

As stated at the beginning of this book, using the provided test environments won't incur any cost. As such, since we require an object storage bucket for our examples, we relied on a project called MinIO, which exposes an S3-compatible API; you can find more information about it at https://min.io/. Configuration-wise, this storage endpoint should be available in the storage instance with the following settings:

```
vagrant@storage:~$ systemctl cat minio
...
EnvironmentFile=/etc/default/minio
ExecStart=/usr/bin/minio server $MINIO_OPTS $MINIO_VOLUMES
...
```

The preceding `systemd` unit file loads the following environment variables:

```
vagrant@storage:~$ sudo cat /etc/default/minio
MINIO_VOLUMES='/var/lib/minio/data'
MINIO_OPTS='--address :9000'
MINIO_ACCESS_KEY='strongACCESSkey'
MINIO_SECRET_KEY='strongSECRETkey'
```

To ensure that you don't have to wait two hours to have blocks to ship into the object storage, the Prometheus server in our test environment has the following settings in place:

```
vagrant@prometheus:~$ systemctl cat prometheus
...
    --storage.tsdb.max-block-duration=10m \
    --storage.tsdb.min-block-duration=10m
...
```

This configuration changes the block duration, setting the interval at which to flush them to disk, from the default two hours to ten minutes. Although setting such a low value is very useful for testing this particular feature, it is completely ill-advised for anything else. To make this crystal clear, there's no good reason to change these values to anything other than two hours, except for testing.

With the specifics for this chapter's test environment out of the way, we can now proceed to introduce each individual Thanos component.

Thanos query

In Chapter 13, *Scaling and Federating Prometheus*, we had the chance to explore the Thanos querier and sidecar to solve the global view problem. For this component, the features we covered then will also be used in this chapter. We'll continue using querier to query several StoreAPI endpoints, taking advantage of the deduplication it provides, and using the query API through its web interface.

The configuration that's available in our test environment is quite simple, as we can see in the following snippet, which was taken from the `thanos` instance:

```
vagrant@thanos:~$ systemctl cat thanos-query
...
ExecStart=/usr/bin/thanos query \
          --query.replica-label replica \
          --store "prometheus:10901" \
          --store "thanos:11901" \
          --store "thanos:12901"
...
```

As you can see in the previous snippet, we specified several `--store` endpoints. To understand which is which, we can point our browser at the Thanos querier web interface, available at `http://192.168.42.12:10902/stores`, and see the available stores, as depicted by following screenshot:

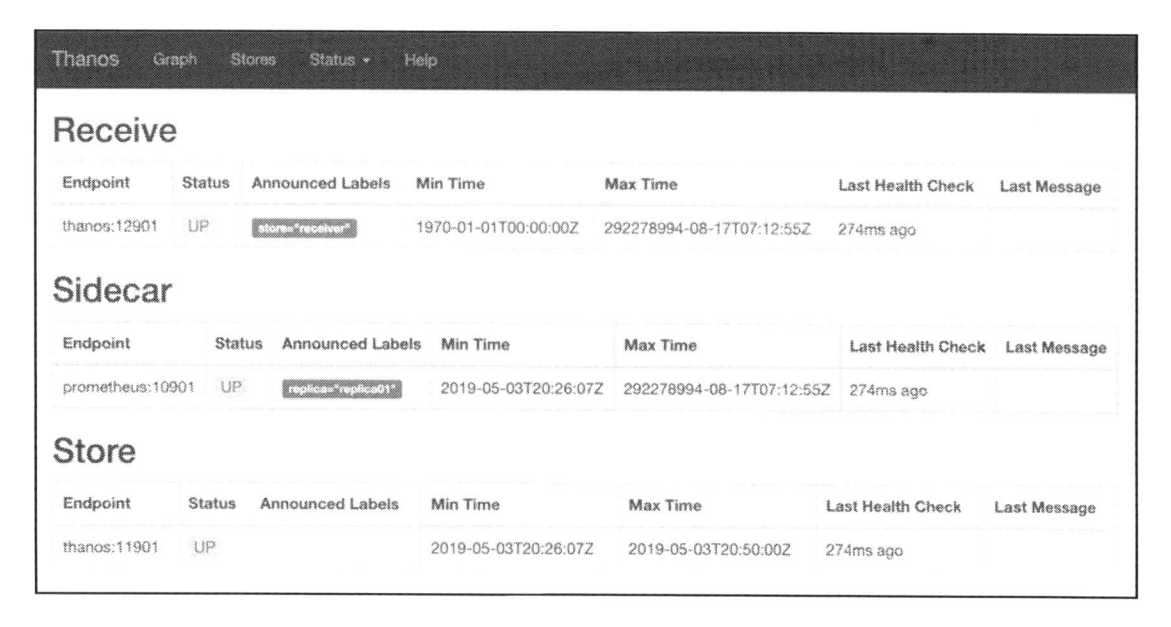

Figure 14.3: Thanos querier /stores endpoint

Integrating Long-Term Storage with Prometheus

The previous screenshot illustrates all the available store APIs in our test environment. These will be the sources of data that will be used any time you execute a query in the Thanos querier.

Thanos sidecar

Besides the Store API that's exposed by the Thanos sidecar we covered previously, this component is also is able to gather TSDB blocks from disk and ship them to an object storage bucket. This allows you to decrease the retention of the Prometheus server by keeping historical data in a durable medium. In order to use the block upload feature in the sidecar, the `--storage.tsdb.min-block-duration` and `--storage.tsdb.max-block-duration` flags need to be set to the same value (two hours to match the default behavior), so that Prometheus local compaction is disabled.

The configuration in use is available on the `prometheus` instance and can be inspected by executing the following instruction:

```
vagrant@prometheus:~$ systemctl cat thanos-sidecar
...
ExecStart=/usr/bin/thanos sidecar \
          --log.level debug \
          --prometheus.url "http://localhost:9090" \
          --tsdb.path "/var/lib/prometheus/data" \
          --objstore.config-file "/etc/thanos/storage.yml"
...
```

As we can see, the `--objstore.config-file` flag loads all the required configuration from the file in order to ship the TSDB blocks to an object storage bucket, such as the bucket name (in our case, `thanos`), the storage endpoint, and access credentials. The following are the contents of that file:

```
vagrant@prometheus:~$ sudo cat /etc/thanos/storage.yml
type: S3
config:
  bucket: 'thanos'
  endpoint: 'storage:9000'
  insecure: true
  signature_version2: true
  access_key: 'strongACCESSkey'
  secret_key: 'strongSECRETkey'
```

Chapter 14

In our Prometheus test instance, a new TSDB block will be generated every 10 minutes, and the Thanos sidecar will take care of shipping it to the object storage endpoint. We can review the available blocks in our bucket by using MinIO's web interface, available at `http://192.168.42.11:9000/minio/thanos/`. After logging in with the `access_key` and `secret_key` shown in the previous code snippet, you'll be greeted with something resembling the following screenshot:

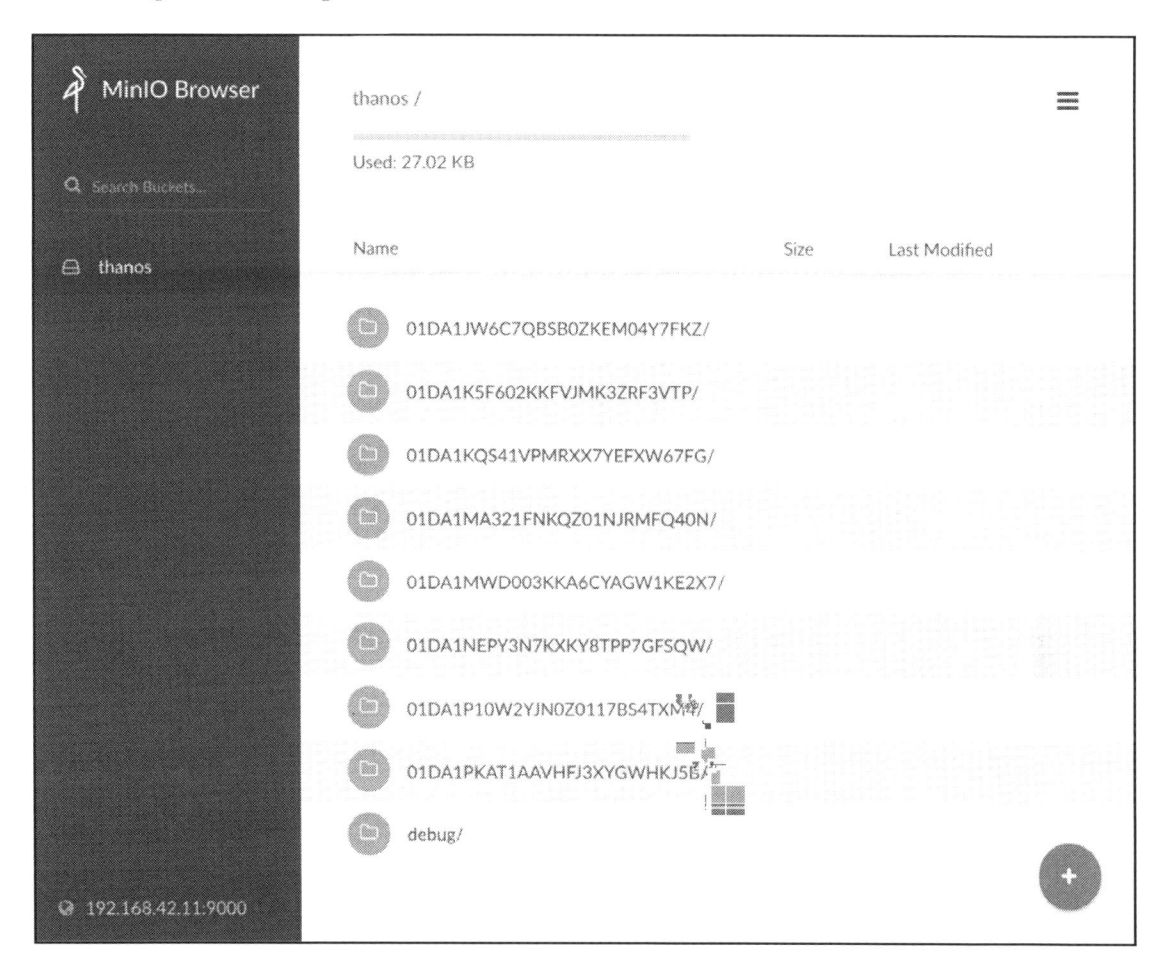

Figure 14.4: MinIO object storage web interface

We should now have some historical data available for testing. We'll need a way to query this data. That's where the Thanos store gateway comes into play.

Thanos store gateway

The Thanos store gateway's main function is to provide access to the historical time series data in the blocks that are shipped to object storage through a StoreAPI endpoint. This means that it effectively acts as an API gateway. All major object store integrations in Thanos store (Google Cloud Storage, AWS S3, Azure Storage) are considered stable enough to run in production. It uses a relatively small local cache of all block metadata, and it keeps it in sync with the storage bucket.

A minimal configuration for this component is available in the Thanos instance in our test environment. The following is the snippet from it:

```
vagrant@thanos:~$ systemctl cat thanos-store
...
ExecStart=/usr/bin/thanos store \
        --data-dir "/var/lib/thanos/store" \
        --objstore.config-file "/etc/thanos/storage.yml" \
        --grpc-address "0.0.0.0:11901" \
        --http-address "0.0.0.0:11902"
...
```

As we can see, object storage configuration is done in its own configuration file. Like most of the other components, a store binds a StoreAPI GRPC port for receiving queries and an HTTP port so that its metrics can be collected by Prometheus.

Thanos compact

Since Prometheus block compaction needs to be turned off for Thanos sidecar upload feature to work reliably, this work is delegated to a different component: Thanos compact. It was designed to use the same compaction strategy as the Prometheus storage engine itself, but for blocks in object storage instead. Since compaction cannot be done directly in object storage, this component requires a fair amount of available space (a few hundred GB, depending on the amount stored remotely) in local disks to process the blocks.

Another important function Thanos compact performs is creating downsampled samples. The biggest advantage of downsampling is querying large time ranges reliably, without needing to pull an overwhelming amount of data. The usage of *_over_time functions (as discussed in Chapter 7, *Prometheus Query Language – PromQL*) is also highly recommended when using downsampled data as the method that's used to downsample does not merely remove samples but also pre-aggregates them using five different aggregation functions. This means that five new time series for each raw series. Something very important to keep in mind is that full resolution data is only downsampled to a five minute resolution after 40 hours. Similarly, one hour's downsampled data is only created after 10 days by using the previously downsampled data with five minute resolution as the source. Keeping the raw data might be useful for zooming into a specific event in time, which you wouldn't be able to do with just downsampled data. There are three flags for managing the retention of data (that is, how long to keep it) in raw, five minute, and one hour form, as shown in the following table:

Flag	Duration
--retention.resolution-raw	The duration keeps data with a raw resolution in the object storage bucket, for example, 365d (it defaults to 0d, which means forever)
--retention.resolution-5m	The duration to keep data with 5-minute in the object storage bucket, for example, 365d (it defaults to 0d, which means forever)
--retention.resolution-1h	The duration to keep data with 1-hour in the object storage bucket, for example, 365d (it defaults to 0d, which means forever)

> Each storage bucket should only have one Thanos compactor associated with it, as it's not designed to run concurrently.

When considering retention policies, bear in mind that, as the first downsampling step aggregates five minutes-worth of data and the aggregation produces five new time series, you'd need to have a scrape interval lower than one minute to actually save space (the number of samples in the interval needs to be higher than the samples produced by the aggregation step).

Integrating Long-Term Storage with Prometheus

The compactor can either be run as a daemon which springs to action whenever it's needed, or as single-shot job, exiting at the end of the run. In our test environment, we have a Thanos compactor running in the `thanos` instance to manage our object storage bucket. It's running as a service (using the `--wait` flag) to make the test environment simpler. The configuration being used is shown in the following snippet:

```
vagrant@thanos:~$ systemctl cat thanos-compact
...
ExecStart=/usr/bin/thanos compact \
        --data-dir "/var/lib/thanos/compact" \
        --objstore.config-file "/etc/thanos/storage.yml" \
        --http-address "0.0.0.0:13902" \
        --wait \
        --retention.resolution-raw 0d \
        --retention.resolution-5m 0d \
        --retention.resolution-1h 0d
...
```

Just like the other components, the HTTP endpoint is useful for scraping metrics from it. As can be seen in the `retention.*` flags, we're keeping the data in all the available resolutions forever. We'll be discussing Thanos bucket next, a debugging tool that helps inspect Thanos-managed storage buckets.

Thanos bucket

This component of the Thanos ecosystem is responsible for verifying, repairing, listing, and inspecting blocks in object storage. Unlike other components, this one behaves as a command-line tool instead of a daemon.

You can try out the following example of its usage: listing the available blocks in our object storage bucket:

```
vagrant@thanos:~$ sudo thanos bucket ls -o wide --objstore.config-file=/etc/thanos/storage.yml
01D9SN3KEBNCB2MHASYXSDF1DE -- 2019-05-01 12:00 - 2019-05-01 12:10 Diff: 10m0s, Compaction: 1, Downsample: 0, Source: sidecar
01D9SNNXCAXWKZ0EH6118FTHSS -- 2019-05-01 12:10 - 2019-05-01 12:20 Diff: 10m0s, Compaction: 1, Downsample: 0, Source: sidecar
01D9SP87A9NZ9DE35TC2QNS7ZZ -- 2019-05-01 12:20 - 2019-05-01 12:30 Diff: 10m0s, Compaction: 1, Downsample: 0, Source: sidecar
01D9SPTH88G9TR4503C4763TDN -- 2019-05-01 12:30 - 2019-05-01 12:40 Diff: 10m0s, Compaction: 1, Downsample: 0, Source: sidecar
01D9SQCV68KVE7CXK4QDW9RWM1 -- 2019-05-01 12:40 - 2019-05-01 12:50 Diff: 10m0s, Compaction: 1, Downsample: 0, Source: sidecar
01D9SQN6TVJ97NP4K82APW7YH9 -- 2019-05-01 10:51 - 2019-05-01 11:50 Diff:
```

```
58m41s, Compaction: 2, Downsample: 0, Source: compactor
```

This tool is very useful for troubleshooting issues and quickly understanding the state of blocks in the storage bucket.

Thanos receive

This component, at the time of writing, is still very experimental. However, as promised in the *Remote write and read* section of this chapter, this component is an excellent example of what remote write is all about, so we decided to show you what it can do. It acts as a target for Prometheus remote write requests, and stores received samples locally. The receiver also implements a StoreAPI endpoint, so it has the ability to act as a store node. Finally, it can also ship blocks to object storage, just like sidecar.

To make more sense of what all of this means, let's explore two scenarios.

A Prometheus server will, by default, generate a block every two hours. Even using Thanos sidecar with block shipping, there's no way for Thanos querier to get to data that is still in the WAL without sidecar having to request it via a remote read API from the Prometheus server. When you get to a scale where Grafana, or another API client, generates a huge request rate against Prometheus, the odds are that it will impact Prometheus' performance and eventually affect alerting, even though Prometheus has some protections mechanisms, as we've seen previously. By using Thanos receiver, you can simply move the client queries to it, ensuring that the Prometheus server's main job is scraping and evaluating rules. In a nutshell, you will effectively be separating the reads from the writes of the Prometheus server. You could continue to use Thanos sidecar just to ship blocks and Thanos receiver to answer all Thanos querier inquiries, just like a fresh cache, protecting the Prometheus write path in the process.

> **TIP**: Thanos receiver generates blocks every two hours and, unlike Prometheus, this value is hardcoded by design.

Imagine another scenario where there are several tenants/teams using the infrastructure you're managing. If they're technically savvy enough, they'll eventually want to manage their own Prometheus servers. You could try to provide all the automation that's required to manage their servers, but you'll quickly encounter a bottleneck. One option would be to give them a Prometheus server to manage, a Thanos receiver endpoint, and a Thanos store endpoint. Thanos receiver would take care of shipping the blocks to object storage, and Thanos store would provide a way to access them, abstracting the complexity of remote storage from the tenant altogether. This would just be the first step in providing long-term storage as a service for your infrastructure.

In our test environment, in the `thanos` instance, we have a Thanos receiver running. In the following snippet, we can see its configuration:

```
vagrant@thanos:~$ systemctl cat thanos-receive
...
ExecStart=/usr/bin/thanos receive \
          --tsdb.path "/var/lib/thanos/receive" \
          --tsdb.retention 6h \
          --labels "store=\"receiver\"" \
          --remote-write.address "0.0.0.0:19291" \
          --grpc-address "0.0.0.0:12901" \
          --http-address "0.0.0.0:12902"
...
```

Since we already have a Thanos sidecar running alongside our Prometheus server, which is sending TSDB blocks to object storage, we disabled the shipping functionality of the receiver just by not adding the `--objstore.config-file` flag. Notice the `--labels` flag, which allows us to specify a label to add to all the time series exposed by this receiver's StoreAPI; this is effectively a way to configure external labels. Another noteworthy flag is `--remote-write.address`, which is used to provide the remote write endpoint. If we look into the `prometheus` instance, we will see the following configuration, which takes advantage of the aforementioned flag:

```
vagrant@prometheus:~$ cat /etc/prometheus/prometheus.yml
...
remote_write:
  - url: http://thanos:19291/api/v1/receive
...
```

To test all of this, we can simply stop the Thanos sidecar in the `prometheus` instance, as follows:

```
vagrant@prometheus:~$ sudo systemctl stop thanos-sidecar
```

After doing this, Thanos querier will no longer be able to access Thanos sidecar and the recent block information won't be flushed to disk. This way, we can validate whether the receiver will provide this data. If we go over to the Thanos querier web interface at http://192.168.42.12:10902/graph and run an instant query such as `up{instance=~"prometheus.+"}`, we are presented with the following output:

Figure 14.5: Thanos receiver showing metrics, even with the Thanos sidecar down

Note the `store` label, indicating that Thanos receiver is providing data while also informing us that Thanos sidecar is currently down. This proves that we can query recent data thanks to the Prometheus remote write API.

The decision to use this component shouldn't be taken lightly, as it has some disadvantages: besides the fact that it is clearly marked as experimental, it is effectively a push-based system, like Graphite. This means that all the downsides from push-based approaches apply, namely difficulty in managing abusive/rogue clients.

Thanos rule

This component allows you to run Prometheus-compatible rules (recording/alerting) against remote query endpoints, such as Thanos querier or sidecar. It exposes a StoreAPI endpoint to make the results of rule evaluations available, which are stored in local blocks, and can also ship these TSDB blocks to object storage. It's tempting to imagine using this component as a solution for the centralized management of rules instead of spreading them across multiple Prometheus instances, but that's not its purpose and would be ill-advised. Throughout this book, we have stressed how critical rules are, especially for alerting. We also underlined the importance of running those rules locally in the Prometheus instance that has the required metrics. We've provided alternatives, such as a hierarchical or cross-service federation, for gathering metrics from different Prometheus instances. By using the Thanos ruler for alerting, you would be adding a number of points of failure to the critical path: other Thanos components, the network, and, in the worst case, object storage. Alerting needs to be predictable and reliable, so you can have a high level of confidence that it will work when you need it the most. Though Thanos ruler can have a legitimate set of use cases, it shouldn't be considered for most alerting needs. Nonetheless, it's important to acknowledge its existence.

> **TIP**
> More information regarding the Thanos ruler can be found at `https://thanos.io/components/rule.md`.

We now have a complete overview of the Thanos ecosystem and how it's configured on the test environment. We invite you to experiment with all the components while evaluating their behavior: for example, stopping all the store APIs except the Thanos store or using the Thanos bucket to understand what data is available in the object storage bucket.

Summary

In this chapter, we were introduced to remote read and remote write endpoints. We learned how the recent remote write strategy using WAL is so important for the global performance and availability of Prometheus. Then, we explored some alternatives for keeping Prometheus local storage under control, while explaining the implications of opting for a long-term storage solution. Finally, we delved into Thanos, exposing some of its design decisions and introducing the complete ecosystem of components, providing practical examples showing how all the different pieces work together. With this, we can now build a long-term storage solution for Prometheus if we need to.

Questions

1. What are the main advantages of a remote write based on WAL?
2. How can you perform a backup of a running Prometheus server?
3. Can the disk space of a Prometheus server be freed at runtime? If so, how?
4. What are the main advantages of Thanos using object storage?
5. Does it make sense to keep data in all available resolutions?
6. What is the role of Thanos store?
7. How can you inspect the data that's available in object storage using Thanos?

Further reading

- **Prometheus HTTP API**: https://prometheus.io/docs/prometheus/latest/querying/api/
- **Thanos official website**: https://thanos.io

Assessments

Chapter 1, Monitoring Fundamentals

1. A consensual definition of monitoring is hard to come by because it quickly shifts from industry or even in job-specific contexts. The diversity of viewpoints, the components comprising the monitoring system, and even how the data is collected or used, are all factors that contribute to the struggle to reach a clear definition.
2. System administrators are interested in high resolution, low latency, high diversity data. Within this scope, the primary objective of monitoring is so that problems are discovered quickly and the root causes identified as soon as possible.
3. Low resolution, high latency, and high diversity data.
4. It depends on how broad you want to make the monitoring definition. Within the scope of this book, logging is not considered monitoring.
5. The monitoring service's location needs to be propagated to all targets. Staleness is a big drawback of this approach: if a system hasn't reported in for some time, does that mean it's having problems, or was it purposely decommissioned? Furthermore, when you manage a distributed fleet of hosts and services that push data to a central point, the risk of a thundering herd (overload due to many incoming connections at the same time) or a misconfiguration causing an unforeseen flood of data becomes much more complex and time-consuming to mitigate.
6. The RED method is a very good starting point, opting for rate, errors, and duration metrics.
7. This is a blackbox approach to monitoring and should instead rely on instrumenting said process directly or via an exporter.

Chapter 2, An Overview of the Prometheus Ecosystem

1. The main components are Prometheus, Alertmanager, Pushgateway, Native Instrumented Applications, Exporters, and Visualization solutions.
2. Only Prometheus and scrape targets (whether they are natively instrumented or use exporters) are essential for a Prometheus deployment. However, to have alert routing and management, you also need Alertmanager; Pushgateway is only required in very specific use cases, such as batch jobs; while Prometheus does have basic dashboarding functionality built in, Grafana can be added to the stack as the visualization option.
3. Not all applications are built with Prometheus-compatible instrumentation. Sometimes, no metrics at all are exposed. In these cases, we can rely on exporters.
4. The information should be quickly gathered and exposed in a synchronous operation.
5. Alerts will be sent from both sides of the partition, if possible.
6. The quickest option would be to use the webhook integration.
7. The Prometheus server comes with an expression browser and consoles.

Chapter 3, Setting Up a Test Environment

1. While the Prometheus stack can be deployed in almost every mainstream operating system, and thus, it will most certainly run in your desktop environment, it is more reproducible to use a Vagrant-based test environment for simulating machine deployments, and minikube to do the same for Kubernetes-based production environments.
2. The `defaults.sh` file located in the `utils` directory allows the software versions to be changed for the virtual machine-based examples.
3. The default subnet is `192.168.42.0/24` in all virtual machine-based examples.
4. The steps to get a Prometheus instance up and running are as follows:
    1. Ensure that software versions match the ones recommended.
    2. Clone the code repository provided.
    3. Move into the chapter directory.
    4. Run `vagrant up`.
    5. When finished, run `vagrant destroy -f`.

5. That information is available in the Prometheus web interface under `/targets`.
6. Under `./cache/alerting.log`.
7. In any chapter, when you are done with the test environment, just run `vagrant destroy -f` under the said chapter's directory.

Chapter 4, Prometheus Metrics Fundamentals

1. Time series data can be defined as a sequence of numerical data points collected chronologically from the same source – usually at a fixed interval. As such, this kind of data, when represented in a graphical form, will plot the evolution of the data through time, with the *x*-axis being time and the *y*-axis the data value.
2. A timestamp, a value, and tags/labels.
3. The **write-ahead log** (**WAL**).
4. The default is 2h and should not be changed.
5. A float64 value and a timestamp with millisecond precision.
6. Histograms are especially useful for tracking bucketed latencies and sizes (for example, request durations or response sizes) as they can be freely aggregated across different dimensions. Another great use is to generate heatmaps (the evolution of histograms over time).
Summaries without quantiles are quite cheap to generate, collect, and store. The main reason for using summary quantiles is when accurate quantile estimation is needed, irrespective of the distribution and range of the observed events.
7. Cross-sectional aggregation combines multiple time series into one by aggregated dimension; longitudinal aggregation combines samples from a single time series over a time range into a single data point.

Chapter 5, Running a Prometheus Server

1. Then, `scrape_timeout` will be set to its default – 10 seconds.
2. Besides restarting, the configuration file can be reloaded by either sending a `SIGHUP` signal to the Prometheus process or sending an HTTP POST request to the `/-/reload` endpoint if `--web.enable-lifecycle` is used at startup.
3. Prometheus will look back up to five minutes by default, unless it finds a stale marker, in which case it will immediately consider the series stale.

Assessments

4. While `relabel_configs` is used to rewrite the target list before the scrape is performed, `metric_relabel_configs` is used to rewrite labels or drop samples after the scrape has occurred.
5. As we're scraping through a Kubernetes service (which is similar in function to a load balancer), the scrapes will hit only a single instance of the *Hey* application at a time.
6. Due to the ephemeral nature of Kubernetes pods, it would be almost impossible to accurately manage the scrape targets using static configurations without additional automation.
7. The Prometheus Operator leverages Kubernetes Custom Resources and Custom Controllers to declare domain-specific definitions that can be used to automatically manage a Prometheus stack and its scrape jobs.

Chapter 6, Exporters and Integrations

1. The textfile collector enables the exposition of custom metrics by watching a directory for files with the `.prom` extension that contain metrics in the Prometheus exposition format.
2. Data is collected from the container runtime daemon and from Linux cgroups.
3. You can restrict the number of collectors (`--collectors`) to enable, or use the metric whitelist (`--metric-whitelist`) or blacklist (`--metric-blacklist`) flags.
4. When debugging probes, you can append `&debug=true` to the HTTP GET URL to enable debug information.
5. We can use `mtail` or `grok_exporter` to extract metrics from the application logs.
6. One possible problem is the lack of high availability, making it a single point of failure. This also impacts scalability, as the only way to scale is vertically or by sharding. By using Pushgateway, Prometheus does not scrape an instance directly, which prevents having the `up` metric be a proxy for health monitoring. Additionally, and like the textfile collector from `node_exporter`, metrics need to be manually deleted from Pushgateway, via its API, or they will forever be exposed to Prometheus
7. In this particular case, the textfile collector from Node Exporter can be a valid solution, particularly when the life cycle of the produced metric matches the life cycle of the instance.

Chapter 7, Prometheus Query Language - PromQL

1. The comparison operators are < (less than), > (greater than), == (equals), != (differs), => (greater than or equal to), and <= (less than or equal to).
2. When the time series you want to enrich are on the right-hand side of the PromQL expression.
3. `topk` already sorts its results.
4. While the `rate()` function provides the per-second average rate of change over the specified interval by using the first and last values in the range scaled to fit the range window, the `irate()` function uses the last two values in the range for the calculation, which produces the instant rate of change.
5. Metrics of type info have their names ending in `_info` and are regular gauges with one possible value, `1`. This special kind of metric was designed to be a place where labels whose values might change over time are stored, such as versions (for example, exporter version, language version, and kernel version), assigned roles, or VM metadata information.
6. The `rate` function expects a counter, but a sum of counters is actually a gauge, as it can go down when one of the counters resets; this would translate into seemingly random spikes when graphed, because `rate` would consider any decrease a counter reset, but the total sum of the other counters would be considered a huge delta between zero and the current value.
7. When a CPU core is being used 100%, it uses 1 CPU second. Conversely, when it's idle, it will use 0 CPU seconds. This makes it easy to calculate the percentage of usage, as we can utilize the CPU seconds directly. A virtual machine might have more than one core, which means that it might use more than 1 CPU second per second. The following expression calculates how many CPU seconds per second each core was idling in the last 5 minutes:

```
rate(node_cpu_seconds_total{job="node",mode="idle"}[5m])
```

A simple way to calculate the average CPU idle seconds per second for the last five minutes is to average the value for each core:

```
avg without (cpu, mode)
(rate(node_cpu_seconds_total{job="node",mode="idle"}[5m]))
```

As CPU seconds used, plus CPU seconds idle, should total 1 CPU second per second per core, to get the CPU usage, we do the following:

```
avg without (cpu, mode) (1 -
rate(node_cpu_seconds_total{job="node",mode="idle"}[5m]))
```

To get a percentage, we just need to multiply by 100:

```
avg without (cpu, mode) (1 -
rate(node_cpu_seconds_total{job="node",mode="idle"}[5m])) * 100
```

Chapter 8, Troubleshooting and Validation

1. Prometheus is distributed with `promtool` which, among other functions, can check a configuration file for issues:

   ```
   promtool check config /etc/prometheus/prometheus.yml
   ```

2. The `promtool` utility can also read metrics in the Prometheus exposition format from `stdin` and validate them according to the current Prometheus standards:

   ```
   curl -s http://prometheus:9090/metrics | promtool check metrics
   ```

3. The `promtool` utility can be used to run instant queries against a Prometheus instance:

   ```
   promtool query instant 'http://prometheus:9090' 'up == 1'
   ```

4. You can use `promtool` to find every label value for a given label name. One example is the following:

   ```
   promtool query labels 'http://prometheus:9090' 'mountpoint'
   ```

5. By adding `--log.level=debug` to the start-up parameters.
6. The `/-/healthy` endpoint will tell you (or the orchestration system) whether the instance has issues and needs to be redeployed, while the `/-/ready` endpoint will tell you (or your instance's load balancer) whether it is ready to receive traffic.
7. While the Prometheus database is unlocked (for example, when no Prometheus is using that directory), you can run the `tsdb` utility to analyze a specific block of data for metric and label churn:

   ```
   tsdb analyze /var/lib/prometheus/data 01D486GRJTNYJH1RM0F2F4Q9TR
   ```

Chapter 9, Defining Alerting and Recording Rules

1. This type of rules can help take the load off heavy dashboards by pre-computing expensive queries, aggregate raw data into time series that can then be exported to external systems, and assist the creation of compound range vector queries.
2. For the same reasons as in scrape jobs, queries might produce erroneous results when using series with different sampling rates, and having to keep track of what series have what periodicity becomes unmanageable.
3. `instance_job:latency_seconds_bucket:rate30s` needs to have at least the `instance` and `job` labels. It was calculated by applying the rate to the `latency_seconds_bucket_total` metric, using a 30-second range vector. Thus, the originating expression could probably be as follows:

   ```
   rate(latency_seconds_bucket_total[30s])
   ```

4. As that label changes its value, so will the identity of the alert.
5. An alert enters the *pending* state when it starts triggering (its expression starts returning results), but the `for` interval hasn't elapsed yet to be considered *firing*.
6. It would be immediate. When the `for` clause isn't specified, the alert will be considered firing as soon as its expression produces results.
7. The `promtool` utility has a `test` sub-command that can run unit tests for recording and alerting rules.

Chapter 10, Discovering and Creating Grafana Dashboards

1. Grafana supports automatic provisioning of data sources by reading YAML definitions from a provisioning path at startup.
2. Steps to import a dashboard from the Grafana gallery are as follows:
   1. Choose a dashboard ID from the `grafana.com` gallery.
   2. In the target Grafana instance, click on the plus sign in the main menu on the left-hand side and select **Import** from the sub-menu.
   3. Paste the chosen ID in the appropriate text field.

3. Variables allow a dashboard to configure placeholders that can be used in expressions and title strings, and those placeholders can be filled with values from either a static or dynamic list, which are usually presented to the dashboard user in the form of a drop-down menu. Whenever the selected value changes, Grafana will automatically update the queries in panels and title strings that use that respective variable.
4. In Grafana, the building block is the panel.
5. No, it does not. The dashboard ID will remain the same, but the iteration will be incremented.
6. Consoles are custom dashboards that are served directly from a Prometheus instance.
7. They are generated from console templates, which are written in raw HTML/CSS/JavaScript and leverage the power of the Go templating language, making them endlessly customizable. Since the templating runs inside Prometheus, it can access the TSDB directly instead of going through the HTTP API, which makes console generation amazingly quick.

Chapter 11, Understanding and Extending Alertmanager

1. In the case of a network partition, each side of the partition will send notifications for the alerts they are aware of: in a clustering failure scenario, it's better to receive duplicate notifications for an issue than to not get any at all.
2. By setting `continue` to `true` on a route, it will make the matching process keep going through the routing tree until the next match, thereby allowing multiple receivers to be triggered.
3. The `group_interval` configuration defines how long to wait for additional alerts in a given alert group (defined by `group_by`) before sending an updated notification when a new alert is received; `repeat_interval` defines how long to wait until resending notifications for a given alert group when there are no changes.
4. The top-level route, also known as the catch-all or fallback route, will trigger a default receiver when incoming alerts aren't matched in other sub-routes.

5. The webhook integration allows Alertmanager to issue an HTTP POST request with the JSON payload of the notification to a configurable endpoint. This allows you to run a bridge that can convert notifications from Alertmanager to your chosen notification provider's format, and then forward them to it.
6. The `CommonLabels` field is populated with the labels that are common to all alerts in the notification. The `CommonAnnotations` field does exactly the same, but for annotations.
7. A good approach is to use a deadman's switch alert: create an alert that is guaranteed to always be firing, and then configure Alertmanager to route that alert to a (hopefully) external system that will be responsible for letting you know whether it ever stops receiving notifications.

Chapter 12, Choosing the Right Service Discovery

1. Managing scrape targets in a highly dynamic environment becomes an arduous task without automatic discovery.
2. Having a set of access credentials with sufficient permissions to list all the required resources through its API.
3. It supports A, AAAA, and SRV DNS records.
4. Due to the large number of API objects available to query, the Kubernetes discovery configuration for Prometheus has the concept of *role*, which can be either `node`, `service`, `pod`, `endpoint`, or `ingress`. Each will make available their corresponding set of objects for target discovery.
5. The best mechanism for implementing a custom service discovery is to use file-based discovery integration to inject targets into Prometheus.
6. No. Prometheus will try to use filesystem watches to automatically detect when there are changes and then reload the target list, and will fall back to re-reading target files on a schedule if watches aren't available.
7. It's recommended to use the adapter code available in the Prometheus code repository, as it abstracts much of the boilerplate needed to implement a discovery mechanism. Additionally, if you intend to contribute your custom service discovery to the project, the adapter makes it easy to incorporate the service discovery code into the main Prometheus binary, were it to gain traction and community support.

Chapter 13, Scaling and Federating Prometheus

1. You should consider sharding when you're sure a single instance isn't enough to handle the load, and you can't run it with more resources.
2. Vertical sharding is used to split scrape workload according to responsibility (for example, by function or team), where each Prometheus shard scrapes different jobs. Horizontal sharding splits loads from a single scrape job into multiple Prometheus instances.
3. To reduce the ingestion load on a Prometheus instance, you should consider dropping unnecessary metrics through the use of `metric_relabel_configs` rules, or by increasing the scrape interval so that fewer samples are ingested in total.
4. Instance-level Prometheus servers should federate job-level aggregate metrics. Job-level Prometheus servers should federate datacenter-level aggregate metrics.
5. You might need to use metrics only available in other Prometheus instances in recording and alerting rules.
6. The protocol used is gRPC.
7. You will lose the ability to use the Thanos deduplication feature.

Chapter 14, Integrating Long-Term Storage with Prometheus

1. The main advantages of basing the remote write feature on the WAL are: it makes streaming of metrics possible, has a much smaller memory footprint, and it's more resilient to crashes.
2. You can request Prometheus to produce a snapshot of the TSDB by using the `/api/v1/admin/tsdb/snapshot` API endpoint (only available when the `--web.enable-admin-api` flag is enabled), and then back up the snapshot.
3. You can delete time series from the TSDB by using the `/api/v1/admin/tsdb/delete_series` API endpoint and then using the `/api/v1/admin/tsdb/clean_tombstones` to make Prometheus clean up the deleted series (these endpoints will only be available when the `--web.enable-admin-api` flag is enabled).

4. Object storage usually provides 99.999999999% durability and 99.99% availability service-level agreements, and it's quite cheap in comparison to block storage.
5. Yes. For example, keeping the raw data is useful for zooming into short time ranges in the past.
6. Thanos store provides an API gateway between Thanos Querier and object storage.
7. Data in object storage can be inspected using the `thanos bucket` sub-command, which also allows verifying, repairing, listing and inspecting storage buckets.

Other Books You May Enjoy

If you enjoyed this book, you may be interested in these other books by Packt:

Zabbix 4 Network Monitoring - Third Edition
Rihards Olups, Patrik Uytterhoeven

ISBN: 978-1-78934-026-6

- Install Zabbix server and an agent from source
- Manage hosts, users, and permissions while acting upon monitored conditions
- Visualize data with the help of ad hoc graphs, custom graphs, and maps
- Simplify complex configurations and learn to automate them
- Monitor everything from web pages to IPMI devices and Java applications to VMware stats
- Configure Zabbix to send alerts including problem severity and time periods
- Troubleshoot any network issue

DevOps with Kubernetes - Second Edition
Hideto Saito, Hui-Chuan Chloe Lee, Et al

ISBN: 978-1-78953-399-6

- Learn fundamental and advanced DevOps skills and tools
- Get a comprehensive understanding of containers
- Dockerize an application
- Administrate and manage Kubernetes cluster
- Extend the cluster functionality with custom resources
- Understand Kubernetes network and service mesh
- Implement Kubernetes logging and monitoring
- Manage Kubernetes services in Amazon Web Services, Google Cloud Platform, and Microsoft Azure

Leave a review - let other readers know what you think

Please share your thoughts on this book with others by leaving a review on the site that you bought it from. If you purchased the book from Amazon, please leave us an honest review on this book's Amazon page. This is vital so that other potential readers can see and use your unbiased opinion to make purchasing decisions, we can understand what our customers think about our products, and our authors can see your feedback on the title that they have worked with Packt to create. It will only take a few minutes of your time, but is valuable to other potential customers, our authors, and Packt. Thank you!

Index

A

absent() function 168
adapter implementation
  reference link 346
addon-resizer
  about 116
  reference link 116
advanced deployment walkthrough
  about 39
  Alertmanager 43, 44
  Grafana 41, 42
  Node Exporter 44, 45
  Prometheus 39
  test environment, validating 45
aggregation operations 174
aggregation operators 165, 166, 167
alert notifications
  customizing 302
  default message format 302, 303, 304
  template, creating 304, 305, 306, 307
alertdump 219
alerting rule
  about 217, 218
  annotations 223, 224
  configuring 218
  delays 225
  file configuration 219, 221, 222
  labels 223, 224
  Prometheus server configuration file 218
  setting up, in Prometheus 217
  testing 230
Alertmanager, amtool command-line tool
  alert 289, 290
  check-config 292
  config 292, 293
  silence 290, 291

Alertmanager, file overview configuring
  global 283
  inhibit_rules 285, 286, 288
  receiver 288
  route 283, 285
  templates 288
Alertmanager, notification integrations
  about 297
  chat 299
  email 298
  null 301
  pager 300
  webhook 300
Alertmanager, notification pipeline
  alert groups, dispatching to 275, 276
  inhibition 276
  routing 278
  silencing 276, 278
Alertmanager
  alert routing 24, 25
  amtool command-line tool 289
  clustering 279, 280
  configuration 281
  file overview, configuration 282
  fundamentals 274
  management 24, 25
  notification pipeline 274
  Prometheus, configuration 281, 282
annotations 223, 224
arithmetic operators 160
automated deployment walkthrough
  about 35
  Alertmanager 38
  cleaning up 38
  Grafana 36
  Prometheus 36

B

binary operator precedence 167
binary operators
  about 160
  arithmetic operators 160
  comparison operators 161, 162
blackbox exporter
  about 129, 130, 131
  configuration 131, 132
  deployment 133, 134, 135
blackbox monitoring
  about 129
  blackbox exporter 129, 130, 131
  versus whitebox monitoring 12, 13
Brendan Gregg's USE method
  about 16
  errors 16
  saturation 16
  utilization 16
built-in service discovery
  Consul service discovery, using 331, 332, 333, 334, 335, 336, 337, 338
  Kubernetes service discovery, using 338, 339, 340, 341, 342
  using 331

C

checks 193
checks, usage
  check config 193
  check metrics 194
  check rules 193, 194
Cloud Native Computing Foundation (CNCF) 20, 323
cloud providers 321, 322, 323
code organization 29, 30, 31
comma-separated value (CSV) 143
comparison operators 161, 162
complex queries
  about 185
  CPU usage, comparing across different versions 186
  Node Exporter, executing 185
  PromQL approach 185, 186
  scenario rationale 185
configuration management database (CMDB) 343
console template basics 266, 267, 268
Consul service discovery
  using 331, 332, 333, 334, 335, 336, 337, 338
Consul
  reference link 331
Container Advisor (cAdvisor)
  about 110
  configuring 111
  deploying 111
  deployment 112, 113, 115
  reference link 110
container exporter
  about 109, 110
  Container Advisor (cAdvisor) 110
  kube-state-metrics 115
container orchestrators 323, 324, 326
Context menus 243
CPU usage
  comparing, across different versions 186
  PromQL approach 187, 188, 189
  scenario rationale 187
cross-monitoring 310
cross-sectional aggregation 63, 64
custom service discovery
  building 342
  fundamentals 343
  recommended approach 344
  reference link 344
  using 347, 348, 349

D

dashboard
  building 249
  creating 253, 254, 256, 257, 258, 259
  discovering 260
  exporting 260
  fundamentals 249
  Grafana dashboards gallery 261, 262, 263
  panel 250
  publishing 263, 264
  time picker 252, 253
  variables 251
data flow

about 51
disk 52
memory 51
write ahead log 51
data source 240, 241, 242
data
  visualizing 25, 26
debug 196
debug, usage
  debug all 199
  debug metrics 199
  debug pprof 197, 198
deduplication 373
Discoverer interface documentation
  reference link 346
dynamic configuration, Prometheus
  about 89, 90
  Kubernetes environment 90
  Prometheus Operator deployment 90
  Prometheus server deployment 92, 94
  targets, adding 94, 97, 98

E

Elastic Compute (EC2) 321
Elasticsearch, Logstash, and Kibana (ELK) 14
emote storage integrations 385
endpoints
  about 200, 201
  validating 200
enum metric 176, 177
environment
  spinning up 34
expanding notation 229
Explore 238, 242, 243
Explore interface 243
exporter
  about 141, 142
  fundamentals 23
  HAProxy exporter 143
  internal state, exploring 22, 23
  JMX exporter 142

F

federation, patterns
  about 365

cross-service 367, 368
  hierarchical 366, 367
federation
  configuring 362, 364
  used, for global view 362
file_sd integrations
  reference link 343
Filter box 288
functions
  about 167
  absent() function 168
  aggregation operations 174
  enum metric 176, 177
  histogram_quantile() function 173
  info metric 176, 177
  irate() function 170
  label_join() function 169, 170
  label_replace() function 169, 170
  predict_linear() function 170
  rate() function 170
  reference link 167
  sort() function 174
  sort_desc() function 174
  time function 175
  vector() function 174

G

global view, components
  about 369, 370
  query 372, 373
  sidecar 371
global view
  federation, used 362
Google's signals
  about 16
  errors 16
  latency 16
  saturation 16
  traffic 16
Grafana dashboards gallery
  about 262, 263
  reference link 261
Grafana
  dashboards 244
  data source 240, 241, 242

[419]

download link 238
executing, on Kubernetes 245, 246, 247, 248, 249
Explore 242, 243
login screen 239
used, with Prometheus 238, 239
grok exporter
about 125
configuring 125, 126, 127
deployment 127, 128, 129
Group box 288

H

HAProxy exporter 143
histogram_quantile() function 173
HyperText Transfer Protocol (HTTP) 10

I

info metric 176, 177
Infrastructure as a Service (IaaS) 321
Inhibited checkmark 288
instant vector 156
internal state
exposing, with exporters 22, 23
Internet Control Message Protocol (ICMP) 13, 101
intersection operator 163
irate() function 171, 172

J

Java agent 142
Java Management Extensions (JMX) 142
Java Virtual Machine (JVM) 142
JMX exporter
reference link 143
job 74

K

kube-state-metrics
about 115
configuring 116
deployment 117, 118, 119, 120
reference link 116
kubectl
about 34

URL, for installing 34
Kubernetes service discovery
using 338, 339, 340, 341, 342
Kubernetes test environment 104, 105
Kubernetes
Alertmanager 294, 295, 296
Prometheus operator 294, 295, 296

L

label matchers 150, 152, 153, 154, 155
label_join() function 169, 170
label_replace() function 169, 170
labels 223, 224
layout 52
logical operators 163, 164, 165
logs
about 201, 202
to metrics 121
validating 200
longitudinal aggregation 63, 64

M

machine requisites
about 32
hardware requisites 32
recommended software 33
Managed Beans (MBeans) 142
meta-monitoring 309
Metrics 243
metrics collection
about 14
approaches, overview 14, 15
measuring 16
push-based monitoring system, versus pull-based monitoring system 15
with Prometheus 19
Metrics list 243
metrics storage
local storage 381, 382, 383
options 381
remote storage integrations 384
Minikube
about 34
URL, for installation 34
monitoring system

[420]

   about 308
   cross-monitoring 308, 310
   meta-monitoring 308, 310
   switch alerts 310, 311
monitoring, components
   about 12
   alerting 12
   logging 12
   metrics 12
   tracing 12
   visualization 12
monitoring
   definition 9
   organizational contexts 10, 11
   value 10
mtail
   about 121
   configuring 122
   deployment 123, 124, 125

N

Nagios Service Check Acceptor (NSCA) 14
Node Exporter
   about 106, 107
   configuring 107, 108
   deploying 108, 109
   executing 185
   reference link 106
node_exporter_basics dashboard 252
notification log (nflog) 279

O

observability 12
offset modifier 158
operating system (OS)
   about 101
   exporter 106
   Node Exporter 106, 107
operators
   about 160
   aggregation operators 165, 166, 167
   binary operator precedence 167
   binary operators 160
   vector matching 162
Out of Memory (OOM) 379

out-of-the-box console templates 265, 266

P

panel 250
panel, types
   gauge 251
   graph 251
   singlestat 251
   table 251
patterns
   about 177, 178
   percentiles 179
   scrape job 180
   service level indicators (SLIs) 178
pitfalls
   about 177, 180
   complex queries, constructing 184
   data type, function selecting 180
   data, working with 182
   matchers, avoiding to select time series 183
   query-of-death 184
   statistical significance, losing 183
   sum-of-rates, versus rate-of-sum 181, 182
   unexpected results 183
port 170
predict_linear() function 170
PromDash
   reference link 265
Prometheus data model
   about 49, 53
   cardinality 54, 55
   metric labels 54
   metric names 53
   notation 53
   Prometheus local storage 51
   samples 54
   time series data 50
   time series database 50
Prometheus local storage
   about 51
   data flow 51
   layout 52
Prometheus metrics types
   about 55
   counter 55, 56, 57

gauge 57, 58, 59
histogram 60
summaries 61, 62
Prometheus server configuration file 218
Prometheus server configuration file, components
 alerting 219
 evaluation_interval 218
 rule_files 218
Prometheus server, visualizations components
 console 27
 expression browser 26
Prometheus
 about 40
 alerting rule, setting up 217
 architecture, high-level overview 20, 21, 22
 cleanup 81
 config section 68
 configuring 67, 68
 console template basics 266, 267, 268
 file, configuring 71
 global configuration 72, 73
 Grafana, used 238, 239
 inspection, configuring 78, 79, 80
 managing, in Kubernetes 81
 managing, in standalone server 77
 metrics collection 19
 mitigating, with Thanos 368, 369
 out-of-the-box console templates 265, 266
 query section 70
 reference link 73
 scrape configuration 74, 76, 77
 server deploy 77, 78
 storage section 68, 69
 visualization 264
 web section 69, 70
PromQL
 functions 167
 fundamental 150
 operators 160
 selectors 150
promtool, features
 checks 193
 debug 196
 queries 194
 unit tests 200

promtool
 exploring 192
pull-based monitoring system
 versus push-based monitoring system 15
pushgateway
 about 136, 137
 configuration 137
 deployment 137, 138, 139, 140, 141
pushing metrics
 about 136
 pushgateway 136, 137

Q

queries 194
queries, usage
 query instant 195
 query labels 196
 query range 195
 query series 196
Query field 243

R

range vector 156, 157, 158
rate() function 171, 172
receiver 379
recommended approach, custom service discovery
 example 344, 345
recording rules
 evaluation, working 211
 naming convention 215, 216, 217
 testing 226, 227, 228, 229, 231
 using 211, 212, 213, 214
Regex field 255
regular expression
 reference link 154
remote read 378, 379, 380
remote write 378, 379
role-based access control (RBAC) 117
route
 alerting 25
rules
 about 211
 alerting rules, testing 230
 recording rules, testing 226, 227, 228, 229, 231
 testing 226

S

scaling, with sharding
  about 356
  consideration 360
  jobs, logical grouping 356, 357
  selecting 360
  single job, issues 358
selectors
  about 150
  instant vector 155
  label matchers 150, 152, 153, 154, 155
  offset modifier 158
  range vector 156, 157, 158
  subqueries 159, 160
service discovery
  cloud providers 321, 322, 323
  container orchestrators 323, 324, 326
  DNS-based service discovery 328, 329
  File-based service discovery 329, 331
  options, executing 320, 321
  system 326, 327
service level indicators (SLIs) 178
service level objective (SLO) 179
service-level agreements (SLA) 386
sharding
  used, for scaling 356
Site Reliability Engineers (SREs) 10
sort() function 174
sort_desc() function 174
Standalone HTTP server 142
static configuration, Prometheus
  about 81
  kubernetes environment 82, 83
  Prometheus server deployment 83, 84, 85, 86
  targets, adding 86, 87, 88
static infrastructure test environment 102, 103
subqueries 159, 160

T

Telegraf, InfluxDB, Chronograph, and Kapacitor (TICK) 14
Thanos components
  about 387
  bucket 394
  compact 392, 393, 394
  query 389, 390
  receive 395, 396, 397
  rule 398
  sidecar 390, 391
  store gateway 392
  test environment, specifications 388
Thanos ecosystem, components
  downsampling 386
  global view 386
  long-term retention 386
  rules 386
Thanos ecosystem
  about 385, 386, 387
  sub-commands 385
Thanos
  global view, components 369, 370
  reference link 385
  used, for mitigating Prometheus 368, 369
time function 175
time series data 50
time series database
  about 50
  analyzing 202
  tsdb tool, using 203, 204, 205
Tom Wilkie's RED method
  about 16
  duration 16
  errors 16
  rate 16

U

unit tests 200
user interface (UI) 214

V

Vagrant
  about 34
  URL, for installing 34
variables 251, 252
vector matching
  about 162
  logical operators 163, 164, 165
  multiple to one 163
  one-to-many 163

one-to-one 162, 163
vector() function 174
virtual machine (VM) 101, 214, 236
VirtualBox
  about 33
  URL, for installing 33

W

whitebox monitoring
  versus blackbox monitoring 12, 13
WMI exporter 106

Printed in Great Britain
by Amazon